THE

INDIAN CONSTITUTION

AN INTRODUCTORY STUDY

THE

INDIAN CONSTITUTION

AN INTRODUCTORY STUDY

BY

A. RANGASWAMI IYENGAR

GYAN

Published by

Gyan Publishing House
5, Ansari Road
Daryaganj, New Delhi-110002
Phone: 011-47034999, 9811692060
E-mail: books@gyanbooks.com

Distribution Network
gyanbooks.com
India, USA, Canada, UK, Australia

ISBN: 978-93-6208-801-7 (HB)
First Published, 1913

2nd Impression 2024

Printed at: Gyan Press, Delhi.

THE INDIAN CONSTITUTION AN INTRODUCTORY STUDY
Author: A. RANGASWAMI IYENGAR

THE
INDIAN CONSTITUTION
AN INTRODUCTORY STUDY

THE INDIAN CONSTITUTION

AN INTRODUCTORY STUDY

BY

A. RANGASWAMI IYENGAR, B.A., B.L.

Assistant Editor, "The Hindu"

Second Edition—Revised and Enlarged

MADRAS : G. C. LOGANADHAM BROS.
MOUNT ROAD

1913

TO

THE MEMORY OF

the late Dewan Bahadur

S. Srinivasaraghava Iyengar, C.I.E.

MY UNCLE

WHOSE STUDY OF INDIAN PROBLEMS

WAS AN INSPIRING AND INVALUABLE EXAMPLE

TO ALL THOSE WHO KNEW HIM

PREFACE TO THE FIRST EDITION

This book is intended to meet a demand which is likely to be increasingly felt with the widening of the political life of the Indian people by the inauguration of the new Reform Scheme. Accessible information on the constitutional aspects of the Government and administration of British India is not found in recognised books treating of the laws and institutions of India. Official publications also hardly go beyond bare summaries of facts and events. A systematic treatment of the features of the Indian Constitution, studied from the point of view of the Indian citizen and of the Indian student of political science, has not so far been attempted. Students of Indian history, as it is taught in our schools and Colleges, hardly obtain an idea of the machinery whereby the Indian Constitution works and the lines on which it has been constructed and developed during more than a century of British rule. Such standard books as Cowell's "Courts and Legislative Authorities in India" and Sir Courtenay Ilbert's "Government of India," do, of course, treat of the Indian Constitutional Laws as they have been enacted, in all their details; but they deal only incidentally with the constitutional or political principles, understandings and conventions, on which so large a part of the working of British institutions all over the world depends.

It is to stimulate the study of the Indian Constitution in this direction that this introductory sketch is primarily placed by the author before the public. It is also attempted in the book to furnish the Indian citizen with a handbook of information to be of use to him in the discharge of his duties. The average Indian who cares to interest himself in politics, gains a knowledge of political problems in a haphazard way. Such knowledge as he obtains by his business contact with other men, the reading of newspapers and the hearing and reading of political speeches, can but give him a slender acquaintance with the subject. Matters are not very much better even in regard to many who take an active, instead of a passive, part in public affairs. The author ventures to hope the present publication will give them some preliminary help in this direction.

The book lays no claim whatever to originality or research except in its method of presenting the leading facts and features of the Indian Constitution. Written, moreover, in the intervals of busy work, it is likely to contain many errors of style and of statement. For fuller information he would refer the readers to the authoritative works of Cowell, Ilbert and others, and to the many State Papers and Proceedings published by Government. A small collection of select constitutional documents is, however, published in the Appendix, which the author trusts will prove useful both to students and to politicians.

MADRAS,
December, 1909. A. R.

PREFACE TO THE SECOND EDITION

In bringing out this enlarged and revised edition of a book intended merely as an introduction to the systematic study of the Indian Constitution and its history under British rule, the author desires to express his obligations to the many kind friends and generous critics whose appreciation and advice have enabled him to enlarge the scope of the book, to revise its contents in the light of later incidents and experiences, and to add to the material collected therein, of which the Table of Contents and the Index, which has now been added to the book, give some idea. The author also regrets that owing to pressure of other duties and to other causes, he was not able to publish this second edition earlier, especially as the copies of the first edition had been exhausted more than 18 months ago.

6th January 1913 A. R.

CONTENTS

APPENDIX

B.—THE INDIAN LEGISLATURES

THE INDIAN CONSTITUTION

CHAPTER I

BRITISH SOVEREIGNTY OVER INDIA

Introductory

The Constitution of British India is, in a strict sense, "made"; yet it cannot be denied that it has also "grown." Unlike the British Constitution, it owes its origin to definite statutes of the Imperial Parliament of Great Britain and Ireland; but like the British Constitution, its progress and present character have not been due to any startling innovation or revolution, but to changes consciously made by British administrators to suit the varying needs of good government in the country and, latterly, to satisfy the growing aspirations of the people of the country for a share in the government of the land. The Indian Constitution, therefore, bears all the marks of British political and institutional arrangements, so far as they could be found applicable to this country. It exhibits, for instance, the results of that distaste for violent or radical change and that disposition to deal with the needs of the hour, as they arise, rather than with the requirements and possibilities of the future, which are associated with the British people. It exhibits, again, that tendency towards "legal" forms of political institutions—*i.e.*, institutions in respect of which legal remedies and judicial control are provided—that regard for the maintenance of what Professor Dicey calls the "Rule of Law," which is a peculiarly British or Anglo-Saxon feature. At the same time, the requirements of the necessarily bureaucratic form of government in India, for more than a century, have also produced and perfected an administrative and constitutional system whose efficiency is its most conspicuous merit, but whose drawbacks from the point of view of constitutional development are not inconsiderable.

Establishment of British Sovereignty in India

British India, as the Statute of 1858 puts it, is governed by and in the name of His Majesty the King-Emperor. How the British Crown came to acquire this vast and wonderful country is a matter of history which is common knowledge among educated people in India. The Charter issued to the East India Company in 1600 by Queen Elizabeth and the successive Charters renewing or amplifying the same, conferred on a trading corporation in England monopolies of trade in the East and, for that purpose, authorised the acquisition of territories, and their fortification and defence by military levies. The Company pushed its fortunes vigorously in the midst of the political chaos in India in the 18th century. "At first the agent, it became the master of princes. It fought and conquered with an army of its own and auxiliary forces hired from the Crown." On its behalf, Robert Clive in 1765 obtained from the Emperor at Delhi, the Diwani of the rich and fertile territories of Bengal, Bihar and Orissa. In the difficulties and troubles which arose over the administration of these provinces, arose the first Parliamentary assertion of rights of control and sovereignty over the Company's affairs in the East. The Regulating Act of 1773 contains the first Parliamentary restriction and definition of the Company's political powers and is the first important constitutional document of the Indian Government. It introduced the system of Parliamentary control over Indian affairs, and at each subsequent renewal of the Company's Charter, whenever necessary, the Parliament enacted laws for expanding and revising the constitution of the Indian Government and for providing for just and impartial administration over its territories.

By the Regulating Act, the Governor of Bengal was raised to the rank of Governor-General and, in conjunction with his Council of four other Members, was entrusted with the authority of supervising and controlling the Governments of Madras and Bombay in important matters. A Supreme Court of His Majesty's Judges was established at Calcutta—similar Courts were established later in Madras and Bombay—and the power of legislation was conferred on the Governor-General in Council. The India Act of 1784, known before it became law as Pitt's Bill, established the Board of Commissioners for the Affairs of India—commonly known as the Board of Control—which virtually absorbed all real power from the Company's Court of Directors. The Act of 1813 did away with the Company's trade monopoly, except in China, and that of 1833 took the latter also away and introduced various reforms in the constitution of the Indian Government, among others, the addition of a Law Member to the Council of the Governor-General, the first appointment made to this office being that of Thomas Babington Macaulay. It also accorded the authority of Acts of Parliament to the laws and regulations passed by the Governor-General in Council. The Act of 1853 practically announced the forthcoming death of the Company and its rule as such, and laid down the principle that "the administration of India was too national a concern to be left to the chances of benevolent despotism." Finally, the Act of 1858 for the Better Government of India vested the executive administration of India in the Crown. The Indian Councils Act of 1861 defined and extended the constitutions and powers of the Executive and Legislative Councils in India; and the High Courts Act established the High Courts of Judicature in the Presidency towns under Charter from the Crown by combining the old Supreme and Sadar-adalat Courts. The Acts of 1892 and 1909 have extended the principles embodied in the Act of 1861.

Constitutional aspects of British Indian History

Students of Indian history are usually familiar with the wars and the treaties, the adventures and incidents and the policies and plans carried out by British pro-consuls in India which resulted in successive additions of territories and secure subordination of Native Rulers to the British Raj. But very few of them are conversant with the course of constitutional development which took place side by side and which has resulted in the establishment of that settled and orderly form of government which is firmly associated with the administration of British India. It would, therefore, be useful to take a rapid survey of these aspects of British Indian history and to note some salient features in the constitutional documents relating to India.

The First Charter

It was in the spacious days of the Great Queen Elizabeth that a Company of London Merchants met together in Founders' Hall in the year 1599 for the purpose of trading with the East. They only contemplated at the outset the very modest object of carrying on single trade voyages with India and resolved to ask that Puissant Sovereign to grant them "a privilege in succession and to incorporate them in a company, for that the trade of the Indias being so far remote from hence, cannot be traded but in a joint and a united stock." The hesitancy of the Queen's Privy Council to grant the privilege only increased the ardour of the Company, who prepared an elaborate document showing the parts of the earth, East of the Cape of Good Hope, not actually in the possession of Spain—then the only competitor in the trade with the East Indies—and petitioned for the grant of a Charter to trade exclusively in these 'rich and golden' countries, by means, not of a single voyage or voyages, but of an armed and chartered monopoly for the permanent Indian Trade. On the last day of the year 1600, Queen Elizabeth granted the famous Charter of the East India Company "for the Honour of our Nation, the Wealth of our People, the Increase of our Navigation, and the advancement of lawful Traffick for the benefit of our Common-wealth." It constituted the petitioners into 'one body corporate and politick, in deed and in name, by the name of the Governor and Company of Merchants of London trading into the East Indies,' with legal succession, the power to purchase lands, to sue and be sued and to have a common seal. The Charter secured for 15 years the exclusive privilege of the Indian Trade, that is with all countries beyond the Cape of Good Hope and the Straits of Magellan, except such territories or ports as were in the actual possession of any Christian prince in amity with the Queen. It also empowered the Company to make bye-laws, and to punish offenders against them by fine or imprisonment, as far as consistent with the laws of the realm. All the Queen's subjects were "prohibited from trading within the geographical limits assigned to the Company, unless under its express license, on pain of forfeiting ship and cargo, imprisonment or other punishment." These powers were supplemented by considerable privileges granted as against the Crown in respect of export and import duties.

The Regulated and Joint Stock Companies

The body corporate thus created, as the late Sir William Hunter wrote, represents both as to the nature of its business and as to the mechanism for conducting it, the final stage of sea-enterprise and the final expression of the co-operative principle in the Elizabethan period. The nature of the organization, as he put it, "was rather that of a modern syndicate formed to obtain from the Crown a concession of the East India trade for a certain number of years, and then to work the concession by means of successive new syndicates or groups of subscribers from among its own members for separate voyages, but under its complete control", than that of a joint stock Company as it is understood in modern times. The Company, it has been pointed out, belonged at the outset to the simpler and looser form of associations, to which the City Companies then belonged, known by the name of the

Regulated Companies. The members of such a Company were subject to certain common regulations and were entitled to certain common privileges, but each of them traded on his own separate capital and there was no joint stock.

The trading privileges of the East India Company were reserved to the members, their sons, apprentices, factors and servants. It was, however, soon found that this form of organization under which the Company worked on the principle of each subscriber contributing separately to the expense of each voyage and reaping the whole profits of his subscriptions was insufficient to carry on the Eastern Trade with, and after 1612 the subscribers threw their contributions into a joint stock and thus converted their organization from a regulated Company into a joint stock Company, as it was then understood. The powers and privileges granted to the Company by the first Charter, including as they did the power of subordinate legislation, were supplemented and enlarged by successive Charters. The growth of the business of the Company as well as the contest and rivalry for valuable markets in the East with other European Powers, which was daily growing, necessitated the acquisition of territories for settlement by grant or cession from the Potentates in India.*

In 1669 King Charles II granted by Charter the port and Island of Bombay which had in 1661 been ceded to the British Crown as a part of the dower of Catherine of Braganza,

---

* Sir Alfred Lyall, in his "British Dominion in India," [London : Murray, 1905] p. 18 has explained the position of the Companies in this respect in the following terms :—

"Trade was more valuable, to the maritime folk, than territory, and commerce than conquest. But traffic with distant lands could not be carried on without taking up stations and arming ships ; since the understanding among European nations was that regular diplomatic relations did not practically extend beyond certain well-known lines of longitude....The Chartered Companies, therefore, represented a device, invented to suit these conditions of existence, for extending commerce and for securing it by territorial appropriations, without directly pledging a Government to answer for the acts of its subjects. The Charter expressed the delegation of certain sovereign powers for distinct purposes; it amounted from one point of view to a license for private war ; and the system has since had a long, eventful and curious history, which has as yet by no means ended."

to be held of the Crown "as of the Manor of East Greenwich, in the County of Kent, in free and common soccage" at an annual rent of £10.

Territorial and Trade Privileges

Along with the acquisition of such territories and of powers and privileges for the regulation and administration of affairs therein, the Company also acquired powers of fortifying these places, for maintaining forces both on sea and on land for the protection of its trade, for the enforcement of martial law whenever circumstances needed, for the establishment of Mayor's Courts and of Judges to administer law and justice to the King's subjects within the Company's territories. As the Company thus virtually acquired sovereign powers of civil and military government over its settlements in the East from the Crown, it was soon found that its territorial acquisitions, which by the end of the 17th century had become fairly considerable, were becoming more important than its trade monopolies. The position of affairs of the Company at the end of the 17th century was such that the Company was able to record in a Minute quoted by Macaulay as having been written by Sir Josia Child, the then Governor of the Company, the following:— "The increase of our revenue is the subject of our care as much as our trade; 't is that must maintain our force when twenty accidents may interrupt our trade; 't is that must make us a nation in India...and upon this account it is that the wise Dutch, in all their general advices that we have seen, write ten paragraphs concerning their government, their civil and military policy, warfare, and the increase of their revenue, for one paragraph they write concerning trade."

The Rival Company and the Intervention of Parliament

In the meantime the Company had to face the acute rivalry of what was known as the New Company in England and found considerable difficulties in getting its Charters successively renewed. Both the Companies, however, amalgamated under Lord Godolphin's award and formed themselves into 'the United Company of the Merchants of England trading with the East Indies'.

The English Revolution of 1688, combined with the rivalry of the New Company and of interlopers, had, however, already effected a material alteration in the constitutional position of the Company and its relation to the mother country. The old method of obtaining Charters from the Crown, granting monopolies of trade and of powers pertaining to the Sovereign, by presents or grants of money to the Crown, had disappeared in the midst of the difficulties which the Company had to contend with and the constitutional struggle which ensued in England at this time. The new doctrine then arose that the Crown had no right to grant privileges or powers of the kind which till then had been unquestionably given to, and exercised by the Company. What was known as the affair of the 'Red Bridge' brought this question for discussion before Parliament in 1794 and the House of Commons passed a Resolution disclaiming the right of the Company to detain the "Red Bridge" on the Thames because the latter suspected that it was going to trade within the preserves of the Company. They declared that all subjects of England have equal rights to trade with the East Indies unless prohibited by Acts of Parliament. It has ever since been held, wrote Macaulay, "to be the sound doctrine that no power but that of the whole legislature can give to any persons or to any society exclusive privilege of trade to any part of the world." This was the first assertion of the right of the British people through their Parliament to interfere in the affairs of the Company, and it led, as would be seen presently, to material consequences in the further progress of British Rule in India. As Sir C. P. Ilbert puts it, "the question whether the trading privileges of the East India Company should be continued was removed from the Council Chamber to Parliament and the period of control by Act of Parliament over the affairs of the Company began."[1] The United

1. The Government of India by Sir C. P. Ilbert. [Oxford: Clarendon Press, 1907.] P. 26.

Company which was formed in 1702 was thus an organization which owed its rights and powers to statutory authority, supplemented by Charters based on legislative enactments. Whatever, therefore, may have been the position before the Revolution of 1688, we may for practical purposes take it as settled that the authority of the Supreme Government in India from that time forward, as well as its constitution and powers, have to be derived from successive Acts of Parliament.

Territorial Acquisitions

With its internal constitution and powers well secured in 1702, the Company progressed both in its trade and its trade settlements and began to cast a longing glance at the then political condition of India. By the middle of the eighteenth century it was every day leading to startling developments. It is not necessary here to recapitulate at any length the political events between the years 1700 and 1773 in consequence of which the Company found itself the master of extensive territories and deemed it necessary and expedient to take upon itself the responsibility of administering the affairs of some of the great provinces of the Indian Continent. The political condition of India at the time when the Company had become settled in a number of factories on the Indian sea board was at once the opportunity and the necessity for the Company to strengthen and augment its power by further acquisitions, to maintain them by military levies and to administer them for the peace and security of their inhabitants and for the profit of the Company's shareholders in Europe and its subordinates in India. Half a century of autocratic misrule on the part of Aurangazebe had produced a persistent and contagious spread of Hindu revolt in which the Mahrattas formed the most powerful organization, and the death of that fanatic Emperor of Delhi was the signal for the political chaos within the country which then ensued and the visible loosening of the bond of administration—more especially in the distant provinces of the Empire. The feebleness of the Government in

India was a fact recognised by all the European Powers which made their way to the East in search of commercial expansion, and in the rivalries and jealousies of these powers in regard to the acquisition of territory in India at this time of political disintegration, in their attempts to ally themselves with one or other of the many petty potentates, the foundations of Britain's Empire in India were firmly laid.

The grant of the Diwani of Bengal, Bihar and Orissa

The facts and incidents are well known to all students of Indian history, of the eventful struggle between France and England in South India which is known as the war in the Carnatic, the net result of which, from the constitutional standpoint, was that the East India Company thereby established itself as a land power, equally with the other chiefs and subadars of the titular Emperor at Delhi. At the conclusion of this war, however, the scene of Indian history shifted from Madras to Calcutta where, as well as in Bombay, the new policy of the acquisition of territories by taking up the quarrels of the warring country powers, was sought to be imitated on a larger scale. The Nawab of Bengal of the 'Black Hole' fame, in an unwise moment during his short period of misrule, sought to interfere with the possessions and the rights of the Company, and this led to a small military operation, the full value of which was only realised after the Battle of Plassey. At this historic, but not insignificant, battle, the old Nawab of Bengal was defeated, and the Company put upon the throne a new Nawab who was at the mercy and at the service of the Company and its officers. When his successor attempted to assert authority over the extremely recalcitrant and thoroughly corrupt servants of the Company, he found himself signally defeated, in spite of the support of the Emperor, at the Battle of Buxar, in 1764, the result of which brings the next notable fact in the constitutional history of British Rule in India, *viz.*, the obtaining of the *firman* granting the Diwani of Bengal, Bihar and Orissa to the East India Company by Shah Alum, the blind and infirm Emperor of Delhi. The political history of the Company in India from this time ceased to be one connected with the acquisition of commercial preponderance or of strips of territory and spheres of influence along the sea board,—but one for supremacy, as one among the ruling powers,' over all India. The results of the Mahratta wars, of the Pindari and the Afghan wars, and of the Sikh and Burmese wars are of importance to the student of the Constitution only for the purpose of understanding how the Company and the Crown adjusted the mechanism of administration to the growing needs of the enormous increase in the territories which thereby came under their sway. On the other hand, in the particular province of constitutional history, he has to examine certain other facts and incidents usually relegated to a secondary place in the histories of India now extant, but whose significance it is necessary to grasp in order to know how the present system of government has been evolved.

Its effect in England

It was after Robert Clive laid the foundations of territorial sovereignty of the Company by the acquisition of the Diwani of Bengal, Bihar and Orissa that public attention began to be generally excited in England as to the affairs of India. The circumstances that gave rise to the agitation for a more direct control on the part of the Government in England of the affairs of the Company are well-known, and may be summarised in the following words of Mr. Forrest in his 'Introduction to the Selections from State Papers of the Governors-General of India' relating to Warren Hastings :—

"Meanwhile the management of the Company drifted from bad to worse, and its pecuniary affairs were getting straitened so far as to necessitate the special appointment of Warren Hastings as Governor of Bengal where the Company had resolved directly to start forth as Diwan, to put an end to the Dual Government of the Company and the Nawab and to rescue the province from chaos, destitution and decay. Hastings did great work as Governor of Bengal and the steps which he took, though some of them were subsequently the matter of acrimonious controversy, resulted in strengthening the authority and the rule of the Company over the province, but it hardly enabled the Company at Home to tide over its financial embarrassments—which became so great that they were obliged to solicit help and receive a loan from the public of £1,400,000. This was the opportunity for the public and the Ministry to definitely interpose in Indian affairs, and in the same year Parliament passed an Act for the better management of the affairs of the East India Company *as well in India as in Europe*. It was by the Regulating Act that for the first time "the British nation as a nation assumed the actual responsibility of the Government of the territories won by a trading corporation. .... This first experiment on the part of Parliament to regulate and control the affairs of India was soon found to possess serious defects which led to good deal of acrimonious controversies and administrative deadlocks, to avoid which Parliament had eventually to pass another Act in 1784, but the period of ten years between the passing of the Regulating Act and the enactment of Pitt's India Act of 1784 is crowded with historical and stirring incidents both in the affairs of England and of India, in consequence of which Indian affairs became inextricably associated with political and party affairs in England. The Regulating Act made the Governor-General dependent not only on the aid and support of the Court of Directors but also that of the Ministry, and it was soon found that he could only obtain their favour by a compliance with their claims for a share of Indian Patronage. It imposed direct interference by Parliament in the Local Government of India, a task which at all times difficult, was particularly so in the circumstances of the time...The exercise, moreover, of the newly born spirit of Parliamentary control over the affairs of the Company was not easily acquiesced in by the Court of Directors or of Proprietors and this dispute was also inextricably bound up with the quarrels of Hastings with his Councillors, into which also the rival political parties of the time entered with zest."

The establishment of the Board of Control

The Act of 1784 by which the Board of Control was established was but the legitimate result of the conviction that had been growing in the people of England at the time that the Company had acquired territories in India which made them virtually masters of that continent, that they had grown too powerful for a trading association and that their privileges and powers were an anomaly under the British Constitution. The Parliamentary enquiries at the time revealed serious defects and wholesale corruption in the administrative affairs of the country despite Warren Hastings' great efforts to introduce efficiency. But unfortunately the main question was mixed up with a number of party issues, with the exercise of patronage by the Crown, the Company and the political parties in England. The result was that, though the incongruous India Bill of Charles James Fox was defeated, the Bill of William Pitt which was passed in 1784 established the system of double Government in India—that of the Company with the Court of Directors, and that of the Board of Control acting through a Minister directly responsible to Parliament—a system which lasted till 1858. The alterations in the Constitution of the administrative machinery in India effected by the Acts between 1773 and 1784 have been described by Sir Alfred Lyall in the following terms:—"In the year 1786, therefore, we find the English sovereignty openly established in India under a Governor-General invested with plenary authority by the representatives of the English nation. The transformation of the chief governorship of a chartered commercial company into a senatorial pro-consulship was now virtually accomplished; and with the accession of Cornwallis there sets in a new era of accelerated advance."

Further territorial extension and Consolidation

At the end of the eighteenth century, therefore, we may take it that India and its peoples had already begun to feel the sense of a stable and enduring dominion, within the territories administered by the British Nation. The prevailing sense of political insecurity of the previous century gave way to a feeling of confidence in the peaceful and orderly government of a Western Power. So far, the relations between the British and the territorial powers which yet subsisted with varying degrees of independence in the land, was one of apparent equality, though the superiority of the British power was fully recognized and its assertion in growing proportions was found inevitable. William

Pitt perceived the danger of the indefinite expansion of the territory of the Company in India in the moribund state of many of the principalities in India, and with the express object of restraining the warlike and adventurous ardour of the Company's servants in the East and their ambitious efforts for the expansion of territory the following express declaration was inserted in the Act of 1793 which renewed the Company's Charter:—"Forasmuch as to pursue schemes of conquest and extension of dominion in India are measures repugnant to the wish, the honour, and the policy of this nation, it shall not be lawful for the Governor-General in Council to declare war, or to enter into any treaty for making war, or for guaranteeing the possessions of any country, Princes or States (except where hostilities against the British nation in India have been actually commenced or prepared), without express command and authority from the Home Government." In spite of all these protestations, however, the European situation at the close of the 18th century only too easily lent itself as a pretext and a motive for very large expansions of territory in India under the Governor-Generalship of Marquess Wellesley. Whether in consequence of Napoleon's wars with the English nation, which imperilled England's position in her over-seas dominions, or in consequence of the intrinsic difficulties of maintaining a strong Government of large territories in the midst of a number of weak authorities exercising precarious sway, Marquess Wellesley soon convinced himself that it was absolutely essential that the British nation should not only be *primus inter pares* among the States into which India was then partitioned, but should be the paramount power with which all the rest of the States in India should be either in a state of subsidiary alliance or become merged. The declared object of the Marquis of Wellesley was to establish the ascendancy of the English Power over all other States in India by a system of subsidiary treaties so framed as to deprive them of the means of prosecuting any measure or of forming any confederacy hazardous to the security of the British Empire, to preserve the tranquillity of India by exercising general control over the fast disappearing spirit of restless ambition which existed. This general control he desired to impose, through the medium of alliances contracted with those States, as the best security and protection of their respective rights. The manner in which the subsidiary treaties which originated in Europe during the Napoleonic wars were adapted to the situation in India and subsequently developed into the system of Protected States on the one hand and the policy of maintaining a buffer State on the frontiers on the other, belongs more to the diplomatic than to the constitutional history of India. It is sufficient here to note that the subsidiary system of Lord Wellesley and its subsequent complications have been the main means by which British territories expanded and British protection was imposed over the Native States.

The Charter Acts and Constitutional progress

The process of internal consolidation and external expansion of territory in the first half of the 19th century, however, was more or less unconnected with the changes in the constitutional machinery of Indian Government both in England and in India. The changes which it underwent at the time of the renewal of the Company's Charter in 1813, 1833 and 1853 were entirely dissociated from the external politics and policy of the Home Government. Each of these renewals of Charters, like those of 1773 and 1793, were preceded by careful and elaborate parliamentary enquiries into the affairs of the Company and the reforms that were effected as a result of such enquiries by the Charter Acts of these years introduced improvements and alterations in the various institutions established for the good government of the country, in conformity with those principles of progress and reform with which British constitutional methods of those times have become associated and which will be more particularly referred to in the subsequent chapters. The principal steps, however, which were taken to complete the process of converting the Government of India by a Chartered Company under the supervision of the Crown, into one of the direct Government by the Crown of its Indian territories may be shortly summed up here.

The constitution and powers of the Board of Control

The first assertion of the right of superintendence of the King's Government over the administration of India commenced, it may be noted, not with the Act of 1784 but with an earlier Act of 1781, by which the Court of Directors of the East India Company were required "to deliver to the Lords Commissioners of His Majesty's Treasury a copy of all orders which they intended to send to India relating to the management of the revenues of the Company, and to one of the principal Secretaries of State a copy of all intended orders relating to the civil and military officers and Government of the Company; and the Court was bound to obey such instructions as they might receive from one of the Secretaries of State so far as related to the transactions of the Company with the country powers in the East Indies and to the levying of war and making peace." The Act of 1784 constituted the Board of Commissioners over the Affairs of India consisting of "any persons not exceeding six in number being of the Privy Council," of whom one of the Secretaries of State and the Chancellor of the Exchequer were always two. The constitution of the Board was altered by the Act of 1793 so as to admit any number of Privy Councillors (of whom the two principal Secretaries of State and the Chancellor of the Exchequer were always to be three) and any other two persons. The Act of 1833 empowered the Sovereign "to appoint as Commissioners any number of persons whether of the Privy Council or not, and provided that the Lord President of the Council, the Lord Privy Seal, the first Lord of the Treasury, the Principal Secretaries of State and the Chancellor of the Exchequer shall be by virtue of their offices, Members of the Board." It was not, till 1793 that any sum was assigned by Parliament for the expenses of the Board, but since that date handsome salaries have been provided for the ministers and the staff of the India Offices, out of the Indian Revenues.

The Act of 1784 increased the powers of the Crown over the Company and its administration of Indian affairs considerably, by authorizing the Board of Control to superintend, direct and control all acts, operations and concerns which in any wise related to the civil or military Government or revenues of the Indian possessions, and made elaborate provisions in this behalf to regulate the relations between the Board of Control and the Court of Directors of the East India Company. Subsequent extensions were made in the powers of the Board as representing the Crown, between 1784 and 1833, and in the last mentioned year, they were considerably augmented by the provision that all orders, letters or other communications whatsoever relating to Indian affairs or to any public matter shall not be sent or given by the Directors until the same shall have been approved by the Board. At the same time, the Home Treasury of the East India Company was transferred to the control of the Board from that of the Court of Directors, as the Company no longer possessed any trade privileges or appreciable trade revenues. The only powers which were still withheld from the Board in respect of the Government of India at this time were those relating to the appointment and dismissal of particular servants, though even here sanction was required for the total number of civil and military officers annually appointed. The Board also had not the power to interfere with the Home Establishment though, similarly, their sanction was required for the total sum to be annually expended on that establishment.

The system of 'Home' control under the Board

The principal duties which the Board of Control discharged in the days of its greatest activity were described by Mr. Waterfield, Senior Clerk of the Board of Control, before the Parliamentary Committee of 1853. It gives an insight into the manner of conducting Indian official business in England in those' days' and explains many of the peculiar features of administration which still subsist in the India Office. It is abridged below :–

" The following is the mode in which this superintendence is conducted :—

The general business of the office is divided into six departments :— 1. Revenue :—To which belongs all matters relating to the assessment and collection of the revenues of India. 2. Finance and Accounts :— Taking cognizance of the public expenditure, remittances of revenue and the management of the mints of the three Presidencies. 3. Military. 4. Marine, Ecclesiastical, Public or Miscellaneous. 5. Political. 6. Judicial and Legislative.

There is, besides these, the Secret Department, which is under the immediate management of the President himself. The Despatches in this department are prepared by him, and not at the India House; and in the preparation of those Despatches, it will readily be understood that the events of late years have rendered necessary the careful perusal of a very voluminous and important correspondence.

In all the other Departments the Despatches are prepared at the India House. A proposed Despatch comes to the Board, first, in the shape of what is technically called a " previous communication "; that is, the Chairman of the East India Company communicates his views to the President, previously to submitting them to the Court of Directors. " The previous communication " is accompanied by one or more " collections, " that is, volumes of papers containing all the correspondence which has passed between the various officers in India or between England and India on the subjects treated of in the proposed Despatch. The " previous communication " is sometimes a bulky document ; and the accompanying " collections " often extend to a considerable number of pages. A financial Despatch had 416 folio pages. Mr. Canning mentioned in the House of Commons one in the Military Department, to which were attached 13,511 pages of " collections ;" and there has recently been one in the Revenue Department with 16,263.

In the same department there was in 1845, a Despatch to which there appertained more than 46,000 pages of " collections;" and the Senior Clerk's notes on which occupied 49 closely written sides of folio papers,

The President reads the "previous communication" and all the notes and comments which have been written upon it, and, if necessary, refers to the "collections." Having considered these various papers, he gives his decision. . . . .

This plan of "previous communications" has been found very advantageous to the conduct of the public business, by enabling the Board to exercise, with much less of controversial discussion, their invidious duty of controlling the proceedings of the 24 Directors.

When the "previous communication" is returned to the India House, the Chairman takes into his consideration the alterations made by the President; perhaps he acquiesces in them; perhaps he entirely dissents from them; perhaps he is inclined to a modification of them; in whatever way he decides, the proposed Despatch is copied in conformity thereto, and is submitted to the whole body of Directors. In the Court, it may receive further alteration; and when it has passed that ordeal, it is sent with the "collections" again to the Board, in the form now technically called a "draft". This "draft" is compared in the proper department at the India Board, with the "previous communication" as settled by the President. If they agree, that fact is reported by the Senior Clerk, and the formal approbation of the Board to the proposed Despatch is signified to the Court as a matter of course. If the "previous communication" and the "draft" do not agree, the variations are specified. Reference is, if necessary, again had to the "collections;" comments are again made; the President must again peruse the papers, and after such further consideration, decide whether to alter it; the reasons for alterations must be stated in a formal letter to the Court. Should they not be specified with those reasons, they address to the Board a letter of remonstrance, and that letter must then be considered and answered. When the discussion is at an end, and the Despatch has been transmitted to India by the Court of Directors, a copy is sent to the Board, in order that they may see that their final instructions have been obeyed.

In addition to the duties before detailed, the President has to communicate frequently in private with almost every other department of Government; and, since the year 1811, he has always been a Member of the Cabinet.

He finds it, moreover, indispensable to the due discharge of his functions to carry on an uninterrupted correspondence with the

Governor-General of India, and other high functionaries, which occupies no small portion of his time."

The Charter Act of 1853 was preceded as usual by the elaborate Parliamentary enquiry to which we have above referred, and it virtually announced the death of the Company by simply providing that the Indian territories should remain under the government of the Company in trust for the Crown and until Parliament should otherwise direct. Alterations were made in the machinery of administration in India in various directions to which reference will be made subsequently. The Act remained in force till 1858. After the Mutiny, it was superseded by the Government of India Act of 1858 which vested the direct government of India in the Crown.

Government by and in the name of the Crown

With the transference in 1858 of the control of affairs of the East India Company from the Board of Control and the Court of Directors to a Secretary of State responsible to Parliament, assisted by a Council of persons conversant with Indian affairs, the constitutional character of British rule in India underwent a marked change. The authority of Parliament was recognised, at the time when the transfer was made, as of special importance, and though the hopes which were entertained in 1858 in regard to the great and beneficent influence of Parliament in Indian affairs have not been realised, a good deal of progress has been made in the development of constitutional machinery within India itself. In 1861, the Legislatures of India were established on a new and broader footing and in 1892 they were enlarged, the elective element being recognised and provision being made for Members to interpellate the Executive Government and to discuss the Budget within limits. A great advance in the constitutional position assigned to the Councils in 1892 has been made by the Indian Councils Act, 1909, by which the number of Members in the Imperial Council and in the Provincial Councils has been more than doubled, and by the Regulations made under the Act, the non-official element has been largely increased, fuller play has been given to the elective principle, and more extended powers have been vested in the Councils to consider and discuss financial and administrative questions and to express their opinions thereon in the form of Resolutions.

Changes have also been made from time to time in the constitution of the executive authorities in India. The Viceroy's Executive Council which in 1858 consisted of four Ordinary Members and the Commander-in-Chief now contains five Ordinary Members, of whom one is in charge of the Finances. Before the Mutiny, the Council worked as a collective Board. At present it conducts its business on what are commonly described as the lines of a modern Cabinet. Four Lieutenant-Governorships have been formed and a new Chief Commissionership has been added. The gradually increasing business of the country has also necessitated the delegation of large powers upon Provincial Governments and of some small portions of public functions to Local Bodies. Further changes in the same direction have been recommended by the Royal Commission upon Decentralisation in India and these recommendations are now being considered and carried out.

Some main landmarks

The foregoing brief sketch has been given with a view to the recognition of three or four main landmarks in the constitutional history of British India. In the history of British Rule in India till the close of the 17th century, constitutional progress mainly centres round the organisation, the functions and the fortunes of the Company and its Courts of Proprietors and Directors. The growth of legislative, administrative and judicial authority in the few settlements of the Company in India is closely affected by the amount of interest which successive Stuart Kings could be induced to take in the affairs of the Company, and it was more the prerogative of the King combined with the enterprise of the merchants, than the interest of the British Nation that led to the acquisition and settlement of territories in the East and the development of executive and legislative authority for their government. With the beginning of the 18th century, however, Parliament steps on the scene and begins to assert its authority to control the exercise of the prerogative by the King in respect of all territories acquired by British subjects beyond the seas, a claim which had been fully established in the affair of the " Red Bridge".

The rapid acquisition of territories on behalf of the Company in India in the subsequent period and the equally rapid acquisition of enormous wealth by all manner of means by the servants of the Company, combined with the extremely unsatisfactory state of the affairs of the Company itself in London and of the government of the people in its territories in the East, attracted pointed Parliamentary attention to Indian affairs in the seventies of the eighteenth century. The Regulating Act was enacted "for the better management of the affairs of the East India Company as well in India as in Europe," and because the earlier Charters of the Company establishing Mayor's Courts "did not sufficiently provide for the administration of Justice." The successive renewals of the Charters since that date every twenty years, afforded opportunities for Parliament to institute periodical inquiries into the affairs of the Company and into the state of the countries which were under its administration. The marked growth of the power of Parliament and of the Ministers who had become responsible to Parliament is a regular and noticeable feature, not only in the Charter Acts which were passed from time to time, but also in many intermediate measures of legislation proposed and carried through Parliament by the King's Government.

The Acts of 1833 and of 1858 may be justly regarded as the next important land-marks in the progress of the Indian Constitution. The Act of 1833 definitely and finally recognised the equality of status, of rights and of duties of the Indian subjects of His Majesty with the British subjects, and it laid down principles for the carrying out of a broad and liberal policy of education and of political and moral progress for India. The Act of 1858 placed this country in direct relation to Parliament, and the responsibility of the Government in India to Parliament was made, so far as constitutional theory could make it, as direct and effective as that of any other Secretary of State in charge of any other department of administration in England. Subsequent constitutional progress, therefore, as observed already, is directed to the growth and development of the organs of administration in India and the furtherance to some extent of the principles of popular self-government.

In the following pages an attempt will be made to give a concise and connected account of the main principles which underlie the constitution and functions of the various legislative, executive, judicial, and administrative bodies in India. These, it would be seen, have to be gathered from the Parliamentary enactments and administrative regulations of over a century and a half. The proposal to consolidate the former has been allowed to drop, and the admirable and authoritative exposition of them by Sir Courtenay Ilbert in "the Government of India", remains the only safe guide to this mass of statutory enactments. Parliamentary legislation, as is usual, has not attempted consolidation, but has continued the course of legislation by reference. The latest enactments introducing very important changes in the constitutional system of India, *viz.*, the Indian Councils Act of 1909 and the Government of India Act of 1912, can only be understood and construed with reference to previous statutes.

CHAPTER II

INDIA AND PARLIAMENTARY SOVEREIGNTY

Legal Sovereignty vested in Parliament

We may begin with what is indeed a truism of the British constitutional system, that the legal sovereignty of the British Empire in India, as elsewhere, vests in the British Parliament—Parliament, in legal phraseology, including King, Lords and Commons. It is the British Parliament that possesses the unrestricted power of legislating on Indian affairs, affecting the interests and welfare of all the Indian subjects of His Majesty. To those laws every body or authority in India is bound to pay unquestioned obedience. The exact date at which the British Parliament actually claimed and exercised this supreme authority has usually been placed in the year 1767, when it interfered in the affairs of the Company and passed a statute allowing the Company to retain their territorial acquisitions and revenues for 2 years in consideration of the payment of an annual sum of £4,00,000. The constitutional theory on which Parliament chose to exercise this power, was thus enunciated by the great Lord Chatham at that time:—"No subjects could acquire the sovereignty of any territory for themselves, but only for the nation to which they belonged." Robert Clive in fact proposed at the time that the Crown should take possession of the territorial acquisitions of the Company, and Chatham agreed with him that "it was both the right and the duty of the

Crown to take the Government of India under its direct control."*

While the legal sovereignty of Parliament over British India has thus been an established fact since 1767, nowhere in the enactments of over a century and a half do we find an express declaration of such sovereignty. The Regulating Act of 1773, which may be deemed to have laid down the extent of this authority as clearly and as widely as possible, proceeded to declare in cautious terms "that the whole civil and military government of the Presidency of Fort William and also the ordinary management and government of all the territorial acquisitions and revenues in the kingdoms of Bengal, Bihar and Orissa should, during such time as the territorial acquisitions and revenues remained in the possession of the Company, be vested in the Governor-General and Council of the Presidency of Fort William,

* The practical considerations and events which led to this direct assertion of the authority of the Crown over the affairs of India were, however, many and various. In 1765, public attention in England had been roused by the colossal fortunes brought home by the servants of the Company and by the reports of the huge corruption which was practised by them in acquiring them. The news of the vast riches with which Bengal was said to abound led the Directors to declare enormous dividends, in spite of the heavy debts of the Company, owing to which it was advancing by rapid strides to bankruptcy. The demand of the public to interfere was thus based primarily on the belief that some portion of the wealth believed to be involved in the gift of the Diwani of Bengal, Bihar and Orissa could and should be diverted into the English Exchequer. The compact with the Company in 1767 above referred to, as embodied in a statute, thus began by asserting this right to control and command both the territorial acquisitions and revenues of India. The interference of the Parliament eventually led, as subsequent history has shown, to the complete absorption of British India as part of the territories of the Crown subject to the legal sovereignty of British Parliament. This indeed was inevitable as well in theory as in fact, as every student of colonial history could testify to. Experience has shown, as Sir C. P. Ilbert puts it, "that whenever a chartered company undertakes territorial sovereignty on an extensive scale, the Government is soon compelled to accept financial responsibility for its proceedings and to exercise direct control over its actions. The career of the East India Company as a territorial power may be treated as having begun in 1765, when it acquired the financial administration of the provinces of Bengal, Bihar and Orissa. Within seven years, it was applying to Parliament for financial assistance. In 1773, its Indian operations were placed directly under the control of a Governor-General appointed by the Crown, and in 1784 the Court of Directors in England were made directly subordinate to the Board of Control, that is, to a Minister of he Crown".

in like manner as they were or at any time theretofore might have been exercised by the President and Council or Select Committee in the said kingdoms ".

The process of absorption of the authority, privileges and monopolies of the Company and its Directors by the Ministers of the Crown and Parliament, proceeded in this indirect fashion till 1853, when the Charter Act of that date provided that the Indian territories should remain under the Government of the Company in trust for the Crown until Parliament should otherwise direct. The Act of 1858 for the Better Government of India, which is the basis of the present authority of the Secretary of State for India who is responsible to Parliament, therefore, recites :—

" Whereas, by the Government of India Act of 1853, the territories in the possession and under the Government of the East India Company were continued under such Government, in trust for Her Majesty, until Parliament should otherwise provide, subject to the provisions of that Act, and of other Acts of Parliament, and the property and rights in the said Act referred to are held by the said Company in trust for Her Majesty for the purposes of the said Government : And whereas it is expedient that the said territories should be governed by and in the name of Her Majesty ° ° ° ° ; the Government of the territories now in the possession or under the Government of the East India Company and all powers in relation to Government vested in, or exercised by, the said Company in trust for Her Majesty, shall cease to be vested in, or exercised by, the said Company ; and all territories in the possession or under the Government of the said Company, and all rights vested in or which, if this Act had not been passed, might have been exercised by the said Company in relation to any territories, shall become vested in Her Majesty, and be exercised in her name ; and for the purpose of this Act, India shall mean the territories vested in Her Majesty as aforesaid, and all territories which may become vested in Her Majesty by virtue of any such rights as aforesaid".

In a legal, as well as in a moral sense, therefore, the destinies of this country are committed to the care of Parliament. But in India as in England, legal sovereignty is not the same thing as political sovereignty. "That body is *politically* sovereign, or supreme in a state", writes Professor Dicey in his 'Law of the Constitution', "whose will is ultimately obeyed by the citizens of that State. In this sense of the word, the electors of Great Britain may be said to be, together with the Crown and the Lords, or perhaps in strict accuracy, independently of the King and the Peers, the body in which the sovereign power is vested. The matter, may, indeed, be carried a little further and we may assert that the arrangements of the Constitution are now such as to ensure that the will of the electors shall, by regular and constitutional means, always in the end assert itself as the predominant influence in the country. But this is a political and not a legal fact." So far as England is concerned, the electors constitute the bulk of the people of the land and the will of the people, therefore, can rightly be stated to be supreme in the government of their country. In respect of the government of India, however, it cannot be said that the will of the people of India is supreme, and though it is in a sense true that the electors of Great Britain are the political sovereigns of India, it cannot be said either that the will of the British electors has regularly and constitutionally, or ever, asserted itself on questions of Indian administration. As a matter of fact, at the present time, the conduct of the Indian Government depends on the policy and measures taken from time to time by the Ministers of the Crown commanding the confidence of the House of Commons in the first instance, and thus of the electors ultimately. The time at which the electors of Great Britain assert their political sovereignty with regard to questions concerning themselves is at General Elections. But the time seems yet to be far distant when a purely Indian question will be fought out at a General Election, the prevailing policy of both the great political parties in England being to treat Indian affairs as non-party matter.*

---

* Though the legal supremacy of the House of Commons over all Indian affairs, and the manner in which it may be enforced is quite well established, diverse opinions have been recently expressed as to the extent to which and the metheds by which the House of Commons should exercise its authority in the direct control of the administration of Indian affairs. For, any body can see, as Lord Morley

A three-fold origin of powers

Subject, therefore, to the legal sovereignty of the British Parliament and the political sovereignty of the Ministers of the King, for the time being chosen by the electors of Great Britain, the superintendence, direction and control of the civil and military Government of India is in England vested in the Secretary of State for India, assisted by a Council in England and the Governor-General in Council in India. The Governor-General in Council exercises in India the delegated authority of the Crown and the Parliament over Indian affairs, but the actual powers exercised by all these authorities have been inherited from different sources. Though there could be no limit to the authority of Parliament from a constitutional point of view, it is still useful in obtaining a proper idea of the usual course of Britain's administration of India, to bear in mind the three-fold origin of the powers of the Government in India, *viz.*, consisting of those arising from the authority of Parliament, those inherited from the East India

---

stated in a recent article in the "Nineteenth Century and After" [February 1911] "that, however decorously veiled, pretensions to oust the House of Commons from part and lot in Indian affairs—and this is what the tone now in fashion on one side of the controversy really comes to—must lead in logic as in fact, to the surprising result of placing what is technically called the Government of India in a position of absolute irresponsibility to the governed. Now, this, whatever else it may be, is at daggers drawn with the barest rudiments of democratic principle. So, for that matter, is it incompatible with divine right or the autocracy of the sword. Even the fiercest Oriental tyrant always ran some risk of having his throat cut or his coffee poisoned if he pushed things too far."

It has, moreover, to be borne in mind, as Lord Morley has subsequently pointed out in the same article, that the responsibility of the Government in India and the Secretary of State to Parliament, is not the same thing as the responsibility of the executive to the legislature in other countries. The Government of a country under responsibility to the people of that country, through its legislature, is a very different thing from the Government of one country under responsibility to the people of another through their legislature. The responsibility of the paramount authority in India to the legislature in England is thus very different in its effects from the responsibility of the executive to the Parliament in England. John Stuart Mill has laid down the proposition that while the responsibility to the governed is the greatest of all securities for good government, responsibility to somebody else not only has no such tendency, but is as likely to produce evil as good. It is somewhat unfortunate that Lord Morley in his article above referred to, though he casts doubts upon this proposition of Mill, yet refrains from discussing it further, on the ground that " ill would it

Company and those derived from the Mughal Emperors and other territorial rulers whose powers the Company succeeded to by cession or conquest. The Government of India Act, 1858, refers to these when it recites in section 3 :—

"One of His Majesty's principal Secretaries of State shall have and perform all such or the like powers and duties in anywise relating to the Government or revenues of India, and all such or the like powers over all officers appointed or continued under the Government of India Act, 1858, as if that Act had not been passed, might or should have been exercised or performed by the East India Company, or by the Court of Directors or Court of Proprietors of that Company, either alone or by the direction or with the sanction or approbation of the Commissioners for the Affairs of India, in relation to that Government or those revenues and the officers and servants of that Company, and also all such powers as might have been exercised by the said Commissioners alone."

His Majesty's Secretary of State with his Council thus exercises on behalf of the Crown, all the powers of control over the authorities in India previously exercised by the East India Company through its Court of Proprietors and Court of Directors. He also represents, as a Member of the Cabinet responsible to

---

become me to lay hands on my father Parmenides." Students of political institutions in India have, therefore, to be content with his endorsement of Mill's final conclusion on this matter as to the actual value of the responsibility of the British Government in India to the House of Commons in England. The responsibility of the British rulers of India to the British nation is chiefly useful, according to Mill, "because, when any acts of Government are called in question, it ensures publicity and discussion, the utility of which does not require that the public at large should comprehend the point at issue, provided there are any individuals among them who do—or, a merely moral responsibility, not to the collective people, but to every separate person among them who forms a judgment. Opinions may be weighed as well as counted, and the approbation or the disapprobation of one person well versed in the subject may outweigh that of thousands who know nothing about it at all. It is doubtless a useful restraint upon the immediate rulers that they can be put upon their defence, and that one or two of the Jury will form an opinion worth having about their conduct, though that of the remainder will probably be several degrees worse than none. Such as it is, this is the amount of benefit to India from the control exercised over the Indian Government by the British Parliament and the people."

Lord Morley considers that this view of Mill as to the constitutional position of the House of Commons towards the people of India, "though set out with something less than his usual lucidity and force, and by no means exhausting the case, may content us : no Government can be trusted, if it is not liable to be called before some Jury or another, compose that Jury how you will, and even if it should unluckily happen to be dunces".—Would it content the people of India for ever?

Parliament, the supreme and ultimate authority of Parliament, formerly exercised through the Board of Control. The powers, rights, and duties inherited from the previous rulers of the land are in practice exercised by the Viceroy and Governor-General of India. This may seem a valueless distinction in the face of the omnipotence of Parliament to deal with Indian affairs as it chooses. But it assumes importance with reference to the actual means and methods of administration in India. We may say, for instance, that the Secretary of State by himself, in a sense, succeeded to the powers of the Board of Control, but with a more direct authority over the affairs of India and a more direct responsibility to Parliament. The Council of India established by the Act of 1858 to advise and assist the Secretary of State in the transaction of Indian business is also, in a similar sense, the successor to the old Courts of Directors and Proprietors of the Company. To the extent to which this Council assists and interposes in the Secretary of State's action or policy in regard to the affairs of India, the position of the Indian Secretary of State differs in some respects markedly from that of other Secretaries of State of His Majesty. Similarly, though his office is the creature of a British statute, the Governor-General has and exercises rights, powers and privileges which do not come within those enumerated in the statutes of Parliament, but which have accrued to the Government of India as the successor of the previous Native Rulers in the land and as the representative of the Crown and the accredited agent for its prerogatives in India. The important rights of the State to the land revenue in India arise, for example, from what is claimed to be the customary and ancient Indian right to the *Rajabhagam* or the King's share of the produce of the land in India.

Indifference of Parliament in practice

It may, therefore, be inferred from the above that Parliamentary control over Indian affairs, even from the constitutional point of view, must needs be imperfect owing to the complicated origin of British authority in India and the difficulty of exercising direct supervision. In actual fact, moreover, the indifference of Parliament and the British electors to the Government of India—the brightest Jewel in the British Crown—is astounding and their ignorance of Indian affairs is 'abyssmal.'* The extent and the limits of the authority ordinarily exercised by Parliament over Indian administration, as fixed by statute, are comprised in the following provisions:—(1) that, "although the whole of the Indian revenues are at the disposal of the Secretary of State and the Council, to be by them drawn upon for all expenditure required for the service of India, they must make known to Parliament all expenditure incurred and may not increase the debt of India without the sanction of the House of Commons; (2) that, on the other hand, although the Indian Budget is annually laid before that House with a report on the 'Home accounts' by an independent auditor and a statement showing the moral and material progress of India—to enable its members to offer suggestions, ask for information, and generally criticise the policy of the Government in relation to India—the financial statement is followed by no application for any vote to control or influence the taxation of India, but merely by a certain formal resolution setting forth the actual revenue and expenditure in India for the current year"; (3) that, except for preventing or repelling actual invasion of His Majesty's Indian possessions, or under other sudden and urgent necessity, the revenues of India are not, without the consent of both Houses of Parliament, applicable to defraying the expenses of any military operation carried on beyond the external frontiers of those possessions by His Majesty's forces or charged upon those revenues and (4) that

* The intention, however, of the framers of the Act of 1858, which transferred the rule of India from the Company to the Crown, appears to have been that the House of Commons should exercise a direct and regular supervision over the Government of India. The history of that measure is, from a constitutional point of view, interesting and an admirable summary of it by the late Mr. George Yule in his Presidential Address to the fourth Indian National Congress is reproduced in a Note at the end of this chapter.

all proclamations, regulations and rules made under the Indian Councils Act, 1909, other than rules made by a Lieutenant-Governor for the more convenient transaction of business in his Council, shall be laid before both Houses of Parliament as soon as may be after they are made.

While it is true that Parliamentary control over Indian affairs has thus tended to become unreal, because of its difficulty, it has been maintained by no less an authority than Mr. Leonard (now Lord) Courtney in his book on the 'Working Constitution of the United Kingdom', "that it has been part of the overruling mind which has shaped the organisation of Indian Government to make it not too responsive to the varying temper of the House of Commons, though in the end, the national will must have its way." How both these could be secured by placing the Indian Secretary of State's salary on the British Estimates, is explained by Mr. (now Lord) Courtney as follows:—

"The Secretary of State is a Member of the Cabinet which must possess the confidence of the House of Commons. . . . In the end, the national will must have its way here as elsewhere ; but checks and obstacles are interposed which, perhaps insensibly, moderate its force. No part of the expense involved in the Government of India comes before the House of Commons in Committee of Supply. The salary of the Colonial Secretary is voted by Parliament and there is thus a possibility of annually reviewing his policy in the full activity of the Parliamentary Session. The salary of the Indian Secretary of State is paid by India and never comes before the House of Commons. At the end of the Session, generally after the Appropriation Bill has been read a second time, the Indian Budget is submitted ; and this consists of the review of the financial situation in India followed, after a desultory discussion, by a Resolution simply affirming that the Indian Accounts show certain totals of income and expenditure. It may be doubted whether this does not betray too great a jealousy of the House of Commons. If the salary of the Indian Secretary of State were submitted like the Colonial Secretary's to a vote, the opportunity for a real debate would be given which, experience suggests, would be used rather than abused."

NOTE

(Extract from the Presidential Address of Mr. George Yule, as President of the Fourth Indian National Congress held in Allahabad in December 1888.)

" When the sole government of this country was taken over by the Crown in 1858, it fell to the lot of Lord Palmerston who was then Prime Minister, to introduee into the House of Commons, a Bill which was afterwards known as India Bill No. 1. The main provisions of this Bill were, that the Government of India was to vest in a Viceroy and Council in India and a Council of eight retired Indian officials presided over by a Secretary of State in London. The proceedings of these two separate bodies, each of whom had certain independent responsibilities, were to be subject to the review and final decision of the House of Commons. The chief objection to this Bill was that no provision was made for the representation of the people of the country. Mr. Disraeli, who was leader of the Opposition, objected to it on the ground of the insufficient check which it provided ; and he said that with such Councils as those proposed, ' you could not be sure that the inhabitants of India would be able to obtain redress from the grievances under which they suffered, that English protection ought to insure.' Almost immediately after the introduction of the Bill, Lord Palmerston was defeated upon a side question and Lord Derby became Prime Minister with Mr. Disraeli as Leader of the House of Commons. No time was lost by the new Ministry in introducing India Bill No. 2. Mr. Disraeli dwelt upon the desirability of having the representative principle applied to the Government of the country and his scheme was to increase the Council in London, which was proposed by Lord Palmerston, from eight to eighteen Members, half of whom were to be elected and were in all other respects to be entirely independent of Government. He regretted that the unsettled state of the country did not admit of a representation of the people in India itself, and all that could be done in the meantime was to approach as near to that form of government as the circumstances would permit. The provisions of his Bill to effect that purpose were briefly these. Four of the elected half of the Council were to be Members of the Indian Civil and Military services of ten years' standing and the remaining five must have been engaged in trading with India for at least five years. The constituency electing the four Members connected with the services was to consist of all officers of both branches of the India Service and also of all residents in India owning £2,000 of an Indian Railway or £1,000 of Government Stock. The five mercantile members were to be elected by the Parliamentary constituencies of London, Belfast, Liverpool, Manchester and Glasgow. So deeply ingrained is this notion of government by representation in the minds of Englishmen that, rather than leave it out of sight altogether in dealing with the affairs of India, the Government of that day made the proposal I have stated. Although the intention underlying these proposals was applauded, the scheme itself was felt to be, from the imperfect character of the constituencies, wholly inadequate to secure the check that was desired. It was clear or rather it soon became clear, that the interests of one set of voters were adverse to the interests of the mass of the people and that the other set knew absolutely nothing of the country or its wants. Received with favour at first, the Bill soon became the object of jest and derision on the part of the Opposition and even its more impartial critics said of it that it was useless offering to the people of India under the name of bread, what would certainly turn out to be a stone. At the suggestion of Lord John Russell, the Bill was withdrawn and the House proceeded by way of resolutions to construct the frame work of another Bill. The plan finally adopted was this—the legislative and administrative powers were to be entrusted to a Viceroy and a Council in India and the check upon them was to be a Council of fifteen Members sitting in London. This Council was to be responsible to the Cabinet through a Secretary of State, who was to be responsible in turn to the House of Commons. This arrangement was regarded merely as a provisional one and the policy to be pursued was to work up to the constitutional standard. Education was to be largely extended and improved and the natives of the country were to be drafted into the service of Government as they became qualified with the view, among other reasons, to fit them for the anticipated enlargement of their political powers. The provisions made and the prospects held out in the debates in Parliaments derived a lustre from the famous Proclamation of the Queen—that half-fulfilled Charter of Indian rights—which was first read and published to the people of India in this very city of Allahabad thirty years ago.

Now, what I wish to impress upon your mind by this brief narrative, is the great importance that was attached at that time to some sort of constitutional check. Failing to have it in the form that the

English people themselves approved and followed in the management of their own affairs, they devised the substitute with its three-fold check that I have mentioned. Parliament itself was full of gushing enthusiasm as to the part it would take in the business. In the absence of a representative body in India, the House of Commons was to play the *rôle* of one on our behalf. It was to regard the work as a great and solemn trust committed to it by an all-wise and inscrutable Providence, the duties of which it would faithfully and fully discharge. Such was the style of language employed both in and out of Parliament at the time I allude to. And now what is the actual state of the case? it is summed up in a single sentence: there is no check. The ill under which our affairs are administered appears like many other Bills to be open to more than one interpretation. The interpretation put upon it at the time, and what was probably the intention of Parliament, was, the Government of India was to have the right of initiative; the Council in London the right of revision and the Secretary of State, subject to the ultimate judgment of the House of Commons, the right of veto. And this was practically the relation of the parties until 1870. In that year, the Duke of Argyll was Secretary of State; and in a controversy on this subject with Lord Mayo who was then Viceroy, he laid down quite another doctrine. He held that the Government in India had no independent power at all and that the prerogative of the Secretary of State was not limited to a veto of the measures passed in India. 'The Government in India,' he maintained, 'were merely executive officers of the Home Government, who hold the ultimate power of requiring the Governor-General to introduce a measure and of requiring also all the Official Members of the Council to vote for it.' This power-absorbing Despatch is dated 24th November 1870. The supposed powers and privileges of the Council in London have been similarly dealt with and the Council is now regarded merely as an adjunct of the offiee of the Secretary of State, to furnish him with information or advice when he chooses to ask for it. The present position is this: the Government of India has no power; the Council in London has no power; the House of Commons has the power, but it refuses or neglects to exercise it. The 650 odd Members who were to be the palladium of India's rights and liberties have thrown 'the great and solemn trust of an inscrutable Providence' back upon the hand of Providence to be looked after as Providence itself thinks best."

CHAPTER III

THE CROWN AND THE INDIA OFFICE

The Colonies and India: a distinction

The executive authority of the Crown over India is not a thing which arose with the Act of 1858. As has been pointed out in the last chapter, it has existed from the middle of the eighteenth century and been exercised through various bodies from time to time. What the Act of 1858 did was to vest that authority directly in a Secretary of State, assisted by a Council, newly created. It is in this respect that the framers of the Act made a departure from the methods followed as regards the Colonies. The reasons therefor were then indicated to consist in a desire to have expert advice and guidance on, and to some extent control over, the affairs of India entrusted to the Secretary of State. In respect of the Colonies, the constitutional theory has been that the authority of the Crown in regard to legislation and administration, is exercised by the King in Council (*i.e.*, the Privy Council). Parliament, of course, is supreme and might intervene and make provision for the Government of any Colony—for, in the words of Lord Mansfield, "there cannot exist any power in the Crown exclusive of Parliament." But, ordinarily, it has been deemed to be specially within the province of the 'King in Council' to deal with the good government of the overseas Empire. This theory, to a large extent, held good in respect of India too, and vestiges of it still remain in the matter of issuing military commissions. With the passing, however, of the Regulating Act in 1773, the

Parliament came upon the scene and the authority of the King in Council receded and was practically thereafter confined to the "settled prerogative of the Crown to receive appeals in all colonial causes"—a power which is now statutorily vested in the Judicial Committee.

Thus, while the authority of the Crown over Colonial affairs continued to be exercised by the King in Council, that over India came to be exercised through special bodies, such as the Board of Control and the Secret Committee of the Court of Directors, the main reason being, it may be presumed, to keep a zealous watch over the Company and to provide well-informed and expert guidance in the administration of such a vast and varied territory as the Indian Empire. The evolution of the Colonial Secretary, therefore, became associated with the King's Council, while that of the Indian Secretary became associated with a special and new body known as the Council of India. In his book on "The Law and Custom of the Constitution," Sir William Anson has laid down this distinction in the following terms :—"Apart from the legislative supremacy of Parliament, which is the same for all parts of the King's dominions, the Colonies are governed by the King in Council, or by the King acting on the advice of the Secretary of State for the Colonies. But India is governed by the Emperor of India acting on the advice of the Secretary of State for India in Council. The Secretary of State, no doubt, represents the King-Emperor of India in the exercise of the royal prerogative, but his *Council* is not the Privy Council, but the *Council of India*".

The Indian Secretary of State

The Act of 1858 which inaugurated the direct Government of India by the Crown, recites that all rights which, if the Act had not been passed, might have been exercised by the East India Company in relation to any territories, may be exercised by and in the name of His Majesty as rights incidental to the Government of British India. In virtue of his position, the Indian Secretary is always a Member of the Cabinet—the body in whom the ultimate executive authority of the Crown over the whole of the British Empire is by constitutional convention vested. The Secretary of State for India advises the Sovereign, according to legal theory, in his capacity of Privy Councillor, having been 'sworn of the Privy Council' as a matter of course. The Cabinet, therefore, in its solidarity, joins in his counsels and shares in his responsibilities. The Act of 1858, however, as we have seen, has associated with the Indian Secretary a Council whose function it is "to conduct, under his direction, the business transacted in the United Kingdom in relation to the Government of India and the correspondence with India." Its concurrence, moreover, on some important matters relating to Indian affairs, has been made essential to the Secretary of State taking any action in respect thereto.

His position : In theory

The constitutional position of the Indian Secretary of State has thus been made to differ somewhat markedly from that of other Ministers. According to constitutional usage, he is the person responsible to Parliament for the administration of India. But in regard to certain specified questions—one of them being the appropriation of the revenues of India—the determination thereof is reserved by statute to the Secretary *and* a majority of the India Council, a body which is unrepresented in Parliament and is statutorily disqualified from direct representation in Parliament. The only exception to this rule is that no appropriation of Indian revenues for any military operations beyond the Indian frontiers can be made without the sanction of Parliament. This, of course, is of very rare occurrence. It would, therefore, seem as if the principle of ministerial responsibility to Parliament could not be enforced against the Indian Secretary in such cases—which would virtually mean that Parliament could not exercise effective control over the finances and expenditure of India. A discussion arose on this question in the House of Commons some time after the Act of 1858 was passed, in 1869, and the matter has been virtually settled by the statement of a late Secretary of State for India. The proper mode of regarding the India Council would appear to be to treat it as a body deputed by Parliament to exercise a species of *quasi*-Parliamentary control in certain matters over the Secretary of State, and the authority so delegated is, in this view, liable to be revoked. "The House of Commons is so overwhelmed with business nearer home," he said, "that it has no opportunity of making itself acquainted with all those vast fields of knowledge that will enable it to exercise an efficient influence over the Secretary of State for India. Therefore, it has instituted this Council to be its deputy, as it were, to watch him and see that the powers placed in his hands are not abused. It ought, however, to be clearly understood that the moment the House steps in and expresses an opinion on a subject connected with India, that moment the jurisdiction of the Council ought to cease. It is not to be endured in this constitutional country for a moment that the Council should set itself against the express opinion of the House."

In practice

The student of Indian constitutional history has yet to look for the development and subsequent use of a constitutional convention such as is indicated in the above words. The consciousness that the will of the House of Commons is ultimately bound to prevail has not acted so much in the direction of preventing the Council of India from assuming a factious or obstructive attitude in the exercise of its powers, as in that of strengthening the hands of the British Cabinet, which could rely on the support of the House to subordinate and sometimes to sacrifice the interests of India—now unrepresented in the House—to British or Imperial exigencies or interests. "While the object, and to some extent, the effect of the Act was," writes Sir C. P. Ilbert, "to impose a constitutional restraint on the powers of the Secretary of State with respect to the expenditure of money, yet this restraint could not be effectively asserted in all cases, especially where Imperial interests are involved. For instance, the power to make war necessarily involves the expenditure of revenues, but it is a power for the exercise of which the concurrence of a majority of votes at a meeting of the Council cannot be made a necessary condition. The Secretary of State is a Member of the Cabinet and in Cabinet questions, the decision of the Cabinet must prevail." The belief that the Act of 1858 had vested in the India Council the power to veto absolutely any expenditure which they considered India should not be charged with, was soon discovered to be unfounded. In practice, the Council has often been overborne and sometimes not even consulted. The Secretary of State has had to bow to the decision of the Cabinet in these matters irrespective of the interests of India.

The India Council ineffective

This fact was clearly brought out in the examination of the Marquis of Salisbury, when Secretary of State for India, by the Parliamentary Committee on Indian Finance of 1871—74. "If, with the support of the Council, the Secretary of State should oppose a demand from the Treasury," said Lord Salisbury, "the result would be 'to stop the machine'." He was thereupon asked: "You must either stop the machine or resign or go on tacitly submitting to injustice." "I should accept that statement", he replied, "barring the word, 'tacitly.' I should go on submitting with loud remonstrances." "Remonstrances, however loud," remarks an authority, * "might be unavailing unless backed by the force of external opinion. And here was the constant difficulty indicated by another of Lord Salisbury's replies. Under the pressure applied by the House of Commons, every department desires to reduce its estimates. It is, therefore, tempted, without any desire to be unjust, to get money in the direction of least resistance. So long as the House of Commons is indifferent to Indian finance, there will, therefore, be a steady temptation to shift burdens upon India. The zealous watchfulness of the House of Commons, said Lord Salisbury, would be the best protection of the people of

* Leslie Stephen—Life of Henry Fawcett.

India against such injustice, and he spoke of the desirability of exciting public opinion in England 'up to the point of integrity'."

The Constitution of the Council

It has thus happened that the body constituted by Parliament to watch over and act as a check on the Indian Secretary in the exercise of his powers has been, by the Parliament's own subsequent action, deprived of its power and that the object of the framers of the Act has been defeated. The India Council, in fact, possesses little real power and its only function is to constitute itself into a body of advisers to the Indian Secretary, who are deemed specially conversant with Indian affairs. The constitutional distinction, however, between the Secretary of State in Council and the Secretary of State is still, in many cases, of practical importance. The powers of the Secretary of State, of the India Council and of the Secretary of State in Council will be found fully set out in the Act of 1858, and the subsequent amending Acts which are published in the Appendix; only a brief reference to a few noteworthy points is here necessary. In general, under the terms of the Charter Act of 1833, the Secretary of State may, as inheriting the powers of the Board of Control, "superintend, direct and control all acts, operations and concerns which in any wise relate to or concern the Government or revenues of India." The Council of India, under the terms of Section 19 of the Act of 1858, conducts under his direction "the business transacted in the United Kingdom in relation to the Government of India and the correspondence with India." The Council of India, as at present constituted, is to consist of not more than fourteen Members and not less than ten Members. These are appointed by the Secretary of State to hold office—with the exception of one having professional or peculiar qualifications who may be appointed Member during good behaviour—for a term of ten years which may for special reasons be extended for a further term of five years. The Secretary of State may also appoint to the Council a Member having professional or other special qualifications. The Members of the India

Council can only be removed, like His Majesty's Judges in England, by an address of both Houses of Parliament. All powers required to be exercised by the Secretary of State in Council and all powers of the Council may be exercised at meetings of the Council at which not less than five Members are present. The Secretary of State is authorised to divide the Council into committees for the more convenient transaction of business and to appoint a Vice-President.

The Control of the India Office

The Indian Secretary and his Council, between them, have succeeded, as we have seen, to all the powers previously exercised by the Board of Control, with and without the Courts of Directors and Proprietors of the East India Company. The nature of the control which, prior to 1858, this Board exercised over the administration in India was thus described by John Stuart Mill:—

"It is not" he said, "so much an executive as a deliberative body. The Executive Government of India is and must be seated in India itself. The principal function of the Home Government is not to direct the details of administration, but to scrutinise and revise the past acts of the Indian Government, to lay down principles and issue general instructions for their future guidance and to give or refuse sanction to great political measures which are referred Home for approval."

Sir John Strachey * is of opinion that this description holds good even at the present day. "The work of the Secretary of State," is, according to Sir John, "mainly confined to answering references made to him by the Government in India and apart from great political and financial questions, the number and nature of those references mainly depend on the character of the Governor-General for the time being. Some men in that position like to minimise personal responsibilities and to ask for the orders of the Home Government before taking action. Others prefer to act on their own judgment and on that of their

* India: Its Administration and Progress. Third Edition, [Macmillan] p. 78.

Councillors. The Secretary of State initiates almost nothing." The last statement, however, appears too broad. Though it is supported in principle by the pronouncement of the present Viceroy that in the matter of the new reforms, the initiative came from the Government of India and not from Lord Morley, still instances can be quoted in which the Secretary of State initiated measures of reform owing to pressure of public opinion in India and England, in opposition to the views of the Government in India. Other instances can also be quoted in which the "Home" Government initiated and forced on this country measures of financial or fiscal policy under the pressure of powerful interests in England and against the declared intentions and policy of the Government in India as well as of public opinion in this country.

The Business of the Council

The work of the Council of India is usually to deal with such business as is placed before it by the Secretary of State. He may overrule his Council in all matters where there is difference of opinion between him and his Council, except as to those in which their concurrence is obligatory under the statute. He may despatch letters and issue orders directly to the authorities in India in the "Secret Department", wherever the matter is, in his opinion or in that of the Indian authorities, one requiring secrecy or urgency, or concerns the making of war or peace, or the policy respecting the Native States and Princes, or for which a majority of votes of the Council is not declared to be necessary. A majority of such votes is necessary for decisions on the following matters:—

(i) Appropriation of the revenues of India or properties.

(ii) Exercise of borrowing powers and entering into contracts.

(iii) Alteration of salaries, furlough rules, etc.

(iv) Appointments of Natives of India to offices reserved for the Indian Civil Service and the making of provisional appointments to the Governor-General's Council.

For the purposes of the exercise in England of the financial powers and duties in respect of the revenues of India or other properties which are by law vested in the Crown, and the incurring of rights and liabilities under contracts, the Secretary of State has been declared by the Act of 1858 a juristic person. The Act has also provided that the Secretary of State in Council may sue and be sued as well in India as in England as a body corporate and that every person has the same remedies against the Secretary of State in Council as he might have had against the East India Company.

An interesting distinction in law

In this respect, an important constitutional distinction exists between him and the other Secretaries of State. In England, an action does not lie against the Crown. The only legal remedy against the Crown is by Petition of Right. On the other hand, Ministers in England are not protected, except where expressly so provided by statute, in respect of legal wrongs by pleading the authority of the Crown, whereas in respect of India, the Secretary of State and every Member of the India Council are expressly exempted from personal liability in respect of all contracts, covenants or other engagements entered into by them in their official capacity, and "all costs and damages in respect thereof are borne by the revenues of India." Moreover, as Sir C. P. Ilbert points out*, it has been held that a Petition of Right does not lie for a wrong committed, in pursuance of the maxim that the King can do no wrong; and for a wrong done by a person in obedience or professed obedience to the Crown, the remedy is against the wrong-doer himself and not against the Crown. But, in India, it would seem as if a statutory remedy will lie against the Secretary of State in Council as a body corporate, not merely in cases in which a Petition of Right will lie in England, but in all cases in which the right of suit is given by statutes and in respect of acts done in the conduct of undertakings which might be carried on by private individuals without sovereign powers.

* The Government of India—Second Edition, p. 171.

CHAPTER IV

THE IMPERIAL GOVERNMENT

The Executive authority in India

We have dealt, in the last two chapters, with the powers, functions and ordinary business of the Supreme Legislative and Executive authority over the Indian Empire, vested in the Parliament of Great Britain and Ireland and the Crown of the United Kingdom. The direct administration of an Empire like British India could not, however, be conducted by a body or bodies constituted in London and it is to the organs and institutions, evolved and established in India during more than a century and a half, that we must next look to obtain an idea of how the administration is carried on. In doing so, we may first of all deal with the executive authority, as being the older in point of origin and as the one from which the legislative authority subsequently expanded and became distinct. The 'superintendence, direction and control' in India of the civil and military Government of British India is vested in the Viceroy and Governor-General of India in Council. Statutorily, of course, the old provision in the Regulating Act of 1773 requiring and directing the Governor-General in Council "to obey all such orders as they shall receive from the Court of Directors", of the East India Company is still operative and vests in the Secretary of State—who has succeeded to the powers of the Court of Directors under the Act of 1858—the power of requiring similar obedience to his orders.

The constitutional question, however, in this connection is not so much as to the subordinate or delegated executive authority of the Governor-General in Council, which is undisputed, as to the extent and limits of such authority. The relations between the Secretary of State and the Government of India are now regulated, according to Sir Courtenay Ilbert, by constitutional usage. Sir John Strachey, however, as stated before, seems to think that the usage is not quite settled, at least so far as the every-day administration is concerned, and that it varies with the character of the Governor-General for the time being. It is not possible for those not directly acquainted with the administrative business and methods of the Imperial Government to venture any opinion on this subject. Nor could any definite and petrified usage in this respect be expected to outlive the requirements of the daily progressive and expanding administration of India. There are those who believe implicitly in "the man on the spot" theory, while there are others who believe in the corrective influences of control from the democracy in England and its agents, the Ministers of His Majesty, under the guidance of public opinion and progressive ideas.

The position of the man on the spot

Whatever be the right principle in this respect, we may refer to one or two understandings which have become settled in regard to the relations between the Governor-General in Council and the Secretary of State, as a result of controversies which arose after the Acts of 1858 and 1861 were passed. The interpretation put upon the Act of 1858 at the time it was passed by Parliament was, as Mr. George Yule pointed out in the speech quoted in the Note to the last Chapter, that the Government of India was to have the right of initiative, the Council in London the right of revision and the Secretary of State the right of veto, subject to the ultimate judgment of the House of Commons. Similarly, the Indian Councils Act of 1861 vested the power of previous sanction necessary for the introduction of certain important measures in the Legislative

His initiative in Legislation

Councils, in the Governor-General, and not in the Secretary of State—the power of subsequent disallowance by the Crown, exercised through the latter, being the only check retained in his hands under the Statute. Disputes, however, arose over this division of powers. The first of its kind was in 1870, when the Duke of Argyll was Secretary of State for India and Lord Mayo the Viceroy. There were differences of opinion between the Secretary of State and the Government of India in connection with some of the legislative proposals of the latter, then before the Legislative Council. Among these the Punjab Drainage and Canal Act which set the whole subject of irrigation works on a legal footing as regarded the Punjab, was the subject of a great controversy between Lord Mayo and the Duke of Argyll. In a Despatch, dated the 24th November 1870, the Duke of Argyll laid it down that the prerogative of the Secretary of State was not limited to a veto of the measures passed in India. "The Government of India," he observed, "were merely executive officers of the 'Home' Government, who hold the ultimate power of requiring the Governor-General to introduce a measure and of requiring also all the Official Members to vote for it." The Punjab Canal Act was afterwards repealed and re-enacted with modifications.

The next important dispute was in 1874 and was but the natural development of what took place in 1870. If the Secretary of State could and ought to do what the Duke of Argyll said he had the power of doing in respect of the legislative proposals of the Government of India, it follows that in order effectually to exercise such a power, action subsequent to the passing of measures by the Councils in India, either by exercise of veto or by requiring the Governor-General to repeal and re-enact them with the necessary modifications, is not sufficient. This was exactly how it struck the Marquis of Salisbury who was Secretary of State for India in 1874. In a Despatch to Lord Northbrook, the Governor-General, the Secretary of State directed that the Government of India should in future communicate to him—in order that he may have an opportunity of previously expressing his opinion and directions thereon—information regarding any measures, except those of slight importance or those requiring urgent action, which they might intend to introduce into the Legislative Council. A similar course was to be followed in case any important alterations were made during the progress of a measure through the Legislative Council and the orders of the Secretary of State were to be awaited thereon. The Provincial Governments were also asked similarly to follow the same procedure. The Government of India pointed out difficulties in following this course, after once a measure had been launched, and suggested that the understanding should be that the measure might be proceeded with, if no reply were received to their communications within two months; and in regard to the Provincial Legislative Councils, Lord Northbrook's Government pointed out that the course proposed by the Secretary of State was likely to interfere with the power and the obligation, imposed by statute upon the Governor-General, of sanctioning or rejecting prior or subsequent to enactment the legislative proposals of the Provincial Governments. As a result of the correspondence that took place, the Government of India promised to bear carefully in mind the wishes of the Secretary of State, more especially as he had assured them that his instructions were not intended to fetter the discretion which the law had vested in the various legislative authorities in India or in the Governor-General. The Secretary of State accepted the arrangement. But in 1875, in consequence of the financial state of the country, the Tariff Act was passed as an urgent measure without reference to the Secretary of State, imposing a duty of 5 per cent. on imported cotton and other goods, and it had the effect of checkmating the Secretary of State in reference to a matter on which he had expressed contrary views before and in which the interests of the Lancashire cotton manufacturers were involved. He, therefore, censured the Government of India for having passed the Tariff Act without reference to him. He refused to accept the contention of the Government of India that the urgency of the case was their justification and that an additional reason for immediate action lay in the difficulty of carrying on prolonged discussions, pending a reference to the Secretary of State, with regard to measures 'involving alterations of customs duties without a disclosure of the intentions of Government which would be productive of considerable inconvenience to trade.' Lord Salisbury considered that the Government of India had over-rated the difficulty of keeping an official secret and re-affirmed his former position that the import duty on cotton manufacturers should be removed as soon as the condition of the revenues enabled the Government of India to part with it. In regard to legislative measures, he directed for the future that whenever the Government of India found it necessary to pass an Act urgently, telegraphic intimation should be given to him beforehand without delay.

This decision led to the immediate resignation of Lord Northbrook and the appointment of Lord Lytton to the Viceroyalty, with a mandate on this and other questions—a mandate, however, which he found difficult to carry out and which he carried out eventually only by the exercise of his extraordinary power of overruling the majority of his Councillors. The effect of the Marquis of Salisbury's orders in connection with this question was considered to be, according to a high authority, "to transfer to a great extent the initiative of the measures required for the good government of India from the Viceroy's Council to the Secretary of State," and the Despatch on the subject, though approved by a majority of the then members of the Council of India, was dissented from by such distinguished administrators as Sir Erskine Perry and Sir Henry Montgomery.*

His executive powers.

It may, therefore, be inferred that while the statutory powers vested in the Governor-General in regard to legislation have come to be controlled by the Secretary of State in the manner indicated

* The main Despatches in connection with this controversy which set forth the constitutional understandings between the Secretary of State and the Government of India will be found in the Appendix.

7

in the foregoing paragraphs, his powers are even more liable to be interfered with in regard to executive administration, where the occasions for interference in the interests of good government or otherwise are likely to be more frequent. On all questions relating to foreign affairs, the Government of India equally with the self-governing Colonies, have no foreign policy of their own, because India's foreign relations must necessarily be co-ordinated with those of the Empire. The power of declaring war, commencing hostilities or concluding treaties is vested in the Crown, and in cases where questions connected with its exercise arise in connection with India, they have been subject, as we saw in the last chapter, to some amount of Parliamentary control where expenditure is involved. In regard to India's neighbouring Asiatic powers, the initiative in the conduct of foreign affairs must, to a large extent, be in the hands of the Government of India; but the summary manner in which Mr. Brodrick (now Lord Midleton), Secretary of State in 1904, revised the treaty, concluded by Colonel Sir Frank Younghusband with the Tibetan Government at the instance of the Government of India, is one example to show how limited the power of the Government of India might become should the Secretary of State choose to interfere. The Curzon-Kitchener controversy of 1905 is the latest instance which furnishes a measure of the extent to which even a powerful Viceroy may have to yield in respect of large questions of administrative policy to the Secretary of State's views.*

* In respect of executive functions and administration, the control which, if he chooses, the Secretary of State could exercise over the authority of the Governor-General in Council may be expressed by the words used in the Imperial Gazetteer, Vol. IV, p. 36 that "the Secretary of State has the power of giving orders to every officer in India including the Governor-General." Apart from specific restrictions imposed by the Secretary of State on the financial powers of the Viceroy and his Council, his sanction is required :—

(i) to any reduction or increase of taxation or other measure which would substantially affect Indian revenues,

(ii) to any important new departure in financial policy, such as matters relating to currency operations or debt,

(iii) generally, to any matters, which raise important administrative questions or involve considerable expenditure or outlay of an unusual or novel character.

The Governor-General and his Council are appointed from "Home," and the former is usually a politician or administrator of experience from England.

Extent of the Viceroy's responsibility.

The utmost effect, therefore, of his subordination to the Secretary of State could only be that, if he felt disposed to differ from the policy of the Secretary of State, he must, yield up his private opinion or resign. If he yields, he becomes in effect a mere creature of the "Home" Government. If he resigns, there is no constitutional means in India by which he can vindicate his position, or have carried out the policy which he deems necessary for the welfare of India. It is to be noted that in this respect the Government of British India differs from that of the self-governing Colonies. If the Secretary of State for the Colonies, through the Governor or Governor-General of that Colony, vetoes any legislation or other proposal, the members of the Colonial Government can resign and appeal to their constituencies and, if the latter support them, the "Home" Government becomes virtually powerless to proceed further. The responsibility of the Government of a self-governing Colony rests upon and could be enforced by the will of the people of the Colony and not that of the "Home" Government. The Governor-General in India may resign, but the Government of India, consisting of the Councillors and his successors, are bound to carry out the orders of the "Home" Government. The legal and political responsibility of the Government of India is only towards the "Home" Government, and there is no constitutional arrangement by which they could be made responsible to the people of India. The Government in India is primarily based upon principles of benevolent despotism and such responsibility as the Government of India might feel towards the people of India is only moral and based upon their sense of justice and righteousness and upon the effect of such expressed public opinion in the country as could, if possible, make itself felt through the now enlarged Legislative Councils and otherwise.*

Wide powers of Viceroy

Yet, when all has been said as to the measure of subordination of the Governor-General to the Secretary of State, the fact remains that British India is under the immediate administration of the Viceroy and his Council. In the ordinary course of business, where the Secretary of State is not disposed unduly to interfere with the Governor-General and his Council, the powers of the latter are practically unlimited for efficient administration and the furtherance of the welfare and progress of the country. In a country where personal government

* It has been claimed by no less an authority than Sir Valentine Chirol ('Indian Unrest' Macmillan & Co., 1910) that the effect of the recent constitutional reforms introduced by Lord Morley and Lord Minto, designed as they are to give some responsible share to the representatives of the people, in the work not only of legislation but of every day administration, is calculated to lead to further developments in the direction of increasing the responsibility of the Governor-General and his Council to the representatives of the people in India itself, and that in furtherance of this purpose it is necessary that the control of the 'Home' Government must diminish. In this view the interference of Parliament in the details of Indian Administration is, he has contended, undesirable. He writes: "The peculiar conditions of India exclude the possibility of Indian self-Government on Colonial lines, but what we may, and probably must, look forward to at no distant date is that, with the larger share in legislation and administration secured to Indians by such measures as the Indian Councils Act, the Government of India will speak with growing authority as the exponent of the best Indian opinion within the limits compatible with the maintenance of British Rule and that its voice will therefore ultimately carry scarcely less weight at home in the determination of Indian policy than the voice of our self-governing Dominions already carries in all questions concerning their internal development." There can be no doubt that to the extent the executive administrations in India develop a sense of constitutional responsibility to the representatives of the people in the Councils, to that extent it would become unnecessary for the Parliament to exercise control which it has now the power to do and sometimes does. But whether and how far it is possible and safe to anticipate such development and dispense with that control in advance and how far such a process is likely of itself to defeat the purpose in view are questions which arise for discussion. It is unnecessary for our purpose to pursue this political speculation further. Sufficient has been said, it is believed, to give an idea of the constitutional view to be taken of the position of the Viceroy and Governor-General of India and his Council in relation to the Secretary of State and the Parliament of the United Kingdom to whom he is constitutionally responsible, and the right political principles by which this question has to be examined and discussed.

has played so large a part, the personality of the Viceroy and Governor-General, as the representative of His Majesty the King-Emperor in India, has always been looked upon to a great extent as the sign of just and benevolent Government, though the tendency of departmentalism, as we shall see presently, has steadily gone to reduce his personal factor in administration. The Governor-General, moreover, as we have observed in a former chapter, is the repository of all those legal prerogatives and powers, privileges and immunities, which have become vested in him as the representative of the British Crown and as the successor on behalf of the Crown, to the old territorial rulers and princes of the land. These rights which the Governor-General in person and the Executive Government collectively have inherited, vary from the important rights of the State to the land revenue in India, to receiving formal *nuzzers*, which are touched and returned, from chiefs and princes. The prerogative of pardon and mercy reside in the Governors and in the Governor-General, and the Imperial and Provincial Governments have been expressly strengthened in the exercise of this power by the Criminal Procedure Code. The Governor-General, and the provincial heads of Government too, can claim the priority of Crown debts over other debts. They are also entitled to the benefit of the rule that the Crown is not bound by statute unless expressly named therein. The Governor-General in Council has also, by virtue of delegated authority and subject to the control of the Secretary of State, the powers of making treaties and arrangements with Asiatic States, of exercising jurisdiction and other powers in foreign territory, and of acquiring and ceding territory.

'Council Government': Its History

In the exercise of such vast and varied powers and the discharge of responsibilities so great and growing, towards the people in India and the Government in England, as those which the Acts of 1858 and 1861 and the subsequent series of administrative regulations have imposed on the Governor-General in Council, it is hardly to be expected that the plan of conducting the business of the Government of India should not from time to time undergo marked changes. This plan has, however, throughout proceeded upon what has been termed a scheme of "Council Government." Its evolution in different parts of the British Empire is full of interest to the student of political institutions, while its peculiar evolution in India as a mode of conducting the highest class of administrative business is, according to John Stuart Mill, "one of the most successful instances of the adaptation of means to ends which political history, not hitherto prolific in works of skill and contrivance, has yet to show". It is worthwhile therefore to go in somewhat more detail than might be thought necessary, into the origin and development of Council Government generally in the British Empire in this connection, as it will serve to explain many important features of the Indian Constitution and will have an important bearing in the discussion of questions as to the future trend of this institution in India.

The early Council-governed Colonies

Council Government, as such, may be described as an even older institution than that of the Cabinet and, indeed, represents the first rudimentary form of Colonial Government with which Great Britain began her territorial expansion in the East and in the West. As early as King James' reign, Sir Francis Bacon in his essay on "Plantations" observed :—"For Government, let it be in the hands of one assisted with some counsel." It was the Council-governed Colony or plantation of the earliest type on which the first settlements of the East India Company in India were modelled. Before the close of the 18th century, however, the Council-governed Colonies in the West had approximated to a single type of government, and they came to comprise most of the important British Colonies in America and in the West Indies. According to Professor Lowell, the author of the "Government of England," this type was that of a Governor appointed by the Crown and a legislature with a popular branch elected by the inhabitants of the Colony possessing the power of the purse. "For any people with English political traditions," he observes, "that was the natural form to adopt. Where men of English stock were the predominant element in the population, it was impossible to refuse them an elective assembly empowered to levy taxes and appropriate the proceeds; and, on the other hand, the Governor must be appointed by the Crown if any real connection with the parent state was to be maintained."* So far is this true that, as a matter of course, the same type of government has ordinarily been adopted by the United States for the administration of her territories and dependencies. At the time when British institutions took root in Canada, however, it was decided that circumstances did not permit the creation of representative institutions. The Quebec Act of 1774 set up instead a legislative council of persons appointed by the Crown. The further history of Canada lies in the direction of the acquisition of responsible self-government, but, at the close of the 18th century, both in that Colony and in other Colonies, the government consisted of the familiar type of a royal governor and an elected assembly.

Councils in early Indian Charters

In the Charters which were granted to the East India Company at the time of their early settlements and acquisitions in the seventeenth and eighteenth centuries, this familiar type was modified to the extent of omitting the elective assembly which, under the circumstances of the British occupation of territories in India,—an occupation then made more for trade purposes than for permanent colonial settlement—could not be established among a population of non-British antecedents amidst whom the British settlers numbered but a handful. The earlier Charters, therefore, established institutions consisting of a Governor and a Council for

* The Government of England by A. Lawrence Lowell [Macmillan] Vol. II, page 393.

the administration of territories in and around Madras, in and around Bombay, and in and around Calcutta, with their dependencies. The Governor-in-Council, in the absence of an elected Council, was given the power to legislate along with the power to administer, and the distant factories subordinate to these 'Presidencies, as they came to be called were administered by a Chief' and Council or by Residents according to their importance.

The Councils under the Regulating Act, 1773

The Regulating Act which was passed about the same time as the Quebec Act, took further steps in the same direction by providing a consolidated constitution for all the territories under the rule of the Company in India. The original system of government by mutually independent and unwieldy Councils of merchants with Presidents at the Presidency towns, not merely gave rise to gross abuse but was found hardly adequate for the management of the local affairs, even of a large trading corporation. The system became quite impossible as soon as the Company was called upon to fill a more important *rolé*. The governing body which till then consisted of a President or a Governor and a Council composed of the senior servants of the Company, exercising their powers collectively and issuing their orders in accordance with the votes of the majority, was, therefore, altered by the Regulating Act which, as its preamble stated, was enacted 'for the better management of the affairs of the East India Company as well in India as in Europe'.

Executive Councils : Advisory and Administrative

The form of Council Government which that Act provided for the government of India and Bengal, as well as for that of the other two Presidencies, made a departure from one or two important features in the prevailing type of colonial constitutions then in vogue, which they have subsequently retained to the present day in most of the Crown Colonies. The general outward marks of a Colony then, as now, have been that it is administered by a Governor assisted by an advisory body called the Executive Council which includes the official heads of the principal departments, while the power of legislation is vested in a separate legislative council. In many of the Crown Colonies at the present time, the members of the Legislative Council either serve in virtue of their offices or are nominated by the Governor. In others, the nomination of a limited number of members is entrusted to public bodies. In some, there are representative members elected in local constituencies by electors having a prescribed qualification. Other Council-governed Colonies have a nominated legislative council and a separate representative assembly—a system which once prevailed more extensively but, as in all other cases, has been voluntarily surrendered as less suitable to the needs of the Colony than that of a single legislative body. In some cases, representation has been surrendered altogether and Colonies which once elected their legislature have accepted government by a legislative council wholly consisting of official and nominated unofficial members. Only governments having a legislative council of this description are, in the proper sense of the term, Crown Colonies, but all Council-governed Colonies as distinguished from self-governing Colonies are, however, described in popular usage as Crown Colonies.

The Regulating Act, on the other hand, provided that the whole Civil and Military government of the Presidency of Fort William shall vest in the Governor-General in Council, who was to be bound by the votes of the majority of those present in their meetings. This power of the Council to over-ride the wishes of the President who was only given an additional or casting vote, is not expressly found to exist in the system of Council-Government in the Crown Colonies, where the councils have been treated as more or less advisory. In many of them—and of these the earlier African and American Colonies, as well as Ceylon and Cyprus in later times, may be taken as typical—the executive councils consist of but the subordinate officials of the Government.

In others, such as Malta, Mauritius, British Guiana and Hong-Kong, it includes these as well as paid or unpaid members from outside—in the former two elected, and in the two latter nominated—as representatives of the legislatures established in the Colonies. One consequence of this difference is that whereas the acts of Government in all Crown Colonies are the acts of the Governor, Lieutenant-Governor or High Commissioner as the case may be, and the Councils are treated as advisory only, in India, the acts of Government are legally the acts of the body consisting of the Governor or Governor-General and his Council.

Councils, Executive and Legislative

The second marked difference to be noted is that while the normal type of constitution in a Crown Colony always included the establishment of a legislative council on a more or less representative basis, both the Regulating Act which established the Imperial Council and the earlier Acts which established the Provincial Councils, in India did not proceed to set up such separate councils for legislative purposes. This significant deviation is difficult to explain, but it may be surmised that as the settlements of the British in India started only as commercial *entrepôts* and not as Colonies proper, where Englishmen proposed to take a permanent habitation, the need and the desire for a representative council may not have been felt. Besides, it has to be remembered that the Governors and Councils professed to act as the agents of a trading corporation, and as this corporation itself, under its Charter and through its Courts of Proprietors and Directors, had the power of making regulations and ordinances for the government of the corporation and its dependencies, the establishment of a separate legislative assembly for and in the trade settlements themselves was not thought of until the necessity for specific law making itself arose in India. Accordingly, when at the time of the Regulating Act, it was found necessary to invest some power of legislation in the local authorities, for the good order and civil government of the growing settlements of the British in India, it was vested in the Governor-General in Council. But this power was probably treated as a mere process of legislation supplemental to the laws of the realm of England which, it was assumed, were applicable to all the territories subject to the East India Company and to all the subjects of Great Britain resident therein. The Governor-General in Council was thus invested with powers, 'to make and issue such rules, ordinances, and regulations for the good order and civil government of the Company's Settlement at Fort William and the subordinate factories and cities as should be deemed just and reasonable and should not be repugnant to the laws of the realm and to set, impose, inflict and levy reasonable fines and forfeitures for their breach.' This extremely limited power of law-making was further subject to the important restriction that these rules and regulations were not to be valid until duly registered and published at the Supreme Court of His Majesty, which was then established at Calcutta with the assent and approbation of the Court of Directors, while they could be set aside by the King-in-Council. A copy was to be kept affixed conspicuously in the India House and copies were also to be sent to His Majesty's Principal Secretary of State.

Council-Government is Committee-Government

The later development of the legislative councils in India and the acquisition of plenary powers by them will be dealt with in a subsequent chapter. It is only necessary here to lay stress on the fact that Council-Government as established in India by the Regulating Act was a 'Committee Government,' and not a 'one-man-government' with an advisory Executive Council such as was established in the Crown Colonies. Subsequent events, however, have gone to strengthen the position of the Governor or Governor-General as the responsible head of the executive, as also the position of members of the Executive Council as administrative heads of important departments of State. But the essential characteristic of Committee-Government has continued to attach to the forms of executive administration in India. As already observed, all acts of the Governments in India, Imperial or Provincial, always issue in the name of the Governor-General or Governor in Council as the case may be.

Committee-Government, an old and familiar constitutional expedient

The method of putting governmental authority into commission as it may be called is, however, not an innovation which began with the growth of governmental machinery in India. It is a familiar constitutional arrangement in all British institutions and may be traced far into the past of English constitutional history. Students of the English constitution will easily recall that, at the close of the Revolution in 1688, the practice of putting the high appointments of State into commission was a very well-known expedient. The appointments of Lord High Treasurer and Lord High Admiral in England were, after that period, entrusted respectively to the Committee of the Lords of the Treasury of the Privy Council and to the Committee of the Lords of the Admiralty of the Privy Council. In quite recent times, in the case of the War Office, the appointment of the Commander-in-Chief of His Majesty's forces to which the members of the Royal family long clung, was abolished in 1904 with the death of the Duke of Cambridge, and supreme authority over the Military forces of the Empire was then entrusted to an Army Council assisted by the Committee of Imperial Defence. Again, in respect of the new departments of State and administration which have grown up during the last and present centuries, we have had Boards or Committees of the Privy Council established and entrusted by statute with the administration of the departments of Local Government, Education, Trade, and Agriculture, and though the work of the departments is virtually carried on by a single Minister, he is yet styled the President of the Board of Local overnment, Education, Trade, or Agriculture as the case may be, and the idea of Committee administration, is still kept up by the manner and style of issuing orders and proceedings.

Merits and demerits of one-man and Committee-Government

It is, of course, not possible to trace any further analogy between the growth in England of these later Boards of the Privy Council, and their Presidents who have now become members of the Cabinet, and the developments which Council-Government has undergone in India, but it is necessary to bear in mind that both of them originated in the process of substituting a committee in place of a single individual holding executive authority. The relative advantages and disadvantages of either are differently appraised at different times. When monarchy was put into commission in ancient Greece and Rome and the offices of high Ministers of the Crown in England were constituted into Boards in the seventeenth century, such action was prompted more by the fear of the consequences—which people owing to past experience dreaded—of concentrating full discretionary power in the hands of a single individual than by a belief in the maxim of experience enunciated by Mill, "that in the multitude of counsellors, there is wisdom and that a man seldom judges right, even in his own concerns, still less in those of the public, when he makes habitual use of no knowledge but his own, or that of some single adviser". Whether either or both of these considerations operated on the minds of those who, in the Colonies of Great Britain vested government "in the hands of one assisted with some counsel"—as Bacon put it—it is unnecessary to discuss. But when by the Regulating Act of 1773, the British Parliament proceeded to set up for the whole of the Company's territories in India, a system of Council-Government by which the authority over, and administration of those possessions was directed to be carried on by the vote or opinion of the majority of the Council over which the Governor-General presided, it certainly underrated the advantages of the other general principle laid down by Mill that "every executive function, whether superior or subordinate, should be the appointed and responsible duty of a given individual."

Council - Government in Mill's day

The administrative difficulties and deadlocks which arose in working the provisions of the Regulating Act in this and other respects, led next to the development of the idea that, while effective power and full or final responsibility should reside in the hands of one, the counsellors or advisers should occupy a position of responsibility for the advice tendered or opinion given. At the time, therefore, when Lord Cornwallis was appointed to succeed Warren Hastings as Governor-General, the Regulating Act was modified so as to empower the Governor-General to over-ride the majority of his Council in special cases and act on his own responsibility. In fact, Lord Cornwallis, mindful of the bickerings which had impeded Warren Hastings in his administration, went so far as to give it as his opinion to Mr. Dundas, President of the Board of Control, at the close of his administration, that "nobody but a person who had never been in the service and who was essentially unconnected with its members, who was of a rank far surpassing his associates in the Government, and who had the full support of the Ministry at Home, was competent for the office of Governor-General." These considerations have, with a single exception, been kept in view since, and an Act passed in 1793 further strengthened the position of primary responsibility and power which the Governor-General thenceforth assumed. The system of "Council-Government," as thus established, was deemed by John Stuart Mill to possess peculiar merits.

In his essay on "Representative Government," he observes :—

"The Councils should be consultative merely, in this sense, that the ultimate decision should rest undividedly with the minister himself; out neither ought they to be looked upon, or to look upon themselves as ciphers, or as capable of being reduced to such at his pleasure. The advisers attached to a powerful and perhaps self-willed man ought to be placed under conditions which make it impossible for them, without discredit, not to express an opinion, and impossible for him not to listen to and consider their recommendations, whether he adopts them or not. The relation which ought to exist between a chief and this description of advisers is very accurately hit by the constitution of the Governor-General and those of the different presidencies in India. These Councils are composed of persons who have professional knowledge of Indian affairs, which the Governor-General and Governors usually lack, and which it would not be desirable to require of them. As a rule, every member of Council is expected to give an opinion, which is, of course, very often a simple acquiescence ; but if there is a difference of sentiment, it is at the option of every member, and is the invariable practice, to record the reasons of his opinion ; the Governor-General or Governor doing the same. In ordinary cases the decision is according to the sense of the majority ; the Council, therefore, has a substantial part in the Government, but if the Governor-General or Governor thinks fit, he may set aside even their unanimous opinion, recording his reasons. The result is that the chief is, individually and effectually, responsible for every act of the Government. The members of Council have only the responsibility of advisers ; but it is always known, from documents capable of being produced, and which, if called for by Parliament or public opinion, always are produced, what each has advised, and what reasons he gave for his advice ; while from their dignified position and ostensible participation in all acts of Government, they have nearly as strong motives to apply themselves to the public business, and to form and express a well-considered opinion on every part of it, as if the whole responsibility rested with themselves."

Its present altered character

The progress of Indian Government since Mill's day has made his language to some extent inapplicable to the actual methods of business and manner of administration pursued by the Government of India. The distribution of business amongst the Members of Council that has taken place since Mill wrote has devolved greater responsibility on them in regard to ordinary business. The Governor-General, of course, is nominally associated with every act of the executive Government. Neither the Governor-General individually nor the Council collectively is actually responsible for much of the ordinary business of administration, which is transacted by the Member in charge of the particular department. So much as regards what Mill termed the chief's *individual* responsibility for every act of the Government. Turning now to *effectual* responsibility, Mill derived this characteristic of Council-Government from the power possessed by the chief to override even a unanimous verdict of the Council. This power still exists on the statute-book, but is gradually falling into disuse. The power was originally vested in the Governor-General with a view to counteract factious opposition in the Council. The most notable exercise of it during the last 30 years was by Lord Lytton when he repealed the Indian Cotton duties in pursuance of a mandate from the 'Home' Government. Since then the power has lain dormant mostly and a tendency has developed in most Governors-General to embark on a policy only if a majority of the Council concur in it and not to take on themselves the sole responsibility of initiating and carrying it out. This is only natural. The task of Indian Government is becoming every day more complicated and an English statesman fresh from 'Home,' with no knowledge of India, has, of necessity, to defer to the opinions of his colleagues. This may mean in some cases the surrender of his better judgment and wider outlook to the views of colleagues, most of whom are nurtured in a narrower groove and have not at any time in their career felt the restraining hand of popular control. On the other hand, it also acts as a curb upon a Governor-General who may wish to introduce and carry out in India measures unsuited to local conditions. At the same time, the existence of the power to override the Council has in cases in which the Viceroy's determination to use it, if necessary, becomes known, usually sufficed to induce the members to withdraw factious or ineffective opposition.

It is therefore apparent that, while the *individual* and *effectual* responsibility of the chief for every act of Government cannot be said to be a correct representation of the actual methods of Council-Government at the present day, the status of the Councillors themselves has changed from that of mere advisers to that of heads of important departments of the State, responsible indidually for all *ordinary* business relating to their particular departments. In this latter respect, the Governor-General and his Council have approximated to the position of Ministers in England in charge of great departments of administration, held together by a system which has been frequently compared to that of Cabinet Government in England, but which is in fact very different from it.

Its disadvantages

It is worth while to go somewhat more fully into this question. The changes that have been brought about in the system of Council-Government, as described by Mill, are the natural outcome of the rapid progress of the Indian Government and the changes it underwent in the middle of the nineteenth century. To us in the twentieth century, it is no doubt obvious that if every case or paper was supposed to be laid before the Governor-General and the whole Council, and to be decided by them collectively, a "more cumbrous and impossible system," as Sir John Strachey says, could hardly have been invented. But those who had grown up under the system could not perceive its inconveniences as acutely. Moreover, the reason that enabled such a system to last so long was that in matters requiring prompt and vigorous action, it was not really acted upon. Events, however, precipitated the change after the Mutiny. The growth of administrative business became very great and Lord Canning availed himself of a power to make rules under the Indian Councils Act, 1861, to improve the usefulness of the Members of Council and the efficiency of administration. Section 8 of the Act empowered the Governor-General to make rules and orders for the more convenient transaction of business in his Council, and every order made or act done in accordance therewith was directed to be treated as being the order or the act of the Governor-

General in Council. Rules were made by Lord Canning assigning to each Member of the Council a separate department, the Governor-General himself keeping the Foreign Department in his hands. The change, however, does not seem to have gone far enough, for we find Sir Henry Maine complaining of the cumbrous manner in which business was done during the time of Lord Elgin, Lord Canning's successor, in the following terms:—

"A division of business was made between the Governor-General in the Upper Provinces (whither he had gone on account of military and political business) and the President in Council at Calcutta. Everything which was of importance was referred directly to the Governor-General, and there was either a rule or an understanding that if any matter which came before the President in Council assumed, contrary to expectation, the least importance, it should be sent on to the Governor-General . . . Except in regard to matters belonging to the Foreign Department, of which it was usual for the Governor-General himself to undertake the primary management, the severance of the Governor-General from the Council dislocated the whole machinery of Government. I believe it to be impossible for any human arrangement to have worked more perversely. Lord Elgin was distinguished by remarkable caution—though I doubt whether his caution was practically greater than that which any man comparatively fresh from England would display under similarly vast responsibilities—and all or most important matters were transferred by him over a distance of 1,500 miles for the opinions of his Council. The result was that a great deal of work was done twice over, and a great deal not done at all."

Its development

The reform of procedure, however, was completed by Lord Lawrence and the mechanism of the Supreme Government of India as it worked during the time of the successor of Lord Lawrence has been graphically described by Sir William Hunter in his valuable biography of the Earl of Mayo, from which we take the following passages, as they serve to illustrate the next stage in the development of Council-Government.—

"Lord Mayo, besides his duties as President of the Council, and final source of authority in each of the seven departments, was therefore in his own person Foreign Minister and Minister of Public Works. All routine and ordinary matters were disposed of by the Member of Council, within whose department they fell. Papers of greater importance were sent, with the initiating Member's opinion, to the Viceroy, who either concurred in or modified it. If the Viceroy concurred, the case generally ended, and the Secretary worked up the Member's note into a letter or resolution, to be issued as the orders of the Governor-General in Council. But in matters of weight, the Viceroy, even when concurring with the initiating Member, often directed the papers to be circulated either to the whole Council, or to certain of the Members whose views he might think it expedient to obtain on the question. In cases in which he did not concur with the initiating Member's views, the papers were generally circulated to all the other Members, or the Governor-General ordered them to be brought up in Council. Urgent business was submitted to the Governor-General directly by the Secretary of the Department under which it fell; and the Viceroy either initiated the order himself, or sent the case for initiation to the Member of Council at the head of the department to which it belonged.

"This was the paper side of Lord Mayo's work. All orders issued in his name. Every case of any real importance passed through his hands, and either bore his order, or his initials under the initiating Member's note. Urgent matters in all the seven departments went direct to him in the first instance. He had also to decide what cases could be best disposed of by the departmental Member and himself, and what ought to be circulated to the whole Council or to certain of the Members. In short, he had to see, as his orders ran in the name of the Governor-General in Council, that they fairly represented the collective views of his Government.

"The Viceroy also gives one day a week to his Executive Council. In this Oligarchy, all matters of Imperial policy are debated with closed doors before the orders issue; the Secretaries waiting in an ante-room and each being summoned into the Council Chamber to assist his Member when the affairs belonging to his department come on for discussion. As the Members have all seen the papers and recorded their opinions, they arrive in Council with their views accurately matured, and but little speechifiying takes place. Lord Mayo, accustomed to the free flow of Parliamentary talk, has left behind him an expression of surprise at the rapidity with which, even on the weightiest matters, the Council came to its decision, and at the amount of work which it got through in a day. His personal influence here stood him in good stead. In most matters, he managed to avoid an absolute taking of votes, and by little compromises won the dissentient Members to acquiescence. In great questions he almost invariably obtained a substantial majority, or put himself at the head of it; and under his rule the Council was never for a moment allowed to forget that the Viceroy retained the constitutional power, however seldom exercised, of deciding by his single will the action of his Government."*

Its present tendencies

It will be seen from this that, though the Council was remodelled after the Act of 1861, it continued for long to retain the essential characteristic which Mill claimed for the system of 'Council-Government,' *viz.*, that the chief is individually and effectually responsible, if not for every act of Government, at least for all really important acts of the Government, the Members having only the responsibility of advisers therein. Now, if we next take a later description of the manner in which the executive business of the Governor-General has been carried on, we find a few more changes. Sir John Strachey describes the system as follows :—

" Although the separation of departments in India is less complete than in England, and the authority of the Member of Council much less extensive and exclusive than that of an English Secretary of State, the Members of Council are now virtually Cabinet Ministers, each of whom has charge of one of the great departments of Government. Their ordinary duties are rather those of administrators than of councillors. The Governor-General regulates the manner in which the public business shall be distributed among them. He usually keeps the Foreign Department in his own hands; the other departments are—Home, Revenue and Agriculture, Finance and Commerce, Military, Public Works, and Legislative. While the Member of Council takes the place of the English Secretary of State, there is in each department a Secretary holding a position analogous to that of a permanent Under-Secretary in England.

* Life of the Earl of Mayo. By Sir William Wilson Hunter.

It is the duty of this Secretary to place every case before the Governor-General or Member in charge of his department, in a form in which it is ready for decision. He submits with it a statement of his own opinion. In minor cases, the Member of Council passes orders which are final. If the matter be one of greater importance, he sends on the papers, with his own orders, to the Governor-General for his approval. If the Governor-General concurs and thinks further discussion unnecessary the orders are issued. If he does not concur, he directs that the case shall be brought before the Council, as in England an important case might come before the Cabinet. The duty rests upon the Secretary, apart from his responsibility towards the Member of Council in charge of the department, of bringing personally to the knowledge of the Governor-General every matter of special importance."*

On the other hand, Lord Curzon, with all his bias towards pro-consular authority, was inclined to the view that the Government of India was a Committee-Government, and not one by the responsible head of it. In one of his farewell speeches in India, he said :—

" Never let it be forgotten that the Government of India is conducted not by an individual but by a Committee. No important act can be taken without the assent of a majority of that Committee. In practice this cuts both ways. It is the tendency in India as elsewhere, but much more in India than anywhere else that I have known, to identify the acts of Government with the head of the administration. The Viceroy is constantly spoken of as though he and he alone were the Government. This is, of course, unjust to his colleagues, who are equally responsible with himself, and very often deserve the credit which he unfairly obtains. On the other hand, it is sometimes unfair to him ; for he may have to bear the entire responsibility for administrative acts or policies which were participated in and perhaps originated by them . . . In the previous records of Indian Government, I have often come across sparring matches between illustrious combatants, and contentious minutes used to be fired off like grape-shot at the head of the Secretary of State . . . The Viceroy has no more weight in his Council than any individual Member of it".†

* India—its Administration and Progress. Second Edition [Macmillan] p. 60.

† Lord Curzon's Indian Speeches, edited by Sir Thomas Rayleigh [Macmillan] Vol. II, p. 299.

If the Council or the system under which the Council works has come to wield the power which even such a strong Viceroy as Lord Curzon is prepared to attribute to it, we may form some idea of the extent to which departmentalism and devolution have tended to remove the Viceroy and Governor-General from that position of primary responsibility which the statutes intended to vest in him.

It is no doubt true, as a former Member of the Viceroy's Executive Council wrote, that the old system involved an amount of minute writing which seems now hardly conceivable, and that fifty years ago, the Governor-General and the Council used to perform work which would now be disposed of by an Under-Secretary. But the evolution of departmentalism, even if inevitable or necessary in administrative progress, is by no means a merit in the political progress of Governments unless it is the result of popular or legislative control over the executive. If carried too far in the administration, it will tend to diminish, if not the sense of personal responsibility to the public in India and to the Government in England in the head of the Indian Government, at least the opportunities for his personal initiative in the several departments of administration, while it is also likely to reduce his personal factor in an impersonal system which is subject to no regular constitutional checks.

It may be noted in this connection that Lord Morley, with whose name as Secretary of State the recent political reforms have become associated, like the profound student of Mill that he is, has apparently adopted the older view of the political philosopher as regards the character of the Executive Councils. In his well-known Reform Despatch of the 27th November 1908, dealing with the proposals for the creation of Executive Councils in the Provinces under Lieutenant-Governors, he has expressed the opinion that the functions of the Councils should be, more especially in view of the enlargement of the powers and duties of the Legislative Councils, to ensure that "the judgment of the

Lieutenant-Governor should be fortified or enlarged by two or more competent advisers, with an official and responsible share in his deliberations."

Council - Government, not Cabinet Government

Whether this is so or not, it must be clear that 'Council' Government, whether of the old or the new type, is not Cabinet Government nor the Members of Council Cabinet Ministers—as Sir John Strachey seems to put it—and students of the Indian Constitutional system should note the distinction. The necessary implication of the words, "Cabinet Government," is, government by a body of people constitutionally responsible to the Legislature—a thing which is entirely absent in the Indian Executive. "The essence of responsible government," said an eminent English statesman, the late Lord Derby, "is that mutual bond of responsibility to Parliament one for another, wherein a Government acting by party go together, frame their measures in concert, and where, if one member falls to the ground, the others almost, as a matter of course, fall with him." This is as far from being the case in regard to India as could be possible. The Members of Council are mainly of the permanent Civil Service and do not and need not resign if their policy is disapproved. For instance, when in consequence of the censure of the Marquis of Salisbury referred to earlier in the chapter, Lord Northbrook resigned, Lord Lytton had to take the headship of a Council in which he found himself in a permanent minority as to the policies on which he came with a mandate*. With the power to overrule the majority which he possessed, with the support of the Home Government and with the exercise of a great deal of tact and good feeling, he managed to get on, though in one important matter he had to exercise his extraordinary powers. The political conception of a Cabinet, on the

* "From day to day and hour to hour," wrote Lord Lytton to the Marquis of Salisbury as soon as he arrived in India ; "I found as I approached Calcutta, that the spirit of anticipative antagonism to the new Viceroy was so strong on the part of the Council here that any appearance of scolding or lecturing them would have been fatal to our future relations".

other hand, is the reverse of this state of things. A Cabinet has been defined "as a body necessarily consisting (*a*) of members of the legislature, (*b*) of the same political views and chosen from the party possessing a majority in the lower House of Legislature, (*c*) prosecuting a concerted policy, (*d*) under a common responsibility to be signified by collective resignation in the event of Parliamentary censure; and (*e*) acknowledging a common subordination to one chief minister".

This description cannot by the boldest flight of imagination be attributed to either the Imperial or Provincial Governments in India, and the recent reforms, so far at least as their main principles are concerned, have hardly aimed at making them approach Cabinet Government, or indeed attempted their approximation to any form of Parlimentary Executive. The semblance to it, such as there is, exists only in the form. In essence and in spirit, the Government of India is as unlike Cabinet Government as could be imagined.

The British Cabinet is, moreover, a body unknown to law and no record is kept of its proceedings. In Continental constitutions, Cabinets have a legal existence, but like the British Cabinet, they have not been invested with that corporate capacity with which the Parliamentary statutes have invested in India the Councils with their Governor-General, Governors or Lieutenant-Governors as their Presidents. All acts of the Central Government, Imperial or Provincial, even of the most trivial nature and disposed of by an Under or Assistant Secretary, proceed as from the Lieutenant-Governor, Governor or Governor-General in Council, and all alike are included and recorded in their proceedings. The Executive Government in India is thus pre-eminently a "Government by record", not a Government by understandings, which is what the British Cabinet Government stands for. This characteristic of Indian Council-Government is, in the absence of any control proceeding from the people at once its real merit and one of the actual securities for good government in India. It was aptly described as such nearly sixty years ago by Mr. H. T. Prinsep and it has been certainly for the welfare of the country that it maintains this characteristic to this day. In one of those periodical Parliamentary enquiries into the affairs of India and of the East India Company which brought together such a valuable mass of evidence and information, Mr. Prinsep, in the course of the evidence which he gave before the Select Committee of the House of Commons in 1853 as to the advantages and disadvantages of having Councils for Provincial Governments, was asked :—

"Q.—What do you consider to be the checks against abuses, if there are any, in the constitution and the Government of India at present ?

A.—I think the best security you have for good government is in the necessity of recording everything that is done, and copying on the record every letter that is written to Government and every answer ; the necessity of reporting all matters and transmitting them periodically for review by the Court of Directors, appears to me also to be a very wholesome check and such a check as has never, I believe, been applied in any other Government : We in India consider that as the best security that can possibly be established against misconduct or irregularity of any kind.

Q.—Is it necessary to keep a constant record and make full report of everything that occurs ?

A.—Yes, it is necessary to place everything on record, no discretion is vested in any member of the Government or in the Secretary, of changing or withholding from the record anything which is addressed to the Government and the exact nature of the reply to it.

Q.—Has the Governor-General any power of omitting in his report anything that occurs ?

A.—Certainly not ; it would be considered unconstitutional if he did so"

Departmentalism and centralisation

Council Government, being thus a Committee Government and a Government by record, the departmentalisation of the work of Government, which is really what has been effected since 1861, the distribution of that work among the various departments and the procedure regulating their relations to one another, are governed by the rules and orders above referred to, made by the Governor-General, and are treated as confidential by the Government. They are collected together in the "Rules of Business" and are also supplemented by subsidiary regulations termed "Secretariat Instructions." Any important alteration in the former would in practice require the sanction of the Secretary of State. Their general effect will be gathered from the quotations which have been cited. There are now nine departments, namely, Home, Foreign, Finance, Legislative, Revenue and Agriculture, Public Works, Commerce and Industry, Army, and Education and minor departments. All minor questions are settled departmentally by the Secretary who is at the head of each department, or by the Member of Council in whose charge the department is placed. All important questions, questions involving any difference of opinion between two departments, or raising any general question of policy or gravity, are brought before the Council which meets generally once a week, and the Secretaries in charge then take note of the orders passed and issue them as resolutions or proceedings. The Report of the Royal Commission on Decentralisation in India gives the following authoritative description of the manner in which the business of the Government of India is transacted:—

"In regard to his own department, each Member of Council is largely in the position of a Minister of State, and has the final voice in ordinary departmental matters. But any question of special importance and any matter in which it is proposed to overrule the views of a local Government, must ordinarily be referred to the Viceroy. This latter provision acts as a safeguard against undue interference with the local Governments, but it necessarily throws a large amount of work on the Viceroy. In the year 1907-08, no less than 21·7 per cent of the cases which arose in, or came up to the Home Department required submission to the Viceroy. The Home Department is, however, concerned with questions which are, in a special degree subject to review by the Head of the Government, and we believe that in other departments the percentage of cases referred to the Viceroy is considerably less. Any matter originating in one department which also affects another must be referred to the latter and in the event of the departments not being able to agree, the case would have to be referred to the Viceroy.

The Members of Council meet periodically as a cabinet—ordinarily once a week—to discuss questions which the Viceroy desires to put before them, or which a Member who has been overruled by the Viceroy has asked to be referred in Council. The Secretary in the department primarily concerned with a Council case attends the Council for the purpose of furnishing any information which may be required of him. If there is a difference of opinion in the Council, the decision of the majority ordinarily prevails but the Viceroy can overrule a majority if he considers that the matter is of such grave importance as to justify such a step.

Each departmental office is in the subordinate charge of a Secretary whose position corresponds very much to that of a permanent Under-Secretary of State in the United Kingdom, but with these differences, that the Secretary as above stated, is present at Council meetings, that he attends on the Viceroy, usually once a week, and discusses with him all matters of importance arising in his department: that he has the right of bringing to the Viceroy's special notice any case in which he considers that His Excellency's concurrence should be obtained to action proposed by the departmental Member of Council : and that his tenure of office is usually limited to three years*.

The Secretaries have under them Deputy, Under and Assistant Secretaries together with the ordinary clerical establishments. Taking the departments with which we are concerned, that is to say the Home, Revenue and Agriculture, Finance, Commerce and Industry, and Civil Public Works Secretariat—the Secretaries, Deputy Secretaries and Under Secretaries in all but the last are members of the Indian Civil Service.

Rules of business Foot note to Rule 10

* In cases where the Government of India while differing from a local Government express their view in the form, not of a command but of a suggestion, it is unnecessary merely on this account, to submit the case to the Viceroy for orders at this stage. Similarly, where the proposals of a local Government contravenes standing orders or accepted principles and the reply of the Government of India merely refers to such orders (as in cases where the Local Government may wish to anticipate the sanction of the Secretary of State or to give retrospective effect to some financial sanction). It is not necessary merely on this account to take the Viceroy's instructions.

The Assistant Secretaries where these exist and the subordinate staff are men permanently connected with the department."

Centralisation and State Functions

It is not possible within the limits set for this book to deal exhaustively with the administrative mechanism—tracing it from the Crown downwards to the District Officer and the Village Headman and Panchayat. The mechanism itself is subject to frequent changes and divergent tendencies, now veering towards centralisation and again towards decentralisation. The process of consolidation which the Indian Government underwent, immediately after the transfer of the rule from the Company to the Crown, has tended to unify the Indian Empire in respect of administrative policy and methods, while the measures of decentralisation from time to time adopted have tended to increase the authority and the initiative of subordinate authorities subject to such control. The functions of the Government in India, moreover, are in many respects much wider than in the United Kingdom and have been described by the Royal Commission on Decentralisation in the following terms:—

"The Government claims a share in the produce of the land and save where (as in Bengal) it has commuted this into a fixed land tax, it exercises the right of periodical re-assessment of the cash value of its share. In connection with its revenue assessments, it has instituted a detailed cadastral survey, and a record of rights in the land. Where its assessments are made upon large land-holders, it intervenes to prevent their levying excessive rents from their tenants: and in the Central Provinces it even takes an active share in the original assessment of landlord's rents. In the Punjab and some other tracts it has restricted the alienation of land by agriculturists. It undertakes the management of landed estates when the proprietor is disqualified from attending to them by age, sex or infirmity, or occasionally by pecuniary embarrassments. In times of famine it undertakes relief works and other remedial measures upon an extensive scale. It manages a vast forest property, and is a large manufacturer of salt and opium. It owns the bulk of the railways of the country and directly manages a considerable portion of them; and it has constructed and maintains most of the important irrigation works. It owns and manages the postal and telegraph systems. It has the monopoly of note issue, and it alone can set the mints in motion. It acts for the most part as its own banker and it occasionally makes temporary loans to Presidency banks in times of financial stringency. With the co-operation of the Secretary of State it regulates the discharge of the balance of trade, as between India and the outside worlds through the action of India Council's drawings. It lends money to municipalities, rural boards, and agriculturists, and occasionally to the owners of historic estates. It exercises a strict control over the sale of liquor and intoxicating not merely by the prevention of unlicensed sale, but by granting licenses for short periods only and subject to special fees which are usually determined by auction. In India, moreover, the direct education, medical and sanitary operations, and ordinary public works, are of a much wider scope than in the United Kingdom. The Government has further very intimate relations with the numerous Native States which collectively cover more than one-third of the whole area of India and comprise more than one-fifth of its population. Apart from the special functions narrated above, the Government of a sub-continent containing nearly 1,800,000 square miles and 300,000,000 people is itself an extremely heavy burden and one which is constantly increasing with the economic development of the country and the growing needs of populations of diverse nationality, language and creed."

Division of administrative duties

The administrative work of the Imperial Government thus divides itself into two groups, namely, that in which its action is only by way of supervision and control and that which it directly deals with. The Secretariats, of course, are only concerned with control, but the public services controlled by them are divided into Provincial and Imperial. The former are the larger and more important group, but they are performed by Local, or as we should more accurately describe, Provincial Governments, while the latter are conducted by the officers under the Government of India. The latter comprise such departmental services as for Imperial, fiscal or administrative reasons the Imperial Government has deemed necessary to keep in its own hands. Under the former group, the ordinary functions of administration, the maintenance of law and order, the collection of revenues, education and sanitation, provincial and local finance, agriculture, roads, forests, &c., are included. Under the latter, are included : (i) the Railways, Posts and Telegraphs and the Opium Department, all of which may be described as coming under the quasi-commercial functions of the Government; (ii) the Political, Foreign and Military Departments, which, for obvious reasons, have not been provincialised. The Finance Department also derives its authority from the Government of India and exercises a control over finance, Imperial, Provincial and Local, over currency, general taxation, tariffs and debt, and an outside audit over public accounts, which is all the more necessary in India in the absence of a systematic legislative check.

The duties of the group of officers immediately under the Government of India, outside the Secretariat, who form the connecting link between the Provincial officers and the Imperial Government, differ according to the group of services with which they are connected. In regard to the matters under the control of the Provincial Governments and Administrations, comprising such work as that of the new offices created during Lord Curzon's régime, namely, the Inspectors-General of Agriculture, Forests, Irrigation, &c., the Directors-General of Education, Medical Service, &c.,—their function is mainly that of advisers of the Provincial and Imperial Governments, with some amount of control derived from the latter as their administrative advisers and guides. In regard to the other matters directly under the Government of India, the officers such as the Directors-General of Posts and Telegraphs, the Railway Board, the Surveyor-General and others, exercise authority all over India and conduct the business of their departments in direct subordination to the authority of the Governor-General in Council.

CHAPTER V

PROVINCIAL GOVERNMENTS

Gradation of Governmental authority in India

An Imperial Government like that of British India cannot be conducted on the same plan of administrative machinery as that which is usually found in states which possess what is known as a unitary constitution. In such states, Governmental functions are usually and clearly divisible into central and local ones, the former comprising those of the immediate executive agents of the sovereign authority at the seat of Government, and the latter comprising those of the delegates or agents, official and non-official, of the Government on the spot or locality concerned. Such a simple division does not and cannot exist in India. Nor can the present system of administration in India be described as partaking of the nature of federal constitutions like those of the United States or the German Empire. A federal constitution is usually formed by the voluntary or historical association of a number of states for common purposes and interests and for common national ends, and the Indian Constitution does not owe its existence to any voluntary or historical association of such separate states for any national objects.

Provincial Governments not Federal

Federalism, as Professor Dicey points out, implies the existence of what is known as the federal sentiment, consisting of a desire for union without a desire for unity. A federal state is, therefore, a political contrivance intended to reconcile national unity and power with the maintenance of state rights, and a federal constitution necessarily involves a distribution of sovereignty and the powers which sovereignty implies. This distribution is usually found in two forms. In the first of these, the common government of the part-states is invested with specific powers and the residuary powers are left in the hands of the part-states. In the second, the common state retains all the residuary powers and gives over only specific powers of sovereignty to the part-states. It is, of course, obvious that in a country like India, where the legislative sovereignty is vested in the British Parliament and executive authority is entirely in the hands of officials not responsible to the legislatures in India—where the constitution possesses that particular mark of dependency which Sir George Cornwall Lewis defines as that of being part of an independent political community, which is immediately subject to a subordinate government—the organs of administration would not exhibit those marks of federalism which consist in a distribution of sovereignty. A federal constitution, moreover, almost always implies a written constitution, strictly defining the powers of the federated State and the part-states, not alterable by either of them, and alterable, if at all, only by a superior authority and by a procedure specially provided. This is a state of things which cannot exist in India in the face of the express and absolute controlling and appellate authority given to the Government of India and the Secretary of State in all administrative matters, and to the Parliament of the United Kingdom in all matters legislative and administrative.

Provincial Government based on devolution

The principle, therefore, on which the gradation of powers in India, both in legislative and administrative affairs, has to be viewed, is not that of federalism but that of what in more recent times has come to be called, the principle of devolution and decentralization. This principle is not necessarily inconsistent with that of self-government on the part of the authorities to whom power and responsibility may be devolved. It only implies that the ultimate control of the Imperial authority, in legislative as well as in executive matters, is kept intact and in reserve to be used whenever necessary. A better illustration of this principle cannot be found than in the Home Rule Bill which has been introduced in the House of Commons this year for conferring self-government on Ireland, by the present Liberal Government. In an authoritative exposition of the new Irish Constitution proposed by the Bill, Professor Morgan points out that the Bill is quite outside the category of federalism in that while it proposes a delegation of authority, both executive and legislative, there is none of the distribution of sovereignty which is the distinguishing characteristic of a federation. The executive power in Ireland will "continue vested in His Majesty. The legislative authority will be subject to an Imperial veto and to the supremacy of the Imperial Parliament with its powers of concurrent legislation, and the Irish courts will be subject to the appellate jurisdiction of an Imperial court". In other words, "the Imperial power will be supreme in the executive, the legislative and the judicial sphere." The position of the executive and legislative authorities in India is quite similar and although the element of self-government in every one of them is more or less non-existent, the legal relation between the Imperial and the Provincial Governments is based on the same principle.

Before describing this relation, it is necessary, briefly, to deal with the history of the Provincial Governments and Administrations. In India, the Provincial Governments of Madras, Bombay and Bengal, though they owe their later organisation and development to political and administrative causes, are historically of an earlier origin and were of

History of Provincial Governments: the old Presidencies

more importance in the early history of British rule in India than the Government of India. Until the acquisition of Bengal and the passing of the Regulating Act, the system of government in India was that known as the Presidency system, viz., that in which a group of factories and their adjoining acquisitions within a certain area were placed under the administrative control of a President and Councillors, otherwise known as the Governor and Council. The three Presidencies which the territories of the East India Company originally comprised were, till 1773, distinct from one another and under the direct control of the Court of Directors. In 1773, under the Regulating Act, the Bombay and the Madras Presidencies were placed in subordination to the Governor of Bengal, which had no separate Governor, and he was thereafter styled Governor-General of Bengal. This Presidency system endured till 1833. As fresh territories came into the possession of the Company, they became attached to one or other of the Presidencies according to their proximity, but the additions to the Presidency of Bengal, which was in the hands of the Governor-General himself, became so heavy, especially after the beginning of the nineteenth century, that the Charter Act of 1833 authorized the creation of another separate Presidency, to be styled the Presidency of Agra. The provisions in this behalf were, however, suspended by a statute of 1835, which directed that during such suspension the Governor-General in Council might appoint any servant of the Company of not less than ten years' service to "the Office of Lieutenant-Governor of the North-West Provinces now under the Presidency of Fort William in Bengal." Thus was the first Lieutenant-Governorship created. Very soon after this, the further growth of the work of the Governor-General made it imperative that he should cease to directly administer the Presidency of Fort William or of other territories. The Act of 1853, therefore, provided that the Governor-General of India (not of

Bengal, as he was till then called) should not be Governor of the Presidency of Fort William thereafter, that a separate Governor should be appointed thereto, but that until this was done the Governor-General was not to appoint a Deputy Governor from his Council—as was done till then—but to appoint a Lieutenant-Governor for such portion of the territories of the original Presidency as was not under the Lieutenant-Governor of the North-West Provinces. The Act also authorised the creation of one more new Presidency and the appointment of one more Lieutenant-Governor similar to those of the two Bengals.

The later Lieutenant-Governorships

The origin of the Lieutenant-Governorship of the North-West Provinces and Lower Provinces was thus a tentative one, the constitution of Presidencies with Governors and Councils being then deemed the normal method of administering a Province. This idea, however, was subsequently given up, and the two Bengal Lieutenant-Governorships remained. A third was added to them in 1859, by constituting the Punjab into a Lieutenant-Governorship, the first appointment in which capacity was held by Sir John Lawrence. Further powers of constituting new Lieutenant-Governorships have been given by Section 46 of the Indian Councils Act, 1861, but, according to Sir C. P. Ilbert, they are exercisable only when a new Legislative Council is established. Burma in 1897, and Eastern Bengal and Assam in 1905, became Lieutenant-Governorships under this provision. The tendency, however, to the creation of Lieutenant-Governorships without Councils in preference to the Presidencies with Governors and Councils, received a marked check with the passing of the Councils Act of 1909, which has authorised the creation of Executive Councils for the Lieutenant-Governors. Apparently, the advantages of "Council Government" as opposed to pro-consular Government, as Lord Curzon would put it, seem to have again acquired importance with the political and administrative changes which are now coming into operation.

Further changes in the constitution of the Provinces were announced on the occasion of His Majesty's visit to India to hold the Delhi Durbar in December 1911, and they have since been carried out by the Government of India Act, 1912. The result of the changes thus introduced has been to revive the old Presidency of Bengal with a Governor and Executive Council, as in the days prior to 1835, to abolish the territorial division made in 1905 of Bengal and East Bengal and to substitute, instead, the new province of Bengal with a Governor and Council, the new province of Behar and Orissa with a Lieutenant-Governor and an Executive Council to assist him, and the old Chief Commissionership of Assam which existed prior to 1905. The capital seat of the Government of India was also removed from Calcutta and located in Delhi, which, with a small surrounding area, has been created into an *enclave*, with a Chief Commissioner at its head and certain special administrative arrangements.

The latest re-distribution of territories

Besides the Presidencies and Lieutenant-Governorships, there are also the territories and provinces administered by Chief Commissioners under the more direct control of the Governor-General in Council. There are now eight administrative charges of this class. There are thus, generally speaking, in all, fifteen separate provincial administrations at present consisting of three Governorships, four Lieutenant-Governorships and eight Chief Commissionerships. Of the latter, the Chief Commissionership of the Central Provinces very nearly approximates to that of a Lieutenant-Governorship in respect of executive administration, and if the power conferred by the Government of India Act of 1912 to create a Legislative Council in the Chief Commissionership territories is to be immediately given effect to in the Central Provinces, as has

The existing Provinces and their Governments

been announced—it would differ from the Lieutenant-Governorships very little except perhaps in respect of the exercise of patronage. The legal and constitutional position of these Local Governments or Local Administrations, as they are called according to their importance, varies both according to their status and according to the powers and responsibilities specifically entrusted to them. Taking, however, the Presidency Governments as the type of the fully developed Provincial Governments, we may deduce a few general characteristics.

The Presidency Governments

Historically, the authority of the Government of India over these Presidency Governments is one super-imposed by later legislation. These Provincial Governments had therefore the fullest plenary powers to start with, for the good government of their various Presidencies—subject, of course, to the control of the Court of Directors and the ultimate sovereignty of Parliament. It was seen in an earlier chapter how the Regulating Act of 1773 originally imposed the superintendence, direction, and control of the Governor-General and his Council in Bengal over the Presidency Governments of Madras and Bombay. This superintendence and control was strengthened by successive declarations in the Acts of 1793 and 1813, but apparently they did not go far enough in the direction of securing effective control, and the Charter Act of 1833, therefore, reiterated this power of control on the part of the supreme Government with an additional proviso to the effect that " the Governments of Madras and Bombay are required to obey the orders and instructions of the Governor-General in Council in all cases whatsoever ".

The extent o Imperial control over them

The exact interpretation to be given to this higher authority and control of the Government of India over the Local Governments, has been sought to be laid down in the instructions issued by the Court of Directors in a Despatch which accompanied the Act of 1833 to the

Government of India in 1834, and in another Despatch in 1838. As they have been declared on behalf of the Government of India to contain an authoritative statement of the principles applied in the regulation of the relations between the Imperial and the Provincial Governments, it is reproduced below along with certain observations from the report of the Royal Commission on Decentralization:—

"The control of the Government of India is, moreover, not confined to the prescription of policy and to action taken upon reports and inspections. It assumes more specific forms to scrutinize and when necessary modify the annual budgets of the local Governments.

Every newly created appointment of importance, every large addition even to minor establishments, every material alteration in service grades has to receive their specific approval and in many cases, reference to the Secretary of State is likewise necessary. The practical result is that no new departure in provincial administration can be undertaken without their preliminary sanction, and in important matters without that of the Secretary of State also. Moreover, the general conditions of Government service, such as leave, pension and travelling allowance rules, and the public works and Forest codes are all strictly prescribed by the central government either *suo motu* or on instruction from the Secretary of State. Lastly, there is a wide field of appeal to the Government of India as also to the Secretary of State from persons who may deem themselves aggrieved by the action of the local government.

Instruction to the Court of Directors in 1834-1868 as to the character of this control

44. The essential point to be borne in mind is this; at present even in matters primarily assigned to the Provincial governments these act as the agents of the Government of India, who exercise a very full and constant check over their proceedings. The general principles which should govern the relations between the Government of India and the subordinate Provincial Government of India and the subordinate Provincial Governments were laid down in 1834, in a letter addressed by the Court of Directors to the Government of India on the subject of the Charter Act of 1833, the essential portions of which we subjoin as well as extract from a later Despatch of 1833. We are informed by the Home Secretary to

the Government of India that these pronouncements may be taken as an authoritative statement of the principles applied to-day.

Extract from Despatch (accompanying the Government of India Act 1833) from the Court of Directors to the Government of India No. 44, dated 10th December 1834.

76. We have now completed all that we deem it necessary to say at present regarding the legislation to be exercised and laws to be made in India. We will proceed to consider the new relation in which we will be placed with reference to the subordinate Governments not by means of your legislative supremacy but in other respects.

77. The words of the 39th clause were very comprehensive: The superintendance, direction, and control of the whole Civil and Military Government of all the said territories and revenues in India shall be vested in the said Governor-General in Council.

78. The powers here conveyed when the words are interpreted in all their latitude, include the whole powers of Government. And it is of infinite importance that you should well consider and understand the extent of the responsibility thus imposed upon you. The whole Civil and Military Government of India is in your hands and for what is good or evil in the administration of it, the honour or dishonour will redound upon you.

79. With respect to the exercise of your legislative powers in the several presidencies what we have adduced of a general nature on that subject will, for the present, suffice.

80. With respect to other powers which you are called upon to exercise, it will be incumbent upon you to draw with much discrimination and reflection, the correct line between the functions which properly belong to a local and subordinate Government and those which belong to the general Government ruling over and superintending the whole. The only local Governments which then existed were the presidencies of Madras and Bombay. The Bengal presidency was at that time directly under the Governor-General in Council.

81. When this line is improperly drawn, the consequence is either that the general Government interferes with the province of the local Government and enters into details which it cannot manage, and which preclude its consideration of more important objects or that it withdraws its attention from the evidence of many things which may be right or wrong in the general course of the local administration and

thus partially deprives the state of the benefit of its superintendence and control.

82. It is true that the former Acts of Parliament, which made the local Government of Bengal a Supreme Government, gave the Governor-General in Council a control and superintendence over the other Presidencies as complete and paramount as it was possible for language to convey and this we must assume to have been the intention of the legislature. In practice, however, the Supreme Government made little exercise of its superintending authority and the result has been that even that little exercise of it has been generally made when it was too late to be made with real effect, namely, after the subordinate Government had taken its course, thus losing the character of control and responsibility and retaining only that *ex post facto* intervention—a sort of intervention always invidious, and in most cases nothing but invidious, because what was already done, however open to censure, was beyond the reach of recall or correction.

83. It is evidently the object of the present Act to carry into effect that intention of the legislature to which we have alluded. Invested as you are with all the powers of government over all parts of India and responsible for good government in them all, you are to consider to what extent and in what particulars the powers of Government can be best exercised when retained in your own hands. With respect to that portion of the business of government which you fully confide to the local authorities and with which a minute interference on your part would not be beneficial, it will be your duty to have always before you evidence sufficient to enable you to judge if the course of things in general is good and to pay such vigilant attention to that evidence as will ensure your prompt interposition whenever anything occurs which demands it.

84. In general it is to be recollected that in all cases where there are gradations of authority, the right of working of the system must very much depend on the wisdom and moderation of the supreme authority and also of the subordinate authorities : This is especially of a system so peculiar as that of our Indian Empire. It was impossible for the legislature, and it was equally so for us in our instructions, to define the exact limits between a just control and a petty vexatious meddling interference. We rely on the practical good sense of our Governor-General in Council and of our other Governors, for carrying the law into effect

in a manner consonant with its spirit and we see no reason to have the possibility of preserving to every subordinate government its due rank and power, without impairing or neutralizing that of the highest.

85. The subordinate governments will correspond directly with us as formerly but we think, that you should immediately receive copies of all their more important letters to us, both as part of the evidence of their proceedings which you should have before you, and that we may have the benefit of the observations which you may have to make, and which we desire that you will always despatch to us with the smallest possible delay.

86. It will be for you to determine what part of their records or what other documents it will be necessary for you regularly to receive as evidence of the general proceedings of the subordinate governments, and as an index to the other documents which you will have occasion to call for when anything occurs which you desire to investigate.

Extract from Despatch from the Court of Directors to the Government of India No. 3, dated 28th March 1838.

By the 65th clause of the Act 3 and 4 Wm. IV Cap. 85 the Governor-General in Council is invested with full power to superintend and control the subordinate Governments in all points relating to the Civil and Military Administration of their respective presidencies and those governments are required to obey the orders and instructions of the Governor-General in Council in all cases whatsoever, and in order to enable you to exercise with effect the control and superintendence thus devolved on you, the subordinate governments are required by the 68th section to transmit regularly to the Governor-General in Council true and exact copies of all the orders and Acts of their respective governments and to give intelligence of all transactions which they may deem material to be communicated, or as the Governor-General in Council shall from time to time require. Although a minute interference on your part in the details of the local Administration of the subordinate Presidencies is neither desirable nor practicable, yet we should hold you but ill-acquitted towards whose interests are committed to your charge, if you should allow to pass without comment and if necessary without effective interference, any measures having in your opinion, an injurious tendency either to one Presidency or to the Empire at large.

The present situation as regards the control exercised on the Government of India

It is thus laid down that the Government of India are responsible for everything done in the provinces, but it would be seen from paragraphs 80 and 83 of the Despatch of December 1834 that they were intended to discriminate between matters which would be primarily within the scope of the local governments where their interference would be of a very exceptional character and matters in regard to which their control would be more detailed and constant. No definite steps towards the immediate attainment of this object appear, however, to have been taken and the present discrimination between the functions of the Imperial and local governments, and the extent of the control normally exercised by the former over the latter are the results of gradual administrative evolution.

Political and military exigencies, and the growth of services generally recognised as suitable for direct management by a central Government have given the Government of India a number of functions exercised independently of the provincial Governments. As regards the departments which have been recognised as lying primarily within the scope of local governments, the control exercised by the Government of India has differed at various periods. Speaking generally, it may be said that although the powers of the Madras and Bombay Governments, the only subordinate administrations then existing, were materially reduced in 1833, those of all the present major provinces, including the two presidency Governments, are decidedly larger than were the prerogatives of any local Government fifty years ago, when the Crown took over the Government of India. For example, no province had any separate powers of legislation, any separate financial resources or practically any power of creating or modifying any appointment in the public service; and the references to the Government of India which this last restriction involved gave that Government the opportunity of interference with all the details of provincial administration."

Tendency towards closer control

In actual experience, however, the carrying out of the principles and instructions of the Court of Directors has varied from time to time, but the tendency has steadily been towards strengthening the power and authority of the Imperial Government by various means. In the solution of the difficult question of defining the exact limits between 'a just control and petty, vexatious and meddling interference', the Government of India have generally had the advantage on their side. One reason for this may perhaps lie in the fact that the Local Governments as such do not yet represent the people of the province and are not therefore constitutionally backed up by that popular feeling and public support which would have sustained effectually the claims of local freedom and action. On the other hand, the authority of the Imperial Government, backed up by the Secretary of State, is usually sustained by the authority of the King's Ministers who represent the will in the last resort of the Parliament and the people of the United Kingdom. However this may be, it is essential to remember, as the report of the Royal Commission on Decentralization has put it, " that the mutual relations of the Indian Governments are not those of states or colonies voluntarily associated in a federal system where a written constitution is necessary to preserve original rights of the contracting portions ".

Nature and Methods of Present Control

The gradual evolution of the administrative control of the Government of India has been established and exercised, according to the Commission, in the following manner :—

i By financial rules and restrictions, including those laid down by Imperial departmental codes.

ii. By general or particular checks of a more purely administrative nature, which may (*a*) be laid down by law or by rules having the force of law, or (*b*) have grown up in practice.

iii. By preliminary scrutiny of proposed Provincial legislation, and sanction of Acts passed in the Provincial legislatures.

iv. By general resolutions on questions of policy, issued for the guidance of the Provincial Governments. These often arise upon the reports of Commissions or Committees, appointed from time to time by the Supreme Government to investigate the working of departments with which the Provincial Governments are primarily concerned.

v. By instructions to particular Local Governments in regard to matters which may have attracted the notice of the Government of India in connexion with the departmental administration reports periodically submitted to it, or the proceedings-volumes of a Local Government.

vi. By action taken upon matters brought to notice of the Imperial Inspectors-General.

vii. In connexion with the large right of appeal possessed by persons dissatisfied with the actions or orders of a Provincial Government.

Presidency Governments possess unenumerated powers

The position of the Provincial Governments is thus one of subordination, no doubt, to that of the Governor-General in Council, but it cannot be said that the Presidency Governments at any rate, are mere delegates or agents of the Imperial Government. It would seem indeed that they must be deemed to be free, in all those departments of administration which are not specially reserved for the Imperial Government's direct administration, to exercise the functions which have statutorily devolved upon them from the earliest times. Applying the language of political phraseology used with reference to European Constitutions, we may say that the unenumerated powers in India seem to rest in the Presidencies with the Provincial Governments, subject to a power of concurrent action on the part of the Imperial Government. This view is strengthened by the fact that under the Indian Councils Acts the position of the Provincial Legislative Councils is made one of a concurrent and plenary character, subject to some special reservations and the right of veto on the part of the Imperial Government and the Secretary of State.

The special position of Presidency Governments

Madras and Bombay and, since this year, Bengal, as Presidency Governments, are in a somewhat special position. Though the tendency has been, till recently, to treat them in the same way as the other large Provinces subsequently created, they retain the following vestiges of their separate origin and former independence :—

i. They are under a Council Government, consisting of a Governor usually appointed from home, with two Civilian and one Indian colleagues, who are nominated by the Crown, on the advice of the Secretary of State. The ordinary business of Government is distributed between the members of these Councils in much the same way as in the larger Council of the Governor-General, but the distinction of portfolios is not so definite. The Governor can, like the Viceroy, overrule his colleagues in cases of emergency ; otherwise decisions of the Governor in Council are by a majority.

ii. The Presidency Governments have the right of direct correspondence with the Secretary of State, except in matters which raise financial issues and can appeal to him against orders of the Government of India ; but such an appeal must go through, or be communicated to that Government.

iii. They have full discretion in the selections for certain posts, which in other Provinces rests finally with the Government of India, (*e. g.*,) nominations to the Board of Revenue and to the Provincial Legislative Councils, and the appointment of Chief and Superintending Engineers in the Public Works Department, and Conservators of Forests.

iv. They have, in practice, a free hand in the details of their district land revenue settlements which in other provinces are subject to control by the Government of India. Similarly they are less supervised in forest administration.

The Lieutenant-Governorships: their origin and greater subordination

The authority of the Governor-General and his Council over the Presidency Governments is thus exercisable only with reference to the statutes which have given them the power of superintendence and control, but their power over the Lieutenant-Governors and their administration of the provinces entrusted to them, has been made much more specific and direct and is capable of being increased or diminished according to circumstances. The provinces of the Lieutenant-Governors have been carved out of the territories which were previously under the direct administration of the Governor-General in Council, and therefore, their administrators necessarily derived their authority, through the Governor-General and not independently of him. In the next place, Section 4 of the Act of 1854 which created the two older Lieutenant-Governorships has laid down that "it shall be lawful for the said Governor-General of India in Council with the like sanction and approbation, that is, of the Court of Directors and the Board of Control from time to time, to declare and limit the extent of the authority of the Governor in Council, Governor or Lieutenant Governor of Bengal, of Agra or the North-Western Provinces who is now or may be hereafter appointed." This applies in terms only to Bengal and the United Provinces, but, according to Sir C. P. Ilbert, would seem to give power to the Governor-General in Council to "declare and to limit" the extent of the authority of any Lieutenant-Governor. Lastly, the appointment of Lieutenant-Governors rests in the hands of the Governor-General, subject to the approval of His Majesty, and this gives him a power of personal control which in the case of the Presidency Governments he does not possess, as their Governors are usually appointed from among politicians "at Home".

The Chief Commissionerships: primarily delegations of imperial authority

The Chief Commissioner is even more restricted in his authority as the head of his local Administration. The territories under the administration of a Chief Commissioner are legally speaking those which are placed "under the immediate authority and management of the Governor-General in Council, who thereupon gives all necessary orders and directions respecting the administration of that part or otherwise provide for the administration thereof." A Chief Commissionership, therefore, consists of territories which were either already under the direct administration of the Governor-General or which come under his administration at the time it is constituted. Territories which are already under the administration of Governors or Lieutenant-Governors, according to the interpretation of the statutes, could not be brought by the Governor-General under the direct administration of a Chief Commissioner, under the powers vested in him to alter the limits of provinces. A Chief Commissionership, apparently, is viewed as a less developed form of Government than that of a Governorship or Lieutenant-Governorship. It is usually created by means of a Resolution of the Government of India—followed by a Proclamation, whenever a territory previously under the Viceroy's direct control is made over to the Chief Commissioner, who, according to the view taken of his functions by the Government of India, merely administers a territory on behalf of the Governor-General in Council, and the latter does not divest himself of any of his powers in making over the Provincial administration to a Chief Commissioner. (*Vide* "Ilbert," page 194.)

General Character of Imperial Supervision and Control

The undefined nature and character of the supervision and control of the Government of India over the Presidency Governments, have, as in that of the latter to the India Office, led to many historic disputes and is regulated by the specific rules which have been quoted above and also by usage and precedents, some of which are treated as more or less confidential. The position of partial freedom and prestige which the Presidency Governments have enjoyed has not been without administrative difficulties even in recent years. A masterful personality like Lord Curzon—who disbelieved in devolution and decentralisation, who had a firm faith in a strong Government of India, "gathering into its hand and controlling all the reins," and who "would ride local governments on the snaffle," though not on the curb—was able to boast that there never had been a time when the relations between the Supreme and the Presidency Governments had been so free from friction or so harmonious, as in his days. But other masterful rulers like Lord Mayo or Lord Lytton were not able to avoid the frequency of "peppery letters or indignant remonstrances," or "the spectacle of infuriated pro-consuls strutting up and down the stage." During the famine of 1877 in Madras, for example, Lord Lytton was hard put to it to manœuvre a astisfactory arrangement with the Duke of Buckingham in Madras, in regard to an efficient and uniform famine policy, for, as he said, he was unable "to force upon the Madras Government advice which it will neither invite nor accept." Presidency Governments, it would then seem, were often "more strongly represented than the Supreme Government, not only in the India Council, but throughout the whole region of Anglo-India." The danger of provoking the resignation of provincial pro-consuls even by the use of slight pressure from above, which Lord Lytton feared, is perhaps less likely now than before, but the opportunities therefor have also become less owing to the growth of system, routine and uniformity in administrative methods. In truth, however, the legal powers of compelling obedience in the case of obstructive Provincial Governments in the ordinary course of business are, as Lord Lytton found out, much feebler and fewer than might be supposed. Now-a-days much more depends on diplomacy and influence and the personal qualities and characteristics of the Supreme and the Provincial rulers than on statutory powers and rules, in enforcing the due limits to the authority of the Supreme Government on the one hand and the amount of independence and autonomy of the Provincial Governments on the other.

The checks against the wrongful exercise by the Lieutenant-Governor of arbitrary powers are, however, much more complete than in respect of Governors and Councils. There is no branch of the administration, according to Sir John Strachey, in which he is not bound either by the positive law or by the standing orders of the Supreme Government or by the system which has gradually grown up under his predecessors. Any great changes which he may desire to introduce must first receive the approval of the Governor-General in Council. It is not perhaps so well known that this tendency to secure the previous approval of the Government of India is silently, but steadily, finding expression in the methods of the Provincial Governments of the two older Presidencies also, a tendency which, if allowed to persist, will destroy independence of action even in the limited sphere in which they are at present able to exercise it. The freedom of action of the Chief Commissioner is still more restricted, for it merely exists at the discretion of the Supreme Government to whom the Chief Commissioner has not only to look for the support which is necessary to carry on his administration, but for the approval and credit on which his future and further prospects depend.

Provincial departmentalisation

The Executive Councils of Madras and Bombay and of Lieutenant-Governors who have been provided with Executive Councils are modelled on similar lines to those of the Governor-General. The Governors, who like the Governor-General, are usually appointed from England from among distinguished politicians or administrators, and the Lieutenant-Governors, have the power of overruling their Councils under circumstances similar to those defined in the case of the Governor-General. Administrative work in their provinces has also been "departmentalised," more or less in the same way as that of the Governor-General in Council, under the powers given by the Acts of 1861 and 1909 to them to frame rules for the efficient conduct of business. The Lieutenant-Governors' provinces which have no Executive Councils are assisted by Boards of Revenue, or as in the Punjab and Burma, by Financial Commissioners. Each Provincial Government has a Secretariat of varying strength according to its needs, and the departments of administration are presided over by heads variously termed in different provinces, while there are also special departments presided over by special officers.

CHAPTER VI

DISTRICT ADMINISTRATION

The Imperial and Provincial Executive authorities in India owe their constitution and powers, more or less directly to statutes of Parliament. The departments of administration which carry on the work of the Central Government, Provincial and Imperial, as well as the Local and Municipal bodies which perform functions of local administration, depend for their authority, on the other hand, on laws passed by the Indian legislatures and on administrative regulations, organisation and tradition, not easily susceptible of general treatment. But while a description and study of the functions performed by the many ministerial officers directly under the Government is not of much constitutional importance, the division of administrative functions between the Imperial, Provincial and Local authorities in its general outlines ought to be noted. From the standpoint of political development, the form of Local, Provincial and Imperial organisation will undoubtedly react with momentous effect on the national character. *

Division of administrative functions

* As a recent writer on constitutions has put it:—" The citizen who from boyhood expects to take some time or other of his own free will, an active part in the administration of local affairs, is likely to be found a very different citizen from the man who may be authoritatively commanded at the most inconvenient juncture of affairs to serve his locality without remuneration, and both from the citizen who perpetually finds himself cabined, cribbed, confined by the cramping influences of an all-pervading bureaucracy ". (Leonard Alston, M.A., in his 'Modern Constitutions'.)

Central isation and Devolution

An attempt has been made in the last chapter to deduce from the statutes and the prevailing practice, traditions and understandings, the exact relations which subsist between the Provincial and the Imperial Governments in the exercise of executive authority and the general division of executive functions which have flowed therefrom. Apart from statutory provisions, the distribution of executive functions in India, does not exactly follow the lines which are to be found in ordinary unitary Constitutions in the West on the one hand, or in the federal Constitutions on the other. The reason for this lies, in the first place, in what has been explained in detail in the last chapter *viz.*, that the division of powers in India is in the nature of devolution and not of federation. In the next place, it arises from the fact that executive authority in India has proceeded from the centre outwards in all the provinces and started with a more or less highly centralised administrative machinery. Administrative authority was, first of all, devolved upon the agents of the Central Provincial Governments, and only later on entrusted in small and varying measures to Local and Municipal Councils subject to a deal of supervision and control on the part of the central authority and its agents. The principle that it is but a small portion of the public business of a country which can be well done or safely attempted by the central authorities, was but slowly and but too cautiously recognised in this country, where the capacity for self-Government even in local affairs on the part of the people was assumed to be less than the minimum. The primary principle on which District and Provincial administration may be said to rest in India, is one of division of labour. Popular control over the performance of Local and Provincial administrative duties was a matter of later and slower growth.

Devolution and local Self-Government

Thus the existing system, while it has secured better organisation, has left less liberty to the citizens than in other countries where British institutions have grown. That the growth of popular institutions, and the grant of some measure of popular control over the exercise of administrative functions is inevitable in the growth of all modern forms of government, is not only an inference easily drawn from the lessons of history in the past, but is one which necessarily arises from the very nature of the progress of modern administrations. The growth and persistence of the kind of subordinate government which implies popular control, is due, as Professor Montague once observed, "practically to the need of relieving the central authority in the State and to experience of failure of a completely centralised bureaucracy" *

Local Self-Government and Political Education

Indeed, "the administration of a civilized State is so serious a task as to demand all the powers of bureaucracy and Self-Government combined." The steps, therefore, which have been taken in India from time to time for associating the people in the actual administration of the country, both in the

* Professor Ashley in his book on "Local and Central Government" has elucidated the same position in the following terms :—

"Whatever may have been the previous course of their constitutional history the persistent and rapid growth of the functions of the State, and the constant assumption of new and onerous duties and responsibilities in the last century have rendered some attempts at decentralization and some grants of Self-Government absolutely necessary, if the national administration is to be carried on with success. Experience, ancient and modern alike, has shown conclusively that a completely centralised bureaucracy—that is, a self-recruiting body of officials working from a single centre, and responsible only to itself—cannot carry on infinitely the administration of a large country ; it tends to ignore the varieties of local conditions, to become stereotyped in its ideals and methods, and overburdened ; and sooner or later a breakdown becomes inevitable. And where the people have been discouraged from taking an interest in the task of Government, where they have not been habituated to the management of public affairs, the collapse, when the bureaucracy fails, is so much the greater, since there is nothing which can be substituted for the broken-down official organisation. For these practical reasons, amongst others of a more theoretical and political character, in all progressive States, dating the last century, attempts have been made at decentralization and the development of Self-Government in two ways: (a) by entrusting the inhabitants of localities, or their chosen representatives, with the conduct (under greater or less control) of those matters of public interest and utility which concern the localities chiefly or entirely ; and (b) by providing for the participation of unofficial citizens in the management of some at least of those other matters of administration which are supposed to belong particularly to the sphere of the Central Government."

Legislative Councils and in the Local and Municipal bodies, are but the necessary consequences of a devolution which became inevitable with the growing burden of administration. There are, however, along with these purely administrative requirements, other considerations of a more theoretical and political character which have also to some extent influenced the association of the people in the task of Government. These are usually summed up in the phrase, "political education," which it is deemed to be the duty of all modern progressive governments to impart to the citizens of the State. The importance of that portion of the operations of political institutions which is comprised in the political education of the citizens has been the theme of all writers on politics since the days of Mill. Both these aspects of Local Government have been well summed up by the late Professor Sidgwick in the following terms :—

"Most internal executive functions whether coercive or industrial, obviously need officials locally dispersed,—policemen and soldiers for the maintenance ,of order, collectors of taxes direct and indirect, managers of roads and public land of all kinds, postmasters and other officials occupied in conveyance and communication, relieving officers, sanitary inspectors and so forth. In speaking however, of "local governments" in a unitary state, we chiefly mean organs which, though completely subordinate to the central legislature, are independent of the central executive in appointment and to some extent, in their decisions and exercise a partially independent control over certain parts of public finance.

The primary reason for this local independence is that it is required to realise the full advantages of that reaction of the governed on the governing organs which representative or responsible government seeks to bring about. Such advantages may lie in the direction either of greater efficiency or of greater economy. First, as we say, the theory of responsible government rests on the principle that the interests of any group of governed persons will be most safely entrusted to governing persons whom they have the power, from time to time, to dismiss directly or indirectly. It is an obvious inference from this principle that governmental functions which affect solely or mainly the inhabitants of a limited portion of a State should be placed under the special control of this section of the community; in order that the criticism of this section, backed by the power of appointment and dismissal, may bring about a closer adaptation of administrative activity to its peculiar needs. Especially in matters—such as education and poor-relief—in which valuable aid can and should be given to governmental work by the voluntary efforts of private persons, we may expect to secure important gains by localising the control of the electorate over the work. Again, so far as any class of governmental services are rendered exclusively or mainly to a group of persons who live within a certain district, it is obviously equitable to throw the whole or main expense of such services on these persons; and—so far as this expense cannot conveniently be met by payments voluntarily made by the recipients of the services the comparison of cost with utility is likely to be more accurately performed if the financial management of this department of governmental business is entrusted to a separate locally-elected organ.

But there are other reasons why a vigorous development of local government is important, if not indispensable, to the effective working of representative institutions in a community as large as most modern states are overcentralisation, in such a community, introduces two opposite dangers. In the first place, if the only action that an ordinary citizen is called upon to take, in reference to public affairs of any great interest or importance, is that of voting at intervals of several years, as a unit in a group of many thousand electors, for a member of the central legislature—or even for the head of the executive—there is a danger that the control of the citizens generally over their government will become slack and ineffective; so that their exercise of the vote will be especially liable to be perverted by the sinister influences which we have before examined. But again the same cause that tends to render the political consciousness of the ordinary citizen too languid at ordinary times also tends to increase the risk from occasional gusts of discontent and excitement, causing unreasonable expectations and complaints of government; since the mass of the community cannot but lack that general diffused knowledge of the real nature of governmental business, and the conditions and limitations under which it is carried on, which results from being brought into intimate social relations with the persons actually responsible for it. In short, whatever educative value is rightly attributed to representative government largely depends on the development of local institutions.

We must also take into account the danger of overloading the central government with work. The importance of this danger grows in proportion as a more extended view is taken of the proper functions of government ; if the tendency actually operative in England towards increasingly extensive and complex governmental interference is in the main justifiable—as we have seen reason to think—it becomes increasingly important that the work to be done should be carefully distributed among different organs so that none may be overburdened". ["Elements of Politics", pp. 511-513].

The principle of popular political education as a *raison d'etre* of Local Self-Government did not find ready acceptance in India for a long time, though it was laid down by Lord Ripon in his famous Resolution on Local Self-Government in India in 1882 in no unambiguous terms. Lord Morley, while Secretary of State for India, reiterated this aspect of the matter in his well-known Reform Despatch in 1908, and it is not yet known, to what extent it will be carried out in the proposals which are now under consideration, in consequence of the recommendations of the Royal Commission on Decentralisation, for the improvement of the machinery of local and district government in India. The association of the people or their representatives in the higher tasks of government above those of district and local administration, is still of a very limited character, but is likely to be appreciably enhanced with the progress of the Reformed Legislative Councils.

Four administrative authorities

A devolution of administrative functions which involves the grant of some measure of Self-Government cannot be in India a mere matter of defining the relations between the local and central government, but involves a division of powers and duties between four different authorities. There is, first of all, the Imperial Government which, as we have seen, has got direct control of certain services. There is next, the Provincial Government in whose hands are entrusted the normal functions of administration within the province, but subject to supervision by the Imperial Government. There are next the district officials who are the agents or deputies of the Provincial Government and exercise their powers under its orders and instructions in the several districts which constitute, more or less, the uniform administrative unit in all the provinces of India. And, lastly, there are the Local and Municipal bodies to whom have been entrusted specific functions of administration in the localities where they are constituted, and whose constitution and powers are also subject to close official supervision.

Division of duties and functions among them

It was seen in the last chapter how difficult it is on general grounds to say what functions of administration should necessarily remain in the hands of the Imperial Government and what should be made over to the Provincial Governments. It is even more difficult to lay down what duties of government and what control over local bodies the central authority in a Provincial Government should undertake, and what could be safely, and should be with advantage, left to local management in the hands of local representatives of the people. Much will, no doubt, depend on the circumstances and conditions of each province and of each locality concerned. To lay down that matters of Imperial, Provincial or local concern should severally be left in the hands of the Imperial, Provincial or Local authorities is merely to re-state the problem. There cannot exist the most exclusively Imperial question which may not, in some way, affect the interests of localities. Nor can there be any matter of local concern which may not conceivably become matter of Imperial concern. Nevertheless, some of the broad lines of general division are easily noticeable and they have, in the main, formed the basis on which the statutory division of powers, which has been referred to in the last chapter, has been largely based. Such questions, for instance, as Military and Naval Defence, Foreign and Political affairs including those connected with the relations of Native States, are necessarily and with advantage, left in the hands of the Imperial Government.

with a highly centralised organization. Such matters, again, as the management of what may be called the State properties and monopolies including the Currency, Railways, Posts and Telegraphs, and Opium, are among what may be called the quasi-commercial functions of Government and, on the score of economy and efficiency and the common interest therein of the citizens of all parts of the Empire, are also left in the hands of the Imperial Government. In the department of Finance and Taxation, controversy has raged for a long time over the proper limits of Provincial and Imperial Finance, to which attention will be drawn in a subsequent chapter. To the Provincial Governments, on the other hand, properly belong such normal functions as the central government usually exercises in a unitary state, as the maintenance of law and order, the collection of revenues, provincial finance, education, sanitation, roads, forests, etc. In respect of the functions which are in Imperial hands, the position of Local Governments becomes one of advice or of carrying out instructions, while in respect of the functions and powers granted to local authorities, the position of the Provincial Governments is one of supervision and control.

Division of Central and Local Functions

The division of administrative powers between the central Provincial authority—exercised either by the central heads of Government departments or their local agents in the districts—and the local and municipal bodies which have been constituted in the local areas is, however, a much more direct result of the principles discussed at the outset of this chapter. In matters connected with the local administration of districts and towns, while the paid official would, no doubt, have the advantage in professional knowledge, professional skill and professional discipline, the unpaid representative has or should have the advantage of familiarity with local requirements, of local patriotism, and of freedom from technical prejudice and routine. An ideal system would, therefore, make the unpaid citizen do as much work for the public as could be got out of him and ensure his doing it properly by providing official information, supervision and audit. It may also be laid down as a general principle that the assurance of a certain independence is necessary to make unpaid work attractive to able and honest men. On the other hand, some duties can never be efficiently discharged by unpaid officers, because they need a special training and special skill. The difficulty, in the case of unpaid work in local self-government is even greater as to how and where to draw the line between 'a just control and meddlesome interference', and scientific classifications are, as a rule, of little value in determining the actual course pursued by various governments.

Onerous and Beneficial, Obligatory and 'Facultative', services

A classification of services into those which are onerous—that is, undertaken by the local authorities on behalf of the national or provincial government at its cost—and those which are beneficial—that is, undertaken by the local authorities for the particular benefit of the locality concerned—does not lead us far in defining the extent of outside control permissible, while the familiar division adopted in Continental States, of services into obligatory and facultative or optional ones, is one which is not useful even as a sound or exhaustive classification of functions. There is no service, as observed before, not even defence, which may not somewhere or other be thrown upon local administration and local funds. There is no service either which is of concern simply to the community as a whole, exclusive of the particular locality in question. The interest of the community is, however, more or less apparent, more or less direct and more or less certain, in some cases than in others. The means and methods by which the interest of the community is to be protected and enforced by the Government as its trustee, must differ from time to time, from place to place and from service to service.

The tendency, however, of the Indian system of local self-government is to accentuate the interference of the central government in the true or supposed interests of the community—a tendency to which all bureaucracies are but too prone—and in the interests of what is also called efficiency. In France and Germany, Belgium and Austria, and generally throughout the Continent of Europe, we find local administration entrusted in the main to salaried officials of special training and high special qualifications, whose work is regularly supervised by and is completely subordinate to, the various departments of the executive government. There are, it is true, representative local councils of various grades and formed in various ways, by which the consent of the inhabitants of the several localities is more or less adequately expressed, and some degree of local control is secured. But the functions and powers of these local councils are narrowly limited and their actual interferences with the day by day administration are in almost all cases subject to the control and approval of the central executive departments. This particular relation between central and local Government has been conveniently termed as the "Bureaucratic System" by Mr. Sidney Webb in his preface to Mr. Walton Grice's book on "National and Local Finance." The characteristics of the Continental system to which Mr. Sidney Webb refers are possessed in no small degree by the local and municipal institutions in India, though there are some fundamental differences between the two to which attention will be directed in the next chapter.

Province of local and central authority in the performance of each administrative service

Nor could we advance further in the discussion as to the proper province of the local and central authorities, if we take all the different functions of administration and attempt to determine on general principles, where the province of the Central Government may end and that of the local authorities may begin in each case. The functions of government in India, as was before stated, are much wider than in the United Kingdom, while even in respect of such functions as are common to England and India, the province of the central authority is at present much wider in India than it ever was in England. Local unpaid agency is necessary and is employed in such primarily protective functions as the administration of justice, the preservation of peace and order as well as the defence of the country, both in England and in India. In the discharge of commercial functions, local boards and councils in India have been permitted to embark upon forms of municipal trading such as the construction of light railways and tramways in the same manner as they have been, though to a larger degree, permitted in England. In regard to the developmental functions, such as education, maintenance of state domains, forests etc., local as well as central organizations have been discharging these functions in varying proportions both in England and in India. In fact, there does not seem to exist a single function coming under any of these categories which could not in some form or other be made to have a local aspect or could possess a local interest without some scope for central control.

To discuss at any length, what are the limits of local effort and local autonomy and of central control in respect of these various functions is to consider each of them separately and in detail. This is the only means of arriving at a satisfactory conclusion both as to the theory on which the province of local and central authorities should be determined and the actual state of things which has been established by the existing administrative arrangements. Such an inquiry is one which is far beyond the limits of a treatise like the present, while much of it would be controversial in character. On many questions raised, no settled conclusions have yet been reached and even in the case of those on which a settled policy or a defined principle has been adopted, it can by no means be treated as the final word on such administrative questions—especially in a country where conditions and circumstances are so rapidly changing.

Description of local official machinery

A description of the official administrative machinery in the districts of British India need not be given here at length. The official heirarchy and the bureaucratic organisation in the administration of India have been one of the most elaborate and complex devised for the administration of Empires, and the success which they have achieved, has blinded many to their defects. It is, however, unnecessary to enter upon the question as to the relative merits and demerits of bureaucracies in the administration of Empires. A fairly comprehensive idea of district administration can be easily gathered from the many extant official publications. The summary of it which appears in the Report of the Royal Commission on Decentralization is, with a few unimportant omissions, reproduced below as being the most authoritative and accurate description of the present system :—

"The principal unit of administration is everywhere the district. British India contains more than 250 districts and the number at present existing in each of the major Provinces has been shown in the statement in paragraph 25. The average area of a district is 4430 square miles or about three-fourths of the size of Yorkshire and the average population 931,000, but the actual districts vary greatly in size and population. They are largest, in point of area, in Burma and Madras and smallest in the United Provinces.

Each district is under a Collector (styled Deputy-Commissioner in the non-Regulation Provinces) who is the local representative of Government in its general dealings with the people and is also the District Magistrate*. As Collector, he is not merely responsible for the

---

* The oft-quoted description of the model Collector-Magistrate, in the first edition of the Imperial Gazetter in 1882, though it requires some alterations in its application at the present day, will still bear repetition here :—

"The District Officer, whether known as Collector-Magistrate or as Deputy Commissioner, is the responsible head of his jurisdiction. Upon his energy and personal character depends ultimately the efficiency of our Indian Government. His own special duties are so numerous and so various as to bewilder the outsider; and the work of his subordinates, European and Native, largely depends upon the stimulus of his personal example. His position has been compared to that of the French Prefect, but such a comparison is unjust in many ways to the Indian District Officer. He is not a mere subordinate of a central bureau, who takes his colour from his chief and represents the political parties or the permanent officialism of the capital. The Indian Collector is a strongly individualised worker in every department of rural well-being, with a large measure of local independence and of individual initiative. As the name of Collector-Magistrate implies his main functions are two-fold. He is a fiscal officer, charged with the collection of most branches of the revenue, but is concerned with the manifold relations existing between Government and the agricultural classes, which represent two-thirds of the total population of British India. Thus he is concerned with questions relating to the registration, alteration, relinquishment or partition of land-holdings which pay revenue direct to Government and in the greater part of India, has to deal in these respects with an immense number of petty peasant-proprietors. He is likewise, in most Provinces, concerned with the adjudication of disputes between land-lords and tenants and also with the administration of estates taken under the management of the Courts of Wards. * He has to keep a careful watch over the general circumstances of his district, and in times of famine or severe agricultural distress, he is responsible for the administration of relief and other remedial measures. He also deals with the grant of loans to agriculturists, and with the preparation of agriculturul and other statistics ; and he has a general control over the working of the Forest Department in his district, in so far as this touches on matters affecting the economic or other interests of the people.

It is his duty to guide and control the working of municipalities and he is often the actual chairman or presiding officer of one or more of these. He usually, also, presides over the district board, which, with the aid of subordinate local boards where such exist, maintains roads, schools, and dispensaries, and deals with vaccination and sanitary improvements, in rural areas. Finally, he has to furnish in-

---

collection of the revenue from the land and other sources; he is also a revenue and criminal judge both of first instance and in appeal. But his title by no means exhausts his multifarious duties. He does in his smaller local sphere all that the Home Secretary superintends in England, and a great deal more, for he is the representative of a paternal and not of a constitutional Government. Police, Jails, Education, Municipalities, roads, sanitation, dispensaries, the local taxation and the imperial revenues of his district are to him matters of daily concern. He is expected to make himself acquainted with every phase of the social life of the natives, and with each natural aspect of the country. He should be a lawyer, an accountant, financier, and a ready writer of State papers. He ought also to possess no mean knowledge of agriculture, political economy, and engineering."

* In Bombay and the Central Provinces, Commissioners of Divisions are Courts of Wards in their respective jurisdictions. In the other major Provinces, except Burma, where there is as yet no Court of Wards the Court is the Board or Revenue or Financial Commissioners to the Province.

formation on all important occurrences in the district and he is called upon to advise on any general schemes affecting it which may be under consideration.

As District Magistrate, he is responsible for all matters affecting the peace of the district, and exercises a general supervision over the local police officers, while he controls the working of subordinate criminal courts, and has himself a certain amount of original and appellate majesterial work.*

Each district is usually split up into a number of sub-divisions which are in charge either of junior officers of the Indian Civil Service or of officers of the 'Provincial' Service (Deputy Collectors or extra Assistant Commissioners)†. The functions of these sub-divisional officers, who are all Magistrates as well as revenue and executive fuctionaries, vary in different Provinces. They are most developed in Madras and Bombay, where the sub-divisional officer exercises within his own charge, most of the functions of a Collector, subject to supervision by and appeal to, the latter. Save in Bengal and Eastern Bengal there are smaller sub-district units, stlyed taluqs or tahsils, administered by tahsildars who belong to the subordinate service. ‡ These officials are, in general, under the immediate control of the sub-divisional officer, where there is one, and they and their assistants (deputy or *naib* tahsildars, revenue inspectors, Kanungos etc.) are in direct relations with the cultivators and the village officials.

In all the major Provinces except Madras, the districts are grouped into divisions, each of which consisting usually of from four to six districts, is under the general superintendence of a Commissioner, who also acts as a Court of appeal in revenue cases.

In Bombay, there is no intermediate authority between Commissioners and the Local Government and the same condition has hitherto applied in the Central Provinces, but here the appointment of a Financial Commissioner has recently been sanctioned. In other Pro-

* Steps are now being taken, in Bengal and Eastern Bengal, towards the dissociation of Collectors and other executive officers from criminal case duties.

† In Bengal and Eastern Bengal the head-quarters sub-division of the district is in the direct charge of the Collector, and in the Punjab there are but few sub-divisions.

‡ These units are called circles in Assam and townships in Burma; and the officers administering them are styled sub-deputy collectors in Assam, *myooks* in Burma, *mamlatdars* in Bombay proper, and *mukhtyarkars* in Sind.

vinces, there is such an intermediate authority, *viz*., a Board of Revenue (or a single Financial Commissioner, as in the Punjab and Burma)—which in subordination to the Local Government, controls the work of Commissioners and Collectors and the general administration of the Province in revenue matters.

Originally Collectors and their subordinates were responsible for almost all the administrative work of their districts, subject to the superintendence of Commissioners and Board of Revenue. During the last 50 years, however, separate administrative departments have been gradually evolved, the most important of which are those dealing with Public Works, Education, Police, Forests, Medical Administration, Sanitation and Prisons. These departments have their own separate staffs and heads in each Province, *viz*. :—

Chief Engineers for (*a*) Irrigation and (*b*) Ordinary Public Works ; The Director of Public Instruction ; The Inspector-General of Police ; Conservators, or, a Chief Conservator of Forests ;

The Inspector-General of Civil Hospitals, (Surgeon-General in Madras and Bombay), the Sanitary Commissioner * ; and the Inspector-General of Prisons. †

The Inspector-General of Police is often an Indian Civilian, but otherwise, the head of each department is usually drawn, either locally or by transfer from another Province, from the departmental service. These departmental heads are in direct subordination to the Local Government‡. As already stated, the Chief Engineers for Public Works and also Secretaries to Government; the other heads of departments address their reports and letters to one or other of the Civilian Secretaries. §

* Outside Bombay, the Sanitary Commissioner works largely through the agency of the District Medical Officers, who, for medical work, are subordinate to the head of the Medical Department.

† There are also Inspectors-General of Registration ; but in most Provinces this function is combined with the management of some other department. When there is extensive famine in a Province, an officer, drawn from the Indian Civil Service, may be appointed to act as a special Famine Commissioner, under the Local Government.

‡ Except, as regards forests, in Madras and Bombay, where conservators of Forests are under the Board of Revenue in the former Province and under the Revenue Commissioners in the latter.

§ In the Punjab the Director of Public Instruction is also *ex-officio* Under Secretary for Education, and appears in that capacity to submit cases direct to the Lieutenant-Governor, while the Inspector-General of Police is also an *ex-officio* Under Secretary to Government but subordinate in that *rôle* to the Judicial Secretary.

As regards the district staffs of these departments, the Collector and District Magistrate, as already noted, has a general outside control, in non-technical matters, over the work of the Local Police and Forest Officers; he is responsible for the minor jails ; and principally in his capacity as President of the District Board (and in some Provinces also of Municipal Councils), he is largely concerned with questions of sanitation, medical relief and elementary education. He has much less concern with the operations of the Public Works Department, and with those branches of education which are under the direct control of the Department of Public Instruction; and the principal local officer of these two departments (Superintending and Executive Engineers and Inspectors of Schools) have charges which do not necessarily correspond with district or divisional limits.

There are other heads of departments who are members of the Indian Civil Service, and who work in closer connection with the ordinary district staff, through whose agency a great deal of the work which they have to supervise is discharged. The chief of these are the Commissioner of Excise, the Director of Agriculture, the Director of Land Records and, in some Provinces, the Commissioner for Revenue Settlements. These officers are under the Board of Revenue or Financial Commissioner, where either exists *

*In Madras the functions of the Excise Commissioner and the Settlement Commissioner are directly exercised by members of the Board of Revenue; and in Bombay the Commissioner of Excise is of the same status as the territorial Commissioners.

CHAPTER VII

LOCAL GOVERNMENT

Modern Boards and ancient Punchayets

We may now turn our attention next to what is, from the constitutional point of view, the more important subject of the organisation of local boards, municipalities and other local authorities in India. It has to be remembered that though the social and historical conditions which have determined the present state of insufficient development of local self-government in India have often been discussed, sufficient stress has not always been paid upon one important fact in connection with the history of local self-government in India. It has often been wrongly assumed to begin with, that the traditional sentiments of the community and their habits of co-operation are against the formation of local self-governing bodies whereas in fact the oldest units of local self-government in all history and among all civilized communities, the unit to which all other modern political organisations could be traced, was found in its vigour of life in this country, when it had ceased to exist or had been superseded long ago by other centralised institutions in other countries. The ancient village community or the panchayet was deliberately disintegrated by the adoption of the administrative measures of the East India Company in India in the early part of the 19th century, and though the unwisdom of it was perceived later, no attempt was made to revive it as a unit of local government in the seventies and eighties of the last century, when steps were first taken towards introducing measures of local self-government in India. As usual, the process in British India began from above and it was only after the exhaustive inquiries of the Royal Commission on Decentralisation two years ago that it was found that to ensure the rapid and permanent improvement of local self-government in this country, it is necessary to build it up from the bottom, that strenuous efforts ought to be made to revive and resuscitate the old village panchayets and turn them into useful units of local administration on modern lines.

History of Modern Local Institutions in India

Before proceeding to consider the characteristics and tendencies which local self-governing institutions in India exhibit, it is necessary to trace briefly the history of the successive measures by which they have been established and their constitution and functions developed or modified from time to time.

Origin in de-concentration rather than in decentralisation

The beginnings of local self-government in India are in some respects similar to those of France and Prussia in that they started after the building up of a consolidated and powerful State by means of a great bureaucracy directed from a single centre and pursuing a uniform policy. Local institutions in both cases mainly have thus owed their origin to the will of the central authorities and were primarily created for the purposes of their administration. They were treated as agencies not so much for the decentralization of administrative functions, as for what Continental authorities describe as de-concentration of authority. These delegations of authority which have been rendered necessary in India from time to time, took the form of entrusting them to purely stipendiary officials, then to committees of officials in particular localities and then to committees composed partly of officials and partly of unprofessional members, nominated by the central authority or selected by the localities or local authorities.

First Municipal Charter 1687

The system of municipal administration had a much earlier origin in the Presidency towns than in the interior of the country. It was first granted to Madras by a Royal Charter in 1687, which resulted in the establishment of a Corporation and Mayor's Court with powers to levy taxes and to try both civil and criminal cases. In 1726 a Mayor's Court with Aldermen was established in each of the Presidency towns. But little was done to introduce municipal institutions generally in the territories acquired by the East India Company though the Charter Act of 1793 contained statutory provisions as to municipal administration in the Presidencies. Between the years 1840 and 1853, the constitution of the municipalities was widened and elective principles, to a limited extent, were introduced. But in 1856 all municipal functions were concentrated in a body corporate, consisting of three nominated and salaried members. Till the year 1861, the system of municipal government was the same all over India, but with the passing of the Councils Act in that year, it was remodelled by enactments local legislatures, thus from that time varying in different provinces and leading through a series of Acts to those now in force. The system of election of representatives by the ratepayers was first established in Bombay in 1872, in Calcutta in 1877 and in Madras in 1878.

Beginnings of Local Institutions in 1842

Outside the Presidency towns, therefore, whose local self-government is complicated by the indroduction of British local institutions from the outset, there was practically no attempt at creating municipal institutions before 1842. In that year, an Act was passed applicable to Bengal to enable the inhabitants of any place of public resort or residence to make better provision for purposes connected with public health and convenience. An Act of 1850 extended this law to the whole of British India and provided for the constitution of Town Committees and the levy by them of certain indirect taxation. This Act was only of an enabling kind and was very little availed of by the inhabitants of localities. In the Presidency of Madras, however, the germs of local self-government were laid by the early voluntary associations formed in the sixties of the last century by the respectable and opulent classes, for maintaining the sanitation and health of urban areas. The Government assisted these associations by contributions of sums equal to those realised by them by private subscriptions. In 1863-64, there were six such associations.

Towns Improvement Acts, 1865

The difficulty of discharging primarily local functions by agents of the central authority grew enormously with the establishment of settled government in the year 1858, while the financial difficulties of the government pointed to the need for devolving local resources and powers on local unpaid authorities. The need for more extensive municipal measures was pointedly referred to by the Army Sanitary Commission in 1863 in consequence of the general unhealthy condition of towns in India. The Towns Improvement Acts of 1865 which were passed for the different provinces, provided for the appointment of Commissioners to manage municipal affairs and authorised the levy of various taxes. As measures of local self-government, the Acts did not proceed far; but they were of great service in improving the sanitary condition of towns. An Act passed in 1863 attempted to bring education within the province of local functions, but did not succeed, while an Act passed in 1866 for the first time authorized the levy of a local rate for providing the funds required for popular education, roads and other objects of a local character in rural areas.

Financial Decentralization and Local Finance

The policy which was thus begun by such incontinent steps was reviewed comprehensively in connection with the decentralization of finances in India carried out under Lord Mayo's scheme. Lord Mayo effected the separation of Provincial from Imperial finance and pointed to the need also of the separation of purely local from Provincial finance—a separation which was completely effected only five years ago. In indicating the necessity for local self-government, he laid down in his resolution of 1870 as follows :—" Local interest, supervision and care are necessary to success in the management of funds devoted to education, medical charity and local public works. The operation of this resolution in its full meaning and integrity will afford opportunities for the development of self-government, for strengthening municipal institutions and for the association of Natives and Europeans to a greater extent than heretofore in the administration of affairs."

Lord Ripon's comprehensive proposals, 1882

The "Towns Improvement Act" which was passed in 1871 did much to provide for the administration of local affairs in towns and municipal areas, particularly in respect of health and sanitation. But though, as the resolution of 1882 observed, considerable progress in the direction of local self-government was made from 1870 onwards and a large income from local rates and cesses was realised, the management of which was freely entrusted to local bodies, there was still a greater inequality of progress in different parts of the country than local circumstances seemed to warrant. In many places, services admirably adapted for local management were reserved in the hands of the central government while charges were levied on municipalities in connection with matters over which they had no executive control. It was in Lord Ripon's time, therefore, that the first really important and decisive step was taken in respect of local self-government by placing it on its true basis, not merely as a means of devolution of authority in administration and in decentralization of financial resources, but as a means of popular and political education by means of which alone progressive communities could cope with the increasing problems of government. The famous and memorable resolution of Lord Ripon on local self-government in India, which will be found in the Appendix, laid down principles which are still being carried out into practice and should be studied by all who desire to have a correct grasp of the real value of local self-government to this country. Subsequent progress in local self-government has not been of any far-reaching character so far as its political and constitutional value is concerned, but the principles on which local self-government has proceeded in this country have not been uniform, nor do they follow entirely those which form the chief distinguishing features of local government in England.

Characteristics of Local Government in England

Local Government in England exhibits certain fundamental characteristics which it is necessary for the Indian student to bear in mind in order to understand some of the features imparted to local institutions in India by the legislative measures of the central government. In their authoritative book on "Local Government in England." Messrs Redlich and Hirst have defined "local government" generally as "the carrying out by the inhabitants of localities or by their elected representatives duties and powers with which they have been invested by the legislature, or which devolve upon them at Common Law."

Local bodies in England possess inherent and independent powers

This definition therefore, postulates the first feature of local government in England *viz.*, that the right of local self-government in England is not a mere creature of express legislation but is an immemorial right at Common Law inherent in every citizen of a locality in the administration of local affairs. Much the larger part of the national administration in England is thus carried on by local authorities under the control, of course, of the central government. The second is that this control exercised over the local authorities by the central government has always assumed the form of an authority expressly derived from Parliament by legislation and enforceable not by the discretionary authority of the executive government, but by the judicial decisions of the courts of the land unless the legislature, as it has done in recent times, expressly armed the executive with discretionary authority. As even in such a case the legislature is in itself but the embodiment of the will of the nation, the principle of self-government is supreme as well in central as in local affairs. The third feature, which is a consequence of the first two, which local institutions exhibit in England is what has been described by Sir C. P. Ilbert in a letter to Dr. Redlich in the following words:—"English Local Councils," he said, "whether County Councils and Borough Councils or District Councils, are public bodies discharging public functions and exercising their powers on lines and within limits defined by Parliament; but they are independent bodies—not agents—as every English Minister knows. They decline to take orders from the central executive except in the limited class of cases in which the legislature has conferred on the executive powers of interference."

Contrast with Continental institutions of bureaucratic origin

In the case of Continental countries like France or Prussia, whatever institutions of local self-government may have existed prior to the régime of the absolute monarchs of the 18th century, they disappeared with the growth of despotism. Consequently, when the countries, on the mainland of Europe threw off the yoke of absolute rule and established for themselves constitutional forms of government, the development of local institutions proceeded by express enactments of the legislatures. But the administrative traditions of Continental countries, coupled with the absence of the self-governing impulse which had long disappeared, did not lend themselves to the investment of local authorities with that power or that form of self-government and self regulation which exists in England. The history of both France and Prussia is, as has been observed before, the record of the building up of a consolidated and powerful state by means of a great bureaucracy directed from a single centre and pursuing a uniform policy, and so in both countries, the people became accustomed to look to that centre, to the monarch and to his officials for guidance in all their affairs. When the local institutions were started or revived, it was at the will and for the purposes of the central authorities and so both in France and Prussia local self-government is regarded rather as a gift from above than as an inherent right. Hence it is naturally weaker in these countries than in England.

In the second place, Continental governments have made a careful separation and classification of public services into local and central and all local affairs are administered by three agents, namely official agents or servants of the bureaucracy acting singly, and in committees, secondly committees composed partly of officials and partly of unprofessional members selected by local authorities and approved by the Central Government and, lastly, the purely elected authorities called into being for other purposes, being made to act as agents for the Central Government. The effect of this arrangement is that local authorities are more or less treated as agents for the Central Government and answerable to that government rather than as statutory bodies administering the powers legally vested in them and liable to be questioned only in a court of law, the authority of the Central Government being limited only to that of general supervision, guidance and advice.

Indian local institutions, partly bureaucratic, partly statutory and self-governing

Considering local institutions in India in the light of these facts, it will be seen that the Indian Government, though unconsciously, has pursued a policy oscillating between that which the traditions of self-government have impelled Englishmen to adopt and that which the tendencies of bureaucratic methods led them to. Indian local bodies, whether they be the rural unions and boards or the municipalities, mofussal and metropolitan, are similar to English local bodies in that they are public bodies discharging public functions and exercise their powers on lines and within limits defined by the legislature. They owe their origin therefore to express creation by means of specific enactments whose interpretation rests in the hands of the courts of the land. But as the framing of these enactments was in the hands of those accustomed to bureaucratic sway, the objective of these laws was circumscribed with the result that both the constitution and the functions of local authorities in India have been rigorously limited and defined and but too cautiously extended. At the same time, the power of interference of the central executive was legally widened so as to admit of a very minute control, whenever necessary, of the operations of these bodies. The result has been a medley of powers and duties, discretionary and obligatory, distributed between the central and local authorities in a way which left not much room for that popular and political education which, in Lord Ripon's eyes, was the main justification for the introduction of local self-government in India.

The policy of control in the initial stages of the path of local self-government would not necessarily be a disadvantage if the object that is kept in view is not mainly that of efficiency but of steadily developing faculties of self-government in local areas so as to eventually and inevitably leave the management of local affairs in the hands of the representatives of the citizens of the locality. The latter object often-times militates against the former and the conflict between the claims of efficiency and of popular government has not been reconciled in this country in a consistent or uniform manner. After Lord Ripon's time, the tendency has been mainly to place the claims of efficiency above those of popular education and this has, in turn, reacted on the constitution and functions of even the Presidency municipalities which, throughout had taken their course on the lines of English local institutions.*

* The origin of the Presidency municipalities in India leads back to the period of the development of boroughs in England in the seventeenth century, when town and borough corporations were being established in England by charters from the Crown in the time of the Stuarts. Madras was one of the earliest of such corporations of the Empire. It was in 1687 that James II conferred signal favour on the East India Company by giving them the power to establish by charter a corporation and a Mayor's Court in Madras. Sir Josiah Child, the celebrated governor of the Company in those days appreciated this favour in its true light as the only means of solving the difficult question of town conservancy which, by that time, owing to the brisk trade of the company round Fort St. George had become a matter

These corporations established in Madras, Bombay and Calcutta had, in their earlier days, a continuous history of corporate life and administration to the same extent as that enjoyed by corporations in England, but with the establishment of Legislative Councils in India on a firm basis, invested with what may be called plenary powers of legislation, the constitution

---

of urgent importance. It is useful to recall the words in which the Directors of the Company described the steps which they desired to be taken in establishing the Corporation and Mayor's Court in Madras, as it lays down principles of equal rights of Indians and Europeans, alike in the clearest manner. The impetus which was given by the Court of Directors in this behalf and the motives and intentions which actuated them in so doing are somewhat mixed but yet noteworthy. They wrote as follows: —

"If you could contrive a form of a corporation to be established of the natives mixed with some English freemen, for aught we know some public use might be made thereof, and we might give the members some privileges and pre-eminences by charter under our seal that might please them as all men are naturally with a little power, and we might make a public advantage of them, without abating essentially any part of our dominion when we please to exert it. And it is not unlikely that the heads of the several castes being made Aldermen and some other Burgesses, with power to choose out of themselves yearly their Mayor and to tax all the inhabitants for a Town hall or any public buildings for themselves to make use of, your people would more willingly and liberally disburse five shillings towards the public good, being taxed by themselves than sixpence imposed by our despotical power (notwithstanding they will submit when we see cause), were government to manage such a society as to make them proud of their honour and preferment and yet only ministerial and subservient to the ends of government which under us, is yourselves. We direct nothing positively in this but refer it to your consideration, and if you think it may redound to the public good, and that you may better adopt it to the good of the place and the establishing of our absolute power over it and unto some similitude to the forms of such like corporations in England where there is always a governor, a superior power, and a garrison we have thought fit to send you a copy of the late charter granted by His Majesty to the Borough of Portsmouth where Sir John Biggs (Judge of the new Court of Admiralty at Madras) was recorder and understands well not only the constitution but the way of proceeding it. We conceive their Court books must always be in the English tongue and the Town clerk must always be an Englishman that can speak Portuguese and Gentoo, and their recorder must be the same. We think it convenient that, in the court of Aldermen, being 12 besides the Mayor, there should never be above three English freemen and three Portuguese ; the other seven to be Moors and Gentoos." (Despatch of 16-6-1687.)

and functions of these bodies have been remodelled from time to time with the result that their self-governing character has been materially altered and except for the form of their old constitution and a few privileges still left, they are more or less subject to the same control of the Central Government which the municipalities and local bodies established by the legislation of 1885-86 are now under.

General classification of Indian local institutions: Rural and Urban

The local Institutions of British India may be classified as in England, into rural and urban bodies. The rural boards, as they are called, consist at present of unions which provide mainly for sanitation, conservancy and public health of the more important and populous of the villages or the less important towns. They are generally under the control of the taluk or sub-district boards which are, what we may call, the normal local administrative units for rural areas in all the provinces. The jurisdiction of the taluk boards extends to one or more taluks, according to the requirements of each taluk. Above the taluk boards are the district boards constituted for each district possessing a general control over the local administration of the district. In the urban or municipal areas all through the country, have been established the municipal councils, which except in Bombay, are unconnected with the boards of the districts or sub-districts in which they are.* This system of local bodies has not been fully introduced in some provinces, such as Assam, the North-West Frontier Province, and in certain other stray areas. There are besides special and particular local authorities like the port trusts of Bombay, Calcutta, Madras, Rangoon and Karachi which are invested with statutory administrative powers in respect of the area of their ports, and there are the cantonments whose local affairs are administered under the provisions of the Cantonment Codes. Both of these institutions we may leave out of consideration as of an exceptional character and not

* In the United Provinces the smaller towns are constituted into what are called "Notified Areas" where municipal functions are performed by nominated committees.

directly connected with the general growth of local self-governing institutions within the country.

General features of their constitution: official and non-official elements, nominated and elected members

In the constitution of these corporate bodies, in whom have been vested the local functions presently to be referred to, certain general characteristics may be noted. In the constitution of every board or council or trust, as the case may be, there are two elements called the official and the non-official. The official element is composed of both members *ex-officio*, *e.i.* holding office in virtue of their official position and authority in the locality, and those who are nominated by the Central Government to represent its interests on that body. The official element exists in varying proportions in the various local bodies which have been constituted, but it is generally of a substantial character. It is found in a much larger degree in the rural and district boards than in the municipal councils. The non-official element in those bodies again consists of two parts, that comprising the nominated section, that is, of non-officials who are appointed to the council by the Government without reference to any legal qualification or claim, and that comprising the elected element consisting of those chosen by the votes of qualified voters of the constituencies in the local areas. The elected element again is found in the largest proportion in the Presidency corporations or municipalities, and in a smaller and a greatly varying proportion among the different mofussil municipalities of the various provinces. The proportion in which the official and non-official elements, as well as the elected and the nominated elements, are represented on local bodies generally, has, to some extent, been regulated by statutes. But it is unnecessary to refer to this, inasmuch as, so far, there has been no tendency to preponderate both the non-official and the elected elements in these councils and boards. Generally speaking, the bulk of the municipalities in the Madras Presidency and in Bengal, possess elective privileges to a greater extent than in other provinces where a large number of municipalities do not possess a substantial elective element.

education chiefly elementary, the supply of good drinking water and the improvement of the sanitary and general condition of towns are all functions which, to a larger or smaller degree, have vested in the various municipal councils. The primary duty of the local boards has usually been deemed, owing to historical causes, to be the maintenance and improvement of the means of communication, that is, of roads and bridges. Other important functions, however, have been gradually added to them, such as medical relief, drainage and water-supply, and sanitation, education and, the provision of other public requirements such as pounds, ferries, markets, etc.

Limited extension of functions and large increase of control since 1882

In respect of these functions generally, it may be noted that the Acts which gave birth to these institutions in 1882 contemplated a very wide extension of the powers as well as of the resources of local bodies. While providing for the obligatory performance of a certain minimum of functions of the kind referred to above they also provided for as large and wide an expansion of such functions and resources, at the instance of the local Governments, as could be conceived to be 'of benefit for the locality in any way or to promote the safety, convenience, comfort and well-being of the local areas concerned.' In actual practice, however, the minimum line drawn has not been appreciably extended so far at the instance of the Central Government. One other characteristic of local bodies in India may be noted as illustrating the influence of British legal and constitutional ideas, viz., that involved in the legal relationship of the local authorities generally to the Central Government. Local bodies, in India as in England, can only exercise powers specifically entrusted to them either by the legislature or by the central executive authority under powers invested by the legislature. All residuary administrative powers, therefore lie in the hands of the Central Government. The resources of these local authorities are provided by the taxes and rates which they are empowered to levy on land and buildings, on the practice of professions and arts, by license fees, tolls and the rest, by income from properties vested in municipalities or boards supplemented by grants from the Central Government specifically assigned for various local purposes.

Present features and tendencies: official leading strings

With constitutions, functions and resources of the kind indicated above, the working of the boards and municipalities in India has more or less uniformly been under official leading strings. One of the most useful and usual ways in which administrative local authorities work in England and on the Continent has been by means of Committees, but generally speaking this species of committee work has not been much developed in the ordinary method of work of these bodies. So far as the local boards are concerned, their official character is pronounced and their work is usually conducted as a branch of the departmental work assigned to the Collector or the Divisional Officer as the case may be, who is its president. The official character of the board preponderates not merely by reason of the official members but also by reason of the number of nominated members who owe their position to the official head therein. This official management is moreover, in turn subject to minute outside control prescribed by the rules and regulations of the Provincial Governments. In the case of the municipalities, official control over their constitution or their subordinate establishment is less complete, but has usually taken the more invidious form of meticulous interference with the proceedings of the municipalities and the exercise of the powers of control which are to be usually held in reserve.

Outside, in place of inside, control contemplated in 1884

The Acts constituting the municipalities and local boards in India in 1884 contemplated the cessation of what has been called inside control by the presence of and regulation of business by officials and the councils, and the substitution of outside control by means of an independent audit, inspection and advice, as in England. To this has subsequently been added the system of grants-in-aid, a form of control by the Central Government over local authorities which has been the chief means by which outside control is exercised in England. Local authorities in England have usually deemed themselves independent of the control and superintendence as well as the advice of the central authority and only subject to the legal limitations imposed on them by the statutes or the common law. "How little the powers conferred by the statute have proved effective in introducing efficiency of administration among the local authorities in England is well-known to students of English institutions. But by what has been termed 'characteristic good luck', England has stumbled on an arrangement by which almost without the notice of political students, a solution has been found in the devise of the grant-in-aid. The National Government in the course of the past three quarters of a century has successively 'bought' the rights of inspection, audit, supervision, initiative, criticism and control in respect of one local service after another by the grant-in-aid of the local finances and therefore of the local ratepayers, of annual subventions from the exchequer." The grant-in-aid has proved in England the corrective element in the administration of local business by a local authority entirely in its own way. It has been the means of rendering aid to the poorer localities. It prevents the cost of government falling upon them as a crushing burden and of affording them the counsel and information of wider experience, while it has also served as a means of urging the negligent or apathetic authorities to bring their administration up to the national minimum, that is called for in the interests of the community as a whole, while all local authorities are now the better for an entirely independent audit of their accounts.

Both outside and inside control now exist in India

In India, the grants-in-aid have not been developed to such a large extent as in England, but the principle applied in the assignment of grants has been the same, in that every grant is earmarked for the purpose for which it is given and implies also in consequence, a certain measure of control over it reserved to the central authority. The central authority, moreover, has provided an independent audit, which has of late been given free, while it has also provided local bodies with inspecting officers and advisers such as the inspectors of local fund accounts, inspectors of schools, sanitary engineers and others whose advice and assistance could be sought after by the local authorities. The powers of inspection, advice and supervision have not however, arisen in India in consequence of the financial help which the Central Government has rendered to the local bodies, but as a part of the close control and supervision which, as was observed before, has been a concomitant and by no means consistent feature of the introduction of representative institutions in local areas. The advice of the supervising officers is bound to be taken by the local authorities in many matters. Their opinions are final or a necessary prerequisite for measures which the local authorities may desire to adopt. Whether in consequence of the readjustment of financial relations between the Imperial and Provincial Governments and the recent policy of making large grants to municipal authorities for sanitation and education is likely to reduce the process of control by direct interference and increase the process of advice, assistance and supervision by means of the grants, it is not easy to foretell.

Extraordinary powers of control over local bodies

The Executive Government in this country also possess certain extraordinary powers in respect of local authorities—powers which in England are vested in the hands of Courts. Neglect or failure on the part of the local authorities to carry out their statutory obligations in England can only be dealt with by means of an application to the Court of King's Bench for a writ of mandamus, which has not always proved effective in the case of obstinate and recalcitrant authorities, while the powers of the Local Government Board in gross cases, though recently strengthened, are hardly ever used. A much larger amount of punitive power, however, is vested in the hands of the Executive Government in India who can compel local authorities to carry out their obligations, and in default, carry them out itself and recover the cost from the local authority, while in cases of inefficiency or maladministration the Executive Government have the power and the entire discretion without resort to adjudication by courts to suppress or suspend a local authority. They possess besides a power of removal of individual members of these bodies for misconduct or for anything which, in the Government's opinion, is likely to bring local administration into contempt.

Indian local bodies statutory corporations

The local bodies in India are, nevertheless, as in England, bodies corporate and could be proceeded against by rate-payers for negligence or default in the performance of their statutory duties, and can sue and be sued in the ordinary course on all contracts or other obligations arising in civil law. In this respect, local bodies in India differ from those of the Continent, where they are merely treated as units of administration, as agents of the Central Government, claims and remedies against whom can only be dealt with under what is called '*droit administratif*' before administrative courts.

CHAPTER VIII

THE INDIAN LEGISLATURES—GENERAL FEATURES

Legislative and Executive functions

In dealing with the powers and functions of the executive authority in India, we began by pointing out that it was of earlier origin than the legislative authority. This is true in a general sense of all political communities, but it is true in a special sense with reference to the origin and growth of British Government in India. Logically, no doubt, the making of the law is antecedent to its execution and to decisions as to its meaning, and the legislative power, as Judge Story put it long ago, " is the great and overruling power in every free government ". Historically, however, it is the decisions of disputes and the specific regulation of the conduct of the individuals composing the community by its ruler or rulers, that have preceded the formulation of general rules to guide the rulers and the ruled. The modern distinction of governmental functions into legislative, executive and judicial—in which the organ representing the legislative function is regarded as supreme and as determining the rules applied by the judicature and carried into effect by the executive—did not find its counterpart in the earlier history of communities, as Sir Henry Maine's great works have demonstrated.

Legislatures and law-making

Even in the case of highly developed modern States, it would be a serious mistake to imagine that the Executive *organ* of Government is confined to the carrying out merely of what may be strictly termed, *Executive functions*. No matter how explicitly and comprehensively laws are made, they must of necessity leave a wide discretionary power in the hands of the Executive. To the extent to which the Executive exercise this discretion, they are really supplementing express legislation. A more modern development of what we may call the legislative side of Executive activity, is the power expressly delegated to them by the legislative *organ* to make rules and regulations, to determine the details of laws to be enforced. We may even go further and state that in the constitutions of the most advanced nations, the legislative function which the strictly legislative *organ* of Government exercises, is not that of *law-making*, but only that of *law-sanctioning*. In those countries, like England, in which the Parliament has developed into what the late Professor Seeley called a Government-making organ, it entrusts most of the work of law-making to the Executive in office. For instance, in England, it is the Cabinet that really makes the laws ; Parliament, however much it may amend, or turn them out of shape, only *sanctions* them. As one writer on Political Science has put it : " It is true that all the work of law-making is done *in* Parliament, but it is misleading at the present day to speak of Parliament as the legislative body in contradistinction to the Cabinet, which is called the Executive, because it leads us to forget that the course of legislation (except in Norway) is habitually regulated by the Cabinet through its influence over its supporters in Parliament. " *

Origin of Indian Legislatures

The possession of large legislative powers by the Executive is, therefore, of much less importance in the progress of modern governments than the existence of substantial responsibility, moral and constitutional,

* Hammond's 'Comparative Politics' [Macmillan] pp. 407, 408.

which that Executive bears to the representatives of the people in the legislature or the constituencies. It need be no matter of surprise that in India the Executive are possessed of large powers, but the historical circumstances which have led to it are different from those which have led to the same state of things in most modern European constitutions. In British India, as was seen in an earlier chapter, it was originally the Executive Government itself that was empowered "to make regulations and ordinances," for the good government of the factories or territories at first acquired in India, "so as they be not repugnant to the laws and customs of the United Kingdom". The earlier charters and the later statutes up to 1853, vested both the executive and legislative functions in the same body of individuals. The power of making regulations thus vested was at first in character the same as that which the Executive is invested with by modern statutes. The only laws, properly so called, which the Governors and the Governor-General and their Councils in their Executive, as well as in their legislative, capacity, were subject to, were the laws of the Parliament in England. The legislative and legal sovereignty of Parliament was, as it still is, the only theoretical and legal safeguard against the executive becoming a law unto themselves.

But the power of regulation-making in India gradually grew as the territories of the British rulers increased, and the need for Indian legislation in India itself became imminent. Thus, the executive function came early to be differentiated from the legislative function even when both were vested originally in the same body or bodies. It was in 1833 that, along with the appointment of a Law Member to the Governor-General's Council, Parliament declared that the laws of the Governor-General's Council were "to have the effect of Acts of Parliament." With the addition, in 1853, of additional members to the Council when sitting for the purpose of making laws and regulations, law-making became a distinct branch of the work of government in India, and laws strictly regarded as rules enforceable by the Courts and to be carried out by the executive, came into existence, admirably codified and enacted.

Ordinary and Additional Members of Councils

The process of joining additional members with the ordinary members "for the better exercise of the power of making laws and regulations vested in the Governor-General (or Governor) in Council," as the statutes have described it, may be said to have begun in 1833 with the addition of a fourth ordinary member to the Council of the Governor-General of India, who was not to be one of the Company's servants, and was not to be entitled to act as Member of Council except for legislative purposes. "His duty" as Sir Barnes Peacock wrote in a minute of 1859, "was confined entirely to the subject of legislation; he had no power to sit or vote except at meetings for the purpose of making laws and regulations; and it was only by courtesy and not by right that he was allowed to see the papers or correspondence or to be made acquainted with the deliberations of Government upon any subject not immediately connected with legislation." This principle of strengthening what may be called the legislative capacity of the Governor-General in Council received further development. When the last Charter Act was enacted by Parliament in 1853, it was found necessary to place the fourth or Legislative Member of the Council on the same footing with the ordinary members by giving him a right to sit and vote at executive meetings, while the Council was further strengthened in the discharge of legislative functions by the addition, as legislative members, of the Chief Justice of Bengal and one other Supreme Court Judge, and four others, being Company's servants of ten years' standing, appointed by the several Local Governments of Madras, Bombay, Bengal and the North-West Provinces. The Indian Councils Act of 1861 proceeded further and provided for the addition to the Councils, not only of officials, excluding the Judges who ceased to be nominated thereafter, but also of non-officials and fixed at the same time the maximum and minimum number of each. Further changes, large and liberal, have been made in the constitution of the Legislative Councils by the Indian Councils Acts of 1892 and 1909 which will be referred to in the next chapter, but the legal character of the Councils and of its members has not altered since. Marked developments, however, have taken place in the constitutional position of the Councils towards the people of India and the Parliament in England, and of their members, official and non-official. The legal status of the additional members of the Councils, Provincial and Imperial, as defined by sections ten and twenty-nine of the Indian Councils Act, is that they are part and parcel of the entity called the Governor-General (or Governor) in Council, *i.e.*, Government in the function of law-making. It may in fact be said that the executive organ of the State expands itself by means of *additional* members into the *legislative* organ. It seems therefore both from a legal and a constitutional point of view to be a mistake to regard the Indian Legislative Councils—as Professor Cowell does, in his "Courts and Legislative authorities in India,"—'as mere committees for the purpose of making laws, committees by means of which the Executive Government obtains advice and assistance and the public derive the advantage of full publicity being ensured at every stage of the law-making process.' Although the Government enacts the laws through its Council, he observes, 'yet the public has a right to make itself heard and the duty of enforcing them belongs to the courts of justice. Such laws are in reality the orders of Government but they are made in a manner which ensures publicity in discussion and are enforced by the courts and not by the executive.' Law-making, as has been pointed out already, is no doubt undertaken by the executive in most modern states and it may be quite correct to say, as Professor Lowell does of the English Constitution, that at present the Cabinet legislates with the advice and consent of Parliament. But it must not be forgotten that the Cabinet is itself but the creature of Parliament and constitutionally responsible to it for all its measures of proposed legislation and administration. It cannot be said similarly that in India the Executive legislates by and with the advice of the Legislative Council. In India, the Executive is no doubt the authority primarily concerned with law-making, but its constitutional responsibility for measures of legislation exists not towards the Legislative Councils in India, but towards His Majesty's Government in India and the Parliament of the United Kingdom. This has been well-explained in Lord Morley's reform despatch in order to deduce therefrom the principle adopted in the constitution of the Imperial Legislative Council, of creating a standing official majority. "It is an essential condition of the reform policy" wrote Lord Morley, "that the Imperial Supremacy shall, in no degree, be compromised. I must, therefore, regard it as essential that your Excellency's Council, in its legislative, as well as in its executive, character should continue to be so constituted, as to ensure its constant and uninterrupted power to fulfil the constitutional obligations that it owes and must always owe, to His Majesty's Government and to the Imperial Parliament."

Indian Legislatures are not mere committees of advice. The Legislative Councils of India are, however, legally as competent law-making bodies with plenary powers as the legislatures in many of the self-governing colonies, subject of course to the veto which is reserved on behalf of the Crown in the Executive. The control of the Executive over the Legislatures in India may of course be said to be in practice as complete as the control of the Legislatures over the Executive is in the colonies. But it is as true of the Indian Councils as of the Imperial Parliament to lay down that a bill or project of law cannot be introduced except by a member of the Legislature and any member can introduce a bill. When a member of Government introduces a bill, he does so not as a representative of the Government, but as a member of the Legislature to which he belongs. Legally, there is no difference between a Government bill, and a bill introduced by any other member. The control over legislation which the Executive Government has obtained in democracies is due to their being the servants of the

Legislature and the repositories of the authority of the ultimate sovereign, *viz.*, the electorates of the country. The control of the Executive over legislation in India is established on no such popular support but upon its ultimate responsibility to the Imperial Parliament in all Indian affairs. This position no doubt involves a certain amount of moral responsibility to the governed in India for all measures of legislation—including those which may be introduced by private members—passed by the Indian Legislatures whose proceedings the Executive is able so effectually to control. But it certainly does not preclude the activity of private members in bringing forward legistative measures, nor reduce the functions of the additional Members of Councils to those of mere criticism and discussion of such measures as may be brought by the Government. "Constituted as the Government of India are," said the Hon'ble Sir Reginald Craddock, the Home Member, in a recent speech in the Imperial Council on certain private bills affecting social legislation," it would be quite impossible for them to shelter themselves from any odium that might attach to an unpopular law behind the plea that the objectionable legislation had been the outcome of a private bill, and in a matter of such importance when far-reaching amendments to the substantive Criminal law of the country are in question, it is in accordance with the fitness of things and with general usage that any changes in the law which meet with the approval of Government should find a place in a Government bill rather than in a private one." This seems to sum up the situation correctly though it is a question how far the moral and legal responsibility of the Government could be deemed sufficiently safeguarded, as some hold, in ordinary cases, by the extensive powers of veto lodged in the Governor-General, the Secretary of State and the Crown. But it is certainly incorrect to proceed further and to assert that the Government in India 'cannot concede to private members the same wide sphere of legislative activity as is possible or even desirable under a system of party government', and that 'the primary duty of non-official members is to assist government in the work of legislation, to aid it with advice, and to bring before it the views of the constituencies they represented.' Rather would it seem that the functions of the members of the Legislative Councils in India are wider and have been more efficient in the sphere of law-making than in the Parliaments of other countries whose functions of law-sanctioning are now much more reduced than they were in the past.

Legislatures and Law-Making

The compact constitution of the Indian Councils and the original restriction of their functions primarily to legislation, lent itself to more thorough, systematic and finished work in the making of laws than is usually found attainable in a popular assembly discharging legislative functions. The functions of Parliament in the earliest times were by no means confined to law-making proper, although every Act of Parliament has throughout been expressed in the form of an enactment. The functions of voting supplies, and of imposing taxes on the people, to name only the most important of them, have throughout assumed the forefront in parliamentary activities and the functions of legislation proper began through the redress of grievances and by means of petitions. It was only after the passing of the Reform Act of 1832 that the activities of Parliament in the sphere of legislation assumed a marked importance, and it would appear that the changed attitude of the Government towards legislation which came in at that time was considered by some who were members of the House of Commons, both in the unreformed and the reformed Parliaments, as defects which required to be remedied. In his book on 'Parliament' Sir Courteney Ilbert quotes the opinion of Sir Charles Wood, afterwards Lord Halifax, given at the time as follows: 'When I was in Parliament', he said 'twenty seven years ago, the functions of the Government were chiefly executive. Changes in our laws were proposed by the independent members and carried not as party questions, by their combined action on both s des. Now when an independent member brings forward a subject, it is not to propose himself a measure but to call to it the attention of the Government. All the House joins in declaring that the present state of the law is abominable and in requiring the Government to provide a remedy. As soon as the Government has obeyed and proposed one, they all oppose it. Our defects as legislators, which is not our business, damage us as administrators which is our business.' Such a conception as to the differentiation of legislative and executive functions, though natural, is no longer practically possible in England, when the bulk of law-making inevitably falls into the hands of the party in power through whom indeed the popular needs surely make themselves felt. Until therefore the responsibility of the Executive Government in India for the work of legislation becomes not merely moral, but also political and constitutional towards the people through duly elected representatives in the Council, the relation of the executive to the legislature cannot be treated as similar in character to that which obtains in England.

Non-sovereign characteristics of Indian Legislature

We may then proceed to briefly summarise the general characteristics of the Indian Legislatures which are, it will be clear, distinct from analogous institutions elsewhere. The Indian Constitution, it may be repeated, is really a creature of the British Parliament. That itself is one mark of the subordinate character of the Indian Legislatures. In the next place, the executive authority in India is constitutionally regarded only as a subordinate agency of His Majesty's Government and by that very fact legally responsible to the paramount authority of the Imperial Parliament and not to that of the Indian Legislatures which are themselves subject to the same authority, deriving their constitution and functions from its enactments. Thirdly, the Executive Government is not only independent of the Indian Legislatures, but possesses also the power of virtually controlling and subordinating the legislatures to its authority by means of a standing official majority and otherwise, in order, as Lord Morley put it 'to ensure its constant and uninterrupted power to fulfil its constitutional obligations to the Home Government and Imperial Parliament.' The relationship of the Executive to the Legislature in India is thus not that which is has usually described as that of " a parliamentary executive," as in the self-governing colonies, but that of a "non-parliamentary executive," virtually capable of controlling the legislatures. Hence we arrive at the same result which we referred to in a former chapter as deducible from the constitutional position of the executive authority in India, *viz.*, that there is at present in India no constitutional arrangement by which the Executive is or could be made responsible to the people of the country or to the Legislatures in which the people are represented.

It follows from what has been stated above that the Indian Legislatures are, according to constitutional theory, strictly non-sovereign law-making bodies; and it becomes necessary to note the characteristics flowing therefrom, before proceeding to discuss their constitution and functions. The general characteristics of such bodies are, according to Professor Dicey: first, the existence of laws affecting their constitution which such bodies must obey and cannot change; hence, secondly, the formation of a marked distinction between ordinary laws and fundamental laws; and lastly, the existence of a person or persons, judicial or otherwise, having authority to pronounce upon the validity or constitutionality of laws passed by such law-making bodies. Each of these three characteristics is noticeable with reference to the Indian Legislatures, Provincial and Imperial. Although the Council of the Governor-General can pass laws as important as any Acts passed by the British Parliament, the authority of the Council in the way of law-making is completely subordinate to, and dependent upon, the Acts of Parliament which constituted the Legislatures. The legislative powers of the Indian Councils arise from definite Parliamentary enactments, the chief of which will be found printed in the Appendix. They form what might be termed the 'constituent' laws of the Indian Government. In the next place, the Indian Councils are also non-sovereign in that they are bound by a large number of regulations and rules which the Executive is empowered to frame under the 'constituent' statutes abovementioned, which cannot be changed by the Indian legislative bodies themselves, but which can be changed only by the Executive Government or by the superior power of the Imperial Parliament. If one for a moment turns to these regulations and rules and observes what they provide for, it will be seen that the executive has been invested with very large powers in framing not only the constitution, fixing the franchise, the qualifications of representatives and so forth, but also in prescribing the functions and the authority exercisable by the Councils themselves. This aspect of the matter will, however, be presently discussed in connection with the more detailed consideration of the constitution and the functions of the Councils. It is sufficient to note here that not only the Acts which created the Councils, but also the rules and regulations framed by the Executive under the sanction of these Acts for the constitution and working of the Councils, could not be changed by the Councils themselves. Again, the powers of the Councils as to law-making proper are also specifically restricted by the rules as well as by the statutes. Thus the Governor-General in Council has no power of making laws which may affect the authority of Parliament or any part of the unwritten laws or constitution of the United Kingdom whereon may depend in any degree the allegiance of any person to the Crown of the United Kingdom or the Sovereignty or dominion of the Crown over any part of India or any of certain specified statutes of the British Parliament applicable to this country. Lastly, the Courts in British India are constitutionally vested with the power of pronouncing upon the validity or constitutionality of laws passed by the Indian Councils.

CHAPTER IX

THE INDIAN LEGISLATURES—THEIR CONSTITUTION

Official and non-official elements in the Indian Legislatures

In proceeding to consider briefly the constitution of the various legislatures, Imperial and Provincial, it is necessary again to advert to the fact that the Imperial Legislative Council and the Legislative Councils of Madras and Bombay are, in legal theory, but expansions of their Executive Councils by the presence in them of additional members nominated or elected for the purpose of making laws and regulations. The Legislative Councils of the Lieutenant-Governors and Chief Commissioners have been separately constituted under statutory powers vested in the Governor-General. It is a curious fact to note in this connection that subsequent to the passing of the Indian Councils Act of 1861, no new Lieutenant-Governorships could be created without Legislative Councils accompanying them. In fact, the power to constitute the latter under the Act seems to be derivable from the former.

The constitution and functions of the Legislative Councils in India are now regulated by the Indian Councils Acts of 1861, 1892, and 1909, and by the regulations and rules framed by the Executive Governments under the last named enactment. The Charter Act of 1853 was the first enactment which permitted of additional members to the Council, besides the members of the Executive Council. into which the Law Member was also by that Act absorbed. The Indian Councils Act of 1861 remodelled and enlarged the Councils by providing for the nomination of nòn-official additional members, though it curtailed some of the powers which the Legislative Council claimed to exercise under the Act of 1853. The Act of 1892 further increased the number of additional members both official and non-official and allowed the Executive Government to make rules for nominating some representatives chosen by local bodies and other corporations representative of particular interests. The Indian Councils Act of 1909 considerably enlarged the constitution of the Councils as fixed by the Act of 1892 and formally vested the right to elect a proportion of the members of the Councils in constituencies of the people, created by the regulations which the Governor-General in Council, with the previous sanction of the Secretary of State, has been empowered to make or mend, and under rules and restrictions similarly framed. These regulations and rules are complicated and likely to be somewhat confusing to the ordinary student of political institutions, and as they are likely to undergo revision from time to time in various particulars and details, a general idea of their scope and character as gathered from the reform despatches and the scheme now in force, is sufficient for the purposes of this preliminary study. An attempt has, however, been made in the Appendix to give an analysis and summary of them with a few critical notes.

In reference to all these Councils, it should be noted at the outset that their constitution consists of two elements, the official and the non-official, and that they are appointed both by nomination and by election. While the Government, Imperial or Provincial as the case may be, is on its part empowered to nominate additional members to the Councils from officials and non-officials alike, the constituencies or electorates are on their part empowered to elect only non-officials as members. Under the amended Regulations of 1912, officials as such have been made ineligible for election by any of the constituencies, though they are entitled to vote in them if qualified.

Their proportion in the several Councils

One of the first things to note in the constitution of all the Legislative Councils is the varying proportion of the official and non-official element in the several provinces. Under the new scheme which has been introduced by the Indian Councils Act of 1909, it has been settled as essential that the official majority in the Viceroy's Council should be retained, in order "to enable the Government of India to discharge the constitutional obligations which it owes to His Majesty's Government and the Imperial Parliament." The principle of a standing official majority is, however, dispensed with in the case of all Provincial Legislatures, but the proportion which bears to the total strength of the Council various in different provinces, according to the view the executive heads of each have taken of their necessities. The Bengal Government, it will be seen, have consented to work with the largest, while that of Madras has provided their Council with the smallest, non-official majority.

Constitutional understanding as to official members' votes

The significance of the distinction between the official and non-official elements in the Indian Councils and the official and non-official majorities which thereby result from it, will be fully realised only when it is understood that it is further based upon what has been deemed to be a legitimate constitutional understanding, that official members are bound to vote with the Government on all Government measures. There does not, however, seem to be any statutory warrant for this rule or any warrant under the rules and regulations framed under the Councils Acts. The understanding, however, has been a somewhat anomalous growth in Indian constitutional development. The position taken by the Executive Government in this matter appears to be this. In respect of all measures of legislation introduced by the Executive Government, the Governor-General and the Members of the Executive Council—either in accordance with the decision at which they may have previously arrived, as embodied in the bill, or in pursuance of the instructions and directions of the Secretary of State, which they are bound to carry out—introduce a bill into the Council as a 'Government measure'. In either case, the Ordinary or Executive Members of the Council find themselves bound to vote in favour of the measure they have introduced, and against any alterations or amendments thereto, if they are not in conformity with the plans of the Government.* In the former case, their vote is based upon their convictions, and in the latter case, their vote is based upon the mandate of the Secretary of State which they are bound to have carried out through the Council. The position in this respect was well explained by Lord Elgin in a speech which he made in the Legislative Council on the 27th December 1894, when he defended the position taken by himself and the other Members of his Executive Council in supporting the Cotton Duties bill in pursuance of a mandate from the Secretary of State, and against their own previously expressed views. He said:—

Position of Members of Executive Councils

"So far as the individual action of my colleagues and myself is concerned, Sir Henry Brackenbury, in the discussions on the last Tariff bill, and again to-day, has said that we are bound to obey the orders given by the proper and constitutional authority. But, for my part, I do not think that exhausts the question. It is claimed that members must be free to speak and vote in this Council for the measure they honestly think best. I can accept that proposition only with the qualification that they duly recognise the responsibility under which they exercise their rights in this Council. Only in an entirely irresponsible body can members act entirely as their inclination leads them. In every legislative body a man must sit, unless he has an hereditary right, by

* In the Despatch referred to in Chapter IV, page 47 dated the 24th November, 1870, the Duke of Argyll laid it down that the Government of India "were merely executive officers of the 'Home' Government who hold the ultimate power of requiring the Governor-General to introduce a measure and of requiring also all the official members to vote for it."

what in modern parlance is called a mandate, and that mandate must be given by some authority. I need not remind you that, in a Parliament, a man is not free to act exactly as he pleases; he is distinctly subject to the mandate he has received from his constituents ; and practice has shown that even this is not sufficient, but that to make Parliamentary government effective it has been necessary to introduce party management ; and the bonds of party, in the present day, certainly show no sign of being relaxed. Here we have no election and I am glad to say no party, but every man who sits here sits by the authority and sanction of Parliament ; and to say that he can refuse to obey the decisions of Parliament would be absurd. But that is not all. Parliament has provided for the government of the Indian Empire. The British Raj can be provided for in no other way. Parliament has allotted his proper place to the Viceroy, as the head of the Executive in India, and it has given him a Council for the purpose of making laws and regulations which cannot have powers in which he does not share. But the Viceroy admittedly is not invested with supreme authority, but, as I understand, it is by distinct enactment entrusted to the Secretary of State and his Council; and to speak of this Council as supreme, if that means that it has independent and unfettered authority—is to say what is not the fact."

"I speak with some deference, after what fell from the Hon'ble Sir Griffith Evans ; but, with all respect for his legal authority, I think that he is not correct in the view he took that a member of this Council is unfettered in the vote he gives here, or that he could 'hand over his responsibility' to the Secretary of State. I am inclined to think that the Hon'ble Mr. Mehta took a more correct view of the matter when he said that he would leave the responsibility with the Secretary of State, because the responsibility which the Secretary of State would exercise would be the responsibility which belongs to him."

Position of other official members

If the Viceroy and the Members of his Executive Council could be brought down to the position which Lord Elgin admitted was the net result of the constitutional arrangements of the Government of India, it follows, as a further extension of the very same theory, that additional members nominated by the Government from among its subordinate officials are bound to vote, on all 'Government measures,' in accordance with the declared intentions or policy of the Government, and in respect of every matter on which they are called upon to vote. In the words of Sir James Westland, spoken in the debate above cited, "if the question before the Council is a 'Government question', the Government will, on the reasons and principles explained, exercise the whole of its voting power."

The position of the Legislatures altered in consequence

The effect of this state of things is to alter the actual position originally assigned to the Legislative Councils in the Constitution, in all cases where the Government has an official majority or a majority which it can create, control or influence. Protests have now and again been made both in and out of the Councils as to this state of things. Sir Griffith Evans and Sir P. M. Mehta adverted to this during the debates in the Legislative Council in 1894 and, in the Madras Presidency, the late Sir V. Bhashyam Iyengar, the distinguished jurist, submitted a strongly worded minute against this procedure, in 1908, when giving his opinion in regard to the new Reform scheme. "We should be careful," said Sir Griffith Evans in the Viceregal Legislative Council, "to maintain the position assigned to us in the Constitution and not to abdicate our functions or allow the Executive to make laws when we only register them. The Secretary of State and the Executive Council have no legislative powers and cannot be allowed to usurp them." Sir P. M. Mehta considered the position of the ordinary Members of Council to be different from that of the additional official Members of Council and claimed that the latter had, for their part, more freedom of action. This, however, Sir James Westland did not concede in respect of what he termed 'Government questions.' Sir V. Bhashyam Iyengar's opinion is entitled to the greatest weight on this subject, as he has occupied the position of both an official and a non-official Member of the Legislative Council and as he could by no means be considered to be biassed against the Executive Government. The text of it appears in a note at the end of this chapter and is well worth perusal by students of Indian constitutional history.

Official votes not analogous to Party votes in England

The enforcement of an understanding to the effect above referred to, with respect to the official Members of the Legislative Councils, is very different from that which prevails under the party system in England, and is as it is worked at present far from conducive to constitutional progress. In England, the Party Whips insist on Members of Parliament voting with or against the Government according to the party to which they belong, in respect of all measures irrespective of their individual opinions. The ultimate sanction for this is the power of the constituencies to compel the Member morally to support the Government whom they desire to keep in power, or the Opposition with whom they side. The Government and the Opposition in turn, rest and count on the support of the constituencies. But, while in the case of Members of Parliament, the submission to the Whip is purely voluntary and based on the principles of party government and the alternations of party politics, the voting to order of the official Members in the Indian Legislative Councils is based upon the official authority exercised by a superior over a subordinate in the public service, which virtually gives power to the former to materially alter the legal character and position of the Legislative Councils and their Members.*

* An esteemed critic and a high authority on constitutional law has expressed the opinion to the author that " there is more to be said from the constitutional point of view, in favour of the convention which requires official members to use their votes in support of the Government, than is to be found in the acute observations of Sir Bhashyam Iyengar." The principle that a Government must be in a position to carry its measures and should not otherwise go on holding office, he rightly points out, "has become firmly established in England in the course of the last century and it is not surprising that it should have found its way to India. You may, of course, argue that it is inapplicable, but there can, I think, be little doubt that it has contributed to bring about the convention of which you complain." The inapplicability of the convention to the Indian Councils and Government, is indeed quite obvious, but is distinct from the question whether its existence and continuance will be favourable or unfavourable to future constitutional progress. In this view, it appears to the author, that while, Sir

Such being the position of the Legislative Councils, we may next consider the qualifications necessary for the Legislative Councillors, Provincial and Imperial. In regard to the Members nominated by the Government, no specific qualification is prescribed under the acts or the regulations. It does

No qualifications for nominated Councillors

Bhashyam Iyengar's observations on its present effects—or rather its effects prior to the establishment of the enlarged and reformed Councils in 1910—are quite justified from the point of view of immediate efficiency and advantage, the growth of constitutional conventions based on the maintenance of a Government by the support of a majority in the Legislatures and its resignation in the withdrawal of that support is no doubt a tendency to be welcomed rather than to be made matter of complaint. But it would indeed seem difficult to say how far the development of such conventions which imply a Parliamentary executive, and as its necessary concomitant, a system of Party Government—is likely to be furthered by the existing constitutional arrangements. In arriving at any conclusion on this matter it is necessary to bear in mind the following considerations :—

1. The growth of the convention as to party voting in England became established in the course of a century, but the introduction of the solid official vote to India was not determined by any such historical causes or political requirements, but by a mere process of transference by British administrators under the circumstances referred to above. In England, the party vote is not the consequence, but the cause and source of the power which sustains the Government, whereas in India the official party vote is not the cause, but the consequence of the power which the Government possesses independently of the vote of elected representatives in the Councils—due to the statutory standing official strength and to the position of constitutional independence of the Indian Executive Government in carrying on the ordinary administration of the country, which will be referred to more particularly hereafter.

2. It is no doubt the experience of modern countries that wherever democratic institutions begin to grow and the number of voters is necessarily large, the system of Government sooner or later involves the permanent existence of political parties. But the distinction of official and non-official votes in the Indian Councils does not rest on the existence of one class of voters supporting the officials and the other class opposing them but on the officials relying on their statutory power and authority, and on the non-officials relying on all the support of the voters. The conception of a party in power and a party out of power is a feature of British Parliamentary institutions and so far only the form and not the substance of it has been introduced into India with the attendant drawbacks referred to above.

3. The non-official opposition in the Indian Councils therefore is not in the same position as "His Majesty's Opposition" in England (*i.e.*), that 'of a party out of power which is recognised as perfectly loyal to the institutions of the state and ready at any moment to come into office without a shock to the political traditions of the nation.' The Indian Opposition is a permanent opposition, perpetually out of office and without the advantages accruing from the exercise of responsible

not seem to be even necessary that the nominees should be literate in English; for, we find that among the rules of business provision is made for having bills or their purport to be translated in Hindustani or other local vernaculars for the use of Members unacquainted with English, and also provision for one Member to speak at the request of and on behalf of another Member who is unable to express himself in English. Such contingencies are, of course, of rare occurrence. It is also to be noticed that the rules and regulations now framed under the Indian Councils Act, 1909, prescribing the qualifications of Members, are applicable only to those elected by the constituents and not to those nominated by the Government. It, therefore, seems to be open to the Government, theoretically at least, to nominate to the Council persons who may be ineligible, to be elected under the Regulations for any of the constituencies, such as bankrupts or convicted persons or others.

Qualifications and disqualifications of elected Councillors

The qualifications and disqualifications of Members elected by the constituencies are, however, prescribed in great detail under the new Regulations. In the first place, there are certain general categories of disqualification. Aliens, females, lunatics, minors, bankrupts, dismissed public servants, convicted persons, persons debarred from practice as lawyers and, lastly, persons who "have been declared by the Government to be of such reputation and antecedents that their election would, in the opinion of the

---

power which they could attain to by persuasion of the Legislatures and the electors. The non-official members cannot so far be said to be divided from the official members on any recognised differences of political principles on public questions, which are to be put in operation as each party attains to power.

4. Party vote in England has led to party Government and the establishment of a Parliamentary executive. In America, on the other hand, it has led to Presidential Government and Congressional legislation and though parties there are more thoroughly organised than in England, they are outside the framework of the Government. In India, the British system of party voting has been introduced into the legislatures, but the British system of party oGvernment which was the origin of such voting in England is yet to grow.

Government, be contrary to public interests,"—are disqualified from being elected. In the next place, any person who is to be elected by any constituency should, except in some rare instances, himself belong to the constituency as a voter entitled to elect the candidate of that constituency. He must, in order to be elected, be also duly nominated under the rules in force for each constituency and he must be duly elected according to such rules. Some of the disqualifications can be relieved against by the Executive Government, but others, from the nature of things, could not be so relieved against. The term of office of Legislative Councillors is, as a rule, three years in the case of all elected Members and three years or less in the case of Members nominated by Government. Every member elected or nominated is to take the oath of allegiance before taking his seat. These, in brief, are the general qualifications necessary for the Members of the Councils. Special qualifications are prescribed for special electorates, but these arise more from the nature of the constituencies which they represent than from the qualifications pertaining to candidates themselves.

Complicated constituencies

The constituencies which are to elect members to the Legislative Councils in pursuance of the new rules and regulations are not so much electoral areas as electoral groups so framed as to secure a certain proportion of representation of classes, interests and areas, and for this purpose the power of nomination is also intended to be used to supplement the elections. It is hardly possible to bring under any systematic treatment, from a constitutional standpoint, these various 'schedules' of electoral arrangements, but readers of this book may be referred to the whole scheme as summarised from the Despatches, resoultions and regulations, which is published in the Appendix. It may be mentioned, however, that, while the object and evident intent of the whole scheme is to secure some amount of real representation of the wishes and intentions of the varied classes of the population in the country, it is doubtful whether the complicated machinery provided, coupled with the intricate manner in which the electoral groups are made to intersect each other and also divide themselves off one from another is likely to work as smoothly and efficiently as its authors expect it to do. One is reminded in this connection of the complicated and chaotic state to which the electoral arrangements in England became reduced at the end of the eighteenth century by the variety and antiquity of the franchise, and which led subsequently to the famous Reform Bill of 1832. It may also be pointed out that the power of enquiring into and deciding the validity of disputed elections, disqualifications of voters and candidates—involving questions of title to property under the personal law of each Hindu, Mahomedan, Malabari or other, and the assessment of their rental values and so forth—is vested in the Executive Government, and not in the Courts, at the instance of the legislature itself, as in England. It is hardly possible to exaggerate the burden which this might increasingly throw on its shoulders as time advances. To quote a remarkable petition which was presented to the House of Commons in the last decade of the eighteenth century on an analogous state of things:—

"Your honourable House is but too well acquainted with the tedious, intricate, and expensive scenes of litigation which have been brought before you in attempting to settle the legal import of the numerous distinctions which perplex and confound the present rights of voting. How many months of your valuable time have been wasted in listening to the wrangling of lawyers upon the various species of burgage-hold, leasehold and freehold. How many committees have been occupied in investigating the nature of scot and lot, potwallopers, commonalty, populacy, resiant inhabitant, and inhabitants at large. What labours and research have been employed in endeavouring to ascertain the legal claim of boroughmen, eldermen, portmen, select men, burgesses, and councilmen; and what confusion has arisen from the complicated operation of clashing charters from freemen, resident and non-resident and from the different modes of obtaining the freedom of corporations by birth, by servitudes, by marriage, by redemption, by election, and by purchase."

It has also to be remembered that the franchise in respect of the constituencies or electoral groups above referred to, is distributed in as unsymmetrical and uneven a manner as the conditions of the country and its people are deemed to demand, so as to secure the proper representative elements in the Councils, and in proper proportions. Generally speaking, the franchise now conferred may be divided into three main classes— that of the normal territorial electorates, that of the electorate composed of the landed interest, and that of the electorate composed of the Mahomedan population whose political importance, it has been decided, requires special representation in excess of their numerical strength. The franchise is also bestowed to a more limited extent on certain other special interests, such as those of European and Indian commerce, the planting, jute and other special industries. The proportion in which representation is given to all these interests and classes is not in accordance with either their numerical strength or their proprietary interests. Reasons of political importance, special minority representation and similar considerations have been set out in the whole scheme as having guided the Government in arriving at its decisions as to the numbers of seats to be allotted to each. The consequence has been that, from a theoretical point of view at any rate, some classes have double and sometimes treble representation in the different constituencies to which they belong, while others have none at all.

No Approximation to Parliamentary Franchise

In defending the arbitrary selection and distribution of parliamentary boroughs and the "various, confused and uncertain franchise which they enjoyed," Edmund Burke to whom the British Constitution was a sacred fabric— "to understand it according to our measure, to venerate where we are not able presently to comprehend"—was much less impressed by the sordid and unpleasant features of its electoral system, by the rottenness and corruption practised therein, than by the strength and stability which the Government built on it exhibited at the close of the eighteenth century. "Our representation," he wrote, "has been found perfectly adequate to all the purposes for which a representation of the people can be desired or devised. I defy the enemies of our constitution to show the contrary". Sir C. P. Ilbert points out in his interesting little book on 'Parliament' in the Home University Library series that, according to Burke, "the variety of franchise in the boroughs and the mode in which the constituencies were controlled roughly represented the various interests of the nation and its ruling forces. The King and his ministers had to rule the discordant elements in the country and the constitution had to be kept together."

Somewhat similar appears to have been the frame of mind of Lord Minto who initiated the Council reforms and the electoral arrangements in 1907-09 as Viceroy. The dread of the French Revolutionary ideas and the corresponding and consequent political agitation in England were hardly more operative on Burke's mind than the dread of professional politicians and of a parliamentary franchise on Lord Minto's mind. In the course of a discussion on a paper read by Sir William Chichele Plowden, K. C. S. I. at a meeting of the East India Association, entitled " Problems of Indian Administration"—in which the latter described the provisions of a Bill he had introduced into Parliament, so early as 1890, to enlarge the representation of the existing Councils on the simple system of a numerical franchise worked through Panchayats and local bodies,—Lord Minto, who presided on the occasion, gave expression to the following views as to the existing electoral machinery adopted under the Indian Councils Act, 1909 :—

" I readily admit that the regulations of the new Councils Act are extremely puzzling and often very confusing ; some of them, I confess, that I have found difficult to understand myself, but I may say at the same time that the principles of Sir William Plowden's Bill differed entirely from those of the Act of 1909. His Bill, as I understand it, was based on the old Panchayet system, a system which

I have always admired as well adapted for many localities in India for traditional reasons and because it is peculiarly suited to the character and manner of life of the people. But though no one recognizes more than I do, the immense importance of encouraging a knowledge of local administration among the people themselves, yet when you come to consider the qualifications of individuals for the higher councils, such as the present Provincial Legislative Councils, the qualifications required of candidates appear to me to be different from those required of members who are only expected to deal with local questions. I am afraid the day is very far distant when the masses of the people of India can expect their interests to be fittingly represented by their own countrymen elected on a purely numerical franchise. I believe at the present moment the best friends of the masses of the people of India are British administrators, and, in addition to their able assistance, the Committee which I appointed aimed at framing a Bill which would provide representation for those great factors in India which have a real stake in the country; we felt that on such lines the representation of the real and general interests of the country would be more soundly assured than by any franchise based on a numerical system alone. In August 1906, when I was about to appoint the Committee I have referred to, to consider the reforms which we then had under discussion, and of which Sir Arundel was the Chairman—whom I am so glad to see here to-day—the very first instruction I gave to my Council when I was appointing that Committee was that I should at present limit myself to only one opinion, namely, that in any proposal for the increase of representation it was absolutely necessary to guard the important interests existing in the country, as expressed in paragraph 7, page 3 of the Report of Sir C. Aitchison's Committee, namely, (*a*) the interests of the hereditary nobility and landed classes who have a great permanent stake in the country; (*b*) the interests of the trading, professional and agricultural classes; (*c*) the interests of the planting and commercial European Community; and (*d*) the interests of stable and effective administration. Those were the lines on which the Committee were first requested to act; they always kept those lines in view, and I think, we may fairly claim that the result has been a great addition of strength to the Government of India. What we aimed at at the time was an addition to the Legislative Councils, especially to the Viceroy's Legislative Council—an addition of strength in the shape of expert knowledge, and in the shape of opinions emanating from men who were really interested in the every day life and welfare of the people of India. I always felt that that would be an enormous assistance to us. You must remember that we were in the face of a very serious political agitation; we were very much criticized and were told over and over again that it was not a time in which any reforms whatever ought to be introduced—that it was absolutely foolhardy to do so. I always refused to admit that. I always said that I believed a great deal of the agitation was justifiable agitation, and that if we were to put that right, a great many people would come down on the right side of the fence. Undoubtedly our action gained for us much additional support throughout the country, and I hope that its results will be permanent for the good of India. At the same time, we were very anxious to avoid any appearance of a Parliamentary franchise. I set my face against any thing that might appear to resemble it. We did not want a Parliament at all; we wanted Councils and the best possible advice we could get on those Councils, but did not want Councils elected on Parliamentary lines. I hope there will be no confusion in any one's mind about that."

It is, however, too early for students of political science to subject the present organisation of the Indian Legislative Councils to the test of scientific criticism as an experiment in formal constitution-making.

Elective element by no means overpowerful

It has moreover to be remembered that, after all, the elective element is only one and by no means an over-powerful element in the Legislative Councils, Provincial or Imperial. Even in regard to the territorial electorates, the franchise is bestowed on a fairly high class of citizens, namely present or past members of Taluq and District Boards and of Municipalities and title-holders, a large proportion of whom owe their qualifications the Executive Government. Again, though the mode of election is based more or less upon the Ballot Act in England, still the power of deciding contested elections is vested in the Executive Government and not either in the Legislative Councils or the Courts as was and now is, the practice in England. Besides, the powers of the Councillors themselves in legislation and in administration, even under the new scheme, are strictly limited. Experience might perhaps show that the power of consolidation of the Indian peoples is stronger than the tendency to isolation and differentiation, on the existence of which the Government has based its scheme. But to the student of politics, the present experiment will be from many points of view an extremely interesting one to watch.

NOTE.

(Extract from a note by Sir V. Bhashyam Aiyangar on the proposed enlargement of the Legislative Councils and establishment of Imperial and Provincial Advisory Councils, submitted to the Government in 1908.)

Both under the Indian Councils Act of 1861 and under the Indian Councils Act of 1892, the Governor-General in Council and the Governors in Council of Fort St. George and Bombay, in exercising the power of making laws and regulations vested in such Councils, respectively, are to consist not only of the Governor-General, the Governor of Fort St. George or the Governor of Bombay as the case may be and the ordinary members of his Council, but also of certain additional members whether in the service of the Crown in India or not, the minimum and the maximum numbers of such additional members having been originally prescribed by the Act of 1861 and since raised by the Act of 1892. The functions of a Government are both executive and legislative and the power of making laws and regulations is no less an important function of Government than its executive functions, and the fundamental principle of the British Indian constitution is, that the Indian Government, in expressing its important function of legislation should consist not only of the individuals in whom the executive functions of Government are vested but of a certain number of additional individuals who, in so far as the passing of laws and regulations is concerned, form as much a component part of Government as the former body of individuals. The only diffierence between ordinary members and the additional members is that the former form a component part of Government not only when the Government is discharging its legislative functions, but also when the Government is engaged in discharging its executive functions, whereas the additional members form a component part of Government only when the Government is engaged in exercising its legislative jurisdiction. It is therefore opposed to the very constitution of Indian Government that at meetings of the Council for the purpose of making laws and regulations, the individuals composing the executive Government should be regarded, or that they should assert themselves, as *the* Government, or as a component part of the Council, separate and distinct from the additional members of the Council.

Up to 1834, the executive and legislative functions of each province were vested in one and the same body of individuals constituting the respective Governments and by 3 and 4 William IV, Chapter 85, the Government of Madras and Bombay were substantially divested of their legislative functions and the Governor-General and his Councillors were empowered as the central legislative authority to legislate for the whole of British India, the duty of one of such Councillors, namely, the fourth ordinary member, being confined entirely to the subject of legislation with no power to sit or vote except at meetings for the purpose of making laws and regulations.

Thus for the first time the principle was introduced enlarging the Council of the Governor-General by the addition of a member, a paid official, who formed a part of Government for purposes of making laws and regulations only. This principle was further developed by 16 and 17 Vic., Ch. 95, by which, the Chief Justice and a Puisne Judge of the Supreme Court of Calcutta, as well as four official representative members chosen by the Governments of Bengal, Madras, Bombay and the Nort-Western Provinces formed additional members of the Governor-General's Council for the purpose of making laws and regulations only, and the fourth ordinary member of the Governor-General's Council was, like the other ordinary members, given a right to sit and vote at executive meetings. Under the Indian Councils Act of 1861 legislative powers were restored to the provincial Governments and it was provided that for the purpose of making laws and regulations the Councils of the Governor-General, as well as of the Governors of Madras and Bombay were to be re-inforced by the appointment of certain additional members, officials and non-officials. It will thus be seen that from 1833 to 1853 there was one additional official member in the Governor-General's Council and from 1853 to 1861 there were six additional members in that Council, who were all officials; such additional members were undoubtedly, for purpose of legislation, as much a part of Government as the ordinary members of the Council,and it was only under the Indian Councils Act of 1861 that provision was made for the appointment as additional members of non-official persons also, and under the Indian Councils Act of 1892 not only was the number of additional members increased, but provision was also made for the introduction of an elective or quasi-elective principle in the nomination of such additional members. But the introduction into the Council of non-official members either by direct nomination, or by election under statutory rules subject to the approval of the Governor-General or Governor as the case may be, can in no way affect the constitutional aspect of the question, namely, that all additional members whether official or non-official, whether nominated or elected, are the colleagues of the Governor-General or the Governor and of the ordinary members of his Council and as such form a component part of the Government in the exercise of its legislative functions, and there is nothing in either of the said statutes affecting the status of the Legislative Council as the Government for the purpose of making laws and regulations.

Another cardinal principle of the constitution is that not less than one-half of the persons nominated as additional members of the Council including the Advocate-General for the time being, shall be non-official persons and that the seat in Council of a non-official member accepting office under Government should be vacated on such acceptance, there being however no corresponding provision that an official additional member vacates his seat on ceasing to be an official. Notwithstanding the provision of the law that not less than one-half of the additional members shall be non-official persons, it is no doubt possible for the Governor-General or the Governor as the case may be, to secure, as has almost invariably been the practice, an official numerical majority in the composition of the Council by appointing only the minimum proportion prescribed by law of additional non-official members, with the result that an official majority can be ensured by reckoning upon the additional official members voting with the ordinary members of the Council. The principle however, of the constitution is not that there *need* be a "numerical official majority" in the Council as now proposed, but that the numerical majority *may* be on the side of non-official members. So far as the relative proportion of non-officials to officials is prescribed by law, it is as already stated that the number of non-official additional members should be at least one-half of the additional members. I may also beg leave to assert emphatically that the notion of an official majority in the Legislative Council, or the notion that the additional official members should vote with the ordinary members of the Council or that the ordinary members of the Council and the President should vote alike, is entirely opposed to the fundamental principles of the constitution as stated above, namely, that so far as legislation is concerned, the Government consists of the Governor-General or Governor, his ordinary members *and* the additional members whether nominated by him or elected, subject to his approval, and all form but one component and indivisible part of Government for the purpose of making laws and regulations : and the division of this body into the Executive Government supported by an official majority and a non-official minority corresponding to an opposition to Government is the introduction of a principle which, in British India, is as unconstitutional as it would be mischievous in the result. Until the enlargement of, and the introduction of a quasi-elective principle into, the Indian Legislative Councils by the Indian Councils Act of 1892, the fundamental principle of the constitution as settled by the Indian Councils Act of 1861 was not departed from, the official and the non-official members of the Councils co-operating as members of one body and there was no feeling that the non-official members were in the opposition or that the official members should vote together any more than they should in executive or other matters outside the Legislative Council. Neither when the Legislative Council and the Executive Council were identical, nor, later on when the Governor-General's Council was for the purpose of making laws and regulations reinforced by the addition of certain official members only, was there or could have been any theory or notion that all the individuals composing the Council should vote unanimously on every measure before it. A reference to the reports in the official gazette of the proceedings of the Legislative Councils as constituted under the Councils Act of 1861, and especially to the proceedings of the Viceregal Legislature would show that, when divisions in the Councils were recorded, it was by no means unusual that official members were as much divided among themselves as the non-officials were. If, in the deliberations of the Executive Council or of the Board of Revenue, the members are expected to, and do in fact, express and assert their individual views if they are unable to agree after consultation and discussion, it seems strange that in deliberations on legislative measures at meetings of the Legislative Council a different theory or practice should prevail by reason of the enlargement of the Council and the presence therein of elected members and that officials should all vote together irrespective of their individual, deliberate and mature opinions. According to the principle of the constitution of the Legislative Councils in India, there is no difference between official and non-official members, and it is because of the importance attached to the Legislative function of Government that in addition to the ordinary members a certain number of additional members are associated with the Governor-General or Governor and the policy of the Act is that legislative measures should be publicly discussed and passed at meetings of such bodies in accordance with the views of the majority and it is a distinct violation of this principle that under the sanction of an unwritten law a theory should prevail and assert itself that officials should all vote solidly irrespective of their convictions and opinions and that non-official members, and the elected members, in particular, should be regarded and treated as belonging to the opposition to Government. Though in regard to unessential matters where there is a difference of opinion, it is a matter of comparative indifference if all the officials should vote together by their deferring to the judgment of the ordinary member in charge of the Bill, yet in controversial matters affecting the principles of the Bill, it will be a distinct violation of the constitutional principle that they should do so. I do not at all consider this matter from the standpoint of the moral philosopher but purely from the standpoint of an Indian constitutional lawyer and politician who is convinced of the wisdom of the constitutional principle in question and apprehends the evil political consequences of ignoring this principle and substituting therefor the principle of a standing official majority accompanied by the creation in the Council of an irresponsible opposition. Such has been the unfortunate and unexpected result of the operation of the Indian Councils Act of 1892 and it is a matter for extreme regret that the Government of India should now explicitly declare in writing that "they consider it essential that the Government should always be able to reckon on a numerical majority and that this majority should be strong enough to be independent of the minor fluctuations that may be caused by the occasional absence of an official member. The principle of a standing majority is accepted by the Government as an entirely legitimate and necessary consequence of the nature of the paramount power in India, and so far as they know it has never been disputed by any section of Indian opinion, that does not dispute the legitimacy of the paramount power itself." That is not an open question and if two men are not able to wield one sceptre, it is idle to dissemble that fact in constructing political machinary. I am however not surprised at this and nothing can be a greater condemnation, by the highest authority in India, of the practical working of the Indian Councils Act of 1892 than that it should publicly declare that the *legislative* function of Government cannot be safely and satisfactorily discharged unless a standing and decisive majority of official votes in the Council can always be reckoned upon. This necessarily implies not only that there should be a numerical official majority in the Council, but that they should all vote together. I was a member of the local Legislative Council for several years prior to 1892 and for several years subsequent thereto, and my humble opinion is that the working of the enlarged Legislative Council has by no means been satisfactory in a political point of view. An opposition has unconsciously been created and the relations between the official members and the non-official members and in particular the elected members are far from being cordial. There is no doubt that legislative measures are debated upon and criticised more ably and freely by the non-official members than was the case prior to 1892, but so far as official members are concerned, though their number has been increased, fewer of them take part in debates and the theory, unwritten though it be, that they should all vote solidly with the ordinary member of Council in charge of the Bill has a most demoralising effect. As a general rule, with the exception of one or occasionally two official members who actively assist the member in charge, the other official members pay little or no attention to the debates in Council and when meetings of the Council are sometimes protracted, they attend the Council much to the detriment of their other duties. Of course, if the theory is that an official member is to vote with the member in charge of the Bill and not according to the opinion which he may form by attending to and following the debate, it is no matter for surprise, that instead of paying close attention to the debates in Council he should, while the debate is going on, prefer to attend to his own office work. Since the enlargement of the Legislative Councils in

1892, there has been a preponderance of leading vakils amongst the non-officials who, by their training at the bar, have a decided advantage over their official colleagues, most of whom belong to the Indian Civil Service the members of which have proved themselves remarkably successful as administrators by reason of the fact that their policy hitherto has been one of decisive action and discreet while their official training is not such as to qualify them to make extempore speeches or to meet debates in Council."

CHAPTER X

THE INDIAN LEGISLATURES—THEIR LEGISLATIVE FUNCTIONS

Legislative and Executive Acts

From what has been said in the previous chapter, it will have been perceived that the Indian legislatures were originally created for a strictly limited purpose, namely, that of making laws and regulations, as a non-sovereign legislative body subordinate to the Imperial Parliament. The progress of constitutional development in India has, however, led to the enlargement of both the constitution and the scope of work of these Councils. Both in the department of legislation and of administration, their functions are becoming enlarged from time to time. The powers of the Councils in regard to the latter, however, are of very recent growth and so far not appreciable in extent. The distinction between the legislative and other functions of Government, namely, those comprised under administration is, no doubt, important from the point of view of political theory, but as is usual in all such cases, the line dividing them is hard to draw and the question whether a particular act done or required to be done is an act of legislation or of administration is not easy of solution. Moreover, it is very necessary to note that the power of a statute enacted by the legislature need by no means be confined to the province of what a jurist or political philosopher would consider the domain of legislation. This is as true of Acts of the Indian Legislative Councils as of the Acts of the Imperial Parliament. Taxation, for instance, in England is the undoubted province of the legislature, to vote by means of an Act, and in India legislation is invariably resorted to whenever fresh sources of raising taxation are required. Similarly, there are many fiscal and administrative enactments both in England and in India which could hardly be classified as legislation. On the other hand, there are many matters in which, as we have indicated in the last chapter, the Executive is empowered to practically legislate by rules and to administer the rules so legislated.

Their distinction one of method

The only legal distinction, therefore, between the acts of the legislature and the acts of the Executive is the method adopted in deciding on and pursuing a course of action with reference to the government of the country. This absence of a clear differentiation of functions between the legislatures and the Executive is accentuated in this country by the fact, to which reference has been made, that the Legislative Council practically grew out of the Executive Council. The Act of 1833 formally enhanced the legislative power of the Governor-General in Council by the addition of a Law Member to it, by abolishing the legislative authority of the Madras and Bombay Councils (an authority which was subsequently restored) and by enacting that the body so constituted "is authorized to legislate for all persons, places and Courts within the Company's territories", and that the laws made by it "are, subject to disallowance by the Court of Directors, to have the effect of Acts of Parliament." The Council was strengthened in 1853 by the nomination of additional members to it when acting for the purpose of making laws and regulations. The Indian Council's Act of 1861 formally consolidated, revised and regulated the legislative powers of the Councils. It also restored subordinate legislative authority to the Madras and Bombay Councils and provided for the creation of further Provincial Legislative Councils in fresh provinces to be created.

Powers of Legislation of Indian Councils

The limitations put upon the power of legislation, which was in general terms bestowed on the Governor-General's Council in 1833 by the statutes of Parliament, will be found in detail in the enactments printed in the Appendix. Generally speaking, the Imperial legislature has power (1) to make laws for all persons, for all Courts and for all places and things within British India, (2) for all Native Indian subjects of His Majesty whether within or without His Majesty's dominions in any part of the world, (3) for all British subjects of His Majesty and servants of the Government of India who reside in parts of India outside British India, (4) for all persons employed in the Military or Marine Service of His Majesty in India and (5) for repealing or altering such laws or other laws and regulations for the time being in force in British India. No law so made is to be deemed invalid by reason only that it affects any of the prerogatives of the Crown or any of the statutes or laws of England not applicable to India. But (i) the Imperial Legislative Council has not power to make any law repealing or affecting the laws by which the Indian Government has been constituted, namely, (*a*) some of the provisions of the Government of India Act of 1833 and all the provisions of the Government of India Acts of 1853, 1854, 1858 and 1859, the provisions of the Indian Councils Act of 1861, and (*b*) any Act of Parliament passed since 1861 extending to British India, and a few minor Acts such as Acts enabling the Secretary of State to raise loans on behalf of India, the Army Act and Acts amending the same; (ii) and it has not power to make any law affecting the authority of Parliament or any part of the unwritten laws of the constitution of the United Kingdom of Great Britain and Ireland whereon may depend in any degree the allegiance of any person to the Crown of the United Kingdom or the sovereignty or dominion of the Crown over any part of British India; (iii) nor has it power, without the previous sanction of the Secretary of State, to pass any law empowering any Court other than the High Court to sentence European subjects of His Majesty to the punishment of death or abolishing any High Court. One restriction referred to above is perhaps of more importance than others, so far as constitutional rights go, *viz*, that which refers to the allegiance to the Crown in clause (ii) above. This has virtually been interpreted as amounting to a compact on the part of the subject to bear allegiance to the Crown and on the part of the King to preserve the constitutional rights of the subject, contained in the unwritten laws of the United Kingdom of Great Britain and Ireland. Mr. Justice Norman, in the case of *In re Ameer Khan*, has explained this aspect of the question in the following words :—

"In order to see what is meant by the words 'unwritten laws or constitution whereon may depend in any degree the allegiance of any person,' it is necessary to consider first what allegiance is. Every one born within the dominions of the King of England or in the Colonies or dependencies, being under the protection of the King, therefore, according to our common law, owes allegiance to the King. Every British subject is born a debtor by the fealty and allegiance which he owes his Sovereign and the State, a creditor by the benefit and protection of the king, the laws and the constitution. 'Allegiance,' says Sir William Blackstone, 'is the tie which binds the subject to the King in return for that protection which the King affords to the subject.' Foremost amongst the privileges assured to the subject by the protection of the Sovereign is liberty and security of the person. The Crown cannot derogate from those rights. Bracton tells us that 'the King is under the law, for the law makes the King.' The King cannot interfere with the liberty of the subject, nor deprive him of any of his rights. How absolute soever the sovereigns of other nations may be, the King of England cannot take up or detain the meanest subject at his will and pleasure.

"I will proceed to consider what 'are the unwritten laws and constitution' of the United Kingdom which are alluded to in the section (*b*). It is well known that the provisions of the Great Charter and the Petition of Right are for the most part declarations of what the existing law was, not enactments of any new law. They set forth and assert the right of the subject, according to what was assumed to be the ancient unwritten laws and constitution of the realm.

" Now if it be true that allegiance and protection are reciprocally due from the subject and the Sovereign, it is evident that the strict observance of the laws which provide for such liberty and security ensures the faithful allegiance of subjects.

" On the faithful observance by the Sovereign of the unwritten laws and constitution of the United Kingdom, as contained in the Great Charter and other Acts which I have mentioned, depend in no small degree the allegiance of the subjects. It would be a startling thing to find that they could be taken away by an Act of the subordinate Legislature. It would be a strange thing indeed if a great popular assembly, like the Parliament of England, had put into the power of a Legislature which has not, and in the nature of things cannot have, any representative character, the power of abrogating or tampering with such fundamental laws."

Powers of Indian Legislatures plenary

The net effect of the powers and restrictions relating to the Indian legislatures cannot be better put than in the words of Lord Selborne in the case of *Queen* v. *Burah*. He says :—

" The Indian Legislature has powers expressly limited by the Act of the Imperial Parliament which created it, and it can, of course, do nothing beyond the limits which circumscribe these powers. But when acting within these limits, it is not in any sense an agent or delegate of the Imperial Parliament, but has, and was intended to have, plenary powers of legislation, as large, and of the same nature, as those of Parliament itself. The established courts of justice, when a question arises as to whether the prescribed limits have been exceeded, must of necessity determine that question ; and the only way in which they can properly do so is by looking to the terms of the instrument, by which affirmatively the legislative powers were created, and by which negatively they are restricted. If what has been done is legislation within the general scope of the affirmative words which give the power, and if it violates no express condition or restriction by which that power is limited (in which category would of course be included any Act of the Imperial Parliament at variance with it), it is not for any court of justice to inquire further, or to enlarge constructively those conditions and restrictions."

Limited power of Regulation-making of the Executive

These plenary powers of legislation, which the Indian Legislatures at present possess, are the result of the series of enactments which we have referred to above, between the years 1833 and 1861 which had changed their original character of being delegates or agents of the Imperial Parliament. The delegated authority, originally in the hands of the Councils, then Executive as well as Legislative, ceased to exist with the constitution of plenary Legislative Councils with additional members, but the exercise of the delegated power of 'regulation-making' by Executive authority, continued without legal warrant for many years, in respect of the administration of territories not brought within the regular administration of British Courts and British laws. The difficulty, however, was found out during the time of Sir Fitz-James Stephen as Law Member in India, who placed the power of so-called regulation-making in the hands of the Executive on a legal and statutory basis. Under the Government of India Act of 1870, the power of making regulations at the instance of the local Governments concerned was vested in the Governor-General in Council in his executive capacity in respect of what are, by a curious contradiction in terms, called non-regulation provinces, or provinces in which, owing to their backward character, the regular Indian law and Law Courts could not be established. The Governor-General in his own person also has been vested with an extraordinary power of making Ordinances having the force of laws in cases of emergency for a period not exceeding six months.

The rule of law in India

These vestiges of the tendency to what may be termed non-legal methods of government in India, are still noticeable here and there in the Indian Statute Book. Peculiar powers of deportation are, for instance, found in Regulations nearly a century old and these have recently been revived and exercised under circumstances, also deemed peculiar, but their exercise has been vigorously challenged both in England and in India. Subject to these exceptions, the Indian Constitution may be deemed to be as much subject to the rule of law as the British Constitution. What this singular advantage of British institutions means to India has not always been grasped by many people who have a fondness for arbitrary methods and personal government; but students of constitutional history will easily discern that this is, perhaps, one of the most signal advantages which the British connection has secured for this country. The value of this constitutional principle to India in fact can hardly be over-estimated and cannot be described better than in the words of Sir Fitz-James Stephen, who was Law Member of the Viceroy's Council during the time of Lord Mayo's Viceroyalty. "Peace and law," he said, "go together; whatever else we do in India, we must keep peace; and this is strictly equivalent to saying that we must rule by law." The remarks of this great jurist on the constitutional question whether India shall be ruled by law according to British traditions, or by arbitrary, personal government, according to what are fancied to be Oriental notions, are so apposite that we extract them in a note at the end of this chapter, from the chapter on 'Legislation' which he contributed to Sir W. Hunter's "Life of the Earl of Mayo."

Province of Indian Legislation circumscribed

While it will thus be seen that the province of legislation has been enlarged with very beneficial results to the people of this country, it has also to be noted that it has been limited by other circumstances. The share of the representatives of the people themselves in shaping the laws enacted is, in the first place, extremely limited. In the next place, it has been the declared policy of the Government not to interfere with the personal law of the various communities inhabitating this country, unless they themselves desire it, but to respect and enforce them, as laid down in their legal text books and as deducible from their settled customs, and to maintain scrupulous regard for the religious and social usages of the people themselves. The province of legislation in these directions is extremely circumscribed, and does not lend itself to assisting social progress to the extent to which it has done in Western countries, except by means of legislation of an enabling character or with a view to relieve disabilities which, changes of social status might entail under the personal law of individuals or classes. Interesting questions, legal and social, arise in connection with this peculiar state of things in India, which it is not the province of a student of constitutional history to discuss or to express opinions upon ; but their existence has to be noted as a constitutional fact tending to show that the domain of legislation in India is not as large as in Western countries where a more homogeneous population exists. Legally, of course, Parliament can legislate with the utmost freedom in respect of social and religious matters in India and in the Indian Legislatures also, measures of legislation affecting social and religious usages may be introduced with the previous sanction of the Governor-General ; but the declared policy of neutrality on the part of the State in such matters, a policy which has been solemnly re-affirmed in the late Queen's Proclamation of 1858, makes any interference by Government in any manner counter to the feelings of the people themselves as unlikely as possible.

Powers of Provincial Legislatures

The powers of the Provincial Legislatures are in general respects co-extensive with those of the Imperial Legislature, but only in respect of the territories made subject to their laws. There are, however, a few important matters excepted from their competence and reserved absolutely for the Imperial Council. Apart from the general restrictions on the powers of the Indian Legislatures which apply equally to the Provincial Legislatures, the latter have not power to deal with matters comprised under Imperial

Finance, Currency, Posts and Telegraphs; and they cannot alter the Indian Penal Code, without the previous sanction of the Governor-General.

Veto on Indian Legislation by the Crown and its representatives

All legislative measures passed by the legislatures in India are subject to the power of veto on the part of the Crown and of the authorities representing the Crown in India, as in the case of all Colonial Legislatures. Every act passed by a Provincial Legislature has to receive the assent of the Governor first and the Governor-General next, whereupon it becomes law. It is, however, subject to subsequent disallowance by the Crown, on communication of which to India it ceases to be law. Every law passed by the Legislative Council of the Governor-General has to receive the assent of the Governor-General and is also subject to similar disallowance by the Crown. According to Sir C. P. Ilbert, assent has usually been withheld on one or more of the following grounds:—(1) that the principle or policy of the Act or of some particular provision of the Act is unsound, (2) that the Act or some provision of the Act is *ultra vires* of the Provincial Legislature and (3) that the Act is defective in form.

Legislative work in India and the Legislative Department

The enactments of the Indian Legislatures are not the only laws in force in British India. The entire body of such laws are divisible into:—(1) the laws expressly made for India by the British Parliament or sovereign as to above, (2) the body of English laws in force in India, though not expressly made for India, (3) the law made by persons or bodies having legislative authority in India (4) Hindu, Mahomedan and other personal laws governing particular classes. The first three of these are with rare exceptions territorial *i. e.*, "they apply generally either to the whole of India or to a given area and to all persons within those limits". The last are personal laws *i.e.*, "they apply only to persons who answer a given description."

There are over 120 Acts of Parliament containing provisions

relating to India, the greater portion of which, as may be inferred, relate to what may be called constitutional law. The principal parts of these are reproduced in the Appendix. The law which may be said to have been made by the Sovereign apart from Parliament is stated by the writer on Indian Law in the latest edition of the Encyclopædia Brittanica, to consist mainly of Charters granted by virtue of statutes or the Common Law, such as those granted to the four High Courts of Bengal, Madras, Bombay and the North-West Provinces. A great many Charters were granted to the East India Company and some of the earlier ones contained very important provisions as to the legislative and judicial authority to be exercised in India, but most of these provisions are now obsolete.

The theory on which the English law in force in India, though not made expressly for India—consisting of a considerable portion of the law of England, both statute law and Common Law—is deemed to have been introduced into India, rests on the assumption that " when courts of justice were established in India, to be presided over by English judges, it followed that they were to administer English law as it stood at the time of the Charter so far as it was applicable ". This is usually supposed to have taken place in 1726.

However much in these various ways both the province and the process of the Indian Legislatures have been restricted, the amount and the character of legislation which they have produced have been extremely valuable and might form examples to other states where more advanced legislatures have hardly succeeded so well in the sphere of law-making proper. Not that the Indian Legislatures have not blundered nor that their enactments are perfect; but they have a record of achievement respectable and creditable. This is due to their possession of a special Legislative Department, as well as a compact constitution, which has enabled the Indian Government to make its laws, whatever they have been, more systematically arranged and more thoroughly worked out than, for instance, in the

United Kingdom. In its Legislative Department, the Government of India possesses an office, the function of which is the superintendence of all matters connected with the enactment and revision of the laws and which is under the charge of a Member of the Council. " The small size of the Indian Legislature," Sir Fitz-James Stephen once pointed out, "the fact that it consists of only one body and the fact that its duties are purely legislative and that it has nothing to do with the Executive Government, expedite its proceedings to an extent which it is difficult for any one accustomed only to England even to imagine. The comparative fixity of tenure of the higher Indian officials and the practice which prevails of carrying on the legislative business continuously and not in separate sessions at the end of which every bill not passed is lost, all give a degree of vigour and system to Indian Legislation unlike anything known in England and which I hope and believe compensate to a considerable extent for its unavoidable defects and shortcomings."

The reforms introduced under the Indian Councils Act of 1909, might to some extent modify the observations of Sir Fitz-James Stephen. Symmetry and system in Legislative enactments are not a *summum bonum* in themselves, nor is simplicity of procedure at all conducive to soundness and suitability of legislative measures. The primary need for making legislation popular and representative of the feelings of the people whom the laws affect, outweighs every such consideration, and there can be no doubt that measures taken towards this result will secure far better the real object of all legislation, *viz.*, to make them suited to the people, render them acceptable to them and obtain willing obedience to the Acts of the legislature.

Mode of transacting Legislative business

The procedure of the Legistative Councils in the making of laws will be found fully set out in the rules for the conduct of legislative business, published in the Appendix. The power of the Government on its part to introduce legislation in the Councils is limited; in the first instance, statutorily, by the provisions which we have referred to in the previous pages and, in the next place, by the Legislative standing orders, which have been framed in conformity with the Acts and in pursuance of the policy laid down from time to time by the Secretary of State and the Government of India. There have been many disputes over questions connected with this matter, affecting the powers of the various Executive authorities responsible for the administration of India, in introducing legislation. Some of these are embodied in the standing orders from which we have extracted important portions in the Appendix. Special attention might be directed to one of these which is of more than administrative significance and has raised and decided a constitutional issue of importance to which we have already referred in Chapter IV, *viz.*, the extent to which the Government of India is responsible to the Secretary of State in the matter of initiating legislation.

NOTE

[*Extract from the Chapter on " Legislation under Lord Mayo " by Sir James Fitz-James Stephen in Hunter's " Life of the Earl of Mayo"*]

Many persons object not so much to any particular laws, as to the Government of the country by law at all. They have an opinion which I have in some instances heard very distinctly expressed by persons of high authority, that the state of things throughout India is such that law ought in all cases to be overridden by what is called equity, in the loose popular sense of the word. That the Courts of Justice ought to decide not merely whether a given contract has been made and broken, but whether it ought to have been made, and whether its breach was not morally justifiable. In short, that there ought to be no law at all in the country as far as natives are concerned, but that in every instance, the District Officers ought to decide according to their own notions, subject only to correction by their superiors.

In the second place, it is a favourite doctrine with persons who hold this opinion that the Government of India possesses the absolute power of the old native states subject only to such limitations as it has chosen to impose upon itself by express law; that every new law is thus a new limitation on the general powers of Government and tends to diminish them, and that there ought to be as few laws as possible, in order that the vigour of the executive power may be maintained at a maximum.

Nothing struck me more in my intercourse with Indian civilians, than the manner in which the senior members of the service seemed to look instinctively upon lawyers of all kinds as their natural enemies and upon law as a mysterious power, the special function of which was to prevent, or at all events to embarrass and retard, anything like vigorous executive action. I was once discussing with a military officer of high rank, and in high civil employ, the provisions of a bill for putting certain criminal tribes in the North-West Provinces under police supervision. When I showed him the powers which it conferred upon executive officers, he said, "It is quite a new idea to me that the law can be any thing but a check to the executive power."

* * *

I may give a few illustrations, which will throw further light upon this way of thinking. One of the commonest of all complaints against Indian law is that it is stiff and inelastic, that it does not adjust itself to the exigencies of real business and so forth. I have heard these complaints perhaps a hundred times and whenever I heard them I asked the same question, 'which particular law do you refer to, and in what manner would you make it more elastic?' If, as was generally the case, I got no distinct answer to this question, I used to ask whether the objector thought that the Penal Code was too definite, and that it could be improved if its definitions were made less precise; and in particular, whether he would like to have the definitions of murder or theft, or of any and what other crime, altered and if so, where and how? These questions were hardly ever answered. I generally found that nearly every one, when closely pressed, gave the same illustrations as to what he understood by the stiffness and want of elasticity of the law. They all referred to those sections of the Code of Criminal Procedure which require the officer presiding at the trial to take down the evidence with his own hand, and their notion of rendering the Code more elastic was that this requirement should be relaxed.

These sections are the chief guarantee that a judge actully does this duty, and does not merely pretend to do it. They are the great security for a fair trial to the person accused. Before they were inserted in the Code, it was a common practice for the judges not to hear the witnesses at all, but to allow four or five native clerks to take down, the evidence of as many witnesses in as many different cases at the same time; and then to form his opinion, not from hearing the witnesses, but from reading, or from having read over to him, the depositions taken by the native clerks. In fact, the elasticity which the critics in question really wished for, appeared to me on full examination to be elasticity in the degree of attention which they were to bestow on the most important of their own duties.

A friend of mine, whilst inspecting an important frontier district, received complaints from the officer in charge of it as to the want of elasticity in the existing system; and on asking what he meant, was informed that he had found it impossible to punish certain persons whom he knew to be guilty of murder. His informants would not come forward as witnesses for fear of the vengeance of the relations of the criminals, and the law did not permit him to move without a regular trial. 'Then,' replied my friend, 'what you want is power to put people to death without any trial at all, and on secret information which is satisfactory to your own mind, of which the persons who give it are not to be responsible'. This, no doubt, was what the officer in question did want. It had not occurred to him that the impunity of a certain amount of crime was a less evil than the existence of an arbitrary and irresponsible power, which would practically have to strike in the dark.

* * *

What I wish to notice is the gross fallacy of condemning law and legislation in general, because the provisions of one particular law which allows land to be sold for debts may be open to question. There is nothing specially refined or technical in the law in question. What is really objected is its stringent simplicity. A law which mediated between the usurer and the landowner, which tried to secure to the one his just claims, and to the other the enjoyment of what he had been accustomed to regard as his ancestral rights, would have to be far more complicated than a law by which a judgment-creditor may sell his debtor's land by auction. In this, as in numberless other instances, the commonplaces about simple and primitive populations and refined systems of law mean merely that particular laws ought to be altered, which is a reason for, not against, legislation. To wish to put an end to legislation because some laws are not wise, is like wishing to put an end to tailors because some clothes do not fit. To argue, that because some English laws are unsuited for some Indian populations, law in general is not the instrument by which India ought to be governed, is to assume that law is not that which a legislator enacts as such, but a mysterious something which is to be found in England, and which must be introduced bodily into India, if India is to be governed by law at all.

The only rational meaning which can be ascribed to such language as I refer to is one which is not expressed, because it cannot be avowed. It is, that the person who uses it would like the law to stand as it is but that the District Officers should use their own discretion about putting it in force. This is only a weak form of the doctrine that India ought to be governed, not by law, but by personal discretion. A law which people may enforce or not, as they please, is not a law at all.

The theory that Government by law is not suitable for India, and that everything ought to be left to the personal discretion of the rulers, that is to say, of the District Officers, is one of those theories which many persons hold, though no one who regards his own reputation will avow it. In England, every one will admit in words that popular education is an admirable thing, whilst many persons couple the admission with qualifications intelligible only upon the supposition (which is undoubtedly true) that in their hearts they believe it to be mischievous. In India, whilst hardly any one will be found to maintain distinctly that the personal discretion of local rulers, free from all law whatever, is the true method of Government, numbers of people qualify their consent to the proposition that the country must be governed by law, by commonplaces like those of which I have given specimens, and which really mean that unfettered personal discretion would be a much better thing. The unavowed influence of this theory acts so powerfully, that it will be by no means superfluous even now to show how baseless and mischievous it is.

In doing this, it is necessary to refer shortly to common places, which are often forgotten because they are so familiar. Often as it has been repeated, it is not the less true, that the main distinction between the government which we have established and the Government which it superseded is, that the one is in the fullest sense of the word a government by law, and that the other was a government by mere personal discretion. It is also true that the moral and general results of a government by law admit of no comparison at all with those of despotism. I do not believe that the people of England, as a whole, would take any sort of interest in supporting a mere despotism, differing from those of the native rulers only in the fact that it was administered by Englishmen.

Government by law is the only real security either for life or property, and is therefore the indispensable condition of the growth of wealth. This is no mere phrase. Before the introduction of law, it admitted of considerable discussion whether property in land existed in India at all. It admits of no discussion that the value of landed property depends entirely upon the limitation of Government demand, and upon the due adjustment of the relations between the cultivators and the zamindars. Laws, therefore, of some kind there must be.

CHAPTER XI

THE LEGISLATURES AND THE EXECUTIVE

Attempted control of the Administration by the Legislature between the years, 1853-1861

The function of legislation was differentiated from that of administration in British India and entrusted to the hands of the Councils expanded for legislative purposes by additional members, between the years 1833 and 1861, as we saw in the last chapter. It was then found that the Councils had to be further strengthened by the addition of Provincial and other representatives to assist in the making of laws. Legislative activity at that period was marked, and, between the years 1853 and 1861, the Indian Legislatures modelled themselves on the procedure of the House of Commons in England, and not only proceeded to deal with matters of legislation, pure and simple, but also with questions of administration. They showed what was then considered, in the words of Sir C. P. Ilbert, an inconvenient degree of independence by asking questions as to, and discussing the propriety of, measures of the Executive Government—deeming themselves competent to enquire into abuses and grievances, calling for reports and returns from the local administrations, debating long on questions of public interest and introducing motions and resolutions independent of the Executive Government. In a despatch of Lord Canning at the time, he pointed out that the Council had become invested with forms and modes of procedure closely imitating those of the House of Commons, that there were 136 standing orders to regulate the procedure of a dozen gentlemen assembled in Council, that, in short, in the words of Sir Lawrence Peel, they had assumed jurisdiction in the nature of that of a grand inquest of the nation. It is needless to say that the Legislative Council came into constant conflict with the Executive Government of those days. The following, among others, may be cited as examples of the power which, whether originally intended to be vested in the Council or not, was actually exercised by the Governor-General's Legislative Council between the years 1853 and 1861 :—

At the meeting of the Council held on the 16th April, 1859, Sir Charles Jackson put the following question :—"Whether the Government have taken any and what steps for the erection of a jail in a suitable climate for the reception of European or American convicts sentenced to terms of penal servitude under Act XXIV of 1855?" In support of the question, he made a long statement giving his reasons for his inquiry ; and the answer was also accompanied by a statement at some length.

On September 6, 1859, the Vice-President (Sir Barnes Peacock) called the attention of the Council to certain observations made by the Madras Supreme Court in the matter of an application by one Gunshamdoss, which observations were considered by Sir Barnes Peacock as a reflection on the Legislative Council. Then, on the 4th February, 1860, the matter was by a motion referred to a select committee and the report of the committee was presented on the 25th February, 1860, when Sir Barnes Peacock moved the following resolution thereon, *viz.*, "the remarks of the learned Judges of the Supreme Court of Madras on Act XVI of 1859 in delivering judgment on the 8th August, 1859 on the case of Gunshamdoss, were unwarranted by the facts and were wholly unjustifiable." In moving the resolution, Sir Barnes Peacock made a very long and interesting speech in the course of which he said that the members of the Legislative Council were as independent as the learned Judges of the Supreme Court of Madras and generally defended the conduct of the Legislative Council against the attacks of the Supreme Court. Mr. Sconce, Sir Charles Jackson and Sir Bartle Frere and the Right Honourable Mr. Wilson all took part in the debate. The original motion was eventually withdrawn and a resolution that the report of the select committee be adopted and transmitted to the Secretary of State for India was unanimously agreed to.

On the 18th August, 1860, Sir Mordaunt Wells rose to call the attention of the Council to the evidence given before the Indigo Commission by the Hon'ble Mr. Eden, a member of the Bengal Civil Service, so far as his evidence referred to the administration of Criminal justice in Her Majesty's Supreme Court. In thus calling the attention of the Council to the subject, Sir Mordaunt Wells made an elaborate speech quoting facts and figures in defence of the Supreme Court of Calcutta against the charge made by the Hon'ble Ashly Eden, that the Supreme Court and the Calcutta Jury were partial to Europeans accused of offences. Sir Bartle Frere, Mr. Forbes, Members for Madras, Sir Barnes Peacock and Mr. Sconce, all spoke on the subject.

On the 15th December, 1860, Sir Barnes Peacock moved that Government be requested to furnish several items of information specified in the notice of motion in respect of certain grant by the Government to the descendants of Tippu Sultan of Mysore. The Vice-President made a most vehement and eloquent speech in support of his motion.

The motion was opposed most vigorously by Sir Bartle Frere and others on behalf of the Executive Government. The Council was divided and the votes were equal in number. Sir Barnes Peacock in the chair as Vice-President gave a casting vote in favour of his motion which was carried.

The information asked for by the resolution was substantially given by the Government on the 22nd December, 1860 when Sir Charles Jackson in the absence of Sir Barnes Peacock expressed his gratification and said that the message granting the information "would increase that confidence which the Council had in the Executive Government and would promote that harmonious action between the Executive Government and the Council which was so greatly to be desired."

Powers of Councils curtailed by Act of 1861

The activities of the Council at this time and the lively disputes which it had with the Executive Government finally led to an address of the Legislative Council for the communication to it of certain correspondence between the Secretary of State and the Supreme Government of India. These, together with the differences which arose between the Supreme Government and the Government of Madras on the Income Tax Bill and the doubts which had been raised as to the validity of laws introduced into non-regulation provinces without enactment by the Legislative Council, finally led to the revision and consolidation of the laws in regard to the Indian Councils in general. The Indian Councils Act of 1861 provided a most effective check against any interference of the Legislative Councils with the Executive even by way of advice or suggestion. Under section 19 of that Act, it was enacted that no business shall be transacted at a Legislative Meeting of the Governor-General's Council other than the consideration of measures introduced or proposed to be introduced into the Council for the purpose of enactment or the alteration of rules for the conduct of business at Legislative Meetings, and that no motion shall be entertained other than a motion for leave to introduce a measure into Council for the purpose of enactment or having reference to a measure introduced or proposed to be introduced into the Council for that purpose, or having reference to some rule for the conduct of business. Similar restrictions were imposed on the Provincial Legislative Councils.

Restrictions slightly relaxed by Acts of 1892 and 1909

These restrictions were somewhat relaxed by the Indian Councils Act of 1892, which permitted (1) the asking of questions in regard to administrative matters, under strictly limited conditions, by the Members of Councils and the eliciting of answers thereto, and (2) the explanation of the annual Financial Statements of the Imperial and Provincial

Governments in the respective Councils and a general discussion of the same by the Members. The Indian Councils Act of 1909 has further relaxed the limitations imposed by the Act of 1861 limiting the business of the Council to purely legislative matters, by empowering the Governor-General in Council and the Provincial Governments to make revised rules (*a*) for allowing supplementary questions to be put along with interpellations in the Council, (*b*) for moving resolutions on the Financial Statements presented to the Councils, and (*c*) for moving resolutions on matters of general public interest at meetings of the Legislative Councils. It is doubtful if the extent of what we may call concessions, thus granted to the Legislative Councils, in allowing them to deal with matters of administration, amount to a restoration of the position which they occupied and exercised under the Act of 1853. It may be pointed out, however, that under the Act of 1853 the powers of the Council, if they existed at all, were unrestricted by any legislative limitation and controlled only by the standing orders above referred to. The express limitation on the powers of the Councils imposed by the Act of 1861 is not repealed by the Indian Councils Act of 1909, but only modified to the extent to which the rules framed by the Governor-General in Council or the Provincial Governments may relax it, while the province of such concessions as the Executive Government may grant in this behalf is expressly forbidden to be widened by the Legislative Councils under their power of making rules for the conduct of business.

Extent of present powers

It is too early to decide to what extent the powers of the Legislative Councils to criticise and control the administration might be developed under the rules now framed by the Executive Government. On the one hand, the Executive Government may not make such rules as to nullify in effect the privileges that have been granted; on the other hand, the Legislative Councils or their members may not so far extend the letter of the rules as to defeat the express limitations imposed on their powers by statute. The rules themselves which have now been framed by the Governor-General in Council for this purpose will be found in the Appendix. They are divisible into two sections, (1) those dealing with the powers which the Legislative Councils are now invested with in discussing and proposing resolutions on the Budget and (2) those dealing with the powers which they are invested with in obtaining information from the Executive Government and in discussing questions of general public interest. The former are dealt with in the two subsequent chapters dealing with Indian Finance. The latter, which concern the more general aspects of administration, may be dealt with here.

Powers and Procedure of House of Commons

The utmost powers which a Legislature could exercise over an executive, whom it can directly or indirectly control, are exemplified in the practice of the British House of Commons towards the Ministers of the Crown and the Departments of State. As the rules which have now been framed have, according to the Government of India, been to some extent framed upon the practice of the House of Commons, it is useful to contrast the exact limits of the steps which have now been taken in India with those which now subsist in Parliament. In theory, of course, the Executive is not in England subject to the control of Parliament, but in practice ministerial responsibility to Parliament has been more completely enforced in England than in any other modern democratic state. As Professor Dicey has pointed out: "There is not to be found in the law of England an explicit statement that the acts of the Monarch must always be done through a Minister, and that all orders given by the Crown must, when expressed in writing, as they generally are, be countersigned by a Minister. Practically, however, the rule exists, as the custody of the various seals of the Crown is in fact vested in several Ministers of State. What the law of England provides is that a Minister who takes part in giving expression to the Royal Will is legally responsible for the act in which he is concerned, and he cannot get rid of his liability by pleading that he acted in obedience to Royal orders ".

Thus, the acts of the Executive are brought under the control of the law of the land, and this constitutional principle equally applies to the acts of the Executive in India, except in so far as the laws themselves may provide immunity from legal consequences in respect of acts done under such statutory powers. The tendency to grant such immunity is, no doubt, very much greater in this country than in England, mainly owing to the fact that a British Parliament is unlikely to tolerate any such infraction of its rights in respect of the affairs of its own country. There are no doubt in England other weapons in the hands of Parliament by which the Executive can be made in the last resort subject to the complete control of the House of Commons, such as the power of impeachment, censuring etc., but the ordinary legal power which enables the House of Commons " to insist that the Ministers shall answer what are deemed proper questions and shall carry out resolutions which are the outcome of the deliberate will of the House of Commons," is, according to the late Professor Maitland, " in the last resort the power of withholding supplies or of refusing to legalise the existence of a Standing Army." In the absence of any such power in the Indian Legislative Councils, it is obvious that the effect which their resolutions may have on the Executive will be conditioned by the merit of the resolutions themselves, by the extent to which they express general or popular will and—this is the most important consideration—by the extent to which the Executive considers itself bound to accede to such expression of popular will in the Councils.

The usual methods adopted by the House of Commons in England in respect of administrative matters fall under three heads, namely, (1) the practice of Parliament in regard to asking for information from the Executive, by means of questions or by motion for papers relating to matters of administration, (2) the exercise of what we may term an inquisitorial power by the House of Commons in respect of the administration of public affairs in any department of State, by the appointment of Select Committees or Commissions—either with a view to make the results of such inquiries the basis for legislation or with a view to introduce administrative reforms—and (3) by the practice of moving resolutions on all matters connected with administration, including motions of censure on the conduct of Ministers or of their departments and motions for adjournment on the refusal of any minister to give information to the House or to comply with other similar requests on the part of members. The general principles on which the above rights are based were long ago laid down by Sir Erskine May in the following terms :—

"The limits, within which Parliament, or either House, may constitutionally exercise a control over the Executive government have been defined by usage upon principles consistent with a true distribution of powers in a free state and limited monarchy. Parliament has no direct control over any single department of the state. It may order the production of papers for its information ; it may investigate the conduct of public officers and may pronounce its opinion upon the manner in which every function of Government has been, or ought to be discharged ; but it cannot convey its orders or directions to the meanest executive officer in relation to the performance of his duty. Its power over the executive is exercised indirectly, but not the less effectively, through the responsible Ministers of the Crown. These Ministers regulate the duties of every department of the State, and are responsible for their proper performance to Parliament as well as the Crown. If Parliament disapprove of any act or policy of the Government, Ministers must conform to its opinion or forfeit its confidence. In this manner the House of Commons, having become the dominant power of the legislature, has been able to direct the conduct of the Government, and control its executive administration of public affairs, without exceeding its constitutional powers.

Every measure of the ministers of the Crown' says Lord Grey, is open to censure in either House', as when there is just or even plausible ground for objecting to anything they have done or omitted to do, they cannot escape being called upon to defend their conduct. By this arrangement, those to whom power is entrusted are made to feel that they must use it in such a manner as to be prepared to meet the criticisms of opponents continually on the watch for any errors they may commit, and the whole foreign and domestic policy of the nation is submitted to the ordeal of free discussion."

Powers of Indian Councils, as to (i) interpellation

We may now proceed to consider how far or how little the new rules framed by the Governor-General in Council in respect of the discussion of administrative matters by the Indian legislatures, bear resemblance to the practice of Parliament. To take the question of giving information to members of the Legislature, we may point out that the English practice is based on the principle "that it is imperative that Parliament shall be duly informed of everything that may be necessary to explain the policy and proceedings of Government in any part of the Empire and the fullest information is communicated by Government to both Houses from time to time upon all matters of public interest." Information is, of course, withheld on the ground that public interests will suffer by their disclosure and Ministers cannot be compelled to give the same; but when Ministers do so withhold, they take the responsibility for so doing and if the House is of a contrary opinion, the member who asks for information can move for the adjournment of the House or move a resolution asking the Minister to furnish the information. The powers of interpellation given to members of the Legislatures in India proceed on the reverse principle that the Government is not bound to give any information except such as it deems necessary to give in the public interests, and it is a question how far the power of moving resolutions now vested in the Councils under the rules extends to moving resolutions asking for information or for adjournment, which is doubtful. The practice of putting supplementary questions in England has been developed into what we may term a fine art, both on the part of those putting the questions and on the part of those Members of Government who answer them. Whether the strictly limited power of putting supplementary questions which has been granted this year to the Indian Councils, subject to the wide discretion vested in the President in respect thereof, could, and is likely to, be developed into a weapon of heckling the Executive, as is done in England, it is too early to prophesy.

(ii) appointment of Select Committees and motions

We may next consider the practice as to the appointment of Select Committees. The appointment of Select Committees in the Indian Legislatures in respect of legislative measures introduced in the Councils has been used with very great benefit to the public interest, and in this respect this practice has been deemed to be a wholesome and advantageous variation from the practice and procedure of Parliament in England with respect to Bills which are usually discussed in committees of the whole House and are voted upon more or less on party lines and passed after the third reading. There seems to be nothing in the new rules preventing the Government or any member to move for the appointment of Select Committees of the Councils to enquire into matters of administrative reform or of administrative abuses, and it is sufficient to note that having regard to the nature of the constitution of the Councils, mixed committees of officials and non-officials appointed for those purposes may be the best suited to advise as to the course of action to be taken by the Government. Of course, there is no scope for discussion of questions of public interest on what are usually termed in the House of Commons, motions to go into committee, or motions for adjournment before the orders of the day are begun, so as to allow discussions in Council on questions of urgent public interest and opportunities to the Executive to furnish the Councils with a statement of its policy or its procedure in regard to urgent administrative matters.

Nature of Parliamentary control

It is, as has been pointed out already, quite possible that if the powers now entrusted to the Councils are used with care, wisdom and discrimination, precedents and procedure analogous to those of the House of Commons might gradually grow up and might serve as a useful means, if not of directly controlling the Executive,—a power which, under the present constitutional arrangements of the Government of India, it is impossible that the Council could possess—at least of directing the Executive into correct and proper channels in regard to administrative policy and administrative action. It is however necessary to remember fundamental characteristics of Parliamentary Government in this connection. In England, Parliament does not govern, but it chooses and appoints the governors and having done so, it supervises their action by means of questions and criticism. They are not changed so long as they maintain the confidence of the party or combination of parties who possesses a majority in the House of Commons. Ministers, therefore, are in constant touch with public opinion, with the finger on the pulse of the nation as well as on that of their party, to realise how far they command such confidence. They are always willing and ready to afford explanation and information within reasonable limits, both in public and private, to consider friendly criticism and advice and to correct abuses. Consequently, on the part of the ministerialists, there is usually no necessity—and it would by no means conduce to efficient working of the system of party Government—to push the powers of supervision, check and criticism constitutionally vested in the House to the point of defeating the Government, unless a change of Government is desired owing to their failure on vital matters on which the nation has come to hold a different opinion. On the other hand, it is the constant study and duty of the Opposition and the members who support them in the House, to attack and discredit the ministry, to push the powers of supervision, check and criticism constitutionally vested in the House to the point of defeating the Government, except on rare and critical occasions affecting the safety of the realm. So long as the numerical support of members is sufficient to sustain them in office, adverse motions pushed to a division result in no evil consequences and rather keep the Ministry fully alive to its duties by the risks and chances of the division list.

Limitations of the right of criticism or discussion

The state of things in India, it must be realized, is very different. The legislatures of the country neither govern nor appoint its governors and the latter are placed beyond all the risks of an adverse vote in the Provincial Councils and beyond the very possibility of an adverse vote in the Imperial Council. The Legislatures so far have only a power of criticism, discussion and suggestion. The executive are bound to defend their policy on any matter raised in debate, but there is a very large power and discretion allowed to them to refuse to allow a matter to be debated or discussed at all. There is absolutely no coercive power held in reserve to constitutionally constrain the Government. The effect of the discussion or criticism is only moral as affording the Government the opportunity of knowing the views of the people and communicating their own views to them through their representatives. It leaves it to the discretion of the Government to reject or accept recommendations, even though they may be found to express a unanimous public opinion on any matter. Nevertheless, the moral force of genuine and accurately ascertained public opinion when it is sought and attained in the Council, must be very great even in the most arbitrary of Governments and it is by greater organisation and effort in this direction that the next step in constitutional progress should be compassed before any power of actual control over the Executive becomes a matter of constitutional reality with them.

CHAPTER XII

THE COURTS AND THE CONSTITUTION

The division of governmental functions

A description of the judicial system of the Indian Empire and the powers and duties of Courts is easily available in many recognised text books. In the pages of Cowell's "Courts and Legislative authorities in India" will be found an exhaustive discussion of how the jurisdiction of Courts, established under the authority of the British Government, arose and became established throughout the country and by what laws and rules they are now regulated. It is, therefore, not attempted to re-produce their substance here, nor to discuss the questions arising out of the Indian Judicial system in itself, which are mainly of interest to the student of law rather than to the student of the Constitution, who is principally interested in the relationship of the Courts to the various executive and legislative bodies. It is usual to talk of the English Constitution as resting on a balance of powers and as maintaining a division between the executive, legislative and judicial bodies. Such a distinction, though not quite accurate as to actual facts, as was pointed out in an earlier Chapter, rests upon the definitely recognised principle of the supremacy of the British Parliament and the supremacy of its laws, to which both the Courts and the Executive are subject. The Executive of the

English Constitution, though distinct from the legislature, have been made completely subordinate to it in actual fact. The growth of constitutional principles and understandings have brought the Crown and its servants, in whom the theory of the English Constitution vests the executive authority, into entire subjection to the authority of the legislature. On the other hand, the position of the Judges, though of unquestioned subjection to the law of the land, has been made independent by placing their office on a permanent tenure and raising it above the direct influence of the Crown or the Ministry to whom they might have owed their original appointment.

This inter-relation of the three organs of Government necessarily underwent alterations when applied to the case of territories governed by non-sovereign legislatures within the British Empire. The legislatures of the Colonies and of India are, as pointed out before, subordinate law-making bodies, and it has, therefore, become the necessary function of the Judges of the Courts of the land to interpret the law made by these legislative authorities as well as the constitutional laws on which this authority is based and to decide whether they are within or beyond of the scope and competence of their respective powers. The Courts, therefore, both in India and in the Colonies, are empowered to pronounce on the validity or constitutionality of laws made by their respective legislatures. The position of the Judges of His Majesty's Courts both in the Colonies and in India has consequently been made one of independence of both the legislatures and of the Executive of these territories.

The authority of His Majesty's Courts

Since the days when Parliament began to seriously take upon itself the responsibility of the administration of this country, it has pursued the definite policy of establishing His Majesty's Courts in India, owing their authority to the Government 'at Home' (and not to the Company in India) and exercising jurisdiction subject to the sovereignty of Parliament. The legal theory was, as was seen in the last chapter, that when Courts of Justice were established by Royal Charter presided over by English Judges, the law which they administered was the whole body of the statute and Common Law of England. It is a matter of some controversy as to how far and to what extent these laws became applicable between 1736 when His Majesty's Courts, in the form of Mayor's Courts, were first established in the presidency towns of India, and 1781 when Parliament definitely legislated to remove the doubts and difficulties as to the jurisdiction of the King's Courts and the Company's Courts. Sir Fitz-James Stephen is of opinion that the English Criminal law was introduced originally to some extent by the Charter of 1661, and the later Charters of 1720, 1753 and 1774 must be regarded as acts of legislation whereby it was re-introduced on three successive occasions, as it stood at these dates. But high judicial authorities, as Sir C. P. Ilbert has pointed out, have " maintained a different view. They hold that British statute law was as first given to Calcutta by the charter establishing the Mayor's Courts in 1726, and British statutes passed after that date did not apply to India unless expressly or by necessary implication extended to this country." Generally speaking, however, the establishment of the King's Courts under Royal Charter to exercise supreme judicial authority has been treated as a valuable and necessary concomitant of the introduction of British institutions into this country, as well as elsewhere in the Empire. The Regulating Act of 1772 recited that the Charter Act which authorised the East India Company, to establish courts did not " sufficiently provide for the due administration of justice in such a manner as the state and condition of the Presidencies do and must require ", and empowered His Majesty to establish by Charter a Supreme Court of Judicature at Fort William, consisting of a Chief Justice and three other Judges exercising all the powers which the King's Courts might exercise in England. How far this Court was deemed to be independent of the Executive and the Legislatures in India- -that is, the Governor-General and his Council—can be easily inferred from the famous disputes which arose betweeen this Court and the Governor-General's Council, which nearly reduced the Government of Bengal to a deadlock and necessitated the interference of Parliament to remove some of the anomalies which then arose. The Supreme Court at Calcutta and those at Madras and Bombay which were later established, were in fact originally created for the purpose of acting as a check upon the powers of the Government then administering the affairs of India, and especially over English residents in India. It was considered at the time, as Sir Fitz James Stephen pointed out, "not without reason, that by establishing courts independent of the local Government, armed with somewhat indefinite powers and administering a system of law of which they were the only authorized exponents, a considerable check might be placed upon the despotic tendencies on the part of the Government. The effect of this policy was, in the first place, to produce bitter dissensions between the Government and the Supreme Courts both at Calcutta and at Bombay and, in the next place, to set the Supreme Courts and the English law of which they were administrators before the eyes of every European in India, as representatives of a power not only different from, but opposed in spirit and principle to, the powers of the Government." This antagonism between the two authorities, the Governor-General in Council possessing legislative and executive' functions and the Courts of His Majesty, both simultaneously established by the Regulating Act, was eventually tided over by a series of enactments which enlarged and differentiated the legislative power from the executive and placed the authority of the Supreme Courts and of the High Courts which succeeded them, within bounds considered compatible with smooth and efficient administration.

The laws they administer

The Judges of the High Courts, with reference to the Indian Legislatures and the Indian Executive, then, do stand in a position of independence. They owe their appointment to Letters Patent from His Majesty, though the Governments in India may be and are consulted as to their choice. They hold office during His Majesty's pleasure, and in this respect essentially differ from the Judges of the British High Court of Judicature, who can only be removed upon an address to His Majesty by both Houses of Parliament. The function of the Indian High Courts is to administer justice according to the law of the land, namely, the laws of the Imperial Parliament and the laws of the Indian Legislatures passed within the scope of their respective authorities, and according to the customs and usages of the communities inhabiting this land.

From the time of the Regulating Act in all charters and statutes these Courts, even in the presidency towns were directed to apply to Hindus and Mahomedans their own laws in regard to all matters of inheritance and succession, family law and matters relating to religion or caste. In the territories outside the presidency towns where Courts of Justice were established by the East India Company acting under the authority of the Emperor of Delhi—" the only assumption", as a writer has put it, "that could be made as to the law to be administered was that it was the law already in existence." Acting on this assumption, the Company's Courts administered the Mahommedan Criminal law which was the general law of the subjects of the Moghul emperor: the revenue system remained, as did also the existing relations of Zemindar and ryot (*i.e.*) of the cultivator and of the persons intermediate between the state and the cultivator. In regard to matters of family law, inheritance and succession, religion and caste, the Company's Courts were expressly enjoined to apply the Hindu law to the Hindus, and the Mahommedan law to the Mahommedans—of course, it was also the duty of these Courts to recognise well-established local usages. Thus practically all the topics of litigation at that time likely to arise were provided for. But as time went on, when by intercourse with Europeans new ideas, and with them new wants sprang up in the native populations, gaps came to be discovered in the law. To such cases the judges had been vaguely told that they were to apply "the rules of equity and good conscience." These were naturally sought in the English law. The consequence has been that in some important matters, the notions of English law have powerfully affected India. Such are the conceptions of a complete separation of the ownership of property from the enjoyment of it by means of trusts of the testamentary power, of the creation of life estates, of the substitution of one owner of property for another on the happening of some future event, of rules of evidence, criminal law, civil and criminal procedure and the subordination of the executive to the ordinary law. Upon all of these topics, the law of India is mainly English. Not that the whole of it rests upon the slender authority above described. Much of it, as will appear presently, was introduced by the Indian Legislatures. Much of it also, although originally introduced by the Courts, has since received legislative sanction.*

Independence of the Judges

The position of the Judges has been made one of security against any improper influence of the Executive in India itself, the corrupt or improper exercise of their own powers was guarded against in the Regulating Act of 1772 by vesting the power to punish them for the same in the Court of the King's Bench in England, and for this purpose the Governor-General and the Governors in Council were made judicial authorities to take evidence and transmit the same to the Court in England when asked to do so. This provision has been reproduced in the collection of Statutes relating to British India, and we presume it applies to the Judges of the present High Courts which have succeeded the old Supreme Courts. The Judicial Committee of the Privy Council, constituted by an Act of 1833, is the highest judicial authority in respect of all judicial matters arising in India.

* Encyclopædia Britannica 11th Edition, Vol. xiv, p. 434.

Combination of executive and judicial functions

The composition of the High Courts and of the Courts inferior to them has, however, to some extent told upon their independence in relation to the executive, which the judiciary was expected to possess under the original statutes. The position of the Judges of inferior courts is, so far as their discharge of judicial functions within their respective spheres is concerned, theoretically at any rate, one of independence of the Executive. The conduct of the Executive and its officers and the constitutionality of Indian Acts, in so far as they may come before them for judicial pronouncement, ought to be treated in the same way as any superior Court ought to treat it. The judges of the inferior courts are subject, no doubt, to the administrative control of the High Court, but the executive government, in the case of a large number of them, has a good deal of voice in deciding their prospects and promotion. In the case of judicial officers who are Magistrates exercising criminal jurisdiction, the position of the executive officers of the Government is such as to permit of interference, sometimes serious, with the independence of the subordinate Magistracy in the discharge of their functions. The combination of executive with judicial functions in the same hands, which so largely prevails, however necessary or expedient in some circumstances it may be, has undoubtedly resulted in making the actual discharge of judicial duties appear much less independent than was intended to be. Legally, of course, the two functions are clearly distinct, and the union of them in the same officer is only a matter of administration. The law does not recognise the prosecutor and the judge acting together in the same person, or in the same body of persons related to each other as superior and subordinate. On the other hand, the law does clearly distinguish between Magistrates and Judges who try cases and the prosecutor and police who prosecute and investigate. It is the union in practice of the two functions that has gone to interfere with the principle of the separation of functions on which all British institutions have been framed.

Special exemptions

There are moreover, in India a few exemptions from the authority of the courts which are mainly of historical importance. The position and prestige of the Governor-General and the Governors of the Presidencies have been enhanced from the time of the Regulating Act by the provision contained in it, that they shall be personally exempt from the original jurisdiction, civil or criminal, of the High Court or from arrest or imprisonment in any suit or proceeding of that Court. The Chief Justices and the Judges of the several High Courts are also similarly exempted. It has also been provided that an order in writing of the Governor-General in Council is a full justification for any act which may be questioned in any civil or criminal proceeding in any High Court, except so far as the act extends to any European British subject of His Majesty. The abuse of the authority or power vested in the Governor-General and the Members of his Council is provided against by vesting an authority to deal with them in the Court of the King's Bench in England and the High Court has been authorised, as the Governor-General and Governors in Council have been in respect of the High Courts, to take and transmit evidence to the said Court in this behalf when asked to do so.

CHAPTER XIII

INDIAN FINANCE

Wide field of Indian Finance

No account of the Indian Constitution can be considered complete without a brief description of Indian Finance. The total revenues of this country amount annually to more than 85 millions strerling and the total expenditure amounts to a like figure. The sources of these revenues are as varied as the purposes to which they are applied. We are not here concerned with the principles according to which the revenues of this country are raised. They vary from the extreme English conception of *laisse faire* to the equally extreme German conception of land and railway nationalisation. The history of Indian Finance is full of examples of financial statesmanship notable alike for resourcefulness and for success. Few modern states will furnish adequate parallels to them. The study of Indian Finance, from a scientific point of view, has yet to be made in any serious fashion by students of Indian Politics or Economics. A proper presentation of its varied features and interesting tendencies during the last half-a-century and more is itself matter for a separate volume. Such a task is beyond the limits of this book. All that is essayed here is merely a brief examination of the relation that, under the present constitution, exists between finance and Government.

Control of Indian Finance

As in administrative so in financial matters we have to recognise four distinct authorities possessing financial powers in varying degrees. These are:—(1) the Secretary of State in Council; (2) the Governor-General in Council; (3) the Provincial Governments; and (4) the local and municipal bodies. Section 2 of the Government of India Act, 1858, declares:—"And all the territorial and other revenues of or arising in India and all tributes and other payments in respect of any territories which would have been receivable by, or in the name of the said campany, if this Act had not been passed, shall be received for, and in the name of, Her Majesty, and shall be applied and disposed of for the purposes of the Government of India alone, subject to the provisions of this Act." Section 41 of the same Act provides that the expenditure of such revenues is placed under the control of the Secretary of State in Council—no grant or appropriation being allowed to be made without the concurrence of the majority of votes at a meeting of the Council of India. Under section 53, the accounts of each financial year are required to be placed before Parliament. The general financial powers of the Governor-General in Council are traceable to section 39 of the Charter Act of 1833 under which "the superintendence, direction and control of the whole Civil and Military Government of all the said territories and revenues in India shall be and are hereby vested in a Governor-General and Counsellors to be styled 'The Governor-General in Council.'" The financial powers of Provincial Governments rest on no statutes, but are derived from executive arrangements in connection with the system of Provincial Contracts or Settlements. The financial powers of local boards and Municipalities rest upon Indian legislation and are therefore the creatures of either the Imperial or the Provincial Legislative Councils.

Delegation of financial control

Indian public expenditure is either incurred in England or in India. Roughly speaking, expenditure in England is incurred only on the authority of the Secretary of State in Council; expenditure in India is incurred by the Government of India according to rules approved by the Secretary of State in Council. The sphere of expenditure, therefore, within which the Government of India may be said to have an unfettered discretion is thus limited. To cite one example, no new appointment carrying a salary of over Rs. 250 per mensem can be created by the Government of India without the Secretary of State's sanction. But though the supreme authority for any appropriation of Indian revenues vests by law in the Secretary of State in Council, the Government of India has been generally authorised, in order to facilitate the transaction of public business, by the Secretary of State, subject to certain restrictions, to incur expenditure without his specific sanction, for the purpose of carrying on the ordinary work of administration. The Governor-General in Council has delegated a considerable slice of the powers he possesses to the Provincial Governments and has imposed his own conditions on their exercise of those powers.

It will thus be seen that there are three distinct spending authorities in respect of the same revenues. The Secretary of State is directly responsible for charges in connection with the Government of India incurred in England and exercises control over the Government of India; the Government of India directly incurs the expenditure on the Imperial Services and controls the Provincial Governments ; and the Provincial Governments are responsible for the charges on Provincial Services and are controlled by the Government of India and the Secretary of State. But the taxes which feed this three-fold expenditure are imposed only by a single authority and they, together with the aggregate of the expenditure by all the 3 spending authorities under each head, are estimated for in one budget and exhibited in one account.

Sources of Indian Revenue

All revenue is raised in India. For constitutional purposes, it is sufficient to classify this revenue under two principal heads (i) that which has a legislative sanction and (ii) that which has not. The revenue derived from salt, customs, excise, assessed taxes, provincial rates, stamps, registration and opium, come under the first head. The two considerable items under the second head are tributes and contributions from Native States, and land revenue. Tributes &c., from Native States form a class of revenue arising from the foreign policy pursued by the Government and foreign policy is, and largely ought to be, least controlled by the Legislature.

No legislative sanction for land Revenue

There appears, however, to be no constitutional reason for removing the item of land revenue from the sphere of those which require legislative sanction. This exclusion is generally justified on the ground that, ever since the days of Manu, the State has been entitled to have a share of the produce of the land from the cultivator. This customary right to a *Rajabhagam* is said to be inherent in the British Government as the successors of the ancient Hindu Kings and is being enforced by such rules and according to such principles as the Executive have chosen to fix for themselves. Whether such a position could be considered sound from a modern financier's point of view is a question that need not be discussed in detail here. One argument may, however, be stated in reply to it. In his Financial Statement presented on the 18th Feb. 1860, the Right Hon'ble James Wilson justified the imposition of fresh taxation by quoting the authority of Manu and proceeded as follows :—"Now, I must say that there is latitude enough here for the most needy Exchequer and for the most voracious Minister : a twenty per cent. income-tax upon profits ; a tax varying from two to five per cent. upon accumulated capital ; a share of almost every article produced . . . I should imagine that revenue laws of the ancient Hindus must have been contributed to the sacred compiles by some very needy Finance Minister of the day !" And yet, though authority is found in Manu for income-taxes, customs and excise, all these have been imposed and are to-day collected only under legislative sanction. If a tax on income—

a share of profits, as Manu put it—requires an Income Tax Act, why should a share of agricultural produce be levied without a legislative enactment? Into the vexed question of whether the land revenue is rent or tax, it is again unnecessary here to enter. Its assessment and collection are dependent purely on executive discretion and no one who pays land revenue has the right to question in a Court of Law the justice of the burden that is imposed upon him for the purposes of the State.

Financial and constitutional drawbacks thereof

The exclusion of land revenue from the province of the Legislature practically removes between 40 and 50 per cent. of the net public revenues from any sort of control. Two considerations may be urged in this connection from a financial and constitutional standpoint :—

(a) The amount realised as land revenue — which over a large part of India is subject to periodical revision—has grown and is growing and the funds at the disposal of Government are thereby swelled. Expenditure, therefore, also tends to increase in order to keep pace with the increased revenue ; *(b)* when a surplus occurs and the Finance Minister casts about for the best means of effecting reduction of taxation, he finds himself unable to give any substantial relief to the class which pays the largest slice of the public revenue and which also really parts with the largest proportion of its income for the needs of the State. And, no wonder, he certainly cannot make any suggestions for reducing the amount taken as land revenue, because the principles of its assessment are not fixed by legislative enactment. He has, therefore, to fall back upon the addition of a few unimportant cesses on land or upon the reduction or abolition of other taxes which have been sanctioned by the legislature. It seems to the present writer unnecessary to further press this constitutional objection against the present method of making land revenue assessments. The recent Royal Commission on Decentralisation has recommended the placing of these assessments on a legal and statutory basis but so far it has not been acted upon.

It may, therefore, be stated that all *taxation* in India, except the one item of land revenue, has to be voted by the Legislative Council. Such, at any rate, has been the practice—the constitutional convention, if we may so put it—though there appears to be no definite statutory prohibition apart from the principles of the English Constitution, in the way of the Executive Government imposing a tax without reference to the Legislative Councils.

Taxation voted by Legislature

With regard to public expenditure, however, the Executive both in practice and in theory has been absolutely uncontrolled. How far the reformed Councils will be able in future to exercise any control in this matter will be discussed in some detail in connection with the Budget.

Executive uncontrolled in expenditure

Originally, the administration of the whole of Indian Finance was vested in the Government of India, a task which on account of the growing development of the country, became both difficult and inefficient. A policy of decentralisation was initiated by Lord Mayo's Government in 1870 and the 'Provincial Contracts' came into existence. This policy has been considerably improved and developed of late. It must be clearly borne in mind, however that the various Provincial Governments are merely repositories of financial powers delegated to them by the Imperial Government. Within the sphere limited by the provincial settlements, they are free to order their own revenue and expenditure subject to various rules as regards the creation of appointments, raising of fresh revenue &c. The following passage taken from the new "Imperial Gazetteer of India" Vol. IV, p. 190, describes the system as it was introduced :—

"The objects aimed at were to give the Local Governments a strong inducement to develop their revenue and practise economy in their expenditure, to obviate the Supreme Government in the details of Provincial Administration and at the same

Decentralisation of Provincial Finance in 1870

time to maintain the unity of the finances in such a manner that all parts of the administration should receive a due share of growing revenues, required to meet growing needs, and should bear in due proportion the burden of financial difficulties which must be encountered from time to time. This problem has been solved by the Government of India delegating to the Local Governments the control of the expenditure on the ordinary provincial services, together with the whole, or a proportion, of certain heads of revenue sufficient to meet these charges. The heads of revenue selected are such as are most susceptible of improvement under careful provincial management." These 'Settlements' with provincial Governments were subject to revision periodically, but recently this policy has given place to a more permanent system, Provincial finance, on the whole, is under the constant check and supervision of the Supreme Government and is only a part—and not independent—of Imperial Finance.

The general features of the existing Settlements effected with the aid of these principles are generally of the following character. The Imperial Government directly administers the obviously common services which everywhere a Central Government undertakes, *viz.*, the Army, Foreign relations, Home Charges, Railways, Posts and Telegraphs. The services appertaining to the internal administration of the country are the care of the Provincial Governments, *viz.*, General Administration, Registration, Law and Justice, Police, Jails, Education, Medical, Stationery and Printing and Provincial Civil Works and Forests. The Imperial Government receives the incidental revenue yielded by the expenditure heads under its control, while the provincial Governments take the receipts from the Provincial heads of expenditure. Of the great revenue heads Opium, Salt, Customs, Mint, Railways, Posts and Telegraphs and Tributes from Native States are Imperial; Forests are entirely provincial; Land Revenue, Excise, Stamps and Assessed Taxes are shared between Imperial and Provincial, generally in equal proportions.

The Provincial Governments possess no borrowing powers and their estimates of revenue and expenditure are subject to alteration by the Government of India. In addition to these is the control resulting from the general and specific financial restrictions contained in various Acts, the Civil Account Code and the Civil Service Regulations. Such in very brief outline is tha existing system. Let us now examine this system from a scientific standpoint.

CHAPTER XIV

BUDGETS AND BUDGETARY RULES

Finance and constitutional Government

"Money is the vital principle of the body politic. He who controls the finances of the State controls the nation's policy. Constitutionalism is the idea, budgets are the means, by which that idea is realised."* These are the words of a well-known writer on Public Finance. They describe most effectively the close relation that subsists between finance and constitutional government. One of the fundamental principles of every state that either recognises constitutional limitations or purports to develop a constitutional form of government, is the vesting of some measure of control of the public purse in the representatives of the people. This control—the measure of which varies with the stage which each particular community and state has arrived at in the development of free institutions—is usually exercised through the Budget.

What is a budget

The Budget, broadly speaking, is an account of the finances of the state presented by the Executive to the legislature. Its presentment is necessary in order that the representatives of the people constituting the legislature may ensure that care and economy are secured in the finances of the nation. In highly

* H. C. Adams' Finance, pp. 115-6.

developed forms of popular government, it passes through two stages. In the first stage, it is a report prepared for the purpose of giving the legislature an idea of the condition of the finances and of what is needed and proposed for the year that is budgeted for. In its second stage, it is treated as a project of law and passed like other legislative measures. With these prefatory remarks, we may proceed to the study of the Budget in India, as a means of exercising control over financial administration.

Control of Parliament over Indian Finance

From what has been said in the earlier chapters of this it will be clear that the Parliament, though it is the ultimate sovereign in respect of all revenue that is raised and authority all expenditure that is incurred by the Government of India, does not, and is unable to, regularly and systematically exercise any control over Indian finances, as it does in the case of the finances of the United Kingdom. Its control is mainly confined to two matters, *viz.*:—(*a*) no expenditure of the revenues of India can be incurred for defraying the cost of any expedition beyond the Indian frontiers (except for preventing or repelling actual invasion) without the consent of both Houses of Parliament; (*b*) it is also directed by the Government of India Act of 1858 that the Indian Budget shall be laid annually before the House of Commons to enable its members to offer suggestions, ask for information and generally criticise the policy of the Government in relation to India. In practice, however, the 'resolution to go into Committee to consider the East India Revenue Accounts' is purely a formal one, consisting of the identical proposition that the Accounts show what they show. Not only is Parliament unable to control Indian Finance, but careful students of the tendencies of constitutional development in India ought also to recognise that, so far as the people of India are concerned, this control should be exercised not in England, but in India. The Indian Constitution, even as it is, clearly points to the latter tendency and rightly too.

Indian Legislature cannot vote or veto a Budget

It is true that the Indian Legislatures possess no statutory powers for voting, much less for vetoing, a Budget. Their functions have been confined to discussing the Budget and criticising the general administration. This right was conceded to them during the Viceroyalty of Lord Mayo when financial administration was decentralised. It was considered at one time that the Resolution of the Government of India on the subject vested the Provincial Legislative Councils with the power of passing the Budget by means of an Appropriation Bill. In Madras, at any rate, in 1871, the Executive Government, under the guidance of Sir Alexander Arbuthnot, took up such a position, but the Government of India subsequently disabused them of that impression. For a long time after, the discussion over the Budget was neither systematic nor regular. Under the law, the Councils could only meet for legislative purposes. In the absence of any Bills imposing fresh taxation there was no legal or constitutional obligation thrown on the Executive to present the Budget or to allow its discussion. The difficulty was obviated by the Indian Councils Act of 1892, which authorised the Governor-General in Council to make rules from time to time permitting the Legislative Councils to discuss the annual Financial Statement of the Governor-General in Council. Similar provisions were enacted for the Provincial Legislative Councils also.

Budget Rules under Act of 1892

Under these rules, the procedure with regard to the preparation and presentment of the Financial Statement to the Imperial Legislative Council was as follows. The Comptroller and Auditor-General prepared the Budget Estimate and forwarded it for approval to the Finance Member. The Finance Member examined the same and suggested or made alterations in the proposals necessary for meeting fresh expenditure or disposing of surpluses. It was then laid before the Governor-General in Council. On being passed by them, a Financial Statement was made by the Finance Member to the Legislative Council. After an interval of at least a week, the Members delivered speeches which generally ranged over the whole field of administration. The President wound up the debate with a speech of his own. No vote was taken; no amendments were allowed. The Budget, for the year at any rate, was neither better nor worse on account of this debate. If the latter had any effect at all, it was only posthumous, so to speak; it might result in improving the statement for the following year.

No 'Budget right' in India

A radical change in this procedure has been effected by the Rules made by the Government under the Councils Act of 1909. These Rules will be found published in the Appendix. The Councils are still far from having obtained anything like the control of the national purse. In the Despatch which the Government of India sent to the Secretary of State in October, 1911 they took care to insist upon one proposition as a constitutional fact, namely, that the power of passing the Budget is vested not in the Legislative Council, but in the Executive, and that it is the latter and not the former that decides any question arising on the Budget. There can be no doubt that, under the law, there is no power in the Legislative Council to claim to meddle with the Financial Statement of the Governor-General in Council. If the constitutional proposition enunciated by the Government of India were accepted literally, it would mean that the Legislative Council has no control over either the raising of revenue or the incurring of expenditure. In other words, the Executive Government would be at liberty to impose a tax and collect it with the same ease as it is able to incur expenditure. As a matter of fact, however, these legally unrestrained powers of the Executive have been considerably modified by constitutional usage. During the last half-a-century and more, no fresh taxation or alteration in existing taxation has been resorted to without the sanction of the Legislative Council. Of course, care has always been taken to present the Bill for a fresh tax as a separate measure and not as part of the Budget and with the official majority in the Councils, the powers of the Executive were practically unlimited. The established constitutional practice will, however, be of advantage in the future, especially in regard to Provincial Legislative Councils. With a non-official majority, these Councils must be able, with sufficient unanimity, to indirectly control Provincial finance by the power they have of consenting to fresh taxation, but it has to be recognised that purely provincial taxation is not a field large enough at present for exercising such control effectively. In the field of expenditure, however, no such constitutional usage has grown up, and the Executive have been supreme therein. The Rules have constituted, however, a distinct step in advance and, if acted upon with care and discrimination, are ultimately likely to lead to the realisation of a fully developed 'Budget right.'

The British Budget Procedure

Let us digress for a moment and consider what 'Budget right' means in England. It is really composed of three distinct rights, *viz.*, the right to determine the annual expenditure, the right to consent to the imposition of a fresh tax or the alteration of an existing one, and the right to decide the extent of national borrowing. The Budget, in England, as in all civilised countries, is drafted by the Executive. The King's Speech opening Parliament informs the latter as to the estimated immediate needs of the State. The House of Commons then votes a supply which enables the ordinary work of administration to be carried on while the details of the Budget are being discussed and settled. The next step is the fixing of a day for a discussion in Committee of the expenditure side of the Budget. The House on that day resolves itself into Committee, called the Committee of Supply, for the purpose of considering the supply that has been already voted. The informal procedure in Committee enables the House to thoroughly thresh out every item of expenditure and a general agreement is arrived at as to the total expenditure to be incurred for the year. The House then goes into Committee again, *viz.*, the Committee of Ways and Means, and the Chancellor of the Exchequer opens discussion in it by making his Budget speech. The Budget has afterwards to be passed into law.

New Indian Budget Procedure

It would be idle to expect all the details of such procedure in a government like India. It is only possible in states which have established constitutional government, in the strict sense of the term, and which recognise the doctrine of ministerial responsibility. The constitution of India, is, however, different. Party government and ministerial responsibility are non-existent and the ultimate right of the Executive to determine the Budget is considered necessary to prevent a deadlock in the work of Government. The Executive in India is permanent and cannot be altered. It can, therefore, not afford, at present, to render its hold over the purse weakened by an adverse vote of the representative body. An adverse vote is the same thing as a vote of censure, but the Executive, being permanent, cannot resign and make way for the leaders of those who have censured. They have to continue in office and must carry on the work of Government. This is the constitutional ground on which the Government of India have, in the present Rules refused to permit the legislatures to vote or veto a Budget. It has, however, been recognised in the Rules that the representatives of the people should be consulted and their advice taken before the Executive decides on the final form which the Budget should assume. Herein lies the cardinal point of difference between the old practice and the new. Formerly, the details of the Budget were determined without any possibility of alteration before it was presented to the Legislative Councils. The latter were, therefore, powerless to effect any amendments in it. Under the present Rules, however, a distinction has been made between the 'Financial Statement' and the 'Budget'. The former may usefully be termed the 'preliminary Budget.' The Imperial Budget is ordered to be presented to the Council with an explanatory memorandum. An interval is then allowed and a day fixed for the first stage of the discussion. The Council has, then, the opportunity of moving any resolution relating to (1) any alteration in taxation, (2) any new loan or (3) any additional grant to Local Governments. The resolutions may be voted on. After all the resolutions on these three items have been fully discussed and disposed of, the Council enters upon the second stage of the discussion. It presumably goes into Committee for discussing groups of financial heads under the guidance of the Member in charge of the particular Department. Resolutions can be moved and voted on at this stage also. After this discussion also is closed, the Budget is decided on by the Executive Government—after giving due weight to such resolutions as the Legislative Council may have passed, but on the responsibility of the Executive only—and presented to the Legislative Council by the Finance Member, and it is followed subsequently by the usual general discussion.

Its constitutional importance

To the present writer, these Rules appear to recognise three very important principles of great constitutional significance. The first stage of the discussion and the matters comprised therein enunciate the important maxim that alteration of taxation must be made with reference to the Budget statement, though the alteration itself will presumably have to be passed by a separate legislative measure. In other words, the Members are given the privilege of discussing *before hand* the question of such alteration with reference to the necessities of the Budget. The second stage of the Budget discussion, for the first time in Indian constitutional history, takes the non-official Members of Council into confidence in regard to the determination of public expenditure. The members have the right of placing on record their views, as to the items not excluded from their cognisance, in the form of resolutions. It is true that a good deal of the value of this concession is lost by the exclusion of important heads of revenue and expenditure from discussion, but the principle has been recognised and it may be hoped that it will gradually be extended in application. The third stage of the Indian Budget is also of very great importance in that it imposes on the Finance Member the obligation to explain why any resolutions that may have been passed in the two first stages have not been accepted by Government. The ability and discretion of Members of the Legislative Council in rendering this particular obligation of real and lasting constitutional significance, will be measured by the soundness of the suggestions and the practicability of the recommendations that they decide to shape in the form of resolutions. It will be difficult for them to get resolutions passed in the Imperial Council with an official majority; but further development of constitutional rights is likely to be retarded and endangered if resolutions of an impossible or unpractical character are moved. A few well-considered resolutions may well prevent the Executive from brushing them aside and help to build up constitutional usage, strengthening the rights of the representatives over Indian finance, while a large number of ill-considered and wild-cat schemes will, on the other hand, help to create a body of precedents which will be a standing obstruction to further constitutional progress. What is required to avoid the latter and to build up the former is a satisfactory organisation of the people's representatives and a readiness in them to choose and to follow the leadership of those who are by their knowledge, their patriotism and their sagacity, pre-eminently fitted to lead them.

Scope for growth of constitutional conventions

The progress of Constitutional Government is not dependent so much upon what is expressly declared to be constitutional rights as upon what is silently built up in the form of constitutional conventions. The Rules now promulgated place the Legislative Councils of British India in a position very much worse than that of the Reichstag in Germany. The theory of the German Constitution is that the Reichstag should control expenditure. In actual practice, the Executive has acted several times in defiance of the Reichstag, but the apology which the Government has, soon or late, to make for such unconstitutional action is really the best guarantee for the people's right. The King of Prussia once carried out a reorganisation of the army in spite of the refusal of the legislature to make an appropriation for the purpose. But four years later, he admitted the unconstitutionality of his act, begged the pardon of the legislature and requested them to legalise his procedure. In India, the legislature has not the power to refuse an appropriation, legally; it can only make a recommendation to the Executive in the form of a resolution that certain expenditure need not be incurred. Of course, the Executive may accept this recommendation or not in its discretion. But it is bound to make an explanation as to why a resolution has not been accepted. The necessity imposed by the Rules for making this explanation is a great moral weapon in the hands of the Legislatures, capable of being wielded with great effect, if only the resolutions which necessitate the apology are such as cannot admit of being explained away.

The Procedure *re* Provincial Budgets

The rules which have been provided for the discussion of Provincial Budgets in the Provincial Legislative Councils are somewhat different in respect of the procedure at the initial stages of Budget-making. But though designed to allow of more active discussion of budget proposals by non-official members, and at an earlier stage than in the case of the Imperial Budget, the actual extent of their usefulness has been much smaller. This results more or less from the subordinate character of Provincial finance itself and from its being but a part of Imperial finance. The Provincial Budgets are in fact included in the Imperial Budget and have to receive the sanction of the Imperial Government before they become executory. The general character of Provincial finance has already been indicated in the last chapter, but in order to show the extent of freedom of discussion permitted in Provincial Councils on Provincial Budget it is necessary to reiterate the fundamental conditions on which the Provincial financial arrangements are worked. In the first place, the Provincial Governments have not the power to levy any additional taxation or remit any extra revenue which may remain. The prohibition in this case is directly derived from the statutory restrictions imposed by

Parliamentary enactments. In the next place, the Provincial Governments possess no borrowing powers and are prohibited from raising loans in the open market. This restriction is imposed by means of the enactments of the Indian Legislature. In the third place, the Provincial Governments have, as it were, to bank with the Government of India. In other words, all revenues, Provincial and Imperial, are paid into a common chest or treasury and all payments are made out of that common chest. The custody of this treasury and the management of the funds thereof are vested in the Financial Department of the Government of India, over all the provinces alike, while the same Department has been invested with the powers of checking and auditing the accounts of revenue and expenditure of all the Governments, Provincial and Imperial.

Their restricted scope

It results from this that neither the Provincial Governments nor their Legislative Councils could exercise any control over the receipt side of the Budget, in respect of nearly all the taxation, direct and indirect, and in respect of the bulk of their revenues. The functions of the Councils, therefore, could not be exercised to any effect or advantage over the raising of revenues, or over their remission if they are over and above the requirements of the Province at any time. It is only on the expenditure side that the activities of the Council could be and have been so far expended, but even here the scope for effective criticism seems to be strictly limited. Though under the present Rules, the draft Budget is placed before a Finance Committee appointed by the Council as early as January every year and discussed by them informally, the heads on which this Committee could give useful assistance by way of criticism or suggestion has been narrowed down by rules which the Executive Government again could so interpret as to bring the powers of the Committee as well as of the Council subsequently to the narrowest limits. For instance, the Executive Government is directed to separate the total amount of expenditure budgeted for the year under "allotted" and "unallotted" heads, much in the same way as the budgets of foreign countries divide the expenditure of the year into "obligatory" and "facultative" expenditure, or as the British Budget divides it, into "the Consolidated Fund charges" and "the Annual Supply charges." The rules, however, in India enable the Provincial Governments to include under the former not only expenditure on existing establishments and schemes as in other countries, but also expenditure on new schemes "the cost of which is not considerable or which the Local Government considers to be of an absolutely obligatory character." It would be easily seen that this Rule could be so worked as to include all the proposals which the Executive Government desires to carry out without discussion or question under the "allotted heads," as being "of an absolutely obligatory character." There are besides certain other rules based upon principles of general finance, the working of which restricts still further the powers of the Members of Council to suggest schemes of alternative or additional expenditure. Schemes involving recurring expenditure it is rightly provided, could only be proposed with due regard to the rate of growth of recurring revenues and recurring expenditure, but while schemes which the Government may desire to put through or place in the "obligatory" list, could be taken outside the operation of this rule by previous sanction of the Government of India, the extent to which the proposals made by non-official members involving recurring is strictly conditioned by the operation of this principle. The consequence has been that, as a matter of fact, in all the Provincial Budgets presented after the new Rules came into force, the amount of this "unallotted" fund which is marked out for attacks or suggestions by non-official Members, bears but an insignificant proportion to the total expenditure provided in the budget. Moreover, consistently with the scheme of Provincial Finance, the discussion of Revised Financial Statements in a Committee of the whole Council which forms the second stage of budget discussion in the Provincial Governments, is not to take place on any alteration in taxation or any new loan or grant, to the Local Government, as in the Imperial Council, but only on the various heads of expenditure in the Statements and on such isolated items of revenue as have not come under the statutory prohibitions referred to above.

Constitutional value of control over expenditure

The control of expenditure, however, in all Budgets is a privilege highly prized in all constitutional governments, and to this extent budget debates in the Provincial Councils under the new Rules have been found to be very useful. They have gone, of course, very little towards altering materially the actual budget provisions of the Provincial Governments, which by the prior sanction they have received from the Government of India, become virtually settled from the earliest stages, but the criticisms during the debates and discussions on the Budget have been valuable in guiding subsequent action and in correcting administrative errors connected with these expenditure heads.

Further development in the powers of control of the Provincial Councils over the Provincial Budgets appear to be more dependent —apart from relaxations in the rigidity of the present Rules—on the development of financial decentralization in close connection with Provincial autonomy, of the powers of Provincial taxation, of Provincial borrowing and of the power of passing Provincial Budgets as annual Legislative measures—than upon any peculiarly financial reforms.

CHAPTER XV

THE NATIVE STATES

'British India' and 'India'

An attempt has been made in the foregoing chapters to give a brief account of the machinery of government and the administrative arrangements of 'British India' *i.e.*, as the Interpretation Act of 1889 defines it, of "all those territories and places within His Majesty's dominions which are for the time being governed by His Majesty through the Governor-General of India, or through any Governor or other officer subordinate to the Governor-General of India". The political system of India, however, comprises not merely these territories and places, but "also the territories of any native prince or chief under the suzerainty of His Majesty, exercised through the Governor-General of India or through any Governor or other officer subordinate to the Governor-General of India". These, together with "British India" proper, constitute "India" as defined by the same statute. "India" thus consists of all that part of the great Indian peninsula which is directly or indirectly under British rule or protection. That both these classes of territories form part of the British Empire in India admits of no doubt; but what exactly are the nature and character of the rights which the British Sovereign exercises in "British India", and "in India exclusive of British India" *i.e.*, in the states and territories of princes under the suzerainty of the British Government in India, is a question which is commonly treated as not falling strictly within the scope of discussions on the political and administrative institutions of India. In a popular sense, moreover, 'India' also includes certain other countries such as Nepa and Bhutan and certain small patches of territory belonging to France and Portugal, which are beyond the legal area defined as 'India' by the Interpretation Act, but whose relations with India are yet a concern of the Foreign Department of the Government of India who appoint agents to reside in the territories concerned.

'British India' and British Law and sovereignty

In another view again, it has been maintained that the term 'British India' includes only the districts subject to British law and not any of the Native States. If we take therefore as a test the applicability of British law, that is, the statutes of Parliament, to bring any area within the sphere of the Indian Constitution, it cannot be said that the Native States of India form part of that Constitution. The legal sovereignty of Parliament implies the unrestricted power of making laws for all territories subject to that sovereignty, and it is argued that if Parliament possesses not the power to make laws for all persons resident within the territories of the Native States and princes of India, it follows that the 'constituent' laws which Parliament has from time to time enacted for the Government of his Majesty's Indian territories have no application to the territories outside British India, except in reference to extra-territorial jurisdiction. Is it then to be assumed from this legal phenomenon that the Native States are not subject to the sovereignty of the British Crown? Such a statement would promptly be denied by any one who is acquainted with the real position of the rulers of these subordinate principalities. As was pointed out at the outset of this treatise, the legal sovereignty of Parliament is a mere legal conception drawn from the doctrine of sovereignty as understood in England, and is very different from the political or the actual sovereignty of the United Kingdom over the British Empire. It was seen how the political sovereignty of the United Kingdom may be said to reside in, the person or body of persons whose will is ultimately obeyed by the citizens of the State and, how they thus consist of the electors of the United Kingdom with or without the Crown and the House of Lords as the case may be. Similarly, in respect of the British Empire overseas, whatever may be the legal theory as to the sovereignty of the British parliament being co-extensive with the prevalence of British law or enactments, the actual powers and rights which flow to and are exercised by that Sovereign, vary greatly in different parts of that Empire. But there is this constant feature present in the case of all, that the rights of external sovereignty of the Empire outside the United Kingdom and of their rulers and Governments have been always recognised in International Law as being exercised by His Majesty's Government—even though Parliament may have long ceased to exercise its legislative powers, and even though the rulers of the states under British Imperial sway or protection or alliance, may not acknowledge in practice the right of Parliament or any subordinate legislature thereto to exercise the power to make laws for them. The dependencies and protectorates which have followed the Colonial expansion of the British race in the various continents of the world are, many of them, under the sway of Native rulers, but are virtually under the control of British agents, consuls, administrators or ministers assisted by certain other British institutions implanted in them for the purpose of efficient government.

Native States and British Sovereignty

The position of the Native States of India, however, is somewhat different and somewhat more peculiar than that of these parts of the overseas Empire, and are a resultant of the special historical circumstances under which they have survived absorption into the territories of British India as such, and have had maintained their integrity and position as separate entities for civil government within their own areas. But the sovereignty of the British Crown over them *i.e.*, the political sovereignty which implies the power of compelling ultimate compliance with the will of the superior authority, does undoubtedly reside in His Majesty's Government, in fact as well as in political theory. In one of the famous resolutions issued by the Indian Government, this sovereignty has been laid down in clear terms. "The principles of international law", declares the resolution of the Government of India No. 1700 E, August 21, 1891, "have no bearing upon the relations between the Government of India as representing the Queen-Empress on the one hand and the Native States under the Sovereignty of Her Majesty on the other. The paramount supremacy of the former presupposes and implies the subordination of the latter."

Native States have no international existence

Starting from this position of unquestioned sovereignty of the British Crown, it is easy to see how the Native States of India can have no International existence in the comity of nations. They can have no separate individuality therein, their own being merged in that of the British Government which acts for them in all matters in which they have to come in contact with Foreign Powers and *vice versa.* The responsibility for the welfare of these subordinate states as to matters of international concern is thus vested in the British Imperial Government. One legal consequence has been that the British Parliament and its subordinate legislatures in India have so far to qualify the theory of legal sovereignty on which they usually act as to take upon themselves the power to legislate for the subjects of these Native princes and states, when they reside outside their own territories. It is on this principle that the Foreign Jurisdiction Acts and the Orders in Councils which have followed them later in England, have included the subjects of Native States, under the term 'British Subjects'. This is defined in those Acts and Orders as including, "not only British subjects in the proper sense of the word but, also any persons in Her Majesty's protection, and in particular, subjects of the several princes and states in India in alliance with Her Majesty residing and being in the parts of Africa mentioned in the Order." The term 'foreigner' is defined as meaning "a person whether a native subject of Africa or not, who is not a British subject within the meaning of the Order."

They have no federal nor constitutional rights and obligations

If the relations between the Government of India as the paramount power and the Native States as subordinate to that power cannot thus be deemed international, neither could they be deemed to be constitutional. The position of the Government of India in relation to the Native States is not that of a regular and constitutionally controlling authority which exercises by definite constitutional machinery powers of supervision over the every-day administration of the States, such as obtains in the case of the various Provincial Governments in India. On the other hand, the settled policy of the Indian Government has been to leave the internal administration of each State as fully and freely as possible in the hands of the rulers themselves, and to limit interference to cases of gross misrule or open rebellion in the states concerned. Nor, again, would we be justified in treating the ties between the Government of India and these Native States, as they are resting at the present time on any federal basis, meaning thereby the existence of a defined sovereign authority in the Imperial Government to deal with specified or unspecified common affairs of the entire joint state of India. It is true no doubt, that the Imperial Government undertakes the common defence of the Empire and the Native States to some extent contribute towards the maintenance of the common Military forces necessary for the purpose. It is true also that the foreign affairs of Native States are entirely in the hands of the Government of India, but there is very little else of common interests which have to be dealt with by the Imperial Government and there is certainly no common organization representative of the interests of the States and the British territories, which might be supposed to be charged with the administration of common affairs. Federalism, it may be repeated here again, implies the existence of two inconsistent ideas simultaneously in operation—namely in a common political entity, the desire for unity, and the desire for separation and existence as separate entities of the part States. The Native States have so far not accepted nor have they been found to exhibit any desire to join, a common organisation calculated to promote national unity, while the maintenance of their integrity is so much their most anxious concern that the slightest interference of the paramount power in the internal affairs of these states even by way of advice is jealously opposed.

Difficulty of defining their relations by a single term

In a treatise like the present, it is unnecessary to discuss what expression would correctly convey the true relations of the Native States to the paramount authority of the British Government in India, so long as the nature of that relation is properly apprehended. To call the states "Our Indian Protectorate", as Sir Louis Tupper has done, may not be satisfactory as it reminds people of the semi-civilized regions in the African Continent now under British control or influence. To call them again Feudatory States is to import a notion of territorial relationship which existed in the Europe of the middle-ages, to which the position of the protected princes does not afford any close parallel. The best thing seems to be to understand the various ties that unite, and the diverse circumstances that separate, these states in the general scheme of the Indian Constitution. As the "Imperial Gazetteer of India" puts it, "the Native States consist of territories in India not being within His Majesty's dominions, yet under his suzerainty—which in the case of 175 States including those of the greatest importance, is exercised by the Supreme Government and in the case of the remainder numbering about 500, is entrusted to the Provincial Governments." The exercise of suzerainty by the paramount power of the British Government is thus the tie which primarily unites while the exercise of separate dominion is the circumstance which primarily separates the Native States. This exercise of separate dominion, however, is not equivalent to the exercise of sovereignty, as it is understood in political science, and in deciding the status of Native States, the extent to which sovereign rights are exercised by them is a material factor in deciding the question as to whether they are separate entities invested with the power to exercise dominion within the territories under them or not.

Native States and the Doctrine of Sovereignty

It has long been recognised that the pure Austinian conception of sovereignty—that there must exist in every community which has advanced beyond the savage and pastoral stage, some determinate person or body of persons whom the members of the state habitually obey and who does not obey habitually any one else, and that such community only is to be called an independent political community and such person only whom they so obey its sovereign—is not of as wide an application as was once sought to be given to it by British political thinkers. Nevertheless, it is generally true that every state, whether composite or simple, should usually possess a government whose power is theoritically at least unlimited and is only restrained, so far as this is effective, by the prevalent moral opinion of the community. The question then where supreme political power resides in a state is one which, as Professor Sidgewick points out, it is most important to ask with regard to any political society, but it is a question to which any simple general answer is liable to be misleading. In the first Chapter of this book, in dealing with the question of sovereignty in British India, the convenient hypothesis was accepted, of what Professor Sidgewick calls the device of Professor Dicey, and the term sovereignty was given a dual application, by distinguishing 'legal sovereignty' from "political sovereignty'. It was laid down that while the legal sovereignty over British India vested in the British Parliament, its political sovereignty might be deemed to rest with the Ministers of the King for the time being chosen by the electors of Great Britain. If we seek, however, to apply this theory of sovereignty to the Native States of India, it is found that even the device of distinguishing legal from political sovereignty is not sufficient. The questions, what are the attributes of sovereignty and whether all of them are comprised in the mere unlimited power of law—making which any state might possess irrespective of its dependence upon another government for its protection from external danger or internal disorder—raise an issue which serves to show that pure legal theory does not always conform to facts.

Sovereignty is shared in Native States

The question, then, as to how far the Native States of India should be deemed as independent political communities in the eye of British law, is distinct from how far they are dependent for their existence and progress in actual practice upon the suzerainty which to a greater or less degree the British power in India exercises over them. Sir Courtenay Ilbert in his "Government of India" seeks to connect the two by adopting the view of Sir Henry Maine in one of his minutes written while he was Law-Member of the Government of India, which was as follows:—

"The mode or degree in which sovereignty is distributed between the British Government and any given Native State is always a question of fact, which has to be separately decided in each case and to which no general rules apply. In the more considerable instances, there is always some treaty, engagement or sunnud to guide us to a conclusion, and then the only question which remains is, what has become of the sovereign rights which are *not* mentioned in the Convention? Did the British Government reserve them to itself, or did it intend to leave the Native Power in the enjoyment of them? In the case of Kattywar, the few ambiguous documents which bear on the matter seem to me to point to no certain result, and I consider that the distribution of the sovereignty can only be collected from the *de facto* relations of these States with the British Government, from the course of action which has been followed by this Government towards them. Though we have to interpret this evidence ourselves, it is in itself perfectly legitimate.

It appears to me, therefore, that the Kattywar States have been permitted to enjoy several sovereign rights, of which the principal—and it is a well-known right of sovereignty—is immunity from foreign laws. Their chiefs have also been allowed to exercise (within limits) civil and criminal jurisdiction and several of them have been in the exercise of a very marked (though minor) sovereign right—the right to coin money. But far the largest part of the sovereignty has obviously resided in practice with the British Government, and among the rights which it has exercised appears to me to be an almost unlimited right of interference for the better order of the States. I mean that, if the interferences which have already taken place be referred to principles, those principles would justify any amount of interposition, so long as we interpose in good faith for the advantage of the chiefs and people of Kattywar, and so long as we do not disturb the only unqualified sovereign right which these States appear to possess—the right to immunity from foreign laws."

Nature of Semi-sovereignty in States

The proportions, therefore, in which Sovereignty in Native States is divided between the British Government and the ruler of each Native State, differ greatly according to the history and importance of each and are regulated partly by treaties or less formal engagements, partly by sannads or charters and partly by usage. "The maximum of sovereignty enjoyed by any of their rulers is represented by a prince like the Nizam of Hyderabad who coins money, taxes his subjects and inflicts capital punishment without appeal. The minimum of sovereignty is represented by the lord of a few acres in Kathiawar who enjoys immunity from British taxation and exercises some shadow of judicial authority.

It has been the deliberate policy of the British Government, since the days of the Great Mutiny not to attempt to absorb the rights of dominion in the states into the rights of ultimate sovereignty possessed by the paramount power, and the result has been the maintenance and existence of these semi-sovereign states under peculiar conditions. To attempt to describe this relationship in the language of political science as deduced from Western institutions has been a matter of much difficulty and Sir William Lee-Warner, himself a higher authority on this subject, has discussed the whole question in a luminous chapter at the end of the latest edition of his book on the "Native States of India." He arrives at the conclusion that these States should properly be termed semi-sovereigns, for, through generally speaking, they have no independent existence in international law, yet they possess the right of immunity from foreign laws whether enacted by the Indian Legislatures or the British Parliament. Such a division of sovereignty, he says, is now recognised in respect of the Ionian Islands whose present international position is safeguarded by an arrangement sanctioned by the European powers in 1875.* He also pleads that

*"By the Convention signed at Paris on the 5th of November 1815, it was provided that the Ionian Islands should form "a single, free, and independent state under the denomination of the United States of the Ionian Islands." By Article II the State was placed "under the immediate and exclusive protection" of the King of Great Britain and Ireland. By the next article the appointment of a Lord High Commissioner was provided for, to enable the King "to employ a particular solicitude with regard to the legislation and the general administration of these States". The next Article dealt with the preparation of a new constitutional charter. By Article V the "rights inherent in the said protection" were explained as giving His Britanic Majesty "the right to occupy the fortresses and places of these States, and to maintain garrisons in the same. The Military force of the said United States shall also be under the orders of the Commander-in-Chief of the troops of His Majesty." The next Article dealt with the payment of the British garrison by the Government of the United States. Article VII introduced an element of contrast: "The trading flag of the United States of the Ionian Islands shall be acknowledged by all the Contracting Parties as the flag of a free and independent state." The colours were then described, and the Article proceeded: "None but commercial agents or Consuls, charged solely with the carrying on commercial relations, and subject to the regulations to which commercial agents or consuls are subject in their independent states, shall be accredited to the United States of the Ionian Islands." The Constitutional Charter amplified the Article just quoted by forbidding subjects of the United States of the Ionian Islands from acting as Consuls or Vice-Consuls of Foreign powers. British consular protection was assured to the subjects of the States on all ports. Rules were

the possession of attributes of semi-sovereignty which past policy and engagements have secured these states, should be rigorously respected and continued as if they were of such validity as international understandings, though strictly speaking international law will be inapplicable to them.

Semi-Sovereignty and Self-Government

It would thus be seen that Sir William Lee-Warner desires to put the Native States of India in a position higher than that of the self-governing colonies of the British Empire. Legally speaking, the powers of self-government which the latter possess rest merely upon a constitutional convention or upon the implied understanding that the British Parliament, whose legal sovereignty is unquestioned, as well as its executive, ought not to interfere with the affairs of the provinces or Colonies to which self-governing organs have been granted for conducting their own affairs; whereas, as Sir William Lee-Warner points out, the powers of internal self-government possessed by the bulk of the Native States it based upon the solemn assurances, express treaties and agreements as well as past traditions and uniform policy. He would therefore describe the Native States as semi-sovereignties rather

---

laid down for the approval of the appointments of all foreign agents and consuls. Vessels sailing under the Ionian flag were to carry the pass of the Lord High Commissioner, while other sections dealt with the national colours and the nationalization of foreign subjects. It may be admitted that although the sovereign attribute of free and uncontrolled agency in external relations was wanting to the Ionian states, still here was a share of diplomatic life left to them in the reception of commercial agents. But in all other respects, such as their deprivation of rights of war, their exclusive protection by Great Britain and the particular solicitude over their administration with which the British power was entrusted, they present a very maked parallel to the relations which in the present day subsist between the Government of India and the dependent Protected states. The precision of modern writers and jurists would not perhaps have tolerated the insertion in the Convention of the phrase, independent, but there are many who still do not hesitate to describe the Ionian Islands, under the Convention of 1815, as semi-sovereignties". [Sir W. Lee-Warner's Native States of India (1910) Macmillan & Co.]

than as self-governing units. It would, however, be an error to go away with the impression that because the legal and political status of the Native States as regards autonomy is higher than that of the self-governing colonies, their standard of administration is necessarily higher than those of the latter or that those free institutions and constitutional principles which have gained for the colonies their rights of self-government are necessarily operative in the constitutions and administrative machinery of the Native States. There are about 700 of these Native States varying very much in extent, in the powers of their rulers, in the advancement of their people, and in the organisation of their institutions. It would be indeed not a particularly profitable task to attempt to classify their administrative arrangements and to deduce the characteristics of the Native States' administration in general, because there are not only no such general principles guiding noticeable, but such principles as do exist are of so variable and so insular a character as would not lend themselves to systematic treatment. After all, the institutions of Native States are dependent on the personality of the ruler on whom rests the responsibility for the good administration of each state, whatever machinery, democratic or bureaucratic, may have been established under him. It is to him that the Government of India look for the proper and efficient government of the peoples under him. From the point of view of the Indian Constitution, therefore the administration of a Native State, is the administration of a Native ruler or a prince--and not that of a system or scheme of administrative machinery or of political institutions, popular or otherwise—which is dependent for its success upon the laws and regulations by which they are constituted and upon the degree of supervision which is exercised by the authorities legally constituted to discharge that task.

It is, however, necessary within the limits afforded in this introductory study, to refer to a few general features that are essentially associated with the political and administrative organisation of Native States, at least for illustrating the differences in the constitutional principles which govern them as against those which govern the political system established in British India.

Will of the Ruler is the source of all Sovereign Power

Generally speaking, all the attributes of internal sovereignty are possessed by the rulers of the major Native States and these for the most part comprise the functions of Legislation and of executive and judicial administration. The functions of external defence, of military organisation and of foreign relations lie beyond the scope of their partial sovereignty. In respect of the functions of internal sovereignty, the one guiding principle which distinguishes the rule of Native States from that of all the provinces in British India, is that the will of the Sovereign is the source of all the power within the State. The Sovereign is no doubt individually responsible to the suzerain power for the government of his country, but towards his own people there is no relation of constitutional responsibility which he bears. It must necessarily follow from this that there can be no formal limitations, arising out of any constitutional checks, on the power of the ruler in a Native State in the government of his subjects, and this applies to all the various functions of government comprised in the exercise of legislative, executive and judicial powers. Whatever, therefore, of administrative machinery in the discharge of these functions may be firmly established in the Native States, they rest solely on the will and sufferance of the ruler concerned, and only as a means of assisting him in the exercise of powers which are absolutely vested in him. In the discharge of legislative functions, there are no doubt legislative councils or assemblies established in some of the more advanced Native States, but their power is strictly a delegated one from the hands of the Native ruler, and a concurrent power to legislate by the direct Proclamation of the ruler himself without resort to the Council, has not only been uniformly reserved in these States, but has frequently been exercised. Similarly, in the discharge of executive functions, the ruler is necessarily assisted by a chief minister commonly called the

Dewan. He is the head of the executive administration and conducts the same under the control of the Chief or Ruler. In certain States, the Dewan and certain other ministers are often formed into a Council of State or Executive Council who deliberate upon the more important questions of administrative policy. But the relation of neither the Dewan nor the Council towards the Chief and towards each other could be deemed to be of a constitutional character, so that the powers of either may be deducible from a specific document or instrument embodying their relative rights and duties or from any constitutional condentions. In other words, no Native State could be described as possessing a Constitution as such, because whatever actual constitutional machinery they possess, is dependent for its existence and continuance entirely on the will of the Native Ruler and also in some cases on that of the Suzerain power.

Personal Rule and Constitutional limitations

The guarantee for good government in a Native State is thus dependent on the personal desire, initiative and enterprise of the Ruler in question, and the only means of influencing his personal temperament in the various Native States towards efficient progress in their internal administration at present lies in the generality of cases, in the choice of a competent Minister to guide him, and the advice of a not too meddlesome Resident. The concentration of Executive authority over all departments in a Native State in the hands of a single high official is, however, as the Government of India pointed out in a famous Despatch, known by experience to be attended with risks and disadvantages. On the other hand, unless the ordinary and every day business of a State can be regularly referred to and supervised by one superior Minister, it has been found to be difficult, especially in India, to maintain expedition, efficiency and uniformity in the administration At the same time, the presence of a Resident and his interference, however useful in the case of a self-willed and perverse ruler, has uniformly been found to be more productive of evil than good and to be directly antagonistic to the pursuit of the primary principle which the existence of these Native States and the maintenance of their integrity involves. Sir William Lee Warner has pointed out in his book how a policy of interference in the name of good government on the part of the suzerain power and its agents inevitably leads to the policy of annexation and how a policy of complete non-interference also necessarily leaves the people of the States in question without any guarantees for good government and progressive administration, except in the event of gross misrule or open rebellion. Attempts have been made to adopt the rule of a golden mean, between these two, but it has been difficult to maintain it in all cases with success.

Formal Instruments of Government could provide no constitutional checks

One solution for such a state of things obviously lies, as Sir William himself in a recent lecture in London admitted, in the direction of the growth of a healthy public opinion within each State, accompanied by the maintenance of an independent local Press, and the education of the people themselves to take a part as well as an intelligent interest in their own affairs. Another solution, which has been tried in the case of Mysore, is an attempt "to embody in a formal instrument certain cardinal principles of good government which the ruler of the State before assuming his office might be required to observe as a condition of his investiture with the full powers of the State, and to prevent the possibility of their impugnment in the future." Such a formal instrument, however, could only be brought into existence when, as in the case of Mysore, the territories in the possession of the British come to be handed over into the hands of a Native ruler—whether after a period of minority during which the administration is vested in the British Government or after a period of sequestration owing to previous maladministration. These contingencies cannot be expected to occur so that advantage may be taken of them, nor could it be said that such a procedure by itself would serve the purpose of bringing up the standard of government in Native States and placing it on the right lines of future progress. In the case of Mysore, while the Instrument of Government laid down certain by no means 'cardinal principles of good government,' as it professed to do—the intrinsic difficulties of prescribing a cut and dry constitution for the observance of a Native Sovereign, whose powers in theory at least were unlimited, were sought to be got over by complicated arrangements in which it was sought to distribute power and responsibility between the Ruler, the Dewan and a Council, and a Resident at the instance of the suzerain power with a general right to advise. It was taken as a fundamental condition that it is necessary to maintain the dignity and comparative independence of the Maharajah, by reserving to him personally some substantial share in the actual administration of the affairs of his State, but this consideration was sought to be subordinated to the still more essential necessity of providing beforehand some positive guarantees and checks against the consequences which would follow a serious misuse of the chief's power. While the executive authority therefore, was concentrated in the hands of the Dewan or the chief executive minister in order to secure vigour and expedition, it was also sought to minimise the risks of such a concentration of power in the hands of a single official by surrounding the Maharajah with counsellors and high officials of known ability and experience.

Nor the establishment of a Council

The consequences expected from this arrangement were that the powers which the Dewan was to exercise would come to be restricted by certain rules of business which will lay down what matters he can decide himself as the immediate directing head of the departments and what must be reserved for consideration in Council. It was hoped that the administration would thus be based upon that broad principle laid down by the Government of India that "in order to guard against chronic misrule and to obviate the necessity of frequent and arbitrary interposition by the Supreme Government, it is expedient to avail ourselves of every opportunity of placing some reasonable limitations upon the personal power of the ruler or of the minister to whom the administration may be entrusted."

Popular control the only feasible remedy

Mysore has progressed and come into line with British standards of administration and in some respects is ahead of it at the present day; but it cannot be said that it is because of the complicated administrative machinery thus set up or of any consequent constitutional limitations which have been evolved in the government of its people. Shortly after this Rendition, the statesman who first became Dewan of Mysore, Mr. Ranga Charlu, made the first efforts to add to this mechanism the only really efficient portion of constitutional machinery in all countries that could in time provide a permanent guarantee for good government—consisting in the creation of an organ for the representation of the wishes of the people themselves in the government of their country. The Representative Assembly which was brought into existence by him was full of promise for the future of constitutional government in Native States and has been imitated elsewhere, in Travancore and Puducottah, and quite recently in Bikanir; but the successors of Dewan Ranga Charlu had not the genius to develop it as part of the constitutional fabric of the Native States and it has been allowed to continue as it started—a mere assembly of representatives to put forth grievances, with no power of direct and effective criticism and with little organisation to make their common opinions, wishes and wants felt upon the rulers or their ministers. The absence of efforts to develop this part of the experiment made in Mysore, along with that which arose with the Instrument of Transfer, has thrown back the administration into the position which by the very nature of the constitutional relation which the Ruler bears to the suzerain power, it is bound to assume. The Council which was established to influence the personal temperament of the sovereign and check the misuse of power on the part of the Minister as the chief executive head in Mysore, has not been the success which it was hoped it would become. The Council has no doubt been useful as an advisory body, but it has otherwise proved, as indeed it was bound to, a failure as an effective part of the constitutional machinery of the State. At the time when administrative arrangements were revised in Mysore in 1895 owing to the untimely death of the late Maharaja, the Government of India had to recognise the fact, as they put it, that owing to various causes the then existing Mysore Council failed as a corporate body to assume that position in the administration which it was intended to occupy. It was found that the Council had indeed been little better than a nonentity, and the necessity was therefore considered "of reverting to some approved form of the original model of an Executive Council with defined functions which should be something more than a body of councillors to be consulted at will and whose opinions carry no weight, without however weakening the legitimate authority of the Dewan and interfering with that vigour and promptitude which is necessary for the despatch of business". Arrangements were therefore made to constitute a Council of three members with the Dewan as President, the three nominated officers being no longer *ex-officio*, but whole-time members, appointed for a term and placed generally in charge of important departments of administration under the control of the Dewan. Rules of business were framed for the re-constituted Council and much ingenuity was exercised in strengthening the power of the Council without weakening the authority or responsibility of the Dewan.

Council Government not compatible with personal Rule

The subsequent experience of this abortive attempt at Council-Government in a Native State is fairly well-known to all who are conversant with the inner working of the administrative system in Mysore. Those who desired to temper the power and influence of an overpowerful or masterful Dewan committed the initial error of ignoring that the source of that power really lay in the absolute authority of the Ruler himself whose trusted minister he becomes. The inherent inconsistency between maintaining to the full the responsibility of a ruler who always acts through a chief minister of his choice, and giving responsible power to a Council which is to administer the affairs of the State, was not sufficiently realised when the experiment was started in Mysore. As a matter of fact, neither a Council, nor a Dewan for that matter, could wield power except to the extent delegated or the latitude allowed to them, by a ruler himself; and neither a Council nor a Dewan could exercise it, if a ruler choses to govern as well as to reign, himself—with or without the chief minister or council, though necessarily with some adviser or other belonging to his establishment or to that of the Resident. As one of the distinguished statesmen of Mysore seems to have observed truly, 'analogies drawn from the constitution of Council Governments in the Presidencies of British India are misleading when applied to a state of limited dimensions under a Native Sovereign with unlimited powers.'

Consequences of Personal Rule

It is this cardinal fact which makes it superfluous to consider in detail the mechanism of government in the Native States. Cynics and reactionaries no doubt might take advantage of this and harp upon retrograde standards of Native rule, noticeable here and there, but it cannot be gainsaid that whatever functions, executive or legislative, may be entrusted to Councils and assemblies, they go only so far and no further as the Native ruler may choose to allow them to exercise. This is why it is that, though legislative and executive councils may exist, the personal factor of the ruler himself in Native States is in standing contrast with the impersonal and bureaucratic system as established in British India. Since the ruler's power of law-making is unlimited, one essential constitutional principle, implied in the rule of Law, is of but limited application, and is found only in the more advanced States. The province of executive interference with the rights and liberties of subjects is also thus theoretically unlimited. At the same time, the possibilities of personal and sympathetic rule, accompanied by benevolent reforms and progressive measures tending to the amelioration of the people, are so much greater within the limits of such defined territories as Native States, where the veneration of the person of the ruler plays a no unimportant part in the attitude of the people towards the Government. It has thus happened that some most interesting experiments in administrative, educational and social reforms have started and have progressed in Native States—though not to the extent which one could wish for in the circumstances—which in British India the Government feels too alien and neutral to commit itself to. Similarly, the limitations which a subjection to the common suzerain imposes in the face of rapid administrative reforms in advance of British Indian standards, though by no means apparent, are none the less real and could not be ignored in judging of the comparative results of administration in British India and in the more progressive Native States. There are, besides, more concrete limitations and somes obstacles imposed in the way of Native States in respect of internal administration which it is neither necessary nor expedient to discuss in the present treatise.

Intervention of Suzerain power

The specific rights and functions which the British Indian Government exercises as the Suzerain power varies greatly from State to State, but certain rights are fairly common and well-established: The first of them is the right of intervention in cases of gross misrule; but what amounts to gross misrule has not been definitely laid down, though easily understood. There are also other rights of intervention expressly ascertained and reserved by treaties, while there is a further large field of intervention entirely undefined and bound by no treaties, but dependent on the general obligations which suzerainty and subjection are interpreted to involve. It varies with the personal temperaments and policies of the rulers and the Viceroys, as well as of the Residents and the Foreign Office officials from time to time. One important branch of this aspect of intervention or interference is that connected with the rights and obligations of European British subjects in Native States and the exercise of jurisdiction over them. The method by which intervention of this kind is effected is through the Residency and the Political Department and the pressure exercised through them has not unoften been found irresistible.

Principles of intervention—gross misrule and open hostility

We may, however, leave these political puzzles as beyond the range of students of institutions and confine ourselves to the constitutional theory on which the right of interference in the interests of good government is based. The depositions and annexations, the renditions and restorations in the past political history of India have evolved a few principles which Sir William Lee-Warner has dealt with in his authoritative book. The relationship of the Native Ruler is treated as one of subordination and acts of hostility on the part of the Native rulers towards the British Government are treated not as acts of war, but as acts of disloyalty or rebellion. In the proclamation connected with the deposition of Mulhar Rao Gaekwar in 1867, it was stated:—"Whereas to instigate such attempt to poison the Resident would be a high crime against Her Majesty the Queen and a breach of the condition of loyalty to the Crown under which Mulhar Rao Gaekwar is recognized as the ruler of the Baroda State, and moreover such an attempt would be an act of hostility against the British Government." In the later case which arose out of the troubles in Manipur in 1891, the rebellion of the chief was treated in an even more drastic form, though the Manipur State claimed theoretically to more independence than Baroda did. The principles established by the Manipur case were, according to Sir William Lee-Warner:—"The repudiation by the Government of India of the application of the international law to the protected States ; the assertion of the right to settle successions and to intervene in cases of rebellion against a chief ; the doctrine that resistance to Imperial orders constituted an act of rebellion ; and the right of the paramount power to inflict capital punishment on those who had put to death its agents while discharging the lawful duty imposed on them. In the exercise of their high prerogatives the Government of India in Manipur as in other protected States have exercised what they have claimed as the unquestioned right to remove by administrative order any person whose presence in the State may seem objectionable, and the rule was therefore laid down that 'any armed and violent resistence to the arrest of such person was an act of rebellion and can no more be justified by a plea of self-defence than the resistence to a police officer armed with a Magistrate's warrant in British India.' The trial of the Manipur chief was made by a special commission and the conviction and sentence of hanging were carried out by the executive orders of the Government of India."

Conclusion

It would thus be seen that this theoretically unlimited power of interference on the part of the Suzerain power, with the rights or liberties of subjects of Native States, coupled with the unlimited power on the part of the ruler himself as against his subjects, would seem to diminish appreciably the extent of that guarantee for the civil rights of citizens which is found to exist in British India and is enforceable at the instance of the Courts in the execution of that rule of Law which is a fundamental characteristic of British institutions. To some extent, the maintenance of the integrity of the Native States has involved the retention of a substantial power of government in the hands of the ruler whose arrangements for the exercise thereof are in consequence not subject to any regular and constitutional control exercised from above by the Suzerain power. At the same time, it has in consequence involved a power of arbitrary interference, under circumstances which might at any time be created, on the part of the Suzerain power. It is not our province here to discuss whether a political system so uncertain and undefined, needs to be replaced by more formal and constitutional arrangements, made and secured by a common Imperial Constitution which might begin, for instance, by the formation of an Imperial Council of States as was once seriously projected; nor is it of any practical importance to discuss whether the evolution of the entire political system established in India consisting of the provinces of British India and the Native States, could be consciously guided in the direction of the growth of an Imperial Constitution. It is sufficient to say that if progress is going to be achieved in the future, it will involve the exercise of statesmanship of a high order, and it is fruitless to attempt to forecast the future at this stage.

CHAPTER XVI

CONCLUSION

The Reforms and Parliamentary Government

The introductory study which has been made in the foregoing chapters hardly pretends either to exactness or thoroughness, but is only intended as a means of directing attention to the systematic study of the Indian Constitutional system, now being enlarged and developed on the lines of Western institutions. It would, of course, be the height of folly to imagine that the steps now taken lead, or are likely to lead, in the immediate future to Parliamentary Government, in the sense in which it is understood in Europe. Lord Morley, at any rate, disclaimed any such intention in the initiation of the reforms with which Lord Minto's and his name will for ever be associated. In the course of a speech, in 1909, in the House of Lords, he observed: "If I know that my days, either official or corporeal, were twenty times longer than they are likely to be, I shall be sorry to set out for the goal of a Parliamentary system in India. The Parliamentary system in India is not the goal to which I for one moment aspire." It seems, however, to be necessary, in view of misconceptions which have prevailed as to this statement of Lord Morley, to have a clear idea of what he has termed the 'Parliamentary system'. It is easy to show from Lord Morley's other speeches in regard to Indian Reforms that what he has said is not to be understood as meaning either that he disfavours the development of representative government or is against the gradual concession of self-governing powers to the people of India in their own country. The words 'Parliamentary system' seem to the present writer to have a special significance and are not merely equivalent to 'popular government'. Representative government, for instance, of one kind or another exists at this movement in most Western countries as well as in all countries which have come within the influence of European ideas. As one writer has put it: "There are few civilised States in which legislative power is not exercised by a wholly, or partially, elective body of a more or less popular or representative character." Representative Government, however, does not mean everywhere one and the same thing. It exhibits or tends to exhibit, according to him, "two different forms or types which are discriminated from each other by the differences of the relation between the executive and the legislature. Under the one form of representative government, the legislature or, it may be, the elective portion thereof, appoints and dismisses the executive which under these circumstances is, in general, chosen from among the members of the legislative body. Such an executive may appropriately be termed a 'Parliamentary executive.' Under the other form of representative government, the executive, whether it be an Emperor and his Ministers, or a President and his Cabinet, is not appointed by the legislature. Such an executive may appropriately be termed a 'non-parliamentary executive'."*

Lord Morley and John Bright

If Lord Morley's words are taken in the above significance, it is plain that a parliamentary system of government for India is a goal to which neither Lord Morley nor anybody who has given more than a superficial consideration to the Indian political problem can aspire in the present state of things. What probably was meant by Lord Morley in the above words—and what possibly

* Dicey's Law of the Constitution, pp. 411-412.

was in his mind when he initiated the reforms—as to the political tendencies which they may foster are explained by what he said in his Budget speech in January 1908, in the House of Commons. He then said :—

"Mr. Bright was, I believe, on the right track at the time in 1858 when the Government of India was transferred to the Crown ; but I do not think he was a man very much for Imperial Dumas. (Laughter.) He was not in favour universal sufferage—he was rather old-fashioned —(Laughter) but Mr. Bright's proposal was perfectly different from that of my honourable friend. Sir Henry Maine and others who had been concerned with Indian affairs came to the conclusion that Mr. Bright's idea was right—that to put one man, a Viceroy, assisted as he might be with an effective Executive Council in charge of such an area as India and its 300 millions of population, with all its different races, creeds, modes of thought, was to put on one man's shoulder a load which no man, of whatever powers, however gigantic they might be could be expected effectively to deal with (Hear, hear.) My hon'ble friend and others who sometimes favour me with criticisms in the same sense seem to suggest that I am a false brother, that I do not know what Liberalism is. I think I do, and I will even say that I do not think I have anything to learn of the principles or maxims, aye or of the practice of Liberal doctrines, even from my hon'ble friend. You have got to look at the whole mass of the great difficulties and perplexing problems connected with India from a commonsense plane and it is not commonsense, if I may say so without discourtesy, to talk of Imperial Dumas."

Now, if we refer to what John Bright has said as to the future political evolution of this country, we find the following :—

"The point which I wish to bring before the Committee and the Government is this, because it is on that I rely mainly, I think I may say, almost entirely, for any improvement in the future of India. I believe a great improvement may be made, and by a gradual process that will dislocate nothing. What you want is to decentralise your Government . . . . You will not make a single step towards the improvement of India unless you change your whole system of Government—unless you give to each presidency a Government with more independent powers than are now possessed. What would be thought if the whole of Europe were under one Governor who only knew the language of the Feejee Islands, and that his subordinates were like himself, only more intelligent than the inhabitants of the Feejee Islands are supposed to be . . . How long does England propose to govern India? Nobody answers that question, and nobody can answer it. Be it 50, or 100, or 500 years, does any man with the smallest glimmering of common-sense believe that so great a country, with its twenty different nations and its twenty languages, can ever be bound up and consolidated into one compact and enduring Empire? I believe such a thing to be utterly impossible. We must fail in the attempt if ever we make it, and we are bound to look into the future with reference to that point. The presidency of Madras, for instance, having its own Government, would in fifty years, become one compact state, and every part of the presidency would look to the city of Madras as its capital, and to the Government of Madras as its ruling power. If that were to go on for a century or more there would be five or six Presidencies of India built up into so many compact States; and if at any future period the sovereignty of England should be withdrawn, we should leave so many presidencies built up and firmly compacted together, each able to support its own independence and its own Government; and we should be able to say we had not left the country a prey to that anarchy and discord which I believe to be inevitable if we insist on holding those vast territories with the idea of building them up into one great empire."

Attempt to define ultimate goal. The Delhi Despatch

Whether or no Lord Morley subscribes to the whole of the position taken by John Bright on the question, it is difficult to say, and if Lord Morley with his profound study and insight into all problems of political progress was unable to express himself more clearly on the goal of India's future political progress, it need not be wondered at that others who have been guiding the destinies of this country since his retirement from the India Office, have failed in the attempt to pierce further into her future political evolution than what the immediate requirements of the situation might warrant. Events and policies which have followed the Reform Scheme of Lord Morley in India have raised in some form or other the question of the future basis of political advancement in India, but Lord Morley's successor at the India Office, Lord Crewe, and Mr. Montagu who has been the Under-Secretary for India both under Lord Morley and Lord Crewe, with the Government of India under His Excellency Lord Hardinge as Viceroy, have also found themselves unable to lay down any exact political theories or practical propositions sufficient to determine the whole future course of the political destinies of this country. To the student of political science, the phenomenon is very familiar that theories always follow facts with a view to justify them, and such theories become as varied as the emergencies of their apologists demand. The enunciation of the goal of Indian aspirations as one of provincial autonomy, by the Government of India * is therefore as valueless for forming a correct estimate of future political progress in India as its subsequent repudiation by Lord Crewe, or its reaffirmation by Mr. Montagu as Under-Secretary. If the disputes which have arisen over the proper construction of paragraph 3 of the Government of India's Delhi Despatch did not in fact occur, it might perhaps have been a document of some constitutional value, but it would even then have been limited only to its being the record of a considered opinion by qualified and experienced administrators as to the basis on which they adopted the course of policy which has been justified thereby. As it is, its value is now considerably less owing to the course which subsequent controversy has taken.

* This was in the following words:—"It is certain that in the course of time, the just demands of Indians for a large share in the Government of the country will have to be satisfied, and the question will be how this devolution of power can be conceded without impairing the supreme authority of the Governor-General in Council. The only possible solution of the difficulty would appear to be, gradually to give the provinces a larger measure of self-government, until at last India would consist of a number of administrations autonomous in all provincial affairs, with the Government of India above them all and possessing power to interfere in case of misgovernment, ordinarily restricting their function to matters of imperial concern."

Colonial parallels and Indian institutions

Dealing this paragraph 3 of the Despatch and the discussions thereon as they really are, namely, as an attempt to discuss the future and to get a rather long peep into it, it is significant to note how prepossessions derived from one set of experiences intrude themselves upon others in the discussion of political problems by administrators. In the various speeches which Lord Crewe made in the House of Lords declaring what in his view was meant by 'provincial autonomy', students of political institutions of the different parts of the British Empire will be struck by the way in which the traditions and notions of the Colonial Office where Lord Crewe was Secretary for a long time, have unconsciously influenced and perhaps assisted or affected his perception of the political problems confronting India. In the British Colonial Office, there were only two conceptions of Imperial institutions, under which all Colonies ranged themselves. Colonies, broadly speaking, either govern themselves or are governed by the mother-country through various agencies *i. e.* they are either dependencies—under which term are also included the Crown Colonies,—or they are self-governing Colonies. The natural, though by no means necessary inference which this gives rise to in the minds of those acquainted only with Colonial administration, is that a Colony can be governed by its own people or it can be governed by the mother-country, but that, under ordinary conditions, it cannot be governed successfully by a combination of the two. The history of the Colonial Empire of England to some extent also tends to support this narrow view and sharp distinction, for, while we find that in most of the self-governing Colonies progress has tended towards more and more complete control of their own affairs, in the Crown Colonies which could not advance in that direction for some reason or other, it has tended towards the loss of the remnants of self-government that they possess. Jamaica and Malta may be cited as illustrations of this tendency.

Imperial Problem and colonial self-government

Another Colonial prepossession which may have influenced Lord Crewe's ideas as to Indian political institutions is the one connected with Imperialism and schemes of Imperial Federation. Now schemes of Imperial Federation, it need hardly be said, did curiously for a long time leave India out of account altogether, and comprised only more or less the self-governing Colonies of the Empire. Dependencies that do not govern themselves, it has been argued, will not be conceded the right to govern others though they might be compelled to join them and on the latters' own conditions. Problems connected with Imperial questions, therefore, have usually been solved by treating India and the Crown Colonies as being represented by England, which must continue to be responsible not only for the good government of the dependencies, but also for the enforcement of their obligations towards the Empire. Moreover, to Liberal politicians—perhaps of the older school only and those who with them believe, that cut and dry schemes of Imperial Federation have no place in the political development of the British Empire—the idea of granting responsible government is one which in these days appears a more thorny question than it appeared to be to the robust and optimistic Radicals of an earlier date. The grant of responsible government to the self-governing Colonies was probably not merely the only course that could have been pursued by English statesmen, Liberal or Conservative at the time, but those Liberal politicians who looked with no dismay at the relinquishment of the control of the mother-country over the Colonies, did in fact contemplate with equanimity the ultimate and complete separation of these Colonies from the mother-country. The modern growth of the Imperial sentiment has, however, rendered this view out of fashion. At any rate, one result of the grant of responsible government to the self-governing Colonies on the old notions has been that it has placed the Colonies in a distinctly advantageous position in which they could not be induced to part with their rights nor persuaded to undertake obligations imposed on them against their consent or interests. A federation of the British Empire, therefore, if it has to be accomplised, could only proceed from the voluntary consent of the Colonies concerned, and as the inducements to it are lesser for them than for the mother-country, the prospect of a closer union has become much more difficult than if complete self-government had not been granted, but some system of devolution had been adopted. In Lord Crewe's view, apparently, the basis of England's Colonial Empire, such as it is according to the view of Liberals, rests on mere sentiment which is at bottom the feeling of a common race, common feelings, common language and common institutions —coupled perhaps with a lively appreciation of the assistance rendered by the mother-country in undertaking the duties of Imperial defence and otherwise.

Imperial organisation and Indian self-government

The absense of these ties as between India and England perhaps makes Lord Crewe sceptical of the prospects of 'a complete form of self-government for India within the British Empire,' as he has put it. In his speech of the 21st July in the House of Lords he said :—

"I repeat categorically that there is nothing whatever in the teachings of history so far as I know them or in the present conditions of the world so far as I understand them, which makes such a dream even remotely probable. We have tried the experiment of a world-wide Empire with members of our own race and all the chapters in that experiment have not been felicitous. One broke down in 1776 when the American Colonies declared their independence. Since then, we have learnt some widsom. We have succeeded in winning into the Empire, the French of Canada, and the Dutch of South Africa and now in an Empire which includes both these different European races, we are trying to face and to solve the tremendous problems of Imperial defence and of giving to the component parts of the Empire some share in the shaping of Imperial policy. Can any body conceive any similar solution of the Imperial problem for hundreds of millions of men altogether different in race from our own ? Is it conceivable that at any time an Indian Empire could exist on the lines, say of Australia and New Zealand with no British officials, no British troops and no tie of creed or blood which takes the places of those material bonds ?"

Discussions as to future goal futile

Such a feeling is no doubt natural to one who is appalled by the perplexities of a problem which he unnecessarily took the trouble to solve, but those who would put aside self-government for India as a dream have not certainly seen the end of their troubles by refusing to accept it as a solution. The question then still remains, what *is* the solution—if you are going to solve it ? If it is inconceivable that an Indian Empire could exist on the lines of Australia or New Zealand, it is still more inconceivable—and it has been declared to be so for more than three-quarters of a century since the days of Lord Macaulay repeatedly by political thinkers and sober students—that an Empire consisting of "hundreds of millions of men altogether different in race from our own," could not continue to be governed by a bureaucratic form of government on the part of an alien ruling race, however gifted. "How long does England propose to govern India ?", asked John Bright, and Lord Crewe has certainly failed to answer it. The truth is that the statesmen and administrators of British India in the past have not worried themselves about ultimate things in the government of this country. It is a peculiarly British characteristic to deal with the needs of the hour and the problems of the immediate present, rather than with the theories or ideals of the future, and though theorists may describe it as a policy of drift, those who believe in the reality of the Empire of Great Britain in the world, would certainly declare it to be the wiser and more successful course to pursue than any attempt to reconstruct or reform political institutions on *a priori* theories. Lord Courtney—himself a good student of the British Constitution, of which the Indian Constitution forms but a part,—truly observed in the course of the debate above referred to that it was "surely unwise in view of what is going on in the East, to attempt to put a limitation to the developments which might occur in the future. It was enough for the present to persevere with what has been the wise policy for some time past and to leave the future on the knees of the Gods." It would be equally wise for students of political institutions in India to confine themselves to forming a correct estimate of the course in which the past and present policy of those who control the affairs of this course has tended, instead of speculating on the tendencies which future developments might exhibit or of laying down the lines of future constitution-making.

In the meanwhile, it is necessary to remember that changes in the mere machinery of Government are but one part, though an important part, of the process which this country has to undergo and is likely to undergo in its political evolution. For the present it has still to be remembered that there are a few essential characteristics impressed on the constitutional arrangements of this country which it will be futile to ignore. The British Government in India is what is generally spoken of as a dependency. A dependency has been defined by Sir George Cornwall Lewis as "a part of an independent political community which is immediately subject to a subordinate Government." The test of a dependency is that it is substantially governed by the dominant country, and a self-governing dependency is a contradiction in terms. Do the Reforms, which have from time to time been made in the constitutional machinery in India, tend towards reducing this "dependent character" of the Indian Constitution? To answer this, it is necessary to look at two aspects of the question. We have to look at the character of the agency of administration and we have next to look at the character of the institutions which are being developed in the process of political re-construction. Perhaps the most important step taken for over half a century as regards the former aspect, viz., that implied in India being a dependency, governed by a dominant foreign agency, has already been taken by Lord Morley in the highest ranks of the public service. Where what has been termed the essentially English element of administration was so

Dependency and Representative Government

long deemed necessary to be preserved, he has introduced changes of utmost far-reaching character. The appointment of Indian Members to the Council of the Secretary of State, to the Executive Councils of the Viceroy and the Governors and Lieutenant-Governors of Provinces and the appointment of an Indian to the Privy Council in its Judicial Committee—these seem to us likely to go a great way towards rendering the differentiation between the ruling and the ruled elements, much less acute than ever before.

Agency and methods of Indian Government

It may, however, be deemed immaterial, from the point of view of constitutional development, what the agency of administration is, if the methods of government continue bureaucratic. The essence of bureaucracy is centralisation, and decentralisation, in its widest sense, necessarily implies co-operation of the representatives of the people, not merely in legislation, but in the actual working of administration. What the outcome of the recommendations in this behalf of the Decentralisation Commission in India will be, cannot yet be stated with any definiteness at present. But the whole feature of the recent reforms may be summed up in (1) the immediate step forward of directly associating Indians in the work of every-day administration, and (2) the attempt to decentralise administrative machinery so as to make Provincial and Local Administrations, if not autonomous, at least self-contained, with a strong infusion of the popular element—(3) based upon what Lord Morley deems to be the essential need of enforcing the central control of the Government of India as the responsible representative of His Majesty's Government and the House of Commons in England. These seem to the present writer the three limitations within which constitutional progress will for some time to come have to advance.

Progress in the future

Whatever the results might be of the new policy, the duty of the Government and the people in the immediate future is clear enough and it cannot be put better than in the words of one of the historic figures who fought in the cause of freedom and of order so early as the beginning of the Civil War in England—John Pym. "The best form of Government," he said, "is that which doth actuate and dispose every part and member of a state to the common good; for as those parts give strength and ornament to the whole, so they receive from it again strength and protection in their several stations and degrees. If, instead of concord and interchange of support, one part seeks to uphold an old form of Government, and the other part a new, they will miserably consume one another. Histories are full of the calamities of entire states and nations in such cases. It is, nevertheless, equally true that time must needs bring about some alterations. . . . Therefore have those commonwealths been ever the most durable and perpetual which have often reformed and recomposed themselves according to their first institution and ordinance. By this means they repair the breaches, and counterwork the natural effects of time."

The true disposition to further the common good in its highest form, so necessary for future progress in India, can only be attained by the rulers of the land ceasing to take narrow views of mere administrative "thoroughness," and by taking and imposing on the administration, broad views. What the people, on the other hand, need at this moment is sound organisation and sage counsel and leadership. They want leaders who possess, in the words of Lord Morley, "the double gift of being at once practical and elevated, masters of tactics and organising arts, and yet the inspirers of solid and lofty principles."

APPENDIX

A—CONSTITUTIONAL DOCUMENTS

I

THE EAST INDIA COMPANY ACT, 1772 (1).

(13, Geo. 3, C. 63).

AN ACT FOR ESTABLISHING CERTAIN REGULATIONS FOR THE BETTER MANAGEMENT OF THE AFFAIRS OF THE EAST INDIA COMPANY, AS WELL IN INDIA AS IN EUROPE.

[*Preamble and Ss. 1-6, rep. as to U.K. 50 and 51 Vict., c. 59* (*S.L.R.*) *Omitted as being obsolete and inapplicable to India*].

A Governor-General and four Counsellors to be appointed

7. And for the better management of the said united Company's affairs in India, be it further enacted by the authority aforesaid, that for the government of the Presidency of Fort William in Bengal there shall be appointed a Governor-General and four Counsellors;

In whom the whole civil and military Government of Bengal, Bihar, and Orissa shall be vested

and that the whole civil and military government of the said Presidency, and also the ordering, management, and government of all the territorial acquisitions and revenues in the kingdoms of Bengal, Bihar and Orissa shall, during such time as the territorial acquisitions and revenues shall remain in the possession of the said united Company, be and are hereby vested in the said Governor-General and Council of the said Presidency of Fort William in Bengal, in like manner to all intents and purposes whatsoever as the same now are or at any time heretofore might have been exercised by the President and Council or Select Committee in the said kingdom (2).

---

(1) This Act is commonly known as "the Regulating Act." For historical notes, see Ilbert's *Government of India*, pp. 43 et. seq, and 278-82.

(2). Modified by 33 Geo. 3, C. 52, S. 43.

8. And * * * * in all cases whatsoever wherein any difference of opinion shall arise upon any question proposed in any consultation, the said Governor-General and Council shall be bound and concluded by the opinion and decision of the major part of those present: and if it shall happen that, by the death or removal, or by the absence of any of the Members of the said Council, such Governor-General and Council shall happen to be equally divided, then and in every such case, the said Governor-General, or, in his absence, the eldest counsellor present, shall have a casting vote, and his opinion shall be decisive and conclusive.

In case of difference of opinion, the decision of the major part to be conclusive; and if votes equal, the Governor or eldest Counsellor to have a casting voice

9. The said Governor-General and Council or the major part of them, shall have, and they are hereby authorised to have power of superintending and controlling the government and management of the Presidencies of Madras, Bombay and Bencoolen respectively, so far and in so much as that it shall not be lawful for any President and Council of Madras, Bombay or Bencoolen for the time being to make any orders for commencing hostilities, or declaring or making war, against any Indian Princes or Powers, or for negotiating or concluding any treaty of peace or other treaty, with any such Indian Princes or Powers, without the consent and approbation of the said Governor-General and Council first had and obtained, except in such cases of imminent necessity as would render it dangerous to postpone such hostilities or treaties until the orders from the Governor-General and Council might arrive, and except in such cases where the said Presidents and Councils respectively shall have received special orders from the said united Company ; (1)

and any President and Council of Madras, Bombay or Bencoolen who shall offend in any of the cases aforesaid shall be liable to be suspended from his or their office by the order of the said Governor-General and Council ;

and every President and Council of Madras, Bombay and Bencoolen for the time being shall and they are hereby respectively directed and required to pay due obedience to such orders as they shall receive touching the premises from the said Governor-General and Council for the time being * * * * * (2) ;

---

(1) Apparently superseded by 3 and 4 Will., 4, C. 85 but not repealed.

(2). Words repealed by 55 and 56. Vict., C. 19 (S. L. R.) have been omitted.

and the said Governor-General and Council for the time being shall and they are hereby directed and required to pay due obedience to all such orders as they shall receive from the Court of Directors of the said united Company, and to correspond from time to time, and constantly and diligently transmit to the said Court an exact particular of all advices or intelligence, and of all transactions and matters whatsoever, that shall come to their knowledge relating to the government, commerce, revenues or interest of the said united Company;

10. And * * * * Warren Hastings, Esquire, shall be the first Governor-General, and Lieutenant-General John Clavering, the Honorable George Monson, Richard Barwell, Esquire, and Phillip Francis, Esquire, shall be the four first Counsellors ;

and they and each of them shall hold and continue in his and their respective offices for and during the term of five years from the time of their arrival at Fort William in Bengal, and taking upon them the government of the said Presidency, * * * * * (1) ;

and from and after the expiration of the said term of five years, the power of nominating and removing the succeeding Governor-General and Council shall be vested in the Directors of the said united Company. (2)

11. [Rep. as to U. K. 50 and 51. Vict. C. 59. (S. L. R.) omitted as being spent.]

12. [Rep. 55 and 56. Vict. C. 19 (S. L. R.)].

13. And whereas his late Majesty King George the Second did by his letters patent, bearing date at Westminster this eighth day of January, in the twenty-sixth year of his reign, grant into the said united Company of the merchants of England trading to the East Indies his royal charter, thereby amongst other things, constituting and establishing Courts of civil, criminal and ecclesiastical jurisdiction at the said united Company's respective settlements at Madras-patnam, Bombay on the Island of Bombay, and Fort William in Bengal, which said charter does not sufficiently provide for the due administration of justice in such manner as the state and condition of the Company's presidency of Fort William in Bengal, so long as the said Company

---

(1). Words repealed by 55 and 56. Vict., C. 19 (S. L. R.) have been omitted.

(2). Seems spent, but is probably the origin of the five years' rule which is still observed in practice.

shall continue in possession of the territorial acquisitions before mentioned, do and must require.

Be it therefore enacted by the authority aforesaid, that it shall and may be lawful for His Majesty, by charter or letters patent under the great seal of Great Britain, to erect and establish a Supreme Court of Judicature at Fort William aforesaid to consist of a Chief Justice and three other Judges, being Barristers in England or Ireland, of not less than five years' standing to be named from time to time by His Majesty, his heirs and successors;

His Majesty may, by charter or letters patent, establish a Supreme Court of Judicature at Fort William, to consist of a Chief Justice and three other Judges

which said Supreme Court of Judicature shall have, and the same Court is hereby declared to have full power and authority to exercise and perform all civil, criminal, admiralty and ecclesiastical jurisdiction and to appoint such clerks and other ministerial officers of the said Court, with such reasonable salaries, as shall be approved of by the said Governor-General and Council; and to form and establish such rules of practice, and such rules for the process of the said Court, and to do all such other things as shall be found necessary for the administration of justice and the due execution of all or any of the powers which, by the said charter, shall or may be granted and committed to the said Court; and also shall be at all times a Court of record, and shall be a Court of oyer and terminer and gaol delivery, in and for the said town of Calcutta and factory of Fort William in Bengal aforesaid, and the limits thereof, and the factories subordinate thereto.

14. Provided nevertheless that the said new charter which His Majesty is hereinbefore impowered to grant and the jurisdiction, powers, and authorities to be thereby established, shall and may extend to all British subjects who shall reside in the kingdoms or provinces of Bengal, Bihar and Orissa, or any of them, under the protection of the said united Company and the same charter shall be competent and effectual;

Extent of the jurisdiction and powers of His Majesty's charter;

and the Supreme Court of Judicature therein and thereby to be established shall have full power and authority to hear and determine all complaints against any of His Majesty's subjects for any crimes, misdemeanours or oppressions, committed or to be committed; and also to entertain, hear and determine any suits or actions whatsoever against

and the Supreme Court of Judicature

any of His Majesty's subjects in Bengal, Bihar and Orissa, and any suit, action or complaint against any person who shall, at the time where such debt or cause of action or complaint shall have arisen, have been employed by or shall then have been, directly or indirectly, in the service of the said united Company, or of any of His Majesty's subjects.

Indictments and informations against Governor-General, etc.

15. Provided also, that the said Court shall not be competent to hear, try or determine any indictment or information against the said Governor-General, or any of the said Council for the time being, for any offence (not being treason or felony) which such Governor-General or any of the said Council shall or may be charged with having committed in Bengal, Bihar and Orissa.

16. [Rep. 55 and 56 Vict. C. 19 and as to B. I. by XIV of 1870 S. 1 and Sch.]

The Governor-General, Council, etc., not subject to be arrested or imprisoned

17. And it is hereby enacted and provided, that nothing in this Act shall extend to subject the person of the Governor-General or of any of the said Council or Chief Justice and Judges respectively for the time being to be arrested or imprisoned upon any action, suit or proceeding in the said Court.

18 to 22. [repealed].

The Governor-General or Council, etc., shall not accept of any present

23. And * * * * no Governor-General, or any of the Council of the said united Company's Presidency of Fort William in Bengal or any Chief Justice or any of the Judges of the Supreme Court of Judicature at Fort William aforesaid, shall, directly or indirectly, by themselves or by any other person or persons for his or their use or on his or their behalf accept, receive or take, of or from any person or persons in any manner or on any account whatsoever, any present, gift, donation, gratuity, or reward pecuniary or otherwise, or any promise or engagement for any present gift, donation, gratuity or reward ; * * * *

24. omitted.

25. omitted.

26 to 29. [Rep. 24 Geo. 3, Sess. 2 c. 25, S. 47 and 33 Geo. 3 c. 52, S 46.]

30 and 31. [Rep.]

32. [Rep.].

33. [Rep.].

34 and 35. [Rep.].

36. [Rep.].

Governor-General and Council to transmit copies of their rules to one of the Secretaries of State

37. Provided always * * * * that the said Governor-General and Council shall, and they are hereby required, from time to time, to transmit copies of all such rules, ordinances, and regulations as they shall make and issue to one of His Majesty's principal Secretaries of State for the time being, and that it shall and may be lawful to and for His Majesty, his heir and successors, from time to time, as they shall think necessary, to signify to the said Company, under his or their sign manual, his or their disapprobation and disallowance of all such rules, ordinances and regulations ;

and that from and immediately after the time that such disapprobation shall be duly registered and published in the said Supreme Court of Judicature at Fort William in Bengal all such rules, ordinances, and regulations shall be null and void ;

but in case His Majesty, his heirs and successors, shall not, within the space of two years from the making of such rules, ordinances and regulations, signify his or their disapprobation or disallowance thereof as aforesaid, that then, and in that case, all such rules, ordinances and regulations shall be valid and effectual and have full force. (1)

38. [Rep.]

If the Governor-General, President, etc., commit offence the same may be tried and determined in the Court of King's Bench

39. And * * * if any Governor-General, President or Governor or Council of any of the said Company's principal or other settlements in India, or the Chief Justice or any of the Judges of the said Supreme Court of Judicature to be by the said New Charter established or of any other Court in any of the said united Company's settlements, or any other person, or persons who now are or heretofore have been employed by or in the capacity or who have or claim or heretofore have had or claimed any power or authority or jurisdiction by or from the said united Company, or any of His Majesty's subjects residing in India shall commit any offence against

(1) Sec. 37 ought perhaps to have been repealed along with S. 36. Apparently superseded by 24 and 25 Vict. 67, S. 21.

this Act or shall have been or shall be guilty of any crime, misdemeanour or offence committed against any of His Majesty's subjects or any of the inhabitants of India, within their respective jurisdiction all such crimes, offences and misdemeanours may be respectively enquired of, heard, tried and determined in His Majesty's Court of King's Bench;

and all such persons so offending, and not having been before tried for the same offence in India shall on connection, in any such case as is not otherwise specially provided for by this Act be liable to such fine or corporal punishment as the said Court shall think fit, and moreover shall be liable, at the discretion of the said Court to be adjudged to be incapable of serving the said united Company in an office, civil or military ;

and all and every such crimes, offence and misdemeanours as aforesaid may be alleged to be committed, and may be laid, enquired of and tried, in the county of Middlesex.

Manner of procedure in cases of indictments and informations laid, in the King's Bench

40 (1). And whereas the provision made by former laws for the hearing and determining in England offences committed in India have been found ineffectual by reason of the difficulty of proving in this Kingdom matters done there;

Be it further enacted by the authority aforesaid, that in all cases of indictments or informations laid or exhibited in the said Court of King's Bench for misdemeanours or offences committed in India, it shall and may be lawful for His Majesty's said Court upon motion to be made on behalf of the prosecutor or the defendant or defendants ; to award a unit or units of mandamus, requiring the Chief Justice and Judges of the said Supreme Court of Judicature for the time being, or the Judges of the Major's Court at Madras, Bombay or Bencoolen, as the case may require, who are hereby respectively authorised and require accordingly, to hold a Court with all convenient speed for the examination of witnesses, and of the agents or Counsel of all or any of the parties respectively, and to adjourn from time to time as occasion may require ; any such examination as aforesaid shall be then and there openly and publicly taken *viva voce* in the said Court, upon the respective oaths of witnesses and the oaths of skilful interpreters, administered according to the forms of their several religions ; and shall, by some sworn officer of such Court, be reduced into one or more writing or

1. Ss. 40-45 extended by 22 and 23 Vict., C. 21, S. 16, See Chitty's Statutes. Tit. Evidence; Taylor on Evidence, Ed. 9, § 500.

writings on parchment in case any duplicate or duplicates should be required by or in behalf of the any parties interested, and shall be sent to His Majesty, in his Court of King's Bench closed up and under the seals of two or more of the Judges of the said Court and one or more of the said Judges shall deliver the same to the agent or agents of the party or parties requiring the same ; which said agent or agents (or in case of his or their death, the person into whose hands the same shall come), shall deliver the same from the hands of one or more of the Judges of such Court in India (or, if such agent be dead, in what manner the same came into his hands) ; and that the same has not been opened or altered since he so received it (which said oath such clerk in Court is hereby authorised and required to administer) ;

and such depositions, being duly taken and returned according to the true intent and meaning of this Act, shall be allowed and read, and shall be deemed as good and competent evidence as if such crimes or misdemeanours as aforesaid in His Majesty's said Court of King's Bench any law or usage to the contrary notwithstanding; and all parties concerned shall be entitled to take copies of such depositions at their own costs and charges.

Offences against this Act committed by the Chief Justices or Judges to be determined by the Court of King's Bench

41. And.........in case the said Chief Justice or Judges of the said Supreme Court of Judicature, or any of them for the time being, shall commit any offence against this Act, or be guilty of any corrupt practice or other crime, offence, or misdemeanour in the execution of their respective offices, it shall and may be lawful for His Majesty's said Court of King's Bench in England, upon an information or indictment laid or exhibited in the said Court for such crime, offence or misdemeanour, upon motion to be made in the said Court to award such writ or writs of mandamus as aforesaid, requiring the Governor-General and Council of the said United Company's Settlement at Fort William aforesaid, who are hereby respectively authorised and required accordingly, to assemble themselves in a reasonable time, and to cause all such proceedings to be had and made as are hereinbefore respectively directed and prescribed concerning the examination of witnesses ; and such examination so taken shall be returned and proceeded upon in the same manner in all respects as if the several directions hereinbefore prescribed and enacted in that behalf were again repeated.

* * * *

II

THE GOVERNMENT OF INDIA ACT, 1833 (1)

(3 & 4, Will, 4, C. 85)

AN ACT FOR EFFECTING AN ARRANGEMENT WITH THE EAST INDIA COMPANY AND FOR THE BETTER GOVERNMENT OF HIS MAJESTY'S INDIAN TERRITORIES, TILL THE THIRTIETH DAY OF APRIL ONE THOUSAND EIGHT HUNDRED AND FIFTY-FOUR.

[28TH AUGUST, 1833.]

[*Preamble recites 53 Geo. 3, C. 155, and the consent of the "United Company of Merchants of England trading to the East Indies" to place their rights and property at the disposal of Parliament.*]

The British territories in India to remain under the government of the Company till 30th April, 1854

1. The territorial acquisitions and revenues mentioned or referred to in the said Act at the fifty-third year of his late Majesty King George the third, together with the port and island of Bombay and all other territories now in the possession and under the government of the said Company except the island of St. Helena, shall remain and continue under such management until the thirtieth day of April one thousand eight hundred and fifty-four;

Real and personal property of the Company to be held in trust for the crown, for the service of India

and all the lands and hereditaments, revenues, rents, and profits of the said Company, and all the stores, merchandize, chattels, monies, debts, and real and personal estate whatsoever, except the said island of St. Helena and the stores and property thereon hereinafter mentioned, subject to the debts and liabilites now affecting the same respectively, and the benefits of all contracts, covenants, and engagements. and all rights to fines, penalties, and forfeitures, and other emoluments whatsoever, which the said Company shall be seized or possessed of or entitled unto on the said twenty-second day of April one thousand eight hundred and thirty four, shall remain and be vested in, and be held, received, and exercised respectively accordingly to the nature and quality, estate and interest, of and in the name respectively by the said Company, in trust for His

(1). The provisions of this statute except Ss. 81 to 86 may not be affected by legislation in India—See 24, 25 and Vict., C. 7. S. and 3 & 33 Vict., C. 98, S. 3. For digest and notes—See Ilbert's Government of India, pp. 299-355.

Majesty, his heirs and successors, for the service of the government of India, discharged of all claims of the said Company to any profit or advantage therefrom to their own use, except the dividend on their capital stock secured to them as hereinafter is mentioned, subject to such powers and authorities for the superintendence, direction and control over the acts, operations, and concerns of the said Company as have been already made or provided by any Act or Acts of Parliament in that behalf, or are made or provided by this Act.

All privileges, powers etc., granted by 53 Geo., 3, C. 155, for the term thereby limited;

2. * * * * all and singular the privileges, franchises, abilities, capacities, powers, authorities, whether military or civil, rights, remedies, methods of suits, penalties, forfeitures, disabilities, provisions, matters, and things whatsoever granted to or continued in the said United Company by the said Act of the fifty third year of King George the Third for and during the term limited by the said Act and all other enactments, provisions, matters and things contained in the said Act, or in any other Act or Acts whatsoever which are limited or may be construed to be limited, to continue for and during the term granted to the said Company by the said Act of the fifty third year of King George the Third, so far as the same or any of them are in force, and not repealed by or repugnant to the enactments hereinafter contained, and all powers of alienation and disposition, rights, franchises, and immunities, which the said United Company now have, shall continue and be in force, and may be exercised and enjoyed, as against all persons whomsoever, subject to the superintendence, direction and control mentioned until the thirtieth day of April one thousand eight hundred and fifty-four.

as also all rights and immunities of the Company, to be in force till 30th April, 1854 subject to control

3 to 18. [Rep. 37 and 38. Vict., C. 35 (S. L. R.)].

19 [Rep. 53 and 54 Vict., C. 33 (S. L. R.)].

20 to 24. [Rep. 38 Vict., C. 35 (S. L. R.)].

The Board of Commissioners to control all acts of the Company concerning India etc.

25...............the said Board shall have and be invested with full power and authority to superintend, direct and control all acts, operations, and concerns of the said Company, which in any wise relate to or concern the government or revenue of the said territories or the property hereby vested in the said Company in trust as aforesaid and all grants of salaries, gratuities and allowances and all other payments and charges whatever out of or upon the said revenues and property respectively except as hereinafter is mentioned,

26 to 35. [Rep. 37 and 38 Vict., C. 35 (S. L. R.)].

* * * *

III

THE GOVERNMENT OF INDIA ACT, 1858 (1)

(21 and 22 Vict., C. 106)

AN ACT FOR THE BETTER GOVERNMENT OF INDIA.

[2ND AUGUST, 1858].

16 and 17 Vict., C. 95

Whereas by the Government of India Act, 1858, the territories in the possession and under the Government of the East India Company were continued under such Government, in trust for Her Majesty, until Parliament should otherwise provide, subject to the provisions of that Act, and of other Acts of Parliament, and the property and rights in the said Act referred to are held by the said Company in trust for Her Majesty for the purpose of the said Government :

And whereas it is expedient that the said territories should be governed by and in the name of Her Majesty * * * *

TRANSFER OF THE GOVERNMENT OF INDIA TO HER MAJESTY.

Territories under the Government of the East IndiaCompany to be vested in Her Majesty

1. The Government of the territories now in the possession or under the Government of the East India Company and all powers in relation to Government vested in, or exercised by, the said Company in trust for Her Majesty, shall cease to be vested in, or exercised by, the said Company ;

and powers to be exercised in her name

And all territories in the possession or under the Government of the said Company, and all rights vested in or which if this Act had not been passed might have been exercised by the said Company in relation to any territories, shall become vested in Her Majesty, and be exercised in her name ;

---

(1). The provisions of this Statute cannot be affected by legislation in India—secs. 24 and 25, Vict., c. 67, s. 22. For digest and notes, see Ilbert's Government of India, pp. 309-313.

And for the purposes of this Act India shall mean the territories vested in Her Majesty as aforesaid, and all territories which may become vested in Her Majesty by virtue of any such rights as aforesaid.

India to be governed by and in the name of Her Majesty, &c.

2. India shall be governed by and in the name of Her Majesty ;

And all rights in relation to any territories which might have been exercised by the said Company if this Act had not been passed shall and may be exercised by and in the name of Her Majesty as rights incidental to the Government of India ;

And all the territorial and other revenues of or arising in India and all tributes and other payments in respect of any territories which would have been receivable by or in the name of the said Company if this Act had not been passed shall be received for and in the name of Her Majesty, and shall be applied and disposed of for the purposes of the Government of India alone, subject to the provisions of this Act.

Secretary of State to exercise powers now exercised by the Company, &c.

Save as herein otherwise provided, one of Her Majesty's Principal Secretaries of State shall have and perform all such or the like powers and duties in anywise relating to the Government or revenues of India, and all such or the like powers over all officers appointed or continued under this Act, as might or should have been exercised or performed by the East India Company, or by the Court of Directors or Court or Proprietors of the said Company, either alone or by the direction or with the sanction or approbation of the Commissioners for the Affairs of India in relation to such government or revenues, and the officers and servants of the said Company respectively, and all such powers as might have been exercised by the said Commissioners alone ;

Counter-signing of warrants, 17 & 18 Vict., C. 77

And any warrant or writing under Her Majesty's Royal Sign Manual which by the Government of India Act. 1854 (1), or otherwise, is required to be countersigned by the President of the Commissioners for the Affairs of India, shall in lieu of being so

(1). S. 1 of the Government of India Act, 1854 (17 & 18 Vict. C. 77) which contained the provision referred to, was repealed as to U. K. by 55 & 56 Vict., C. 19 (S. L. R.).

countersigned be countersigned by one of Her Majesty's Principal Secretaries of State. * * *

4. ° ° ° ° any four of Her Majesty's Principal Secretaries of State for the time being, and any four of the Under Secretaries for the time being to Her Majesty's Principal Secretaries of State, may sit and vote as members of the House of Commons;

Four Principal and four Under Secretaries of State may sit as members in the House of Commons

But not more than four such Principal Secretaries and not more than four such Under Secretaries shall sit as members of the House of Commons at the same time.

5. [Rep. 41 and 42 Vict., C. 79 (S. L. R.)](1)

6. In case Her Majesty be pleased to appoint a fifth Principal Secretary of State, there shall be paid out of the revenues of India to such Principal Secretary of State and to his Under Secretaries respectively the like yearly salaries as may for the time being be paid to any other of such Secretaries of State and his Under Secretaries respectively.

Salaries of one Secretary of State and his Under Secretaries to be paid out of the revenues of India

COUNCIL OF INDIA

7. For purposes of this Act a Council shall be established, to consist of fifteen members, and to be styled the Council of India;

Council of India established.

And henceforth the Council of India now bearing that name shall be styled the Council of the Governor-General of India.

8. [Rep. 41 & 42 Vict., C. 79 (S. L. R.).]

9. [Rep. 55 & 56 Vict., C. 19 (S. L. R.).]

10. The major part of the persons to be elected by the Court of Directors and the major part of the persons to be first appointed by Her Majesty after the passing of this Act to be members of the Council, shall be persons who shall have served or resided in India for ten years at the least, and (excepting in the case of late and present Directors and Officers on the Home establishment of the East India Company who shall have so served or

The major part of the Council to be persons who shall have served or resided ten years in India, &c.

(1). There appears to be a mistake in this connection in the Statutes revised in which 38 and 39 Vict., C. 66 (S. L. R.) is cited as the repealing enactment.

resided), shall not have last left India more than ten years next preceding the date of their appointment;

And no person other than a person so qualified shall be appointed or elected to fill any vacancy in the Council unless at the time of the appointment or election nine at the least of the continuing members of the Council be persons qualified as aforesaid.

Tenure of office of Members of the Council

11. Every member of the Council appointed or elected under this Act shall hold his office during good behaviour;

Provided that it shall be lawful for Her Majesty to remove any such member from his office upon an address of both Houses of Parliament.

Members of Council not to sit in Parliament

12. No member of the Council appointed or elected under this Act shall be capable of sitting or voting in Parliament.

Salaries of Members of Council

13. There shall be paid to each member of the Council the yearly salary of one thousand two hundred pounds out of the revenues of India.

14. [Rep. 32 & 33 Vict., C. 97. s. 5.]

Establishment of the Secretary of State in Council

15. The Secretaries and other officers and servants on the Home establishment of the said Company and on the establishment of the Commissioners for the Affairs of India, immediately after the commencement of this Act, shall on such commencement be and form the establishment of the Secretary of State in Council;

And the Secretary of State shall with all convenient speed make such arrangement of the said establishments, and such reductions therein, as may seem to him consistent with the due conduct of the public business, and shall within six months after the commencement of this Act submit a scheme for the permanent establishment to Her Majesty in Council.

And it shall be lawful for Her Majesty, by the advice of Her Privy Council, upon consideration of such scheme, to fix and declare what shall constitute and be the establishment of the Secretary of State in Council, and what salaries shall be paid to the persons on the establishment;

And the Order of Her Majesty in Council shall be laid before both Houses of Parliament within fourteen days after the making thereof, provided Parliament be then sitting, or otherwise within fourteen days after the next meeting thereof ;

And after such establishment has been formed by such Order in Council, no addition of persons shall be made to such establishment, nor any addition made to the salaries authorized by such Order, except by a similar Order in Council, to be laid in like manner before both Houses of Parliament.

Removal of officers and supply of vacancies in the establisment

16. After the first formation of the establishment it shall be lawful for the Secretary of State in Council to remove any officer or servant belonging thereto, and also to make all appointments and promotions to and in such establishment :

Provided, that the Order of Her Majesty in Council of the twenty-first day of May, one thousand eight hundred and fifty-five, or such other regulation as may be from time to time established by Her Majesty for examinations, certificates, probation, or other tests of fitness in relation to appointments to junior situations in the Civil Service, shall apply to such appointments on the said establishment.

17. [Rep. 41 and 42 Vict., C. 79 (S. L. R.).]

18. It shall be lawful for Her Majesty by warrant countersigned as aforesaid to grant to any such Secretary, officer or servant as aforesaid, retained on such last-mentioned establishment, such compensation, superannuation, or retiring allowance on his ceasing to hold office as might have been granted to him if this Act had not been passed ;

And the transfer of any person to the service of the Secretary of State in Council shall be deemed to be a continuance of his previous appointment or employment, and shall not prejudice any claims which he might have had in respect of length of service if his service under the said Company or Commissioners had continued ; and it shall be lawful for Her Majesty, by warrant countersigned as aforesaid, to grant to any Secretary, officer or servant appointed on the said establishment after the first formation thereof, such compensation, superannuation, or retiring allowance as, under the Superannuation Act, 1834, or any other Act for the time being in force, concerning superannuations and other

4 & 5 Will 4, C. 24.

allowances to persons having held civil offices in the public service, may be granted to persons appointed on the establishment of one of Her Majesty's Principal Secretaries of State.

DUTIES AND PROCEDURE OF THE COUNCIL

Duties of the Council, &c.

19. The Council shall, under the direction of the Secretary of State, and subject to the provisions of this Act conduct the business transacted in the United Kingdom in relation to the Government of India and the correspondence with India.

But every order or communication sent to India shall be signed by one of the Principal Secretaries of State ;

And, save as expressly provided by this Act, every order in the United Kingdom in relation to the Government of India under this Act shall be signed by such Secretary of State ;

And all despatches from Governments and Presidencies in India, and other despatches from India, which if this Act had not been passed should have been addressed to the Court of Directors or to their Secret Committee, shall be addressed to such Secretary of State.

Secretary of State to divide the Council into Committees, and to regulate the transaction of business

20. It shall be lawful for the Secretary of State to divide the Council into Committees for the more convenient transcation of business, and from time to time to re-arrange such Committees, and to direct what departments of the business in relation to the Government of India under this Act shall be under such Committees respectively, and generally to direct the manner in which all such business shall be transacted.

President and Vice-President of the Council

21. The Secretary of State shall be the President of the Council, with power to vote ;

And it shall be lawful for such Secretary of State in Council to appoint from time to time any member of such Council to be Vice-President thereof ;

And any such Vice-President may at any time be removed by the Secretary of State.

Meeting of the Council

22. All powers by this Act required to be exercised by the Secretary of State in Council, and all powers of the Council, shall and may be exercised at meetings of such Council, at which not less than five members shall be present ;

And at every meeting the Secretary of State, or in his absence the Vice-President, if present, shall preside ; and in the absence of the Secretary of State and Vice-President, one of the members of the Council present shall be chosen by the members present to preside at the meeting :

And such Council may act notwithstanding any vacancy therein.

Meetings of the Council shall be convened and held when and as the Secretary of State shall from time to time direct :

Provided that one such meeting at least be held in every week.

Procedure at meetings

23. At any meeting of the Council at which the Secretary of State is present, if there be a difference of opinion on any question other than the question of the election of a Member of Council, or other than any question with regard to which a majority of the votes at a meeting is hereinafter declared to be necessary, the determination of the Secretary of State shall be final ;

And in case of an equality of votes at any meeting of the Council, the Secretary of State, if present and in his absence the Vice-President, or presiding member, shall have a casting vote ;

And all acts done at any meeting of the Council in the absence of the Secretary of State, except the election of a Member of the Council, shall require the sanction or approval in writing of the Secretary of State ;

And in case of difference of opinion on any question decided at any meeting, the Secretary of State may require that his opinion and the reasons for the same be entered in the minutes of the proceedings, and any Member of the Council who may have been present at the meeting may require that his opinion, and any reasons for the same that he may have stated at the meeting, be entered in like manner.

Orders, &c., to be open to the perusal of Members of Council who may record their opinions

24. Every order or communication proposed to be sent to India, and every order proposed to be made in the United Kingdom by the Secretary of State under this Act, shall, unless the same has been submitted to a meeting of the Council, be placed in the Council room for the perusal of all members of the Council during seven days before the sending or making thereof, except in the cases hereinafter provided;

And it shall be lawful for any member of the Council to record in a minute book to be kept for that purpose, his opinion with respect to each such order or communication, and a copy of every opinion so recorded shall be sent forthwith to the Secretary of State.

Secretary of State acting against the opinions of the majority to record his reasons

25. If a majority of the Council record as aforesaid their opinions against any act proposed to be done the Secretary of State shall, if he do not defer to the opinions of the majority, record his reasons for acting in opposition thereto.

Provision for cases of urgency.

26. Provided that where it appears to the Secretary of State that despatch of any communication, or the making of any order, not being an order for which a majority of the votes at a meeting is hereby made necessary, is urgently required, the communication may be sent or order given notwithstanding the same may not have been submitted to a meeting of the Council or deposited for seven days as aforesaid, the urgent reasons for sending or making the same being recorded by the Secretary of State, add notice thereof being given to every member of the Council, except in the cases hereinafter mentioned.

Orders now sent through Secret Committee may be sent by Secretary of State without communication with the Council

27. Provided also, that any order, not being an order for which a majority of votes at a meeting is hereby made necessary, which might, if this Act had not been passed, have been sent by the Commissioners for the Affairs of India, through the Secret Committee of the Court of Directors to Governments or Presidencies in India, or to the officers or servants of the said Company, may, after the commencement of this Act, be sent to such Governments or Presidencies, or to any officer or servant in India, by the Secretary of State without having been submitted to a meeting, or deposited for the perusal of the members of the Council, and without the reasons being recorded, or notice thereof given as aforesaid.

As to communication of secret despatches from India

28. Any despatches to Great Britain which might, if this Act had not been passed, have been addressed to the Secret Committee of the Court of Directors, may be marked "secret" by the authorities sending the same;

And such despatches shall not be communicated to the Members of the Council, unless the Secretary of State shall so think fit and direct.

APPOINTMENTS AND PATRONAGE

Appointments to be made by or with the approbation of Her Majesty

29. The appointments of Governor-General of India* * *and Governors of Presidencies in India now made by the Court of Directors with the approbation of Her Majesty, and the appointments of Advocate-General for the several Presidencies now made with the approbation of the Commissioners for the Affairs of India, shall be made by Her Majesty by warrant under Her Royal Sign Manual;

The appointment of the Lieutenant-Governors of provinces or territories shall be made by the Governor-General of India, subject to the approbation of Her Majesty ; and all such appointments shall be subject to the qualifications now by law affecting such offices respectively.

Appointments now made in India to continue to be made there

30. All appointments to offices, commands and employments in India, all promotions, which by law, or under any regulations, usage or custom, are now made by any authority in India, shall continue to be made in India by the like authority, and subject to the qualifications, conditions, and restrictions now affecting such appointments respectively ;

Powers of Secretary of State in Council as to appointments, etc., in India

But the Secretary of State in Council, with the concurrence of a majority of members present at a meeting, shall have the like power to make regulations for the division and distribution of patronage and power of nomination among the several authorities in India, and the like power of restoring to their stations, offices, or employments, officers, and servants suspended or removed by any authority in India, as might have been exercised by the said Court of Directors, with the approbation of the Commissioners for the Affairs of India, if this Act had not been passed.

31. [Rep. 41 and 42 Vict., C. 79 (S. L. R.).]

Secretary of State in Council to make regulations for the admission of candidates to the Civil Service of India

32. * * * * Regulations shall be made by the Secretary of State in Council, with the advice and assistance of the Commissioners for the time being, acting in execution of Her Majesty's Order in Council of twenty-first May one thousand eight hundred and fifty-five for regulating the admission of persons to the Civil Service of the Crown, for

admitting all persons being natural born subjects of Her Majesty (and of such age and qualification as may be prescribed in this behalf) who may be desirous of becoming candidates for appointment to the Civil Service of India to be examined as candidates accordingly, and for prescribing the branches of knowledge in which such candidates shall be examined, and generally for regulating and conducting such examinations, under the superintendence of the said last mentioned Commissioners or of the person for the time being entrusted with the carrying out of such regulations as may be, from time to time, established by Her Majesty for examination, certificate, or other test of fitness in relation to appointments to junior situations in the Civil Service of the Crown ;

And the candidates who may be certified by the said Commissioners or other persons as aforesaid, to be entitled under such regulations shall be recommended for appointment according to the order of their proficiency as shown by such examinations ;

And such persons only as shall have been so certified as aforesaid shall be appointed or admitted to the Civil Service of India by the Secretary of State in Council :

Regulations made by Secretary of State to be laid before Parliament

Provided always, that all regulations to be made by the said Secretary of State in Council under this Act shall be laid before Parliament within fourteen days after the making thereof, if Parliament be sitting, and if Parliament be not sitting then, within fourteen days after the next meeting thereof.

Other appointments and admissions to service vested in Her Majesty

33. All appointments to cadetships, naval and military, and all admissions to service not herein otherwise provided for, shall be vested in Her Majesty ;

And the names of persons to be from time to time recommended for such cadetships and service shall be submitted to Her Majesty by the Secretary of State.

Regulations to be made for admitting persons to be examined for cadetships in Engineers and Artillery

34. * * * * Regulations shall be made for admitting any persons being natural-born subjects of Her Majesty (and of such age and qualifications as may be prescribed in this behalf) who may be desirous of becoming candidates for cadetships in the engineers and in the artillery, to be examined as candidates accordingly, and for prescribing the branches of knowledge in which such candidates shall

be examined, and generally for regulating and conducting such examinations.

Not less than one-tenth of persons recommended for military cadetships to be selected from sons of persons who have served in India

35. Not less than one-tenth of the whole number of persons to be recommended in any year for military cadetships (other than cadetships in the engineers and artillery) shall be selected according to such regulations as the Secretary of State in Council may from time to time make in this behalf from among the sons of persons who have served in India in the military or civil services of Her Majesty or of the East India Company 1.

Nominations for cadetship to be made by Secretary of State and Members of Council

36. Except as aforesaid, all persons to be recommended for military cadetships shall be nominated by the Secretary of State and Members of Council, so that out of seventeen nominations the Secretary of State shall have two and each Member of Council shall have one :

But no persons so nominated shall be recommended unless the nomination be approved of by the Secretary of State in Council.

Regulations as to appointments and admissions to service

37. Save as hereinbefore provided, all powers of making regulations in relation to appointments and admissions to service and other matters connected therewith, and of altering or revoking such regulations, which, if this Act had not been passed, might have been exercised by the Court of Directors or Commissioners for the Affairs of India, may be exercised by the Secretary of State in Council ;

And all regulations in force at the time of the commencement of this Act in relation to the matters aforesaid shall remain in force, subject nevertheless to alteration or revocation by the Secretary of State in Council as aforesaid.

Removal of officer by Her Majesty to be communicated to Secretary of State in Council

38. Any writing under the Royal Sign Manual, renewing or dismissing any person holding any office, employment, or commission, civil or military, in India, of which, if this Act had not been passed, a copy would have been required to be transmitted or delivered within eight days after being signed by Her Majesty to the chairman or deputy chairman of the

1 But see further 22 and 23 Vict., C. 41.

Court of Directors shall, in lieu thereof, be communicated within the time aforesaid to the Secretary of State in Council.

TRANSFER OF PROPERTY

Real and personal property of the Company to vest in Her Majesty for the purposes of the Government of India

39. All lands and hereditaments, monies, stores, goods, chattel, and other real and personal estate of the said Company, subject to the debts and liabilities affecting the same respectively, and the benefit of all contracts, covenants and engagements, and all rights to fines, penalties, and forfeitures, and all other emoluments, which the said Company shall be seized or possessed of, or entitled to, at the time of the commencement of this Act, except the capital stock of the said Company and the dividend thereon, shall become vested in Her Majesty, to be applied and disposed of, subject to the provisions of this Act, for the purposes of the Government of India.

Powers to sell and purchase, and to enter into contracts, vested in Secretary of State in Council, &c.

40. The Secretary of State in Council, with the concurrence of a majority of votes at a meeting, shall have full power to sell and dispose of all real and personal estate whatsoever for the time being vested in Her Majesty under this Act, as may be thought fit, or to raise money on any such real estate by way of mortgage, and make the proper assurances for that purpose, and to purchase and acquire any land or hereditaments or any interests therein, stores, goods, chattels and other property, and to enter into any contracts whatsoever, as may be thought fit for the purposes of this Act;

And all property so acquired shall vest in Her Majesty for the service of the Government of India : and any conveyance or assurance of or concerning any real estate to be made by the authority of the Secretary of State in Council may be made under the hands and seal of three Members of the Council.

REVENUES

Expenditure of revenues of India subject to control of Secretary of State in Council

41. The expenditure of the revenues of India, both in India and elsewhere, shall be subject to the control of the Secretary of State in Council;

And no grant or appropriation of any part of such revenues, or of any other property coming into the possession of the Secretary of

State in Council by virtue of this Act, shall be made without the concurrence of a majority of votes at a meeting of the Council.

Existing and future debts and liabilities of the Company and expenses to be charged on revenues of India

42. * * * * all the bond, debenture and other debt of the said Company in Great Britain, and all the territorial debt and all other debts of the said Company, and all sums of money, costs, charges and expenses, which if this Act had not been passed would after the time appointed for the commencement thereof have been payable by the said Company out of the revenues of India, in respect or by reason of any treaties, covenants, contracts, grants, or liabilities then existing and all expenses, debts and liabilities which after the commencement of this Act shall be lawfully contracted and incurred on account of the Government of India, and all payments under this Act, shall be charged and chargeable upon the revenues of India alone, as the same would have been if this Act had not been passed, and such expenses, debts and liabilities lawfully contracted and incurred by the said Company ; and such revenues shall not be applied to any other purpose whatsoever ;

And all other monies vested in or arising or accruing from property or rights vested in Her Majesty under this Act, or to be received or disposed of by the Council under this Act, shall be applied in aid of such revenues * * * *

Revenues remitted to Great Britain and monies arising in Great Britain, to be paid to Secretary of State in Council, &c.

43. Such part of the revenues of India as shall be from time to time remitted to Great Britain, and all monies of the said Company in their treasury or under the care of their cashier, and all other monies in Great Britain of the said Company, or which would have been received by them in Great Britain if this Act had not been passed, and all monies arising or accruing in Great Britain from any property or rights vested in Her Majesty by this Act, or from the sale or disposition thereof, shall be paid to the Secretary of State in Council, to be applied for the purposes of this Act ;

And all such monies, except as hereinafter otherwise provided, shall be paid into the Bank of England, to the credit of an account to be opened by the Governor and Company of the Bank of England, to be intituled " The Account of the Secretary of State in Council of India ";

And all monies to be placed to the credit of such account under this Act shall be paid out upon drafts or orders signed by three Members of Council and countersigned by the Secretary of State or one of his Under Secretaries; and such account shall be a public account:

Provided always, that the Secretary of State in Council may cause to be kept from time to time, under the care of their cashier, in an account to be kept at the Bank of England, such sum or sums of money as they may deem necessary for the payments now made out of money under the care of the cashier of the said Company.

44. [Rep. 41 and 42 Vict., C. 79 (S. L. R.).]

Stock accounts to be opened at the Bank

45. There shall be raised in the books of the Governor and Company of the Bank of England such accounts as may be necessary in respect of any stock or stocks of Government annuities; and all such accounts respectively shall be intituled "The stock account of the Secretary of State in Council of India;" and every such account shall be a public account.

46. [Rep. 41 and 42 Vict., C. 79 (S. L. R.).]

Power to grant letters of attorney for sale, &c., of stock and receipt of dividends

47. The Secretary of State in Council, by letter of attorney, executed by three Members of the Council and countersigned by the Secretary of State or one of his Under Secretaries, may authorize all or any of the cashiers of the Bank of England to sell and transfer all or any part of the stock or stocks standing, or that may thereafter stand in the books of the said Bank to the several accounts of the Secretary of State in Council, and to purchase and accept stock on the said accounts, and to receive the dividends due and to become due on the several stocks standing or that may thereafter stand on the said accounts, and by any writing signed by three members of the Council and countersigned as aforesaid, may direct the application of the monies to be received in respect of such sales and dividends.

But no stock shall be purchased or sold and transferred by any of the said cashiers, under the authority of such general letter of attorney, except upon an order in writing directed to the said Chief Cashier and Chief Accountant from time to time and duly signed and countersigned as aforesaid.

48. All Exchequer Bills, Exchequer bonds, or other Government Securities, of whatsoever kind, not hereinbefore referred to, which shall be held by the Governor and Company of the Bank of England in trust for or on account of the East India Company at the time of the commencement of this Act shall thenceforward be held by the said Governor and Company in trust for and on account of the Secretary of State in Council ;

Provision as to Exchequer bills, bonds, and other securities

And all such securities as aforesaid, and all such securities as may thereafter be lodged with the said Governor and Company by or on behalf of the Secretary of State in Council, shall and may be disposed of and the proceeds thereof applied as may be authorized by order in writing signed by three members of Council, and countersigned by the Secretary of State or one of his Under Secretaries, and directed to the said chief Cashier and Chief acountant.

49. All powers of issuing bonds, debentures and other securities for money in Great Britain which, if this Act had not been passed might have been exercised by the said Company, or the Court of Directors under the direction and control of the Commissioners for the affairs of India, or otherwise, shall and may be exercised by the Secretary of State in Council, with the concurrence of a majority of votes at a meeting ;

Powers of borrowing transferred to Secretary of State in Council, &c.

And such securities as might have been issued under the seal of the said Company shall be issued under the hands of three members of the Council, and countersigned by the Secretary of State or one of his Under Secretaries.

50. [Rep. 55 and 56 Vict., C. 19 (S. L. R.)]

51. The regulations and practice now acted on by the Court of Directors on the issue of warrants or authorities for the payment of money shall be maintained and acted on by the Secretary of State in Council of India under this Act until the same be altered by the authority of Her Majesty in Council :

Present system of issuing warrants to be continued

Provided * * * *that warrants or authorities which have heretofore been signed by the two Directors of the East India Company shall, after the commencement of this Act, be signed by three members of the Council of India.

D

52. It shall be lawful for Her Majesty, by warrant under her Royal Sign Manual, countersigned by the Chancellor of the Exchequer, to appoint from time to time a fit person to be Auditor of the Accounts of the Secretary of State in Council, and to authorize such auditor to appoint and remove from time to time such assistants as may be specified in such warrant, and every such auditor shall hold office during good behaviour ;

Audit of accounts in Great Britain

And there shall be paid to such auditor and assistants out of the revenues of India such respective salaries as Her Majesty, by warrant as aforesaid countersigned as aforesaid, may direct ;

And such Auditor shall examine and audit the accounts of the receipt, expenditure, and disposal in Great Britain of all monies, shares and property applicable for the purposes of this Act ; and the Secretary of State in Council shall, by the officers and servants of the establishment produce and lay before such auditor from time to time all such accounts, accompanied by proper vouchers for the support of the same, and shall submit to his inspection all books, papers, and writings having relation thereto;

And such auditor shall have power to examine all such officers and servants in Great Britain of the establishment as he may see fit in relation to such accounts, and the receipt, expenditure, or disposal of such monies, shares, and property, and for that purpose, by writing under his hand, to summon before him any such officer or servant;

And such auditor shall report from time to time to the Secretary of State in Council his approval or disapproval of such accounts, with such remarks and observations in relation thereto as he may think fit, specially noting any case if there shall be, in which it shall appear to him that any money arising out of the revenues of India has been appropriated to other purposes than those of the Government of India to which alone they are declared to be applicable ; and shall specify in detail in his reports all sums of money, shares and property which ought to be accounted for, and are not brought into account, or have not been appropriated, in conformity with the provisions of this Act, or have been expended or disposed of without due authority, and shall also specify any defects, inaccuracies, or irregularities, which may appear in such accounts, or in the authorities, vouchers, or documents having relation thereto;

And all such reports shall be laid before both Houses of Parliament by such auditor, together with the accounts of the year to which the same may relate.

Accounts to be annually laid before Parliament

53. The Secretary of State in Council shall, within the first fourteen days during which Parliament may be sitting, next after the first day of May in every year, lay before both Houses of Parliament an account for the financial year preceding the last completed of the annual produce of the revenues of India, distinguishing the same under the respective heads thereof, at each of the several Presidencies or Governments, and of all the annual receipts and disbursements at home and abroad on account of the Government of India, distinguishing the same under the respective heads thereof, together with the latest estimate of the same for the last financial year, and also the amount of the debts chargeable on the revenues of India, with the rates of interest they respectively carry, and the annual amount of such interest, the state of the effects and credits at each Presidency or Government, and in England or elsewhere applicable to the purposes of the Government of India, according to the latest advices which have been received thereon, and also a list of the establishment of the Secretary of State in Council, and the salaries and allowances payable in respect thereof;

And if any new or increased salaries or pensions of fifty pounds a year or upwards have been granted or created within a year, the particulars thereof shall be specially stated and explained at the foot of the account of such year;

And such account shall be accompanied by a statement prepared from detailed reports from each Presidency and district in India in such form as shall best exhibit the moral and material progress and condition of India in each such Presidency.

When order to commence hostilities is sent to India the fact to be communicated to Parliament

54. When any order is sent to India directing the actual commencement of hostilties by Her Majesty's forces in India, the fact of such order having been sent shall be communicated to both Houses of Parliament within three months after the sending of such order, if Parliament be sitting, unless such order shall have been in the meantime revoked or suspended, and, if Parliament not sitting at the end of such

three months, then within one month after the next meeting of Parliament.

Except for repelling invasion, the revenues of India not applicable for any military operation beyond the frontiers

55. Except for preventing or repelling actual invasion of Her Majesty's Indian possessions, or under other sudden and urgent necessity, the revenues of India shall not, without the consent of both Houses of Parliament, be applicable to defray the expenses of any military operation carried on beyond the external frontiers of such possessions by Her Majesty's forces charged upon such revenues.

EXISTING ESTABLISHMENTS

Indian Military and Naval Forces remain under existing conditions of service

56. The Military and Naval Forces of the East India Company shall be deemed to be the Indian Military and Naval Forces of Her Majesty, and shall be under the same obligations to serve Her Majesty as they would have been under, to serve the said Company, and shall be liable to serve within the same territorial limits only, for the same terms only, and be entitled to the like pay, pensions, allowances, and privileges, and the like advantages as regards promotion and otherwise, as if they had continued in the service of the said Company ; such forces, and all persons hereafter enlisting in or entering the same, shall continue and be subject to all Acts of Parliament, laws of the Governor-General of India in Council, and articles of war, and all other laws, regulations and provisions relating to the East India Company's Military and Naval Forces respectively as if Her Majesty's Indian Military and Naval forces respectively had throughout such Acts, laws, articles, regulations, and provisions been mentioned or referred to, instead of such forces of the said Company.

And the pay and expenses of and incident to Her Majesty's Indian Military and Naval Forces shall be defrayed out of the revenues of India.

Provision for persons hereafter entering Her Majesty's Indian Forces

57. Provided that it shall be lawful for Her Majesty from time to time by order in Council to alter or regulate the terms and conditions of service under which persons hereafter entering Her Majesty's Indian Forces shall be commissioned, enlisted, or entered to serve ;

And the forms of attestation and of the oath or declaration to be used and taken or made respectively on attesting persons to serve in Her Majesty's Indian Forces shall be such as Her Majesty with regard to the European Forces, and the Governor-General of India in Council with regard to the Naval Forces, shall from time to time direct :

Provided that every such Order in Council shall be laid before both Houses of Parliament within fourteen days after the making thereof, if Parliament sitting and, if Parliament be not sitting, then within fourteen days after the next meeting thereof.

Officers, etc., in employ of the company at the commencement of this Act to be deemed to hold offices under Her Majesty

58. All persons who, at the time of the commencement of this Act, shall hold any offices, employments or commissions whatever under the said Company in India shall thenceforth be deemed to hold such offices, employments and commissions under Her Majesty as if they had been appointed under this Act and shall be paid out of the revenues of India ;

And the transfer of any person to the service of Her Majesty shall be deemed to be a continuance of his previous service, and shall not prejudice any claims to pension or any claims on the various annuity funds of the several Presidencies in India, which he might have had if this Act had not been passed.

All orders of the Court of Directors or Board of Control given before commencement of this Act, to remain in force

59. All orders, regulations, and directions lawfully given or made before the commencement of this Act by the Court of Directors or by the Commissioners for the Affairs of India shall remain in force ; but the same shall, from and after the commencement of this Act, be deemed to be the orders, regulations, and directions under this Act, and take effect and be subject to alteration or revocation accordingly.

60 to 62 [Rep. 55 and 56 Vict., C. 19 (S. L. R.)]

Governor-General may exercise his powers before he takes his seat in Council, &c.

63. In case the person who shall be entitled under any provisions for appointment to succeed to the office of Governor-General of India upon a vacancy therein, or who shall be appointed absolutely to assume the office, shall be in India (upon or after the happening of the vacancy, or upon or after the

receipt of such absolute appointment, as the case may require, but shall be absent from Fort William in Bengal, or from the place where the Council of the Governor-General of India may then be, and it shall appear to him necessary to exercise the powers of Governor-General before he shall have taken his seat in Council, it shall be lawful for him to make known by proclamation his appointment, and his intention to assume the said office of Governor-General;

And after such proclamation, and thenceforth until he shall repair to Fort William or the place where the Council may assemble, it shall be lawful for him to exercise alone, all or any of the powers which might be exercised by the Governor-General in Council, except the power of making laws and regulations;

And all acts done in the exercise of the said powers, except as aforesaid, shall be of the same force and effect as if they had been done by the Governor-General in Council;

Provided that all acts done in the said Council after the date of such proclamation but before the communication thereof to such Council, shall be valid, subject nevertheless to revocation or alteration by the person who shall have so assumed the said office of Governor-General;

And when the office of Governor-General is assumed under the foregoing provision, if there be at any time before the Governor-General takes his seat in Council, no Vice-President of the Council authorised to preside at meetings for making laws and regulations (as provided by section 22 of the Government of India Act, 1853), the senior ordinary member of Council therefor sent shall preside therein, with the same powers as if a Vice-President had been appointed and were absent.

CONTINUANCE OF EXISTING ENACTMENTS

Existing provisions to be applicable to Secretary of State in Council &c.

64. All Acts and provisions of law in force or otherwise concerning India shall, subject to the provisions of this Act, continue in force, and be construed as referring to the Secretary of State in Council in the place of the said Company and the Court of Directors and Court of Proprietors thereof;

And all enactments applicable to the officers and servants of the said Company in India, and to appointments to office or admissions to

1. S. 12, and 16 and 17 Vict, c. 95 was repealed by 24 and 25 Vict. c., 67, s. 2, see s. 15 of that Act

service by the said Court of Directors, shall, subject to the provisions of this Act, remain applicable to the officers and servants continued and to the officers and servants appointed or employed in India and to appointments to office and admissions to service under the authority of this Act.

ACTION AND CONTRACT

Secretary of State in Council may sue and be sued

65. The Secretary of State in Council shall and may sue and be sued as well in India as in England by the name of the Secretary of State in Council as a body corporate ;

And all persons and bodies politic shall and may have and take the same suits, remedies and proceedings, legal and equitable, against the Secretary of State in Council of India as they could have done against the said Company;

And the property and effects hereby vested in Her Majesty for the purposes of the Government of India, or acquired for the said purposes, shall be subject and liable to the same judgments and executions as they would, while vested in the said Company, have been liable to in respect of debts and liabilities lawfully contracted and incurred by the said company.[1]

66. [Rep. 41 and 42 Vict., C. 79 (S. L. R.).]

Treaties shall be binding on Her Majesty, and contracts, &c., of company may be enforced

67. All treaties made by the said Company shall be binding on Her Majesty ; and all contracts, covenants, liabilities and engagements of the said Company made, incurred or entered into before the commencement of this Act, may be enforced by and against the Secretary of State in Council in like manner and in the same Courts as they might have been by and against the said Company if this Act had not been passed.

Members of Council not personally liable

68. Neither the Secretary of State nor any member of the Council shall be personally liable in respect of any such contract, covenant, or engagement of the said Company as aforesaid, or in respect of any contract entered into under the authority of this Act, or other liability of the said Secretary of State or Secretary

1 See *P. & O. S. N. Co.* v. *Secretary of State for India*, 4 Bom. H. C. Rep. Appendix, pp. 45 per Peacock, C. J.

of State in Council in their official capacity ; but all such liabilities, and all costs and damages in respect thereof, shall be satisfied and paid out of the revenues of India.

* * * *

Company not to be liable in respect of any claim arising out of any covenant made before the passing of this Act

71. * * * * the said Company shall not, after the passing of this Act, be liable in respect of any claim, demand, or liability which has arisen or may hereafter arise out of any treaty, covenant, contract, grant, engagement, or fiduciary obligation made, incurred or entered into by the said Company before the passing of this Act, whether the said Company would, but for this Act, have been bound to satisfy such claim, demand, or liability out of the revenues of India, or in any other manner whatsoever.

72 & 73 [Rep. 41 & 42 Vict., C. 79 (S. L. R.).]

74 [Rep. 55 & 56 Vict., C. 19 (S. L. R.)]

75 [Rep. 41 & 42 Vict., C. 79 (S. L. R.)]

IV

THE INDIAN COUNCILS' ACT, 1861

[1ST AUGUST 1861]

AN ACT TO MAKE BETTER PROVISION FOR THE CONSTITUTION OF THE COUNCIL OF THE GOVERNOR-GENERAL OF INDIA, AND FOR THE LOCAL GOVERNMENT OF THE SEVERAL PRESIDENCIES AND PROVINCES OF INDIA, AND FOR THE TEMPORARY GOVERNMENT OF INDIA IN THE EVENT OF A VACANCY IN THE OFFICE OF GOVERNOR-GENERAL.

Whereas it is expedient that the provisions of former Acts of Parliament respecting the constitution and functions of the Council of the Governor-General of India should be consolidated and in certain respects amended, and that power should be given to the Governors in Council of the Presidencies of Fort Saint George and Bombay to make laws and regulations for the Government of the said Presidencies ; and that provision should be made for constituting the like authority in other parts of Her Majesty's Indian dominions : Be it therefore declared and enacted by the Queen's Most Excellent Majesty, by and with the advice and consent of the lords spiritual and temporal, and commons, in this present Parliament assembled, and by the authority of the same, as follows :

Short title

1. This Act may be cited for all purposes as "The Indian Councils Act, 1861."

Acts and parts of Acts repealed

2. Sections forty, forty-three, forty-four, fifty, sixty-six, seventy, and so much of sections sixty-one and sixty-four as relates to vacancies in the office of ordinary member of the Council of India, of the Act of the third and fourth years of King William the Fourth, chapter eighty-five, for effecting an arrangement with the East India Company, and for the better Government of Her Majesty's Indian territories, till the thirtieth day of April, one thousand eight hundred and fifty-four, sections twenty-two, twenty-three, twenty-four and twenty-six of the Act of the sixteenth and seventeenth years of Her Majesty, chapter ninety-five, "to provide for the Government of India" and the Act of the twenty-third and twenty fourth years of Her Majesty, chapter eight-seven," to remove doubts as to the authority of the senior member of the Council of the Governor-General of India in the absence of the president," are hereby repealed: and all other enactments whatsoever now in force with relation to the Council of the Governor-General of India, or to the Councils of the Governors of the respective Presidencies of Fort Saint George and Bombay, shall, save so far as the same are altered by or are repugnant to this Act, continue in force, and be applicable to the Council of the Governor-General of India and the Councils of the respective Presidencies under this Act.

Composition of the Council of the Governor-General of India

3. There shall be five ordinary members of the said Council of the Governor-General, three of whom shall from time to time be appointed . . . . . . from among such persons as shall have been, at the time of such appointment, in the service in India of the Crown, or of the Company and the Crown, for at least ten years; and if the person so appointed shall be in the military service of Crown, he shall not, during his continuance in office as a member of Council, hold any military command, or be employed in actual military duties; and the remaining two, one of whom shall be a barrister or a member of the Faculty of advocates in Scotland of not less than five years' standing, shall be appointed from time to time by Her Majesty

by warrant under Her Royal Sign Manual; and it shall be lawful for the Secretary of State in Council to appoint the Commander-in-Chief of Her Majesty's Forces in India to be an extraordinary member of the said Council, and such extraordinary member of Council shall have rank and precedence at the Council Board next after the Governor-General.

Present members of Council to continue

4. The present ordinary members of the Council of the Governor-General of India shall continue to be ordinary members under and for the purposes of this Act; and it shall be lawful for Her Majesty, on the passing of this Act, to appoint by warrant as aforesaid an ordinary member of Council, to complete the number of five hereby established; and there shall be paid to such ordinary member, and to all other ordinary members who may be hereafter appointed, such amount of salary as may from time to time be fixed for members of the Council of the Governor-General by the Secretary of State in Council, with the concurrence of a majority of members of Council present at a meeting; and all enactments of any Act of Parliament or law of India respecting the Council of the Governor-General of India and the members there shall be held to apply to the said Council as constituted by this Act, except so far as they are repealed by or are repugnant to any provisions of this Act.

Appointment of fifth member, and salaries of members, &c.

Provisional appointments of members of Councils

5. It shall be lawful for the Secretary of State in Council, with the concurrence of a majority of members present at a meeting, and for Her Majesty, by warrant as aforesaid, respectively, to appoint any person provisionally to succeed to the office of ordinary member of the Council of the Governor-General, when the same shall become vacant by the death or resignation of the person holding the said office, or on his departure from India with intent to return to Europe, or on any event and contingency expressed in any such provisional appointment, and such appointment again to revoke; but no person so appointed to succeed provisionally to such office shall be entitled to any authority, salary, or emolument appertaining thereto until he shall be in the actual possession of such office.

Provisions during absence of Governor-General in other parts of India

6. Whenever the said Governor-General in Council shall declare that it is expedient that the said Governor-General should visit any part of India unaccompanied by his Council, it shall be lawful for the said Governor-General in Council, previously to the departure of the Governor-General, to nominate some member of the said Council to be President of the said Council, in whom, during the time of such visit, the powers of the said Governor-General in assemblies of the said Council shall be reposed, except that of assenting to or withholding his assent from, or reserving for the signification of Her Majesty's pleasure, any law or regulation, as hereinafter provided; and it shall be lawful in every such case for the said Governor-General in Council by an order for that purpose to be made, to authorize the Governor-General alone to exercise all or any of the powers which might be exercised by the said Governor-General in Council, in every case in which the said Governor-General may think it expedient, to exercise the same, except the power of making laws or regulations.

Provision in case of absence of Governor-General &c. from meeting of Council

7. Whenever the Governor-General, or such President so nominated as aforesaid, shall be obliged to absent himself from any meeting of Council (other than meetings for the purpose of making laws and regulations, as hereinafter provided, owing to indisposition or any other cause whatsoever, and shall signify his intended absence to the Council, then and in every such case the senior member for the time being who shall be present at such meeting shall preside thereat, in such manner, and with such full powers and authorities during the time of such meeting, as such Governor-General or President would have had in case he had been present at such meeting, provided always, that no act of Council made at any such meeting shall be valid to any effect whatsoever unless the same shall be signed by such Governor- General or President respectively, if such Governor-General or President shall at the time be resident at the place at which such meeting shall be assembled, and shall not be prevented by such indisposition from signing the same: Provided always, that in case such Governor-General or President, not being so prevented as aforesaid, shall decline or refuse to sign such act of Council, he, and the several members of Council who shall have signed the same, shall mutually

exchange with and communicate in writing to each other the grounds and reasons of their respective opinions, in like manner and subject to such regulations and ultimate responsibility as are by an Act of the thirty-third year of King George the Third, chapter fifty-two, sections forty-seven, forty-eight, forty-nine, fifty, fifty-one, provided and described in cases, where such Governor-General shall, when present, dissent from any measure proposed or agitated in the Council.

33 Geo 3, c. 52. ss. 47 to 51

Power of Governor-General to make rules for conduct of business

8. It shall be lawful for the Governor-General from time to time to make rules and orders for the more convenient transaction of business in the said Council; and any order made or act done in accordance with such rules and orders (except as hereafter provided respecting laws and regulations) shall be deemed to be the order or act of the Governor-General in Council.

Council, where to assemble

9. The said Council shall from time to time assemble at such place or places as shall be appointed by the Governor-General in Council within the territories of India; and as often as the said Council shall assemble within either of the Presidencies of Fort Saint George or Bombay, the Governor of such Presidency shall act as an extraordinary member of Council; and as often as the said Council shall assemble with any other division, province, or territory having a Lieutenant-Governor, such Lieutenant-Governor shall act as an additional councillor at meetings of the Council, for the purpose of making laws and regulations only, in manner hereinafter provided.

Additional members to be summoned for the purpose of making laws and regulations

10. For the better exercise of the power of making laws and regulations vested in the Governor-General in Council, the Governor-General shall nominate, in addition to the ordinary and extraordinary members above mentioned, and to such Lieutenant-Governor in the case aforesaid, such persons, not less than six or more than twelve in number, as to him may seem expedient, to be members of Council for the purpose of making laws and regulations only; and such persons shall not be entitled to sit or vote at any meeting of Council, except at meetings held for such purpose; Provided, that not less than one-half of the persons so nominated shall be non-official persons, that is persons who, at the date of such nomination shall not be in the civil or military service of the Crown in

India ; and that the seat in Council of any non-official member accepting office under the Crown in India shall be vacated on such acceptance.

Such member to be appointed for two years

11. Every additional member of Council so nominated shall be summoned to all meetings held for the purpose of making laws and regulations for the term of two years from the date of such nomination.

Resignation of additional members

12. It shall be lawful for any such additional member of Council to resign his office to the Governor-General and on acceptance of such resignation by the Governor-General such office shall become vacant.

Power to fill up vacancy in number of additional members

13. On the event of a vacancy occurring by the death, acceptance of office, or resignation accepted in manner aforesaid, of any such additional member of Council, it shall be lawful for the Governor-General to nominate a person as additional member of Council in his place, who shall exercise the same functions until the termination of the term for which the additional member so dying, accepting office or resigning, was nominated: Provided always, that it shall not be lawful for him by such nomination to diminish the proportion of non-directed to be nominated.

No law to be invalid by reason of number of non-official members being incomplete

14. No law or regulation made by the Governor-General in Council in accordance with the provisions of this Act shall be deemed invalid by reason only that the proportion of non-official additional members hereby provided was not complete at the date of its introduction to the Council or its enactment.

Senior ordinary member of Council to preside at meetings for making laws and regulations in absence of Governor-General, &c. Quorum

15. In the absence of the Governor-General and of the President, nominated as aforesaid, the senior ordinary member of the Council present shall preside at meetings of the Council for making laws and regulations ; and the power of making laws and regulations vested in the Governor-General in Council shall be exercised only at meetings of the said Council at which such Governor-General or President, or some ordinary member of Council and six or more members of the said Council (including under the term members of the Council such additional members as aforesaid), shall be present ; and in every case of difference of opinion at meetings of the said Council for

making laws and regulations, where there shall be an equality of voices, the Governor-General, or in his absence the President, and in the absence of the Governor-General such senior ordinary member of Council there presiding, shall have two votes or the casting vote.

Governor-General to appoint first meeting for making laws and regulations

16. The Governor-General in Council shall, as soon as conveniently may be, appoint a place and time for the first meeting of the said Council of the Governor-General for making laws and regulations under this Act, and summon thereto as well the additional Councillors nominated by and under this Act as the other members of such Council; and until such first meeting the powers now vested in the said Governor-General of India in Council of making laws and regulations shall and may be exercised in like manner and by the same member, as before the passing of this Act.

Power to appoint and adjourn meetings for making laws and regulations

17. It shall be lawful for the Governor-General in Council from time to time to appoint all other times and places of meeting of the Council for the purpose of making laws and regulations under the provisions of this Act, and to adjourn, or from time to time to authorize such President, or senior Ordinary Member of Council in his absence, to adjourn any meeting for the purpose or making laws and regulations from time to time and from place to place.

Rules for conduct of business at such meetings

18. It shall be lawful for the Governor-General in Council to make rules for the conduct of business at meetings of the Council for the purpose of making laws and regulations under the provisions of this Act, prior to the first of such meetings; but such rules may be subsequently amended at meetings for the purpose of making laws or regulations subject to the assent of the Governor-General and such rules shall prescribe the mode of promulgation and authentication of such laws and regulations. Provided always, that it shall be lawful for the Secretary of State in Council to disallow any such rule, and to render it of no effect.

Business to be transacted at such meetings

19. No business shall be transacted at any meeting for the purpose of making laws and regulations, except as last herein before provided, other than the consideration and enactment of mea-

sures introduced in the Council for the purpose of such enactment; and it shall not be lawful for any member or additional member to make or for the Council to entertain any motion, unless such motion be for leave to introduce some measure as aforesaid into Council, or have reference to some measure actually introduced therein; Provided always, that it shall not be lawful for any member or additional member to introduce, without the previous sanction of the Governor-General, any measure affecting,—

(i) The Public Debt or public revenues of India, or by which any charge would be imposed on such revenues:

(ii) The religion or religious rights and usages of any class of Her Majesty's subjects in India.

(iii) The discipline or maintenance of any part of Her Majesty's Military or Naval Forces:

(iv) The relations of the Government with foreign princes or states.

Assent of Governor-General to laws and regulations made at such meetings

20. When any law or regulation has been made by the Council at a meeting for the purpose of making laws and regulations as aforesaid it shall be lawful for the Governor-General whether he shall or shall not have been present in Council at the making thereof, to declare that he assents to the same or that he withholds his assent from the same, or that he reserves the same for the signification of the pleasure of Her Majesty thereon; and no such law or regulation shall have validity until the Governor-General shall have declared his assent to the same, or until in the case of law or regulation so reserved as aforesaid Her Majesty shall have signified her assent to the same to the Governor-General, through the Secretary of State for India in Council, and such assent shall have been duly proclaimed by the said Governor-General.

Power of the Crown to disallow laws and regulations made at such meetings

21. Whenever any such law or regulation has been assented to by the Governor-General, he shall transmit to the Secretary of State for India an authentic copy thereof; and it shall be lawful for Her Majesty to signify, through the Secretary of State for India in Council, her disallowance of such law; and such disallowance shall make void and annul such law from or after the day on which the Governor-General shall make known, by

proclamation or by signification to his Council, that he has received the notification of such disallowance by Her Majesty.

Extent of the powers of the Governor-General in Council to make laws and regulations at such meetings

22. The Governor-General in Council shall have power at meetings for the purpose of making laws and regulations as aforesaid, and subject to the provisions herein contained, to make laws and regulations for repealing, amending, or altering any laws or regulations whatever now in force or hereafter to be in force in the Indian territories now under the dominion of Her Majesty, and to make laws and regulations for all persons, whether British or Native, foreigners or others, and for all courts of justice whatever, and for all places and things whatever within the said territories, and for all servants of the Government of India within the dominions of princes and states in alliance with Her Majesty*; and the laws and regulations so to be made by the Governor-General in Council shall control and supersede any laws and regulations in any wise repugnant thereto which shall have been made prior thereto by the Governors of the Presidencies of Fort St. George and Bombay respectively in Council, or the Governor or Lieutenant-Governor in Council of any presidency or other territory for which a Council may be appointed, with power to make laws and regulations, under and by virtue of this Act :

Provided always, that the said Governor-General in Council shall not have the power of making any laws or regulations which shall repeal or in any way affect any of the provisions of this Act :

Or any of the provisions of the Acts of the third and fourth years of King William the Fourth, chapter eighty-five, and of the sixteenth and seventeenth years of Her Majesty, chapter ninety-five, and of the seventeenth and eighteenth years of Her Majesty, chapter seventy-seven, which after the passing of this Act shall remain in force :

Or any provisions of the Act of the twenty-first and twenty-second years of Her Majesty, chapter one hundred and six, entitled, "An Act for the Better Government of India," or of the Act of the twenty-second and twenty-third years of Her Majesty, chapter forty-one, to amend the same :

---

* See also 28 Vict., c. 17, s. 1, & 32 & 33 Vict, c. 95, s. 1.

Or of any Act enabling the Secretary of State in Council to raise money in the United Kingdom for the Government of India :

Or of the Acts for punishing mutiny and desertion in Her Majesty's Army or in Her Majesty's Indian Forces respectively, but subject to the provision contained in the Act of the third and fourth years of King William the Fourth, chapter eighty-five, section seventy-three, respecting the Indian Articles of War:

Or any provisions of any Act* passed in this present session of Parliament, or hereafter to be passed, in anywise affecting Her Majesty's Indian territories, or the inhabitants thereof :

Or which may affect the authority of Parliament, or the constitution and rights of the East India Company, or any part of the unwritten laws or constitution of the United Kingdom of Great Britain and Ireland, whereon may depend in any degree the allegiance of any person to the Crown of the United Kingdom, or the sovereignty or dominion of the Crown over any part of the said territories.

Governor-General may make ordinances having force of law in case of urgent necessity

23. Notwithstanding anything in this Act contained, it shall be lawful for the Governor-General, in cases of emergency, to make and promulgate from time to time ordinances for the peace and good government of the said territories or of any part thereof, subject however to the restrictions contained in the last preceding section ; and every such ordinance shall have like force of law with a law or regulation made by the Governor-General in Council, as by this Act provided, for the space of not more than six months from its promulgation, unless the disallowance of such ordinance by Her Majesty shall be earlier signified to the Governor-General by the Secretary of State for India in Council or unless such ordinance shall be controlled or superseded by some law or regulation made by the Governor-General in Council at a meeting for the purpose of making laws and regulations as by this Act provided.

No law, &c. invalid by reason of its affecting the prerogative of the Crown

24. No law or regulation made by the Governor-General in Council (subject to the power of disallowance by the Crown, as hereinbefore provided), shall be deemed invalid by reason only that it affects the prerogative of the Crown.

---

*_Queen_ v. _Meares_, 14 Beng. 106, 112.

Laws made for the non-regulation provinces declared valid

25. Whereas doubts have been entertained whether the Governor-General of India, or the Governor-General of India in Council, had the power of making rules, laws, and regulations for the territories known from time to time as "Non-regulation Provinces," except at meetings for making laws and regulations in conformity with the provisions of the said Acts of the third and fourth years of King William the Fourth, chapter eighty-five, and of the sixteenth and seventeenth years of Her Majesty, chapter ninety-five, and whether the Governor, or Governor in Council, or Lieutenant Governor of any presidency or part of India had such power in respect of any such territories, be it enacted, that no rule, law, or regulation which prior to the passing of this Act shall have been made by the Governor-General or Governor-General in Council, or by any other of the authorities aforesaid, for and in respect of any such non-regulation province, shall be deemed invalid only by reason of the same not having been made in conformity with the provisions of the said Acts, or of any other Act of Parliament respecting the constitution and powers of the Council of India or of the Governor-General, or respecting the powers of such Governors, or Governors in Council, or Lieutenant-Governors as aforesaid.

Provision for leave of absence to an ordinary Member of Council

26. It shall be lawful for the Governor-General in Council, or Governor in Council of either of the Presidencies as the case may be, to grant to an ordinary Member of Council leave of absence under medical certificate, for a period not exceeding six months; and such member, during his absence shall retain his office, and shall, on his return and resumption of his duties, receive half his salary° for the period of such absence; but if his absence shall exceed six months, his office shall be vacated.

Power of making temporary appointments of Members of Council, &c.

27. If any vacancy shall happen in the office of an ordinary Member of the Council of the Governor-General of the Council of either of the Presidencies, when no person provisionally appointed to succeed thereto shall be then present on the spot, then and on every such occasion, such vacancy shall be supplied by the appointment of the Governor-General in Council, or the

See 3 & 4 Wm. IV, C. 85, Section 77.

Governor in Council as the case may be: and until a successor shall arrive the person so nominated shall execute the office to which he shall have been appointed, and shall have all the powers thereof and shall have and be entitled to the salary and other emoluments and advantages appertaining to the said office during his continuance therein, every such temporary Member of Council foregoing all salaries and allowances by him held and enjoyed at the time of his being appointed to such office; and if any ordinary Member of the Council of the Governor-General, or of the Council of either of the Presidencies, shall, by any infirmity or otherwise, be rendered incapable of acting or of attending to act as such, or if any such member shall be absent on leave, and if any person shall have been provisionally appointed as aforesaid, then the place of such member absent or unable to attend, shall be supplied by such person ; and if no person provisionally appointed to succeed to the office shall be then on the spot, the Governor-General in Council, or Governor in Council, as the case may be, shall appoint some person to be a temporary Member of Council ; and, until the return of the member so absent or unable to attend, the person so provisionally appointed by the Secretary of State in Council, or so appointed by the Governor-General in Council, or Governor in Council as the case may be, shall execute the office to which he shall have been appointed, and shall have all the powers thereof, and shall receive half the salary of the Member of Council whose place he supplies, and also half the salary of his office under the Government of India, or the Government of either of the Presidencies, as the case may be, if he hold any such office, the remaining half of such last named salary being at the disposal of the Government of India, or other Government as aforesaid : Provided always, that no person shall be appointed a temporary Member of the said Council who might not have been appointed as hereinbefore provided to fill the vacancy supplied by such temporary appointment.

Governors of Fort Saint George and Bombay may make rules for the conduct of business in their Councils

28. It shall be lawful for the Governors of the Presidencies of Fort Saint George and Bombay, respectively, from time to time to make rules and orders for the conduct of business in their Councils, and any order made or act done in accordance with such directions, except as hereinafter

provided respecting laws and regulations, shall be deemed to be the order or act of the Governor in Council.

Power to summon additional members to the Councils of Fort Saint George and Bombay for the purposes of making laws and regulations

29. For the better exercise of the power of making laws and regulations hereinafter vested in the Governors of the said Presidencies in Council respectively, each of the said Governors shall, in addition to the members whereof his Council now by law consists, or may consist, termed herein ordinary members, nominate to be additional members, the Advocate-General of the Presidency or officer acting in that capacity, and such other persons, not less than four nor more than eight in number, as to him may seem expedient, to be members of Council, for the purpose of making laws and regulations only; and such members shall not be entitled to sit or vote at any meeting of Council, except at meetings held for such purpose; provided, that no less than half of the persons so nominated shall be non-official persons, as hereinbefore described; and that the seat in Council of any non-official member accepting office under the Crown in India shall be vacated on such acceptance.

Such members to be appointed for two years

30. Every additional member of Council so nominated shall be summoned to all meetings held for the purpose of making laws and regulations for the term of two years from the date of such nomination.

Resignation of additional members

31. It shall be lawful for any such additional member of Council to resign his office to the Governor of the Presidency; and on acceptance of such resignation by the Governor of the Presidency, such office shall become vacant.

Power to fill up vacancy in the number of additional members

32. On the event of a vacancy occurring by the death, acceptance of office, or resignation accepted in manner aforesaid, of any such additional Member of Council, it shall be lawful for the Governor of the Presidency to summon any person as additional Member of Council in his place, who shall exercise the same functions until the termination of the term for which the additional member so dying, accepting office, or resigning, was nominated: Provided always, it shall not be lawful for him by such nomination to

diminish the proportion of non-official members hereinbefore directed to be nominated.

No law to be invalid by reason of incompleteness of number of non-official members

33. No law or regulation made by any such Governor in Council in accordance with the provisions of this Act shall be deemed invalid by reason only that the proportion of non-official additional members hereby established was not complete at the date of its introduction to the Council or its enactment.

Senior civil ordinary Member of Council to preside in absence of Governor of Presidency

34. At any meeting of the Council of either of the said Presidencies from which the Governor shall be absent, the senior civil ordinary Member of Council present shall preside; and the power of making laws and regulations hereby vested in such Governor in Council shall be exercised only at meetings of such Council at which the Governor or some ordinary Member of Council, and four or more Members of Council (including under the term Members of Council such additional members as aforesaid, shall be present and in any case of difference of opinion at meetings of any such Council for making laws and regulations, where there shall be an equality of voices, the Governor, or in his absence the senior member then presiding, shall have two votes or the casting vote.

Governor-General to fix first meeting of councils of Presidencies for making laws and regulations, &c.

35. The Governor-General in Council shall, as soon as convenient may appoint the time for the first meeting of the Councils of Fort Saint George and Bombay respectively, for the purpose of making laws and regulations under this Act; and the Governors of the said Presidencies respectively shall summon to such meeting as well the additional Councillors appointed by and under this Act as the ordinary Members of the said Councils.

Governors of Presidencies to appoint subsequent meetings, and adjourn them

36. It shall be lawful for every such Governor to appoint all subsequent times and places of meeting of his Council for the purpose of making laws and regulations under the provisions of this Act, and to adjourn or from time to time to authorize such senior ordinary Member of Council in his

absence to adjourn any meeting for making laws and regulations from time to time and from place to place.

Rules for conduct of business at such meetings

37. Previously to the first of such meetings of their Councils for the purpose of making laws and regulations under the provisions of this Act, the Governors of the said Presidencies in Council respectively shall make rules for the conduct of business at such meetings, subject to the sanction of the Governor-General in Council; but such rules may be subsequently amended at meetings for the purpose of making laws and regulations, subject to the assent of the Governor: Provided always, that it shall be lawful for the Governor-General in Council to disallow any such rule, and render the same of no effect.

Business to be transacted at such meetings

38. No business shall be transacted at any meeting of the Council of either of the said Presidencies for the purpose of making laws and regulations (except as last hereinbefore provided, other than the consideration and enactment of measures introduced into such Council for the purpose of such enactment; and it shall not be lawful for any member or additional member to make, or for the Council to entertain any motion, unless such motion shall be for leave to introduce some measure as aforesaid into Council, or have reference to some measure actually introduced thereinto: Provided always, that it shall not be lawful for any member or additional member to introduce without the previous sanction of the Governor, any measure affecting the public revenues of the Presidency, or by which any charge shall be imposed on such revenues.

Governors to assent to laws and regulations of Presidencies

39. When any law or regulation has been made by any such Council at a meeting for the purpose of making laws and regulations as aforesaid, it shall be lawful for the Governor, whether he shall or shall not have been present in Council at such meeting, to declare that he assents to, or withholds his assent from the same.

Governor-General to assent to laws and regulations of Presidencies

40. The Governor shall transmit forthwith an authentic copy of every law or regulation to which he shall have so declared his assent to the Governor-General; and no such law or regulation shall have validity until the Governor-General shall have assented

thereto, and such assent shall have been signified by him to and published by the Governor: Provided always, that in every case where the Governor-General shall withhold his assent from any such law or regulation, he shall signify to the Governor in writing his reason for so withholding his assent.

Power of the Crown to disallow laws and regulation of Presidencies

41. Whenever any such law or regulation shall have been assented to by the Governor-General, he shall transmit to the Secretary of State for India an authentic copy thereof; and it shall be lawful for Her Majesty to signify, through the Secretary of State for India in Council, her disallowance of such law or regulation and such disallowance shall make void and annul such law or regulation from or after the day on which such Governor shall make known by proclamation, or by signification to the Council, that he has received the notification of such disallowance by Her Majesty.

Extent of power of Governor of Presidency in Council to make laws

42. The Governor of each of the said Presidencies in Council shall have power, at meetings for the purpose of making laws and regulations as aforesaid, and subject to the provisions herein contained to make laws and regulations for the peace and good government of such Presidency, and for that purpose to repeal and amend any laws and regulations made prior to the coming into operation of this Act by any authority in India, so far as they affect such Presidency: Provided always, that such Governor in Council shall not have the power of making any laws or regulations which shall in any way affect any of the provisions of this Act, or of any other Act of Parliament in force or hereafter to be in force in such Presidency.

Governor of Presidency, except with sanction of Governor-General, not to make or take into consideration laws and regulations for certain purposes

43. It shall not be lawful for the Governor in Council of either of the aforesaid Presidencies, except with the sanction of the Governor-General, previously communicated to him to make regulations or take into consideration any law or regulation for any of the purposes next hereinafter mentioned; that is to say,

1. Affecting the Public Debt of India, or the customs duties, or any other tax or duty now in force and imposed by the authority of the Government of India for the general purposes of such Government;

2. Regulating any of the current coin, or the issue of any bills, notes, or other paper currency :

3. Regulating the conveyance of letters by the post office or messages by the electric telegraph within the Presidency :

4. Altering in any way the Penal Code of India, as established by Act of the Governor-General in Council, No. 42 of 1860* :

5. Affecting the religion or religious rites and usages of any class of Her Majesty's subjects in India :

6. Affecting the discipline or maintenance of any part of Her Majesty's Military or Naval Forces :

7. Regulating patents or copyright :

8. Affecting the relations of the Government with foreign princes or states :

Provided always, that no law or provision of any law or regulation which shall have been made by any such Governor in Council, and assented to by the Governor-General as aforesaid shall be deemed invalid only by reason of its relating to any of the purposes comprised in the above list.

Governor-General may establish Councils for making laws and regulations in the Presidency of Fort William in Bengal, &c.

44. The Governor-General in Council, so soon as it shall appear to him expedient, shall, by proclamation, extend the provisions of this Act touching the making of laws and regulations for the peace and good government of the Presidencies of Fort St. George and Bombay to the Bengal Division of the Presidency of Fort William, and shall specify in such proclamation the period at which such provisions shall take effect, and the number of councillors whom the Lieutenant-Governor of the said division may nominate for his assistance in making laws and regulations ; and it shall be further lawful for the Governor-General in Council, from time to time and in his discretion, by similar proclamation, to extend the same provisions to the territories known as the North-Western Provinces and the Punjab respectively.

* should be "No. 45."

Constitution of such Councils

45. Whenever such proclamation as aforesaid shall have been issued regarding the said division or territories respectively, the Lieutenant-Governor thereof shall nominate, for his assistance in making laws and regulations, such number of councillors as shall be in such proclamation specified; provided, that not less than one-third of such councillors shall in every case be non-official persons, as hereinbefore described, and that the nomination of such councillors shall be subject to the sanction of the Governor-General; and provided further, that at any meeting of any such Council from which the Lieutenant-Governor shall be absent, the member highest in official rank among those who may hold office under the Crown shall preside; and the power of making laws and regulations shall be exercised only at meetings at which the Lieutenant-Governor, or some member holding office as aforesaid, and not less than one-half of the members of Council summoned as aforesaid, shall be present; and in any case of difference of opinion at any meetings of such Council for making laws and regulations, where there shall be an equality of voice, the Lieutenant-Governor, or such member highest in official rank as aforesaid then presiding, shall have two votes or the casting vote.

Power to constitute new provinces, and appoint Lieutenant-Governors

46. It shall be lawful for the Governor-General, by proclamation as aforesaid, to constitute from time to time new provinces for the purposes of this Act, to which the like provisions shall be applicable; and further to appoint from time to time a Lieutenant-Governor to any province so constituted as aforesaid, and from time to time to declare and limit the extent of the authority of such Lieutenant-Governor, in like manner as is provided by the Act of the seventeenth and eighteenth years of Her Majesty, chapter seventy-seven, respecting the Lieutenant-Governors of Bengal and the North-Western Provinces.

Power to alter boundaries of presidencies, &c. by proclamation

47. It shall be lawful for the Governor-General in Council, by such proclamation as aforesaid, to fix the limits of any presidency, division, province, or territory in India for the purpose of this Act, and further by proclamation to divide or alter from time to time the limits of any such presidency, division, province, or territory for the said purposes: Provided always, that any law or regulation

made by the Governor or Lieutenant-Governor in Council of any presidency, division, province, or territory shall continue in force in any part thereof which may be severed therefrom by any such proclamation, until superseded by law or regulation of the Governor-General in Council, or of the Governor or Lieutenant-Governor in Council of the presidency, division, province, or territory, to which such parts may become annexed.

Powers of newly constituted Lieutenant-Governors in Council

48. It shall be lawful for every such Lieutenant-Governor in Council thus constituted to make laws for the peace and good government of his respective division, province, or territory, and, except as otherwise hereinbefore specially provided, all the provisions in this Act contained respecting the nomination of additional members for the purpose of making laws and regulations for the Presidencies of Fort Saint George and Bombay, and limiting the power of the Governors in Council of Fort Saint George and Bombay for purpose of making laws and regulations, and respecting the conduct of business in the meetings of such Councils for that purpose, and respecting the power of the Governor-General to declare or withhold his assent to laws or regulations made by the Governor in Council of Fort Saint George and Bombay, and respecting the power of Her Majesty to disallow the same, shall apply to laws or regulations to be so made by any such Lieutenant-Governor in Council.

Previous assent of the Crown necessary to give validity to proclamation

49. Provided always, that no proclamation to be made by the Governor-General in Council under the provisions of this Act for the purpose of constituting any Council for the presidency, division, province, or territorie hereinbefore named, or any other provinces, or for altering the boundaries of any presidency, division, province, or territory, or constituting any new province for the purpose of this Act, shall have any force or validity until the sanction of Her Majesty to the same shall have been previously signified by the Secretary of State in Council to the Governor-General.

Provision for the supply of the office of Governor-General in certain circumstances

50. If any vacancy shall happen in the office of Governor-General of India when no provisional successor shall be in India to supply such vacancy, then and in every such case the Governor of the Presidency of Fort Saint George or the Governor of the Presidency of Bombay who shall have been

first appointed to the office of Governor by Her Majesty, shall hold and execute the said office of Governor-General of India and Governor of the Presidency of Fort William in Bengal until a successor shall arrive, or until some person in India shall be duly appointed thereto; and every such acting Governor-General shall, during the time of his continuing to act as such, have and exercise all the rights and powers of Governor-General of India, and shall be entitled to receive the emoluments and advantages appertaining to the office by him supplied, such acting Governor-General foregoing the salary and allowances appertaining to the office of Governor to which he stands appointed ; and such office of Governor shall be supplied for the time during which such Governor shall be supplied for the time which such Governor shall act as Governor-General, in the manner directed in section sixty-three of the Act of the third and fourth years of King William the Fourth, chapter eighty-five.

If it appears to the Governor necessary to exercise powers before taking his seat in Council, he may make his appointment, &c. known by proclamation

51. If, on such vacancy occurring, it shall appear to the Governor, who by virtue of this Act shall hold and execute the said office of Governor-General, necessary to exercise the powers thereof before he shall have taken his seat in Council, it shall be lawful for him to make known by proclamation his appointment and his intention to assume the said office of Governor-General ; and after such proclamation, and thenceforth until he shall repair to the place where the Council may assemble, it shall be lawful for him to exercise alone all or any of the powers which might be exercised by the Governor-General in Council, except the power of making laws and regulations ; and all acts done in the exercise of the said powers, except as aforesaid, shall be of the same force and effect as if they had been done by the Governor-General in Council ; provided, that all acts done in the said Council after the date of such proclamation, but before the communication thereof to such Council, shall be valid, subject nevertheless to revocation or alteration by such Governor who shall have so assumed the said office of Governor-General and from, the date of the vacancy occurring, until such Governor shall have assumed the said office of Governor-General, the provisions of section sixty-two of the Act of the third and fourth years of King William the Fourth, chapter eighty-five, shall be and the same are declared to be applicable to the case.

Nothing in this Act shall derogate from the powers of the Crown or Secretary of State for India in Council

52. Nothing in this Act contained shall be held to derogate from or interfere with (except as hereinbefore expressly provided) the rights vested in Her Majesty, or the powers of the Secretary of State for India in Council, in relation to the Government of Her Majesty's dominions in India, under any law in force at the date of the passing of this Act; and all things which shall be done by Her Majesty, or by the Secretary of State as aforesaid, in relation to such Government, shall have the same force and validity as if this Act had not been passed.

Meaning of term "in Council"

53. Wherever any act or thing is by this Act required or authorized to be done by the Governor-General or by the Governors of the Presidencies of Fort Saint George and Bombay in Council, it is not required that such act or thing should be done at a meeting for making laws and regulations, unless where expressly provided.

V

AMENDING AND REVISING ACTS

(i) THE GOVERNMENT OF INDIA ACT, 1865

(28 and 29 Vict., Ch. 17)

AN ACT TO ENLARGE THE POWER OF THE GOVERNOR-GENERAL OF INDIA IN COUNCIL AT MEETINGS FOR MAKING LAWS AND REGULATIONS AND TO AMEND THE LAW RESPECTING THE TERRITORIAL LIMITS OF THE SEVERAL PRESIDENCIES AND LIEUTENANT-GOVERNORSHIPS IN INDIA.

[9TH MAY, 1865]

[*Preamble recites 24 and 25 Vict., Ch. 67, S. 22*]

Power to make laws for all British subjects in territories of allied Princes in India

1. The Governor-General of India shall have power at meetings for the purpose of making laws and regulations, to make laws and regulations for all British subjects of Her Majesty within the dominions of Princes and States in India in alliance with Her Majesty whether in the service of the Government of India or otherwise.

Preceding section to be read as part of section 22 of recited Act

2. The preceding section shall be read with and taken as part of section twenty-two of the said Act of the twenty-fourth and twenty-fifth years of Her Majesty, chapter sixty-seven.

3. [Rep. 41 and 42 Vict., Ch. 79 (S. L. R.)

Power to Governor-General to appoint territorial limits of Presidencies &c. by proclamation

4. It shall be lawful for the Governor-General of India in Council from time to time to declare and appoint, by proclamation, what part or parts of the Indian territories for the time being under the dominion of Her Majesty shall be or continue subject to each of the Presidencies and Lieutenant-Governorships for the time being subsisting in such territories, and to make such distribution and arrangement or new distribution and arrangement of such territories into or among such Presidencies and Lieutenant-Governorships as to the said Governor-General in Council may seem expedient.

5. Provided always that it shall be lawful for the Secretary of State in Council to signify to the said Governor-General in Council his disallowance of any proclamation : and provided further that no such proclamation for the purpose of transferring an entire Zilla or district from one Presidency to another, or from one Lieutenant-Governorship to another, shall have any force or validity until the sanction of Her Majesty to the same shall have been previously signified by the Secretary of State in Council to the Governor-General.

Power to Secretary of State in Council to signify disallowance of such proclamation. Royal Sanction necessary to transfer of entire districts

(ii) THE GOVERNMENT OF INDIA ACT, 1869

(32 and 33 Vict., Ch. 97)

AN ACT TO AMEND IN CERTAIN RESPECTS THE ACT FOR THE BETTER GOVERNMENT OF INDIA.

[*Preamble Recites 21 and 22 Vict., Ch. 106*].

1. After the passing of this Act, all vacancies that shall take place in the said Council shall be filled up by appointment by the Secretary of State.

Vacancies in Council of India

2. Every member of the said Council who shall, after the passing of this Act, be so appointed, shall be appointed for a term of ten years, and except as hereinafter provided, shall not be re-eligible.

Term of office

3. It shall be lawful for the Secretary of State to re-appoint for a further period of five years any person whose term of office as member of Council under this Act, shall have expired, provided such re-appointment be made for special reasons of public advantage, which reasons shall be set forth in a minute signed by the said Secretary of State, and laid before both Houses of Parliament.

Re-appointment of a member for further period of five years

4. Except as herein otherwise provided all the provisions of the said recited Act, and of any other Act of Parliament relating to members of the Council of India, shall apply to members appointed under the provisions of this Act.

Former Acts to apply to future members

5. [...omitted as being spent].

6. Any member of Council may by writing under his hand, which shall be recorded in the minutes of the Council, resign his office ; * * * * * *

Resignation of office

Provision as to future changes in the constitution of Council

7. If at any time hereafter it should appear to Parliament expedient to reduce the number or otherwise to deal with the constitution of the said Council, no member of Council who has not served in his office for a period of ten years shall be entitled to claim any compensation for the loss of his office, or for any alteration in the terms and conditions under which the same is held.

Appointment of ordinary members of the Governor-General's Council and of the Presidencies

8. The appointments of the ordinary members of the Governor-General's Council, and of the members of Council of the several presidencies * * * shall * * * be made by Her Majesty by warrant under her Royal Sign Manual.

(iii) THE INDIAN COUNCILS ACT, 1869

(32 & 33 Vict., Ch. 98)

AN ACT TO DEFINE THE POWERS OF THE GOVERNOR-GENERAL OF INDIA IN COUNCIL AT MEETINGS FOR MAKING LAWS AND REGULATIONS FOR CERTAIN PURPOSES.

Whereas doubts have arisen as to the extent of power of the Governor-General of India in Council to make laws binding upon native Indian subjects beyond the Indian territories under the dominion of Her Majesty,

And whereas it is expedient that better provision should be made in other respects for the exercise of the power of the Governor-General in Council,

Be it enacted by the Queen's Most Excellent Majesty, by and with the advice and consent of the Lords Spiritual and Temporal, and Commons in this present Parliament assembled, and by the authority of the same, as follows :—

Power to make laws for native Indian subjects beyond the Indian territories.

1. From and after the passing of this Act, the Governor-General of India in Council shall have power at meetings for the purpose of making laws and regulations to make laws and regulations for all persons being native Indian subjects of Her Majesty, Her heirs and successors, without and beyond, as well as within the Indian territories under the dominion of Her Majesty.

2. No law heretofore passed by the Governor-General of India, or by the Governors of Madras and Bombay, respectively in Council, shall be deemed to be invalid solely by reason of its having reference to native subjects of Her Majesty not within the Indian territories under the dominion of Her Majesty.

Former laws to be valid

3. Notwithstanding anything in the Indian Councils Act or in any other Act of Parliament contained, any law or regulation which shall hereafter be made by the Governor-General in Council in manner in the said Indian Councils Act provided shall not be invalid by reason only that it may repeal or affect any of the provisions of the said Act of the third and fourth years of King William the Fourth, chapter eighty-five, contained in sections eighty-one, eighty-two, eighty-three, eighty-four, eighty-five and eighty-six of the said Act.

Power to repeal or amend certain sections of 3 and 5, Will. 4, c. 85

(iv) THE INDIAN COUNCILS ACT, 1870

(33 Vict., Ch. 3.)

AN ACT TO MAKE BETTER PROVISIONS FOR MAKING LAWS AND REGULATIONS FOR CERTAIN PARTS OF INDIA, AND FOR CERTAIN OTHER PURPOSES RELATING THERETO.

Whereas it is expedient that provision should be made to enable Governor-General of India in Council to make regulations for the peace and good government of certain territories in India otherwise that at meetings for the purpose of making laws and regulations held under the provisions of the Indian Councils Act, 1861, and also for certain other purposes connected with the Government of India.

Be it enacted by the Queen's Most Excellent Majesty, by and with the advice and consent of the Lords Spiritual and Temporal, and Commons, in this present Parliament assembled, and by the authority of the same, as follows:—

1. Every Governor of a Presidency in Council, Lieutenant-Governor, or Chief Commissioner, whether the Governorship, or Lieutenant-Governorship, or Chief Commissionership be now in existence or may hereafter be established, shall have power to propose to the Governor-General in Council drafts of any regulations, together with the reasons for proposing the same, for the peace and government of any

Power to Executive Government of British India to make regulations for certain parts thereof.

part or parts of the territories under his Government or administration to which the Secretary of State for India shall from time to time by resolution in Council declare the provisions of this section to be applicable from a date to be fixed in such resolution.

And the Governor-General in Council shall take such drafts and reasons into consideration ; and when any such draft shall have been approved of by the Governor-General in Council and shall have received the Governor-General's assent, it shall be published in the *Gazette of India* and in the local Gazettes, and shall thereupon have like force of law and be subject to the like disallowances as if it had been made by the Governor-General of India in Council at a meeting for the purpose of making laws and regulations.

The Secretary of State for India in Council may from time to time withdraw such power from any Governor, Lieutenant-Governor or Chief Commissioner, on whom it has been conferred, and may from time to time restore the same as he shall think fit.

Copies of regulations to be sent to Secretary of State Subsequent enactments to control regulations

2. The Governor-General shall transmit to the Secretary of State for India in Council an authentic copy of every regulation which shall have been made under the provisions of this Act ; and all laws or regulations hereafter made by the Governor-General of India in Council, whether at a meeting for the purpose of making laws and regulations, or under the said provisions, shall control and supersede any regulation in anywise repugnant thereto which shall have been made under the same provisions.

Lieutenant-Governors and Chief Commissioners to be members *ex-officio* of Governor-General's Council for the purpose of making laws and regulations

3. Whenever the Governor-General in Council shall hold a meeting for the purpose of making laws and regulations at any place within the limits of any territories now or hereafter placed under the administration of a Lieutenant-Governor or a Chief Commissioner, the Lieutenant-Governor or Chief Commissioner respectively shall be *ex-officio* an Additional Member of the Council of the Governor-General for that purpose, in excess (if necessary) of the maximum number of twelve specified by the said Act.

Section 49 of 3 and 4, Will. 4, c. 85 repealed

4. Section forty-nine of the Act of the third and fourth years of King William the Fourth, chapter eighty five, is hereby repealed.

5. Whenever any measure shall be proposed before the Governor-General of India in Council whereby the safety, tranquility, or interests of the British possessions in India, or any part thereof, may be, in the judgment of the said Governor-General essentially affected, and he shall be of opinion either that the measure proposed ought to be adopted and carried into execution, or that it ought to be suspended or rejected, and the majority in Council then present shall dissent from such opinion, the Governor-General may on his own authority and responsibility, suspend or reject the measure in part or in whole, or adopt and carry it into execution, but in every such case any two members of the dissentient majority may require that the said suspension, rejection, or adoption, as well as the fact of their dissent, shall be notified to the Secretary of State for India, and such notification shall be accompanied by copies of the minutes (if any) which the Members of the Council shall have recorded on the subject.

Procedure in case of difference between the Governor-General and the majority of his Council

6. Whereas it is expedient that additional facilities should be given for the employment of natives of India, of proved merit and ability, in the Civil Service of Her Majesty in India: Be it enacted, that nothing in the "Act for the Government of India," twenty one and twenty-two Victoria, chapter one hundred and six, or in the "Act to confirm certain appointments in India, and to amend the law concerning the Civil Service there," twenty-four and twenty-five Victoria, chapter fifty-four, or in any other Act of Parliament or other law now in force in India, shall restrain the authorities in India by whom appointments are or may be made to offices, places, and employments in the Civil Service of Her Majesty in India from appointing any native of India to any such office, place, or employment, although such native shall not have been admitted to the said Civil Service of India in manner in section thirty-two first mentioned Act provided, but subject to such rules as may be from time to time prescribed by the Governor-General in Council and sanctioned by the Secretary of State in Council, with the concurrence of a majority of members present; and that for the purpose of this Act the words "natives of India" shall include any person born and domiciled within the dominions of Her Majesty in India, of parents habitually resident in India, and not established there for temporary purposes only; and that it shall be

Power to appoint natives of India to certain offices without certificate from the Civil Service Commissioners

lawful for the Governor-General in Council to define and limit from time to time the qualification of 'native of India' thus expressed ; provided that every resolution made by him for such purpose shall be subject to the sanction of the Secretary of State in Council, and shall not have force until it has been laid for thirty days before both Houses of Parliament.

(v) THE INDIAN COUNCILS ACT, 1871

(34 & 35 Vict., Ch. 34.)

AN ACT TO EXTEND IN CERTAIN RESPECTS THE POWER OF LOCAL LEGISLATURES IN INDIA AS REGARDS EUROPEAN BRITISH SUBJECTS.

Whereas it is expedient that the power of making laws and regulations conferred on Governors of Presidencies in India in Council by the Indian Councils Act, 24 & 25 Vict., c. 67, sec. 42 should in certain respects be extended :

Be it enacted by the Queen's Most Excellent Majesty, by and with the advice and consent of the Lords Spiritual and Temporal, and Commons, in this present Parliament assembled, and by the authority of the same, as follows :—

Power to Local Legislatures to confer jurisdiction over European British subjects to Magistrates in certain cases

1. No law or regulation heretofore made or hereafter to be made by any Governor or Lieutenant-Governor in Council in India in manner prescribed by the aforesaid Act shall be invalid only by the reason that it confers on Magistrates, being justices of the peace, the same jurisdiction over European British subjects as such Governor or Lieutenant-Governor in Council, by regulation made as aforesaid, could have lawfully conferred or could lawfully confer on Magistrates in the exercise of authority over natives in the like cases.

Committal of defendant (being an European British subject) to the High Court. (Indian Act No. XXV of 1881, s. 226)

2. When evidence has been given in any proceeding under this Act before a Magistrate, being a justice of the peace, which appears to be sufficient for the conviction of the accused person, being an European British subject, of an offence for which, if a native, he would under existing law be triable exclusively before the Court of Sessions, or which, in the opinion of the Magistrate is one which ought to be tried by the High Court, the accused person, if such European British

subject, shall be sent for trial by the Magistrate before the High Court.

Power to local Legislatures to amend and repeal certain laws

3. And whereas by an Act passed by the Governor-General of India in Council, Indian Act No. XXII of 1870, it is provided that certain Acts heretofore passed by the Governors of Madras and Bombay respectively in Council, and by the Lieutenant-Governor of Bengal in Council, shall, so far as regards the liability of European British subject to be convicted and punished thereunder, be and be deemed to be as valid as if they had been passed by the Governor-General of India in Council at a meeting for the purpose of making laws and regulations: Be it further enacted, that the said Governors and Lieutenant-Governors in Council respectively shall have power to repeal and amend any of the said Acts to be passed under the provisions of the Indian Councils Act.

(vi) THE INDIAN COUNCILS ACT, 1874

(37 & 38 Vict., Ch. 91)

AN ACT TO AMEND THE LAW RELATING TO THE COUNCIL OF THE GOVERNOR-GENERAL OF INDIA.

Whereas it is expedient to amend the law relating to the Council of the Governor-General of India :

Be it enacted, etc., etc. * * * * * as follows :

Power to appoint ordinary Member of Governor-General in Council for public works purposes

1. It shall be lawful for Her Majesty, if she shall see fit, to increase the number of the ordinary members of the Council of the Governor-General of India to six, by appointing any person, from time to time, by warrant under Her Royal Sign Manual to be an ordinary member of the said Council in addition to the ordinary members thereof appointed under section three of the "Indian Councils Act, 1861," and under section eight of the Act of the thirty-second and thirty-third years of Her present Majesty, chapter ninety seven. The law for the time being in force with reference to ordinary members of the Council of the Governor-General of India shall apply to the person so appointed by Her Majesty under this Act, who shall be called the member of Council for public works purposes.

Power to reduce number of members of the Council of the Governor-General

2. Whenever a member of Council for public works purposes shall have been appointed under the first section of this Act, it shall be lawful for Her Majesty, if she shall see fit, to diminish, from time to time, the number of the ordinary members of the Council of the Governor-General of India to five, by abstaining so long as she shall deem proper from filling up any vacancy or vacancies occurring in the offices of the ordinary members of the said Council appointed under section three of "The Indian Councils Act, 1861," and under section eight of the Act of the thirty-second and thirty-third years of Her present Majesty, chapter ninety-seven, not being a vacancy in the office of the ordinary member of Council required by law to be a barrister or a member of the Faculty of Advocates in Scotland, and whenever the Secretary of State for India shall have informed the Governor-General of India that it is not the intention of Her Majesty to fill up any vacancy, no temporary appointment shall be made to such vacancy under section twenty-seven of "Indian Councils Act, 1861," and if any such temporary appointment shall have been made previously to the receipt of such information, the tenure of office of the person temporarily appointed shall cease and determine from the time of the receipt of such information by the Governor-General.

Power of Governor-General in respect of his Council, not affected

3. Nothing in this Act contained shall affect the provisions of section eight of "The Indian Councils Act, 1861," or the provisions of section five of the Act of the thirty-third year of Her Majesty, chapter three, or any power or authority vested by law in the Governor-General of India in respect of his Council or of the members thereof.

(vii) THE COUNCIL OF INDIA ACT, 1876

(39 Vict., Ch. 7.)

AN ACT TO AMEND THE LAW RELATING TO CERTAIN APPOINTMENTS TO THE COUNCIL OF INDIA.

Whereas by an Act of the thirty-second and thirty-third years of the reign of Her present Majesty, chapter ninety-seven (in this Act referred to as the Act of 1869), it was, among other things, provided that the members of the Council of India were to hold their offices for a period of ten years, and for such further period as is in section three of the said Act mentioned.

And whereas, regard being had to the composition of the said Council contemplated in section ten of the Act of the twenty-first and twenty-second years of Her presept Majesty, chapter one hundred and six (in this Act referred to as the Act of 1858), it is expedient to amend the said first-mentioned Act in certain particulars.

Be it enacted * * * * as follows :

Appointment of persons with professional or other qualifications

1. Notwithstanding anything in the Act of 1869, the Secretary of State for India may, if he thinks fit, subject to the condition as to the number of appointments hereinafter laid down, appoint any person having professional or other peculiar qualifications to be a member of the said Council under this Act ; and every person so appointed shall hold his office in the same manner, and shall be entitled to the same salary, pension, and other rights and privileges, and be subject to the same disabilities, as if he had been elected or appointed before the passiag of the Act of 1869.

Where any person appointed under this Act is at his appointment a member of the Council, his period of his service for the purposes of this Act shall be reckoned from the time of his first appointment to the Council.

The special reasons for every appointment under this Act shall be stated in a minute of the Secretary of State for India, and shall be laid before both Houses of Parliament. Not more than three persons appointed under this Act shall be members of the Council at the same time; nor shall the provisions of sections seven and ten of the Act of 1858, with reference to the members of the Council and the qualifications of the major part of the members, be affected by this Act.

(viii) THE INDIAN COUNCILS ACT, 1892

(55 & 56 Vict., Ch. 14.)

AN ACT TO AMEND THE INDIAN COUNCILS ACT, 1861.

Be it enacted by the Queen's Most Excellent Majesty, by and with the advice and consent of the Lords Spiritual and Temporal, and Commons in this present Parliament assembled. and by the authority of the same, as follows :—

Provisions for increase of number of members of Indian Councils for making laws and regulations

1. (1) The number of additional members of Council nominated by the Governor-General under the provisions of section ten of the Indian Councils Act, 1868, shall be such as to him may seem from time to time expedient, but shall not be less than ten nor more than sixteen; and the number of additional members of Council nominated by the Governors of the Presidencies of Fort St. George and Bombay respectively under the provisions of section twenty-nine of the Indian Councils Act, 1861, shall besides the Advocate-General of the presidency or officer acting in that capacity, be such as to the said Governors respectively may from time to time expedient, but shall not be less than eight nor more than twenty.

(2) It shall be lawful for the Governor-General in Council by proclamation from time to time to increase the number of Councillors whom the Lieutenant-Governors of the Bengal Division of the Presidency of Fort William and of the North-Western Provinces and Oudh respectively may nominate for their assistance in making laws and regulations: Provided always that not more than twenty shall be nominated for the Bengal Division, and not more than fifteen for the North-Western Provinces and Oudh.

(3) Any person resident in India may be nominated an additional member of Council under sections ten and twenty-nine of the Indian Councils Act, 1861, and this Act, or a member of the Council of the Lieutenant-Governor of any province to which the provisions of the Indian Councils Act, 1861, touching the making of laws and regulations, have been or are hereafter extended or made applicable.

(4) The Governor-General in Council may from time to time with the approval of the Secretary of State in Council, make regulations as to the conditions under which such nominations, or any of them, shall be made by the Governor-General, Governors, and Lieutenant-Governors, respectively. and prescribe the manner in which such regulations shall be carried into effect.

Modification of provisions of 24 & 25 Vict, c. 67 as to business at Legislative meetings

2. Notwithstanding any provision in the Indian Councils Act, 1861, the Governor-General of India in Council may from time to time make rules authorising at any meeting of the Governor-General's Council for the purpose of making laws and regulations the discussion of the Annual Financial Statement of the Governor-General

in Council and the asking of questions, but under such conditions and restrictions as to the subject or otherwise as shall be in the said rules prescribed or declared : And notwithstanding any provisions in the Indian Councils Act, 1861, the Governors in Council of Fort St. George and Bombay, respectively, and the Lieutenant-Governor of any province to which the provisions of the Indian Councils Act, 1861, touching the making of laws and regulations, have been made or are hereafter extended or made applicable, may from time to time make rules for authorising at any meeting of their respective Councils for the purpose of making laws and regulations the discussion of the Annual Financial Statement of their respective local Governments and the asking of questions, but under such conditions and restrictions as to subject or otherwise as shall in the said rules applicable to such Councils respectively be prescribed or declared. But no member at any such meeting of any Council should have power to submit or propose any resolution, or to divide the Council in respect of any such financial discussion, or the answer to any question asked under the authority of this Act or the rules made under this Act : Provided that any rule made under this Act by a Governor in Council, or by a Lieutenant-Governor, shall be submitted for and shall be subject to the sanction of the Governor-General in Council, and any rule made under this Act by the Governor-General in Council shall be submitted for and shall be subject to the sanction of the Secretary of State in Council : Provided also that rules made under this Act shall not be subject to alteration or amendment at meetings for the purpose of making laws and regulations.

Meaning of 24 & 25 Vict. c. 67, s. 22; 3 & 4 Will. IV, c. 85; & 16 & 17 Vict. c. 95

3. It is hereby declared that in the twenty-second section of the Indian Councils Act, 1861, it was and is intended that the words "Indian territories now under the dominion of Her Majesty" should be read and construed as if the words "or hereafter" were and had at the time of the passing of the said Act been inserted next after the word "now" and further, that the Acts third and fourth, William the Fourth, Chapter eighty-five, and sixteenth and seventeenth Victoria Chapter ninety-five respectively, shall be read and construed as if at the date of the enactment thereof respectively, it was intended and had been enacted that the said Acts respectively should extend to and include the territories

acquired after the dates thereof respectively, by the East India Company, and should not be confined to the territories at the dates of the said enactments respectively in the possession and under the Government of the said Company.

Repeal

4. Sections thirteen and thirty-two of the Indian Councils Act, 1861, are hereby repealed; and it is enacted that—

Power to fill up vacancy in number of additional members

(1) If any additional member of Council or any members of the Council of a Lieutenant-Governor appointed under the said Act or this Act shall be absent from India or unable to attend to the duties of his office for a period of two consecutive months, it shall be lawful for the Governor-General, the Governor, or the Lieutenant-Governor to whose Council such additional member or members may have been nominated (as the case may be) to declare, by a notification published in the Government *Gazette*, that the seat in Council of such person has become vacant.

(2) In the event of a vacancy occurring by the absence from India, inability to attend to duty, death, acceptance of office, or resignation duly accepted of any such additional member or members of the Council of a Lieutenant-Governor, it shall be lawful for the Governor-General, for the Governor, or for the Lieutenant-Governor, as the case may be, to nominate any person as additional member or members, as the case may be, in his place; and every member so nominated shall be summoned to all meetings held for the purpose of making laws and regulations for the term of two years from the date of such nominaion: Provided always that it shall not be lawful by such nomination, or by any nomination made under this Act, to diminish the proportion of non-official members directed by the Indian Councils Act, 1861, to be nominated.

Powers of Indian provincial legislatures

5. The local legislature of any province in India may from time to time, by Acts passed under and subject to the provisions of the Indian Councils Act, 1861, and with the previous sanction of the Governor-General but not otherwise, repeal or amend as to that province any law or regulation made either before or after the passing of this Act by any authority in India other than that local legislature: Provided that an Act or a provision of an Act made by a local legislature, and

subsequently assented to by the Governor-General in pursuance of the Indian Councils Act, 1861, shall not be deemed invalid by reason only of its requiring the previous sanction of the Governor-General under this section.

Definitions

6. In this Act—The expression, "local legislature", means—

(1) The Governor-in-Council for the purpose of making laws and regulations of the respective provinces of Fort St. George Bombay : and

(2) The Council for the purpose of making laws and regulations of the Lieutenant-Governor of any province to which the provisions of the Indian Councils Act, 1861, touching the making of laws or regulations have been or hereafter extended or made applicable.

The expression "Province" means any presidency, division, province or territory over which the powers of any local legislature for the time being extend.

Saving power of Governor-General in Council

7. Nothing in this Act shall detract from or diminish the powers of the Governor-General in Council at meetings for the purpose of making laws and regulations.

Short title

8. This Act may be cited as the Indian Councils Act, 1892; and the Indian Councils Act, 1861, and this Act may be cited together as the Indian Councils Acts, 1861 and 1892.

(ix) THE INDIAN COUNCILS ACT, 1904

AN ACT TO AMEND INDIAN COUNCILS ACT OF 1874

Whereas it is etc. etc. . . . * * * Be it enacted * * * as follows :—

1. In section one of the Indian Councils Act, 1874, the words "who shall be called the member of council for public works" and in section two of the same Act the words 'for public works' are hereby repealed.

2. The Act shall be cited as the Indian Councils Act, 1904.

(x) THE COUNCIL OF INDIA ACT, 1907

AN ACT TO AMEND THE LAW AS TO THE COUNCIL OF INDIA

Be it enacted by the King's Most Excellent Majesty, by and with the advice and consent of the Lords Spiritual, and Temporal and Commons, in this present Parliament assembled, and by the authority of the same, as follows :—

1. The Council of India shall consist of such number of members not less than ten and not more than fourteen, as the Secretary of State may from time to time determine.

2. In section ten of the Government of India Act, 1858 (21 and 22 Vict. c. 106), the words " more than five years " shall be substituted for the words "more than ten years."

3. Section thirteen of the same Act shall, as regards any member appointed after the passing of this Act, be read and construed as if the words one thousand pounds were substituted for the words one thousand two hundred pounds.

4. Section two of the Government of India Act, 1869 (32 and 33 Vict. c. 97), shall, as regards any appointment made after the passing of this Act, be read and construed as if the word " seven " were substituted for the word " ten."

5. The Council of India Act, 1876 (39 Vict. c. 7), and the Council of India Reduction Act, 1889 (52 and 53 Vict, c. 65), are hereby repealed.

6. This Act may be cited as the Council of India Act, 1907.

(xi) THE INDIAN COUNCILS ACT, 1909

AN ACT TO AMEND THE INDIAN COUNCILS ACTS 1861 AND 1892 AND THE GOVERNMENT OF INDIA ACT, 1838

[*15th May 1909.*]

Be it enacted by the King's Most Excellent Majesty, by and with the advice and consent of the Lords Spiritual and Temporal, and Commons, in this present Parliament assembled, and by the authority of the same, as follows :—

Amendment of constitution of Legislative Councils

1. (1) The additional members of the Councils for the purpose of making laws and regulations (hereinafter referred to as Legislative Councils) of the Governor-General and the Governors of Fort St. George and Bombay, and the members of the

Legislative Councils already constituted, or which may hereafter be constituted, of the several Lieutenant-Governors of Provinces, instead of being all nominated by the Governor, or Lieutenant-Governor in manner provided by the Indian Councils Acts, 1861 and 1892, shall include members so nominated and also members elected in accordance with regulations made under this Act, and references in those Acts to the members so nominated and their nomination shall be construed as including references to the members so elected and their election.

(2) The number of additional members or members so nominated and elected, the number of such members required to constitute a quorum, the term of office of such members and the manner of filling up casual vacancies occurring by reason of absence from India, inability to attend to duty, death, acceptance of office, or resignation duly accepted, or otherwise, shall, in the case of each such Council, be such as may be prescribed by regulations made under this Act :

Provided that the aggregate number of members so nominated and elected shall not, in the case of any Legislative Council mentioned in the first column of the First Schedule to this Act, exceed the number specified in the second column of that schedule.

Constitution and procedure of executive Councils of Governors of Fort Saint George and Bombay

2. (1) The number of ordinary members of the Councils of the Governors of Fort Saint George and Bombay shall be such number not exceeding four as the Secretary of State in Council may from time to time direct, of whom two at least shall be persons who at the time of their appointment have been in the service of the Crown in India for at least twelve years.

(2) If at any meeting of either of such Councils there is an equality of votes on any question the Governor or other person presiding shall have two votes or the casting vote.

Power to constitute provincial Executive Councils

3. (1) It shall be lawful for the Governor-General in Council, with the approval of the Secretary of State in Council, by proclamation, to create a Council in the Bengal Division of the Presidency of Fort William for the purpose of assisting the Lieutenant-Governor in the executive government of the province, and by such proclamation—

(*a*) to make provision for determining what shall be the number (not exceeding four) and qualifications of the members of the Council; and

(*b*) to make provision for the appointment of temporary or acting members of the Council during the absence of any member from illness or otherwise, and for the procedure to be adopted in case of a difference of opinion between a Lieutenant-Governor and his Council, and in the case of equality of votes, and in the case of a Lieutenant-Governor being obliged to absent himself from his Council from indisposition or any other cause.

(2) It shall be lawful for the Governor-General in Council, with the like approval, by a like proclamation to create a Council in any other province under a Lieutenant-Governor for the purpose of assisting the Lieutenant-Governor in the executive government of the province: Provided that before any such proclamation is made a draft thereof shall be laid before each House of Parliament for not less than sixty days during the session of Parliament, and, if before the expiration of that time an Address is presented to His Majesty by either House of Parliament against the draft or any part thereof, no further proceedings shall be taken thereon, without prejudice to the making of any new draft.

(3) Where any such proclamation has been made with respect to any province the Lieutenant-Governor may, with the consent of the Governor-General in Council, from time to time make rules and orders for the more convenient transaction of business in his Council, and any order made or act done in accordance with the rules and orders so made shall be deemed to be an act or order of the Lieutenant-Governor in Council.

(4) Every member of any such Council shall be appointed by the Governor-General, with the approval of his Majesty, and shall, as such be a member of the Legislative Council of the Lieutenant-Governor, in addition to the members nominated by the Lieutenant-Governor and elected under the provisions of this Act.

Appointment of Vice-Presidents

4. The Governor-General, and the Governor of Fort Saint George and Bombay, and the Lieutenant-Governor of every province respectively shall appoint a member of their respective councils to be Vice-

President thereof, and, for the purpose of temporarily holding and executing the office of Governor-General or Governor of Fort Saint George or Bombay and of presiding at meetings of Council in the absence of the Governor-General, Governor, or Lieutenant-Governor, the Vice-President so appointed shall be deemed to be the senior member of Council and the member highest in rank, and the Indian Councils Act, 1861, and sections sixty-two and sixty-three of the Government of India Act, 1833, shall have effect accordingly.

3 & 4 Will. 4. c. 85

Power to extend business of Legislative Councils

5. (1) Notwithstanding anything in the Indian Councils Act, 1861, the Governor-General in Council, the Governors in Council of Fort Saint George and Bombay respectively, and the Lieutenant-Governor or Lieutenant-Governor in Council of every province, shall make rules authorising at any meeting of their respective legislative councils the discussion of the annual financial statement of the Governor-General in Council or of their respective Local Governments, as the case may be, and of any matter of general public interest, and the asking of questions, under such conditions and restrictions as may be prescribed in the rules applicable to the several councils.

(2) Such rules as aforesaid may provide for the appointment of a member of any such council to preside at any such discussion in the place of the Governor-General, Governor, or Lieutenant-Governor, as the case may be, and of any Vice-President.

(3) Rules under this section, where made by a Governor in Council, or by a Lieutenant-Governor, or a Lieutenant-Governor in Council, shall be subject to the sanction of the Governor-General in Council, and where made by the Governor-General in Council shall be subject to the sanction of the Secretary of State in Council, and shall not be subject to alteration or amendment by the Legislative Council of the Governor-General, Governor, or Lieutenant-Governor.

Power to make regulations

6. The Governor-General in Council shall, subject to the approval of the Secretary of State in Council, make regulations as to the conditions under which and manner in which persons resident in India may be nominated or elected as members of the Legislative Councils of the Governor-General, Governors, and as to the qualifications for being,

and for being nominated or elected, a member of any such council, and as to any other matter for which regulations are authorised to be made under this Act, and also as to the manner in which those regulations are to be carried into effect. Regulations under this section shall not be subject to alteration or amendment by the Legislative Council of the Governor-General.

Laying of proclamations, etc., before Parliament

7. All proclamations, regulations and rules made under this Act, other than rules made by a Lieutenant-Governor made for the more convenient transaction of business in his Council shall be laid before both Houses of Parliament as soon as may be after they are made.

Short title, construction, commencement, and repeal. 32 & 33 Vict. c. 98. 33 & 34 Vict. c. 34

8. (1) This Act may be cited as the Indian Councils Act, 1909, and shall be construed with the Indian Council Acts, 1861 and 1892, and those Acts, the Indian Councils Act 1869, the Indian Councils Act, 1871, the Indian Councils Act, 1874, the Indian Councils Act, 1904, and this Act may be cited together as the Indian Councils Acts, 1861 to 1909.

37 & 38 Vict. c. 91. 4 Edw. 7 c. 26

(2) This Act shall come into operation on such date or dates as the Governor-General in Council, with the approval of the Secretary of State in Council, may appoint, and different dates may be appointed for different purposes and provisions of this Act and for different councils.

On the date appointed for the coming into operation of this Act as respects any Legislative Council, all the nominated members of the Council then in office shall go out of office, but may, if otherwise qualified, be renominated or be elected in accordance with the provisions of this Act.

(3) The enactments mentioned in the Second Schedule to this Act are hereby repealed to the extent mentioned in the third column of that Schedule.

SCHEDULES

FIRST SCHEDULE

Maximum Numbers of Nominated and Elected Members of Legislative Councils

Legislative Council.	Maximum number.
Legislative Council of the Governor-General.	60
Legislative Council of the Governor of Fort Saint George ...	50
Legislative Council of the Governor of Bombay.	50
Legislative Council of the Lieutenant-Governor of the Bengal division of the Presidency of Fort William ...	50
Legislative Council of the Lieutenant-Governor of the United Provinces of Agra and Oudh	50
Legislative Council of the Lieutenant-Governor of the Provinces of Eastern Bengal and Assam	50
Legislative Council of the Lieutenant-Governor of the Province of the Punjab	30
Legislative Council of the Lieutenant-Governor of the Province of Burma	30
Legislative Council of the Lieutenant-Governor of any Province which may hereafter be constituted	30

SECOND SCHEDULE

Enactments repealed

Section and chapter.	Short title.	Extent of repeal.
24 and 25 Vict., c. 67.	The Indian Councils Act, 1861.	In section ten, the words "not less than six nor more than twelve in number." In section eleven, the words "for the term of two years from the date of such nomination." In section fifteen, the words from "and the power of making laws and regulations" to "shall be present." In section twenty-nine, the words "not less than four nor more than eight in number." In section thirty, the words "for the term of two years from the date of such nomination." In section thirty-four, the words from "and power of making laws and regulations," to "shall be present." In section forty-five, the words from "and the power of making laws and regulations" to "shall be present." Sections one and two.
55 and 56 Vict., c. 14	The Indian Councils Act, 1892.	In section four, the words "appointed under the said Act or this Act" and paragraph (2).

(xii) GOVERNMENT OF INDIA ACT, 1912

(2 & 3 Geo. 5)

AN ACT TO MAKE SUCH AMENDMENTS IN THE LAW RELATING TO THE GOVERNMENT OF INDIA AS ARE CONSEQUENTIAL ON THE APPOINTMENT OF A SEPARATE GOVERNOR OF FORT WILLIAM IN BENGAL, AND OTHER ADMINISTRATIVE CHANGES IN THE LOCAL GOVERNMENT OF INDIA. [*25th June 1912.*]

Whereas His Majesty has been pleased to appoint a Governor of the Presidency of Fort William in Bengal as delimited by a proclamation made by the Governor-General in Council and dated the twenty-second day of March nineteen hundred and twelve :

And whereas the Governor-General in Council by two further proclamations of the same date has constituted a new province under a Lieutenant-Governor styled the province of Bihar and Orissa, and has taken the province of Assam under the immediate authority and management of the Governor-General in Council.

And whereas it is expedient to declare what powers are exercisable by the Governor and Governor in Council of the presidency of Fort William in Bengal and to make other provisions with respect to the administrative changes effected as aforesaid :—

Be it therefore enacted by the King's Most Excellent Majesty, by and with the advice and consent of the Lords Spiritual and Temporal, and Commons in this present Parliament assembled, and by the authority of the same, as follows :—

Power of Governor of Fort William in Bengal

1.—(1) It is hereby declared that the Governor and Governor in Council of the presidency of Fort William in Bengal shall within that presidency as so delimited as aforesaid, have all the rights, duties, functions, and immunities which the Governors and Governors in Council of the presidencies of Fort St. George and Bombay respectively possess, and all enactments relating to the Governors of those presidencies and the Councils (whether for executive or legislative purposes) thereof and the members of those Councils shall apply accordingly to the Governor of the presidency of Fort William in Bengal, and his Council and the members of that Council :

Provided that,—

(*a*) if the Governor-General in Council reserves to himself any powers now exercisable by him in relation to the Presidency of Fort

William in Bengal, those powers shall continue to be exercisable by the Governor-General in Council in the like manner and to the like extent as heretofore ; and

(b) It shall not be obligatory to nominate the Advocate-General of the presidency of Fort William in Bengal or any officer acting in that capacity to be a member of the legislative council of that Governor of that presidency.

55 Geo. 3. c. 84

(2). The power of the Governor-General in Council under section one of the Indian Presidency Towns Act 1815, to extend the limits of the town of Calcutta shall be transferred to the Governor in Council of the presidency of Fort William in Bengal.

Provisions as to the province of Bihar. 9 Edw. 7. c. 4

2. The provisions of sub-section(1) of section three of the Indian Councils Act, 1909 (which relate to the constitution of provincial executive councils),shall apply to the province of Bihar and Orissa in like manner as they applied to the province of the Bengal division of the presidency of Fort William.

Creation of legislative councils of chief commissioners 17 and 18Vict. c. 77

3. It shall be lawful for the Governor-General in Council by proclamation to extend subject to such modifications and adaptations as he may consider necessary, the provisions of the Indian Councils Acts 1861 to 1909, touching the making of laws and regulations, for the peace and good Government of provinces under Lieutenant-Governors (including the provisions as to the constitution of legislative councils for such provinces and the business to be transacted therein, to any territories for the time being under a chief commissioner, and where such provisions have been applied to any such territories the proviso to section three of the Government of India Act, 1854 (which relates to the alteration of laws and regulations in such territories) shall not apply to those territories.

Amendment and repeal of Acts and saving of 33 Geo. c. 52 and 4 Will. 4 c. 85

4. (1) The enactments mentioned in Part I of the Schedule to this Act shall have effect subject to the amendments therein specified, and section fifty-seven of the East India Company Act, 1793, and section seventy-one of the Government of India Act, 1833 (which relate to the filling up of vacancies in the Indian Civil Service), and other enactments mentioned in Part II of that Schedule are hereby repealed.

(2) Nothing in this Act or in the said recited proclamations shall affect the power of the Governor-General in Council of making new distrubutions and arrangement of territories into and among the various presidencies and lieutenant-governorships, and it is hereby declared that the said power extends to territories under the immediate authority and management of the Governor-General in Council as well as to territories subject to the several presidencies and lieutenant governorships.

Short title and commencement

5. This Act may be cited as the Government of India Act, 1912, and shall come into operation on such day as the Governor-General in Council with the approval of the Secretary of State in Council may appoint.

SCHEDULE

PART I

Amendments.

In section fifty of the Indian Councils Act, 1861 (24 and 25 Vict. c. 67), after the words " then and in every such case," there shall be inserted the words "the Governor of the Presidency of Fort William in Bengal."

In the First Schedule to the Indian Councils Act, 1909 (9 Edw. 7. c. 4), there shall be inserted—

" Legislative Council of the Governor of Fort William in Bengal. 50

" Legislative Council of the Lieutenant-Governor of Bihar and Orissa ... ... 50."

PART II

Repeals.

Sections fifty-three and fifty-seven of the East India Company Act, 1793 (33 Geo. 3. c. 52).

In section sixty-two of the Government of India Act, 1833 (3 and 4 Will. 4. c. 285) the words " and Governor of the Presidency of Fort William in Bengal," and section seventy-one of the same Act.

In section fifty of the Indian Councils Act, 1861 (24 and 25 Vict. c. 67) the words " and Governor of the Presidency of Fort William in Bengal."

In the First Schedule to the Indian Councils Act, 1909 (9 Edw. 7. c. 4), the following words :—

" Legislative Council of the Lieutenant Governor of the Bengal Division of the Presidency of Fort William 50

" Legislative Council of the Lieutenant-Governor of the Province of Eastern Bengal and Assam ... ... 50."

VI

QUEEN VICTORIA'S PROCLAMATION, 1858

The following is the full text of the Proclamation of Queen Victoria in 1858 on the assumption of the direct Government of India by the Crown from the East India Company :—

PROCLAMATION, BY THE QUEEN IN COUNCIL, TO THE PRINCES, CHIEFS, AND PEOPLE OF INDIA (PUBLISHED BY THE GOVERNOR-GENERAL AT ALLAHABAD, ON NOVEMBER 1, 1858).

Victoria, by the Grace of God, of the United Kingdom of Great Britain and Ireland, and of the Colonies and Dependencies thereof in Europe, Asia, Africa, America, and Australasia, Queen, Defender of the Faith.

Whereas, for divers weighty reasons, We have resolved by and with the advice and consent of the Lords Spiritual and Temporal, and Commons, in Parliament assembled, to take upon Ourselves the Government of the Territories in India, heretofore administered in trust for us by the Honourable East India Company :

Now, therefore, We do by these presents notify and declare that, by the advice and consent aforesaid, We have taken upon Ourselves the said Government ; and We hereby call upon all Our subjects within the said territories to be faithful, and to bear true allegiance to Us, Our heirs and successors, and to submit themselves to the authority of those whom We may hereafter, from time to time, see fit to appoint to administer the Government of Our said territories, in Our name and on Our behalf ;

And We, reposing especial trust and confidence in the loyalty, ability, and judgment of Our right trusty and well beloved cousin and councillor, Charles John Viscount Canning, do hereby constitute and appoint him, the said Viscount Canning, to be Our first Viceroy and Governor-General in and over Our said territories, and to administer the Government thereof in Our name, and generally to act in Our name and on Our behalf, subject to such orders and Regulations as he shall, from time to time, receive from Us through one of Our principal Secretaries of State :

And We do hereby confirm in their several Offices, Civil and Military, all persons now employed in the service of the Honourable East India Company, subject to Our future pleasure, and to such Laws and Regulations as may hereafter be enacted.

We hereby announce to the Native Princes of India that all treaties and engagements made with them by or under the authority of the Honorable East India Company are by Us accepted, and will be scrupulously maintained ; and We look for the like observance on their part.

We desire no extension of Our present territorial possessions ; and while we will permit no aggression upon Our dominions or Our rights, to be attempted with impunity, We shall sanction no encroachment on those of others. We shall respect the rights, dignity, and honour of Native Princes as Our own ; and We desire that they, as well as Our own subjects, should enjoy that prosperity and that social advancement which can only be secured by internal peace and good Government.

We hold Ourselves bound to the natives of our Indian territories by the same obligations of duty which bind Us to all Our other subjects ; and those obligations, by the blessing of Almighty God, We shall faithfully and conscientiously fulfil.

Firmly relying Ourselves on the truth of Christianity, and acknowledging with gratitude the solace of religion, We disclaim alike the right and the desire to impose Our convictions on any of Our subjects. We declare it to be Our Royal will and pleasure that none be in any wise favoured, none molested or disquieted by reason of their religious faith or observances ; but that all shall alike enjoy the equal and impartial protection of the Law : and We do strictly charge and enjoin all those who may be in authority under Us, that they abstain from all interference with the religious belief or worship of any of Our subjects, on pain of Our highest displeasure.

And it is Our further will that, so far as may be, Our subjects, of whatever race or creed, be freely and impartially admitted to offices in Our service, the duties of which they may be qualified, by their education, ability, and integrity, duly to discharge.

We know, and respect, the feelings of attachment with which the natives of India regard the lands inherited by them from their ancestors; and We desire to protect them in all rights connected therewith, subject to the equitable demands of the State ; and We will see that generally, in framing and administering the law, due regard be paid to the ancient rights, usages, and customs of India.

We deeply lament the evils and misery which have been brought upon India by the acts of ambitious men, who have deceived their countrymen, by false reports, and led them into open rebellion. Our power has been shewn by the suppression of that rebellion in the field ; We desire to shew Our mercy, by pardoning the offences of those who have been thus misled, but who desire to return to the path of duty.

Already in one province, with a view to stop the further effusion of blood, and to hasten the pacification of our Indian dominions, Our Viceroy and Governor-General has held out the expectation of pardon, on certain terms, to the great majority of those who, in the late unhappy disturbances, have been guilty of offences against Our Government, and has declared the punishment which will be inflicted on those whose crimes place them beyond the reach of forgiveness. We approve and confirm the said act of Our Viceroy and Governor-General, and do further announce and proclaim as follows :—

Our clemency will be extended to all offenders, save and except those who have been, or shall be, convicted of having directly taken part in the murder of British subjects. With regard to such, the demands of justice forbid the exercise of mercy.

To those who have willingly given asylum to murderers, knowing them to be such, or who may have acted as leaders or instigators in revolt, their lives alone can be guaranteed ; but in apportioning the penalty due to such persons, full consideration will be given to the circumstances under which they have been induced to throw off their allegiance, and large indulgence will be shewn to those whose crimes may appear to have originated in too credulous acceptance of the false reports circulated by designing men.

To all others in arms against the Government We hereby promise unconditional pardon, amnesty, and oblivion of all offence against Ourselves, Our Crown and dignity, on their return to their homes and peaceful pursuits.

It is Our Royal pleasure that these terms of Grace and Amnesty should be extended to all those who comply with their conditions before the first day of January next.

When by the blessing of Providence, internal tranquillity shall be restored, it is Our earnest desire to stimulate the peaceful industry of India, to promote works of public utility and improvement and to administer its Government for the benefit of all our subjects residents therein. In their prosperity will be Our Strength ; in their contentment Our security ; and in their Gratitude Our best reward. And may the God of all power grant to Us, and to those in authority under Us, strength to carry out these Our Wishes for the good of Our people.

VII

LORD MORLEY'S REFORM DESPATCH

The following is the full text of Lord Morley's Despatch on the Porposals for Constitutional Reform sent by the Governor-General in Council on the 1st October 1908 :—

INDIA OFFICE, LONDON,
Public, No. 193. *27th November, 1908.*

To

HIS EXCELLENCY THE RIGHT HONOURABLE THE GOVERNOR-GENERAL OF INDIA IN COUNCIL

Proposals for Constitutional Reform

MY LORD,

I have to acknowledge the important Despatch of the 1st October, 1908, in which you had submitted for approval and decision a group of constitutional reforms framed by Your Excellency in Council, in pursuance of a policy initiated more than two years ago. Your proposals in their present shape are the outcome of a tentative project placed, in August last year, in the hands of Local Governments in India with instructions to consult important bodies and individuals representative of various classes of the community before putting their own conclusions before the Government of India. Those instructions, as you are very evidently justified in assuring me, were carried out with great care and thoroughness. After examining, moreover, the enormous mass of material gathered together in a prolonged operation, I gladly recognise the admirable industry, patience, thought and candour with which that material has been sifted by your Government and worked out into practical proposals, liberal in their spirit and comprehensive in their scope. I have taken all the pains demanded by their importance to secure special consideration of them in Council. It is a sincere satisfaction to me to find myself able to accept the substantial part of Your Excellency's scheme, with such modifications as would naturally occur to different minds in handling problems of remarkable difficulty in themselves and reasonably open to a wide variety of solution.

THE IMPERIAL ADVISORY COUNCIL

The original proposal of an Imperial Advisory Council was based on the interesting and attractive idea of associating ruling Chiefs and territorial magnates of British India in guardianship of common and

Imperial interests and as a means of promoting more intimate relations among component parts of the Indian Empire. The general opinion of those whose assent and co-operation would be indispensable has proved adverse, and Your Excellency in Council now considers that the project should for the present not be proceeded with.

You still favour an Imperial Council composed only of ruling Chiefs. Lord Lytton made an experiment in this direction, but it remained without successful result. Lord Curzon afterwards proposed to create a Council composed exclusively of Princes contributing Imperial Service Troops, and deliberating on that subject exclusively. The opinion is pronounced that this also is likely to be unfruitful and ineffectual in practice. Your Excellency's project is narrower than the first of these two and wider than the second. I confess that, while entirely appreciating and sympathising with your object, I judge the practical difficulties in the way of such a Council assembling under satisfactory conditions to be considerable—expense, precedence, and housing, for instance, even if there were no others—yet if not definitely discontinued with a view to assembly it could possess little or no reality. It would obviously be a mistake to push the project unless it commands the clear assent and approval of those whose presence in the Council would be essential to its success, and the opinions expressed in the replies with which you have furnished me lead me to doubt whether that condition can be secured. But in case Your Excellency still favours this proposal, which is in itself attractive I do not wish to express dissent at this stage, and if, after consultation with the leading Chiefs, you are able to devise a scheme that is at once acceptable to them and workable in practice, I am not inclined to place any obstacle in the way of a full and fair trial and, in any event, the doubt I have expressed must not be taken as discouraging consultation with individual Chiefs according to the existing practice, for nobody with any part to play in Indian Government can doubt the manifold advantages of still further developing not only amicable but confidential relations of this kind with the loyal rulers in Indian States, possessed as they are of such peculiar authority and experience.

PROVINCIAL ADVISORY COUNCILS

Next I agree with Your Excellency in the judgment that the question of a Council of notables for British India only should not be entertained. I am inclined, furthermore, for my own part, to doubt whether the creation of Provincial Advisory Councils is likely to prove an experiment of any marked actual value. The origin of the demand for bodies of that character, whatever the strength of such a demand amounts to, is undoubtedly the desire for greater facilities in the discussion of public measures. Your Excellency indicates what strikes me as pointing in a more hopeful direction in the proposition that this claim for increased facilities of discussion should be met "rather by extending the powers of the existing Legislative Councils than by setting up large rival Councils which must to some extent conflict with them." Large or small, such rivalry would be almost certain to spring up, and from the first the new species of Council would be suspected as designed to be a check upon the old. As in the case of ruling Chiefs or of notables in British India, so here, informal consultation with the leading men of a locality would have most or all of the advantages of an Advisory Council without the many obvious disadvantages of duplicating political machinery.

ENLARGEMENT OF LEGISLATIVE COUNCILS

From these proposals I pass to what is, and what you declared to be, the pith and substance of the Despatch under reply. "The enlargement of the Legislative Councils" you say, "and the extension of their function to the discussion of administrative questions are the widest, most deep-reaching and most substantial features of the scheme, which we now put forward." This perfectly correct description evoked and justified the close scrutiny to which these features have been subjected in my Council, and I am glad to believe that the result reveals few elements of material difference.

Your Government have now felt bound to deal first with the Imperial Legislative Council and from that work downwards to the Councils in the Provinces. I gather, however, from your despatch of the 21st March, 1907, that you would at that time have preferred, as Lord Lansdowne had done in 1892, to build up the higher fabric on the foundation of the Provincial Councils. In your circular letter of the 24th August, 1907, you observed that the most logical and convenient mode of dealing with the question would have been first to discuss and settle the composition, the electorates and the powers of the Provincial Legislative Councils, and then to build up on the basis of these materials a revised constitution for the Imperial Council. In the absence of proposals from the Local Governments and Administrations, you were precluded from adopting this course, and, therefore, you set tentatively before them the line on which first the Legislative Council of the Governor-General and thereafter those of Governors and Lieutenant-Governors might be constituted.

In your present letter you have followed the same order, but with the full materials before me such as are now supplied by local opinions, it appears to be both more convenient and, as you said, more logical to begin with the Provincial Councils and afterwards to consider the constitution of the Legislative Council of the Governor-General.

PROVINCIAL LEGISLATIVE COUNCILS

The first question that arises touches the principle of representation. This is fully discussed in paragraphs 18 to 20, 26 to 31, and 34 of your letter. Citing previous discussions of the subject and referring to the precedent of the measures taken to give effect to the Statute of 1892, you adhere to the opinion that, in the circumstances of India, representation by classes and interests is the only practicable method of embodying the principle in the constitution of the Legislative Councils (paragraph 18.) You justly observe that the principle to be borne in mind is that election by the wishes of the people is the ultimate object to be secured, whatever may be the actual machinery adopted for giving effect to it (paragraph 29.) You consider that for certain limited interests, Corporations of Presidency towns, Universities, Chambers of Commerce, planting communities and the like limited electorates must exist as at present, and you foresee no serious obstacle in carrying out arrangements for that purpose. Difficulties come into view when you go beyond these limited electorates and have to deal with large and widespread interests or communities, such as the landholding and professional classes, or with important minorities, such as Mahomedans in most provinces in India, and Sikhs in the Punjab. You dwell upon the great variety of conditions in the various provinces of the Indian Empire and the impossibility of applying any uniform system throughout, and your conclusion generally appears to be that class electorates should be framed where this is practicable and likely to lead to good results, and in their failure or defect, it will be necessary to have recourse to nomination.

With the general principles advanced by Your Excellency in this chapter of our discussion, I am in entire accord. I agree that to some extent class representation must be maintained in the limited electorates to which you refer, and here, as you point out, no serious obstacle is to be anticipated. I agree also that the Legislative Council should reflect the leading elements of the population at large and that no system of representation would be satisfactory if it did not provide for the presence in the Councils of sufficient representatives of communities so important as are the Mahomedans and the landed classes. But, in examining your plans for obtaining their representation, I am struck with the difficulty of securing satisfactory electoral bodies under them and with the extent to which, as you expect, nomination will be demanded to supply the deficiencies of election. The same awkwardness and perplexity appear in obtaining satisfactory representation of the Indian commercial classes were, as is found generally throughout India with very few exceptions, they have not established Associations or Chambers to represent their interests.

The case of landholders is discussed in paragraphs 27 to 29 of your letter with immediate reference to the Imperial Legislative Council, and the situation is just the same—if separate representation is to be secured—for local Councils. You " find it impossible to make any definite proposal which would admit of general application." (Para. 27). You see difficulties in devising a constituency that should consist only of landholders deriving a certain income from land (Para. 28), and you point out with much force the objections to election by voluntary Associations. In these observations I agree, and especially in your remark that the recognition of Associations as electoral agencies should be regarded as a provisional arrangement to be maintained only until some regular electorate can be formed.

The same difficulties, as you observe in paragraph 30, encounter the proposal to have a special electorate for Mahomedans. In some Provinces, as in Bombay the Mahomedans are so scattered that common organisation for electoral purposes is thought impracticable. In other Provinces, it is proposed to found a scheme partly on a property qualification and partly on a literary attainment; in others, again it is suggested that recourse might be had to voluntary associations. One difficulty in regard to Mahomedans is not mentioned in your letter, for, the provision in any Province of a special electorate giving them a definite proportion of the seats on the Councils, might involve the refusal to them in that Province of a right to vote in the territorial electorates of which rural and Municipal Boards will afford the basis. If that were not done, they would evidently have a double vote, and this would probably be resented by other classes of the population.

ELECTORAL COLLEGES

Without rejecting the various expedients suggested by Your Excellency for adoption in order to secure the adequate representation of these important classes on the Councils, I suggest for your consideration that the object in view might be better secured, at any rate in the more advanced Provinces in India, by a modification of the system of a popular electorate founded on the principle of Electoral Colleges. The use of this method is not in itself novel. It already exists in the group of District Boards and of Municipalities, which in several Provinces return members to the Provincial Councils. The election is not committed to the Boards or Municipalities directly. These bodies choose electors, who then proceed to elect the representative of the group. I will briefly describe the scheme that at present commends itself to me, and in order to make the method of working clear I will assume hypothetical figures for a given Province. Let it be supposed that the total population of the Province is 20 millions, of whom 15 millions are Hindus and 5 millions Mahomedans, and the number of members to be elected 12. Then since the Hindus are to Mahammadans as three to one, nine Hindus should be elected to three Mahammadans. In order to obtain these members, divide the Province into three electoral areas, in each of which three Hindus and one Mahammadan are to be returned. Then in each of these areas constitute an Electoral College consisting of, let us say, a hundred members. In order to preserve the proportion between the two religions, 75 of these should be Hindus and 25 Mahammadans. This Electoral College should be obtained by calling upon the various electorates, which might be (*a*) substantial land-owners paying not less than a fixed amount of land-revenue, (*b*) the members of rural or sub-divisional Boards, (*c*) the members of District Boards and (*d*) the members of Municipal Corporations, to return to it such candidates as they desired, a definite number being allotted to each electorate. Out of these offering themselves and obtaining votes, the 75 Hindus who obtained the majority of votes should be declared members of the college, and the 25 Mahammadans who obtained the majority should similarly be declared elected. If the Mussalmans returned did not provide 25 members for the Electoral College, the deficiency would be made good by nomination. Having thus obtained an Electoral College containing 75 Hindus and 25 Mussalmans, that body would be called upon to elect three representatives for the Hindus and one for the Mahomedans. Each member of the College would have only one vote and could vote for only one candidate. In this way, it is evident that it would be in the power of each section of the population to return a member in the proportion corresponding to its own proportion to the total population.

In the same way, the desired proportion could be obtained of any representatives of any particular interest, as for instance, of landowners. All that is necessary would be to constitute the Electoral College in such a way that the number of electors representing the land-owning interest should bear to the total number the same proportion as the members of Council representing the interest to be elected bear to the total number to be elected.

In this manner, minorities would be protected against exclusion by majorities and all large and important sections of the population would have the opportunity of returning members in proportion to their ratio to the total population. Their choice could in that event be exercised in the best possible way, that, namely, of popular election, instead of requiring Government to supply deficiencies by the dubious method of nomination.

I do not wish definitely to prescribe such a scheme for adoption, whether locally or universally, but I commend it to your consideration. It appears to offer an expedient by which the objections against a system of nomination may be avoided, and it would work through a choice freely exercised by the electorate at large instead of by artificial electorates specially constituted for the purpose. No doubt it removes the primary voter by more than one stage from the ultimate choice and it does not profess to be simple. I can only say that it is quite as simple as any scheme for representation of minorities can ever be. The system of a single vote, which is an essential part of it is said to work satisfactorily in places where it is in existence, and it is easy of apprehension by the electors. It would have several great advantages. It would bring the classes specially concerned within the popular electorate, and so meet the criticisms of the Hindus to which you refer in paragraph 30 ; second, it establishes a principle that would be an answer to further claims for representation by special classes or associations ; third, it would ensure the persons chosen being actually drawn from the locality that the Electoral College represents ; fourth, it would provide a healthy stimulus to interest in local self-government by linking up local bodies (rural and Municipal Boards) more closely with the Provincial Legislative Councils. To this end, it might be provided that the candidate for election to the Provincial Council must himself have taken part in local administration.

The due representation of the Indian mercantile community on which you touch in paragraph 31 of your letter might be included in the scheme if the commercial classes fail to organise themselves as you suggest that they may arrange to do, in Associations similar to the European Chambers of Commerce.

To meet possible objections founded on the difficulty of bringing together Electoral Colleges to vote in one place, I may add that this is not contemplated in the scheme. You refer at the close of paragraph 28 to the success of the Calcutta University in organising the election of Fellows by a large number of graduates scattered all over India. The votes of the electors in each College could, I imagine, be collected in the same manner without requiring them to assemble at a common centre.

OFFICIAL MAJORITY TO BE DISPENSED WITH

From the electoral structure I now turn to the official element in the constitution of Provincial Legislative Councils, dealt with in paragraphs 48 to 56 of your letter. I first observe that in all of them you provide for a bare official majority, but you contemplate that in ordinary circumstances, only the number of official members necessary for the transaction of business shall be able to attend. The first question, therefore, is the necessity of maintaining in these Councils the majority of officials.

We have before us to begin with the leading fact that in the important Province of Bombay there is in the Council, as at present composed, no official majority, and that the Bombay Government, even in the smaller of its alternative schemes presented to Your Excellency in Council, is willing to dispense with such a majority. Considering the character of the legislation ordinarily coming before the Provincial Council, is it not possible with due representation given to the various classes and interests in the community to do without a majority of officials. After a careful consideration, I have come to the conclusion that in the Provincial Councils such a majority may be dispensed with provided that a substantial official majority is permanently maintained in the Imperial Legislative Council.

I do not conceal from myself the risks in such an arrangement. The non-official majority may press legislation of a character disapproved by the Executive Government. This should be met by the exercise of the power to withhold assent possessed by the head of the Government. Although the Local Legislature is vested with power to make laws for the peace and good government of the territories constituting the Province, still the range of subjects is considerably narrowed by the statutory exclusions now in force. Thus, for example, the Local Legislature may not without the previous sanction of the Governor-General make or take into consideration any law affecting the Public Debt of India or the customs duties or any other tax or duty for the time being in force and imposed by the authority of the Governor-General in Council for the general purposes of the Government of India, or regulating currency or postal or telegraph business, or altering in any way the Indian Penal Code, or affecting religion or religious rites or usages, or affecting the discipline or maintenance of Naval or Military forces, or dealing with patents or copyrights, or the relations of the Government with foreign Princes or States. It is difficult to see how any measures of such urgency that delay might work serious mischief can come before a Provincial Council, for, mere opposition to a useful and beneficial project would not come within this description. On the other hand, and perhaps more often, there may be opposition on the part of the non-official Members to legislation that the Government desires. With a Council, however, representing divergent interests and realising, together with its increased powers, greater responsibility a combination of all the non-official members to resist a measure proposed by the Government would be unlikely, and some non-officials at least would probably cast their votes on the side of the Government. If, however, a combination of all the non-official members against the Government were to occur, that might be a very good reason for thinking that the proposed measure was really open to objection, and should not be proceeded with.

Your Excellency will recall since you came into the authority of Governor-General, an Act proposed by a Local Government which a representative Legislative Council would almost certainly have rejected. Your Excellency's action in withholding assent from the Act shows that in your judgment it would have been an advantage if the Local Government had been induced by a hostile vote to reconsider their Bill. If, in spite of such hostile vote, the comparatively rare case should arise where immediate legislation were still thought absolutely necessary, then the constitution, as it at present stands, provides an adequate remedy. The Governor-General in Council to-day possesses a concurrent power to legislate for any Province, and though I strongly favour a policy that would leave to each local Legislature the duty of providing for its own requirements, still I recognise in this power an ample safeguard, should, under exceptional circumstances, a real demand for its exercise arise.

CONSTITUTION OF PROVINCIAL COUNCILS

This decision will make it necessary to modify to some extent the constitution of the several Provincial Councils proposed by you and will enable you to secure a wider representation. Subject to consideration of these details (which will not involve the postponement of the proposed Parliamentary legislation for the amendment of the Indian Councils Act, 1892, and for other purposes), I am ready to accept generally the proposals for the numbers and the constitution of the Councils set fourth in your letter.

THE IMPERIAL LEGISLATIVE COUNCIL

Your proposals in relation to the Imperial Legislative Council are necessarily entitled to the greatest weight. I am glad to find myself able to accept them practically in their entirety. While I desire to liberalise as far as possible the Provincial Councils, I recoginse that it is an essential condition of this policy that the Imperial supremacy shall be in no degree compromised. I must, therefore, regard it as essential that Your Excellency's Council, in its legislative as well as its executive character, should continue to be so constituted as to ensure its constant and uninterrupted power to fulfil the constitutional obligations that it owes and must always owe to His Majesty's Government and to the Imperial Parliament. I see formidable drawbacks that have certainly not escaped Your Excellency to the expedient which you purpose, and I cannot regard with favour the power, of calling into play an official majority while seeming to dispense with it. I am unable to persuade myself that to import a number of gentlemen to vote down something upon which they may or may not have heard the arguments will prove satisfactory. To secure the required relations, I am convinced that a permanent official majority in the Imperial Legislative Council is absolutely necessary, and this must outweigh the grave disadvantages that induce us to dispense with it in the Provincial Legislatures. It need not be in any sense an overwhelming majority, and this Your Excellency does not seek, but it must be substantial as it is certainly desirable that the Governor-General should be removed from the conflict of the division list and that the fate of any measure or resolution should not rest on his vote alone.

I have already dealt in the earlier paragraphs of this Despatch with elective principle, and it will be for Your Excellency to consider how far the popular electorate can be utilised for the return to your Legislative Council of landholders and Mahomedans. Some modifications of the scheme suggested for the Provinces will no doubt be necessary and the Electoral Colleges would probably have to be on the basis of Provinces and not of Divisions, and the case of the Central Provinces would probably (in view of the disappearance of Advisory Councils) have to be met by nomination until Local Legislature is provided.

I accept your proposals for securing the representation of commerce, both European and Indian.

I also agree to your proposals as to nomination, but it will be a matter for your consideration whether, to meet requirement of a substantial official majority, the number of nominated officials should not be raised.

Your plan for securing occasional representation for the interests of minorities such as the Sikhs, the Parsis, the Indian Christians, the Buddhists and the Domiciled Community meets with my entire approval, and I am in complete sympathy with your intention sometimes to appoint one or two experts in connection with legislation impending before the Councils.

INCREASED FACILITIES FOR DEBATE

I turn to the proposals contained in paragraphs 57-59 of your Despatch affording further facilities for debate. This subject, as Your Excellency remarks, was not dealt with in the earlier correspondence out of which your present proposals arise, but I am entirely in accord with Your Excellency's Government in regarding it as of cardinal importance.

The existing law which confines discussion, except on the occasion of the Annual Financial Statement, to the Legislative proposals actually before the Council, imposes a restriction that I am convinced is no longer either desirable or necessary. The plan of Your Excellency's Government contemplates a wide relaxation of this restriction, and in sanctioning it generally, I am confident that these increased facilities, judiciously used, will be pronounced of the greatest advantage, not only by Councils and those whom they represent, but also by Government who will gain additional opportunities both of becoming acquainted with the drift of public opinion and of explaining their own actions.

EFFECT OF THE RESOLUTIONS

Taking the proposals in detail, I agree that the Resolutions to be moved should take the form of recommendations to Government, having only such force and effect as Government after consideration shall deem due to them. The introduction and discussion of Resolutions should not extend to subjects removed from the cognizance of Legislative Councils by statute, and must obviously be subject to rules and restrictions. These, as Your Excellency observes, may best be laid down, in the first place, when the rules of business are drawn up and developed thereafter as experience may show to be desirable. Meanwhile, I agree generally with the conditions suggested in paragraph 59 of your Despatch. I must, however, remark upon the first of the suggested conditions that isolated incidents of administration or personal questions may be and often are at the same time matters of public and general importance. It would, in my opinion, be sufficient to lay down that Resolutions must relate to matters of public and general importance, inasmuch as the President of the Council will have the power of deciding finally whether any proposed Resolution does, or does not. satisfy this condition.

INTERPELLATIONS

In respect of rules on the asking of questions, I have come to the conclusion that subject to such restriction as may be found requisite in practice and to the existing general powers of the President, the asking of supplementary questions should be allowed. Without these, a system of formal questions met by formal replies must inevitably tend to become unreal and ineffective and in an assembly in which, under proper safeguards, free discussion and debate is permitted and encouraged, there can be no sufficient reason for prohibiting that method of eliciting information and expressing indirectly the opinions and wishes of the questioners.

DISCUSSION OF THE IMPERIAL BUDGET

Special importance attaches to rules as to the discussion of the Imperial Budget and I recognise with much satisfaction the liberality of the proposals that you have placed before me. The changes under this head constitute a notable step in the direction of giving to the representatives of Indian opinion a part in the most important administrative operation of the political year. I approve the dates suggested for the promulgation of the Financial Statement and for the beginning and ending of its discussion in Committee, and I anticipate valuable results from the knowledge which your Government will acquire in these debates of the views of those whom the proposed measures will chiefly and directly affect, and which it will be able to utilise in shaping its final finacial proposals for the year. Generally, also, I approve the rules sketched in paragraph 64 for the regulation of discussions in Committee and of the moving of Resolutions and I concur in your opinion that the form of procedure should be such as to show clearly that the power of executive action resides exclusively in Government, who, while inviting the free expression of opinion in the form of Resolutions do not thereby forego any part of the power and responsibility which has been and must continue to be in their hands.

PROVINCIAL BUDGETS

Your proposals for the discussion of the Provincial Budgets seem entirely sound. As in the case of the Imperial Budget, so with respect to the Provincial Finances, I observe with satisfaction that provision is made for full and free discussion and for the consideration by Government of the results of such discussion before the final proposals for the year are framed, and I believe that under the system suggested by you the Local Governments will retain that ultimate control over the financial policy of their Provinces, without which not only the authority of the Government of India but also that of the Secretary of State in Council and Parliament would inevitably disappear.

FURTHER REFORMS

Your Excellency claims for your scheme as whole "that it will really and effectively" associate the people of India in the work not "only of occasional legislation but of actual every-day administration." The claim is abundantly justified, yet the scheme is not and hardly pretends to be a complete representation of the entire body of changes and improvements in the existing system that are evidently present to the minds of some of those whom your Government has consulted and that, to the best of my judgment, are now demanded by the situation described in the opening words of the Despatch. It is evidently desirable, Your Excellency will agree, to present our reformed constitutional system as a whole. From this point of view, it seems necessary to attempt without delay an effectual advance in the direction of Local self-Government.

LOCAL SELF-GOVERNMENT

The principles that should inspire and regulate measures with this aim can hardly be laid down in sounder or clearer terms than in the Resolution published by the Government of India on the 18th May, 1882. I do not know where to look for a better expression of the views that should govern our policy under this important head, and I will venture to quote some passages in this memorable deliverance. Explaining the proposal for Local self-Government of that date the Government of India place themselves on ground which may well be our ground also. "It is not primarily," they say, "with a view to improvement in administration that this measure is put forward and supported, it is chiefly desirable as an instrument of political and popular education;" and again, "there appears to be great force in the argument that so long as the chief Executive officers are, as a matter of course, Chairmen of the Municipal and District Committees there is little chance of these committees affording any effective training to their members in the management of local affairs or of the non-official members taking any real interest in local business. The non-official members must be led to feel that real power is placed in their hands and that they have real responsibilities to discharge." This anticipation has been, to some extent, warranted by experience. Funds have not existed for an efficient Executive staff. The official element within the local bodies has been in many places predominant. Non-official members have not been induced to such an extent as was hoped, to take a real interest in local business because, their powers and their responsibilities were not real. If Local self-Government has so far been no marked success as a training ground, it is mainly for the reason that the constitution of the local bodies departed from what was affirmed in the Resolution to be "the true principle" that "the control should be exercised from without rather than from within; the Government should revise and check the acts of local bodies but not dictate them." I have no doubt that the Government of India to-day will affirm and actively shape their policy upon the principle authoritatively set forth by their predecessors in 1882 :—" It would be hopeless to expect any real development of self-Government if the local bodies were subject to check and interference in matters of detail, and the respective powers of Government and of the various local bodies should be clearly and distinctly defined by statute, so that there may be as little risk of friction and misunderstanding as possible within the limit to be laid down in each case. However, the Governor-General in Council is anxious that the fullest possible liberty of action should be given to local bodies."

THE STARTING POINT IN PUBLIC LIFE

Your Excellency will recall that the Resolution from which I have quoted treats the sub-division, taluka or the tahsil as the smallest administrative unit. It is a question whether it would not be a wise policy to go further. The village in India (generally) has been the fundamental and indestructible unit of the social system, surviving the downfall of dynasty after dynasty. I desire Your Excellency in Council to consider the best way of carrying out a policy that would make the village the starting point of public life.

A SPECIAL DEPARTMENT

The encouragement of Local self-Government being an object of this high importance in the better organisation of our Indian system, it remains to be considered how far in each province it would be desirable to create a department for dealing exclusively with these local bodies, guiding and instructing them and correcting abuses in a form analogous to the operations of the Local Government Board in this country. That, however, is a detail, though a weighty one, in a question on which as a whole I confidently expect that Your Excellency will find much light in the forthcoming report of the Royal Commission on Decentralisation.

EXECUTIVE COUNCILS : ADMISSION OF INDIANS

In the closing page of your letter Your Excellency raises a question of a high order of importance. You recognise as you inform me that the effect of our proposals will be to throw a greater burden on the heads of Local Governments, not only by reason of the actual increase of work caused by the long sittings of the Legislative Councils, but also because there will be considerable responsibility in dealing with the recommendations of those Councils. You then suggest the possibility that experience may show it to be desirable to strengthen the hands of the Lieutenant-Governors in the large Provinces by the creation of Executive

Councils and of assisting the Governors of Madras and Bombay by enlarging the Executive Councils that now exist in these Presidencies.

I have to observe with respect to Bombay and Madras that the original scheme under the Act of 1833 provided for the appointment of three members in these Presidencies. It seems conformable to the policy of this Despatch to take power to raise to four the numbers of each of these Executive Councils, of whom one, at least, should be an Indian. I would not, however, propose to make this a provision of a statute, but would leave it to pratice and usage growing into confirmed rule.

MORE EXECUTIVE COUNCILS IN THE LARGER PROVINCES

As to the creation of Executive Councils in the larger Provinces, I am such impressed by both of the considerations that weigh with Your Excellency in throwing out the suggestion and more especially by the second of them. All will depend for the wise and efficient despatch of public business upon right relations between the supreme head of the Executive power in the Province and the Legislative Council. The question is whether these relations will be the more likely to adjust themselves effectively if the judgment of the Lieutenant-Governor is fortified and enlarged by two or more competent advisors with an official and responsible share in his deliberations.

Your Excellency anticipates longer sittings of the Legislative Council with increased activity of discussion, and the effectual representation of Provincial opinion and feeling as a guide to executive authority is the central object of the policy of Your Excellency's Despatch. The aim of that policy is two-fold, at once to enable Government, the better to realise the wants, interest and sentiment of the governed; and on the other hand to give the governed a better chance of understanding, as occasion arises, the case for the Government against the misrepresentations of ignorance and malice. That double object, as Your Excellency fully appreciates, is the foundation of the system in India and all over the world of administration and legislation either through or subject to the criticism of deliberative bodies, whether great or small.

The suggestion for the establishment of Executive Councils for Lieutenant-Governors, as Your Excellency is aware, is not new. A really new problem or new solution is in truth surprisingly uncommon in the history British rule in India and of the political or administrative controversies connected with it. Indeed, without for an instant undervaluing the supreme necessity for caution and circumspection at every step and motion in Indian Government, it may be open to some to question whether in some of these controversies before now even an erroneous conclusion would not have been better than no conclusion at all. They are now considering what was much discussed in obedience to the orders of the Secretary of State in 1868 by men of the highest authority on Indian questions and I do not conceive that after all the consideration given to the subject then and since, further consultations could be expected to bring any new arguments of weight and substance into view.

It has sometimes been argued that the creation of Executive Councils in the major provinces would necessarily carry with it as in Bombay and Madras the appointment in each case of a Governor from Home. This would indeed be a "large departure from the present system of administration," almost amounting to the confusion and overthrow of that system reposing as it does upon the presence at the head of the highest administrative posts of officers trained and experienced in the complex requirements and diversified duties of the Indian Government. I take for granted, therefore, that the head of the Province will be, as now, a member of the Indian Civil Service appointed in such mode as the law prescribes.

THE POWER OF VETO

I propose, therefore, to ask for power to create Executive Councils from time to time as may be found expedient. In this connection, we cannot ignore the necessity of securing that a constitutional change designed both to strengthen the authority and to lighten the labours of the head of the Province shall not impair the prompt exercise of Executive power. It will therefore, be necessary to consider most carefully what degree of authority over the members of his Council in case of dissent should be vested in the head of a Province in which an Executive Council may be called into being. It was recognised by Parliament more than a century ago that the Governors of Madras and Bombay should be vested with a discretionary power of overruling these Councils in cases of high importance and essentially affecting the public interest and welfare. A power no less than this will obviously be required in the Provinces in which a Council may come to be associated with the head of the Executive, and I shall be glad if you will favour me with your views upon its definition. Your Excellency will readily understand that the use of such a power, while not to be evaded in the special cases for which it is designed, is not intended for a part of the ordinary mechanism of Government. Rather in the language of the historical Despatch of 1834, it is my belief that "in a punctual, constant and ever fastidious adherence to your ordinary rules of practice you will find the best security not only for the efficiency and also for the despatch of your Legislative proceedings."

VIII

THE RESOLUTION ON THE REFORMS, 1909

The following Resolution of the Governor-General in Council, dated the 16th November 1909, issued when bringing the Indian Councils Act, 1909 into operation:—

No. 4213.—With the approval of the Secretary of State in Council, the Governor-General in Council has to-day brought into operation the Indian Councils Act, 1909, and has published the rules and regulations relating to the nomination and election of the members of the enlarged Legislative Councils. This act marks the completion of the earnest and prolonged deliberations that was initiated by the Viceroy more than three years ago, when he appointed a Committee of his Executive Council to consider and report on the general question of giving to the peoples of India a larger measure of political representation and wider opportunities of expressing their views on administrative matters.

2. The various stages of inquiry and discussion which followed need not be viewed at length. In the Home Department letter of the 24th August 1907, the Government of India put forward certain provisional and tentative proposals, and invited the local Governments to submit their matured conclusions, after consulting important bodies and individuals representing the various classes of the community. The voluminous opinions elicited by that letter were fully dealt with in the Despatch which the Government of India addressed to the Secretary of State on the 1st October 1908, and in Lord Morley's Despatch of the 27th November following. Since those papers were published, the Government of India have been engaged, in communication with the Secretary of State, working out the principles accepted by him, and the scheme finally adopted for the future constitution of the Legislative Councils is embodied in the Indian Councils Act and in the Regulations which are published to-day. The Governor-General in Council will now proceed to state briefly the extent and nature of the changes introduced and to indicate in what respects they differ from the proposals contained in the papers already published.

3. The maximum strength of each Council is fixed by the first schedule of the Act. Excluding the head of the Government and the members of the Executive Councils, it varies from 60 for the Council of Governor-General, to 30 for the Councils of the Punjab and Burma, the number for each of the other five Provincial Councils being 50. The actual strength of each Council is determined by the Regulations: the statutory maximum will at present be worked up to only in the Imperial and Bengal Councils,

but as will be seen from the annexed statements the numbers are in every case slightly larger than those shown in the Despatch of the 1st October 1908.

4. For the reasons given by the Secretary of State in his Despatch of 27th November 1908, there will continue to be a majority of officials in the Governor-General's Council but the Regulations provide not only that there may be, but that there must be, a majority of non-official members in every Provincial Council. The following statement, from which the head of the Government is in each case excluded, shows the effect of this great constitutional change on the composition of each Council. It will be within the power of a local Government to increase the non-official majority by nominating less than the maximum number of officials and substituting non-officials, but that majority cannot be reduced except to the limited extent indicated below and then only for a specified period or in connection with a particular measure:—

Legislative Council of	Officials.	Non-officials.	Majority.
			Official.
India	35	32	3
			Non-official.
Madras	19	26	7
Bombay	17	28	11
Bengal	17	31	14
United Provinces ...	20	26	6
Eastern Bengal and Assam	17	23	6
Punjab	10	14	4
Burma	6	9	3

These figures relate to the ordinary constitution of the Councils and leave out of account the two experts who may be appointed members of each Provincial Council when the legislation in hand is of a nature to demand expert advice. If these members are non-officials the majority will be strengthened, and even if both are officials it will not be entirely neutralised. The strength of the non-official majority varies with local conditions.

5. Special provision has been made for the representation of the professional classes, the landholders, the Muhammadans, European commerce, and Indian commerce. The first of these interests will be represented on the Governor-General's Council by the members elected by the Provincial Legislative Councils and by the district Councils and Municipal Committees in the Central Provinces; and on the Provincial Councils by the representatives of the District Boards, the Municipalities, the Corporations of the Presidency towns and the Universities. The others will be represented upon all the Councils by members elected by special

electorates or nominated under an express provision of the Regulations. The representative of the Bombay landholders on the Governor-General's Council will be elected at the first, third and subsequent alternate elections by the landholders of Sind, a great majority of whom are Muhammadans, while at other elections he will be elected by the Sardars of Gujerat or the Sardars of the Deccan, a majority of whom are Hindus. Again the landholders of the Punjab consist of about equal numbers of Muhammadans, and non-Muhammadans and it may be assumed that their representative will be alternately a Muhammadan and non-Muhammadan. It has accordingly been decided that at the second, fourth, and succeeding alternate elections when these two seats will presumably not be held by Muhammadans, there shall be two special electorates consisting of the Muhammadan landholders who are entitled to vote for the member who represents in the Governor-General's Council the landholders of the United Provinces an Eastern Bengal and Assam respectively. In some Provinces there are special interests such as the tea and jute industries in Eastern Bengal and Assam and the planting communities in Madras and Bengal, for which special provision has been made. The representation of minor interests and smaller classes will be provided for by nominations made from time to time as the particular needs of the moment and the claims of each community may require.

6. In the Despatch of the 1st October 1908 it was explained that some of the seats there shown as elective might at first have to be filled by nomination, pending the formation of suitable electorates. Further inquiry has shown their course to be unavoidable at present in respect of (1) the representative of Indian Commerce in all Councils except that of the Governor of Bombay ; (2) the representatives of the landholders and the Muhammadan community of the Punjab on the Governor-General's Council ; and (3) the representative of the planting community on the Bengal Council. The Regulations, however, provide that a member must be nominated to represent each of these interests ; and it is the intention of the Governor-General in Council to substitute election for nomination wherever a workable electorate can be formed.

7. It will be seen that the Regulations have been divided into two parts, first, the substantive Regulations, which deal with all matters of general application, and, secondly, a series of separate Schedules defining the constitution of each electorate and prescribing the electoral procedure to be adopted in each case.

8. The qualifications required for both candidates and voters are specified in the Schedules, but the disqualifications, which apply generally, are given in the Regulations. The only voters disqualified are females, minors, and persons of unsound mind, but for candidates wider

restrictions are obviously necessary and these are set forth under nine heads in Regulation IV. The last of these provides that no person shall be eligible for election if he has been declared by the Government of India or the local Government to be of such reputation and antecedents that his election would, in the opinion of the Government, be contrary to the public interest. The Act of 1892 laid down that an elected candidate must be nominated by the head of the Government before he could take his seat on the Council. It thus gave power to execlude a candidate whose presence would bring discredit upon the Council, and although this power was never exercised, yet it served a useful purpose in deterring such persons from coming forward for election. If the dignity and representative character of the Legislative Councils are to be maintained, there must be some means of excluding unworthy candidatures, though recourse to it would be of rare occurrence, and the disqualification imposed would not necessarily be permanent.

9. In accordance with the practice of the House of Commons and of other British Legislatures, members of the enlarged Councils must, before taking their seats, make an oath or affirmation of allegiance to the Crown.

10. If a candidate is elected for more than one electorate he is required by Regulation IX to choose for which electorate he will sit. The votes recorded for him in any electorate for which he decides not to sit will be deemed not to have been given, and the seat will go to the candidate who would have been elected but for such votes. This is in accordance with the procedure prescribed for ward elections in the city of Bombay, and it has the advantages of rendering a fresh election unnecessary.

11. The normal term of office has been extended from two to three years, but a member elected to fill a casual vacancy will sit only for the unexpired portion of the outgoing member's term. This provision is necessary to meet the case of electorates which elect by rotation. To deprive such a constituency of its representation for what might be a considerable portion of the term allotted to it would be unfair ; while to allow the constituency of the out-going member (who might have sat for nearly the full term) to elect another member for a further period of three years would be open to still greater objections. The provision is also required to secure the retention of the advantages of cumulative voting in two-member constituencies.

12. It has been expressly laid down that corrupt practices shall render an election invalid. There is no such provision in the existing Regulations but the great extension of the principle of election and the probability of keen contests render it desirable to provide safe-guards

against the employment of improper practices. The definition of "corrupt practices" is taken from the Bombay District Municipalities Act. It covers false personation on the part of a voter and the use of threats of injury, as well as the actual purchase of votes by the candidate or his agent.

13. Any person who is qualified as a voter or a candidate may question the validity of an election and apply to the Government of India or the local Government, as the case may be, to set it aside. After such inquiry as may be necessary, the Government may declare whether the candidate whose election is questioned was duly elected; or whether any, and if so, what other person was duly elected; or whether the election was void (Regulation XVI). An election will not, however, be set aside on the ground of minor irregularities which do not affect the result (Regulation XV).

14. In most cases the electorates are sufficiently defined in the Regulations; where more detailed information is necessary, this has been given in the Schedules prescribing the electoral precedure. Where the electorates are scattered, as is the case with the landholders and the Muhammadans, provision has been made for the preparation and publication of an electoral roll containing the names of all persons qualified to vote. After the first election this roll will be brought under revision from time to time, when claims and objections will be decided; but the roll actually in force at the time of any election will be conclusive evidence on the question whether any person has the right to vote. The Governor-General in Council regrets that it has not been possible to allow claims to be made or objections to be taken in respect of the first roll. The qualifications upon which each roll is based could not be announced until the Regulations had received the approval of the Secretary of State, and no revision of the roll could be undertaken until the new Act had been brought into operation. At least two months would have to be devoted to the disposal of claims and objections, and it is probable that even at the end of that period some cases would still be pending. It would thus be impossible to constitute the Provincial Councils before March 1910, and the Governor-General's Council could not assemble before the end of that month or the beginning of April. The consequent loss of the whole of the legislative season would cause so much inconvenience that it would be necessary to defer putting the Act into operation and to postpone the assembling of the new Councils until the session of 1910-11. The Governor-General in Council is sensible of the objection to holding an election on a register which has not been subjected to the test of revision, but he is convinced that those objections are greatly outweighed by the keen disappointment that would be caused by further delay in

introducing the constitutional changes which have now been under discussion for more than three years. Moreover, the danger of improper omission or inclusion is comparatively small. The two principal qualifications are payment of land revenue and income-tax, the records of which are detailed and complete and steps were taken before-hand to ensure, as far as possible, that doubtful cases and claims based on other qualifications should be brought to notice. The Governor-General in Council believes that the great majority of those interested in the question will recognise the difficulties of the situation, and will acquiesce in the decision to prefer the possibility of some small degree of error affecting only a few individuals to the certainty of further prolonged delay in the assembling of the new Councils.

15. The qualifications prescribed for electors in the cases of the landholders and the Muhammadans vary greatly from province to province. They are in accordance, for the most part with the specific recommendations of the Local Governments, and these recommendations again were based upon inquiries made by a special officer appointed in each province to ascertain by personal consultation the wishes of the members of the two communities. The Governor-General in Council would have preferred some nearer approach to uniformity; but the principle he has borne in mind is that election by the wishes of the people is the ultimate object to be secured, and he has felt that he must be guided by the advice of the local authorities as to what those wishes are. The status and circumstances both of the landholders and of the Muhammadan community differ widely from province to province, and qualifications which would produce a satisfactory constituency in one case would in another give an electorate insignificant in numbers and deficient in representative character.

16. The qualification for candidates are, as a rule, the same as those prescribed for voters, but in some cases, such as that of candidates for election to the Governor-General's Council by the non-official members of a Provincial Council, any such restriction would be inappropriate. In other instances, there has been some difference of treatment in different provinces, but the object in all cases has been to secure that the member shall really represent the electorate.

17. The different kinds of electoral machinery may be broadly classified under two main heads,—one under which the electors vote direct for the members and the other under which they select direct delegates by whom the members are elected. A subsidiary distinction in each case is that the electors or delegates either vote at a single centre before a Returning Officer, or vote at different places before an Attesting Officer, who despatched the voting papers to the Returning Officer. A

further distinction in the case of delegates is that in Bengal each delegate has a varying number of votes, the number depending in the case of District Boards and Municipalities upon the income of those bodies, and in the case of a Muhammadan community upon the strength and importance of the Muhammadan population of a district or group of districts. Elsewhere the same object has been attained by varying the number of delegates on like grounds, each delegate then having only one vote. In the Central Provinces, however, the number of delegates to be elected by each District Council and Municipal Committee has been fixed, not with sole reference to income or population, but with regard to a number of factors, of which those two are perhaps the most important.

18. A special case of voting by delegates is that of the election of a member of the Governor-General's Councils to represent the Muhammadan community of Bombay. The delegates in this case are not appointed *ad hoc*, but consist of the Muhammadan members of the Provincial Council. This exceptional method has been admitted on the assurance of the Governor in Council that the Muhammadan community of the Presidency as a whole would be better represented by the Muhammadan members of the Provincial Council than by any form of direct electorate that could be devised.

19. The procedure for voting is generally similar to that prescribed by the English Ballot Act. In some cases, however, such as the elections by the Corporations of the Presidency Towns, the Chambers of Commerce and the Trades' Associations, the voting will, as at present, be regulated by the procedure usually adopted by those bodies for the transaction of their ordinary business.

20. The rules authorising the moving and discussion of resolutions, the discussion of the Budget, and the asking of questions have been framed in accordance with the decisions on these matters which have already been announced. In the rules relating to the discussion in the Governor-General's Council of matters of general public interest it is provided that no discussion shall be allowed in regard to subjects removed from the cognisance of the Council by the Indian Councils Act of 1861, or matters affecting the foreign relations of His Majesty's Government or the Government of India, or matters which are *sub-judice*. The President may also disallow any resolution on the ground that its introduction is opposed to the public interest, or that it should be moved in the Legislative Council of a Local Government. Subject to these necessary restrictions, a resolution may be moved regarding any matter of general public interest and all such resolutions may be fully discussed and put to the vote. The President may assign such time as

he may consider reasonable for the discussion of resolutions or of particular resolution.

The examination of the annual financial proposals in the Governor-General's Council will be divided into three parts. There will first be opportunity for discussing any alteration in taxation, any new loan, or any grant to Local Governments proposed or mentioned in the financial statement or the explanatory memorandum accompanying it. In the second stage, each head or group of heads of revenue or expenditure not excluded from discussion will be explained by the member in charge of the administrative department concerned and any member may then move a resolution relating to these subjects. The final stage consists of the presentation of the Budget by the Finance Member, who will explain why any resolutions passed by the Council have not been accepted. A general discussion of the Budget will follow, but at this stage no resolution may be moved.

The rules for the asking of questions are substantially the same as those hitherto in force, with the important exception that they permit a member who has asked a question to put a supplementary question.

In respect of these matters each Provincial Council is governed by rules of its own, which in essentials differ but little from those of the Governor-General's Council. One distinguishing feature, however, is that the Local Financial Statement is first examined by a Committee of the Council consisting of the twelve members, of whom six will be nominated by the head of the Government and six elected by the non-official members of the Councils.

21. The Governor-General in Council is conscious that many of the details of the scheme which is being introduced may be found on trial to be unsatisfactory or capable of improvement. Experience alone can show how far methods which are new to India give to the different classes and interests a measure of Representation proportionate to their importance and influence, and to what extent an untried electoral machinery is suitable to the varying circumstances of the different provinces and the numerous electorates. Defects will no doubt be discovered when the rules are put into operation, but, if this proves to be the case, the law admits of the regulations being amended without difficulty.

22. Under the arrangements that have been made the new Provincial Councils will assemble at the beginning of January 1910, and the Council of the Governor-General in the course of that month. It is a source of great satisfaction, both to the Viceroy personally and to the Members of his Council, that the deliberations which have extended over the greater part of Lord Minto's Viceroyalty should have achieved their purpose before he lays down the office of Governor-

General. The constitutional changes that have been effected are of no small magnitude. The Councils have been greatly enlarged; the maximum strength was 126: it is now 370. All classes and interests of major importance will in future have their own representatives. In the place of 39 elected members there will now be 135; and while the electorates of the old Councils had only the right to recommend the candidate of their choice for appointment by the head of the Government an elected member of the new Councils will sit as of right and, will need official confirmation. Under the Regulations of 1892 officials were everywhere in a majority and the Regulations just issued establish a non-official majority in every Provincial Council. Nor has the reform been confined to the constitution of the councils their functions also have been greatly enlarged. A member can now demand that the formal answer to a question shall by supplemented by further information. Discussion will no longer be confined to legislative business and a discursive and ineffectual debate on the Budget, but will be allowed in respect of all matters of general public interest. Members will in future take a real and active part in shaping the financial proposals for the year; and as regards not only financial matters but all questions of administration they will have liberal opportunities of criticism and discussion and of initiating advice and suggestions in the form of definite resolutions. The Governor-General in Council feels that these momentous changes constitute a generous fulfilment of the gracious intention, foreshadowed in the King-Emperor's message, to entrust to the leaders of the Indian peoples a greater share in legislation and government, and he looks forward with confidence to these extensive powers being loyally and wisely used by them, in association with holders of executive authority, to promote the prosperity and contentment of all classes of the inhabitants of his great country.

IX

THE RESOLUTION ON LOCAL SELF GOVERNMENT, 1882.

The following is the Resolution on Local Self-Government issued by the Governor-General in Council during the Viceroyalty of the Marquis of Ripon initiating measures of Local Self-Government in India, in 1882:—

The Governor-General in Council in the Resolution of the Financial Department, dated the 30th September 1881, set out, for the information of the Local Governments, the principles upon which it was proposed to revise the agreements then in force for the administration of the Provincial Services, and to establish the decentralised system of finance on a uniform and extended basis. It was explained that intimately connected with this general scheme for the decentralisation of finance was the very important question of developing Local Self-Government. Considerable progress in the direction had, it was admitted, been made since 1870. A large income from local rates and cesses had been secured, and in some provinces the management of this income had been freely entrusted to local bodies. Municipalities had also increased in number and usefulness. But there was still, it was remarked, a greater inequality of progress in different parts, of the country than varying local circumstances seemed to warrant. In many places services admirably adapted for local management were reserved on the hands of the central administration, while everywhere heavy charges were levied on Municipalities in connection with the Police, over which they had necessarily no executive control.

Paragraph 11 of the Resolution went on to say :—"His Excellency the Governor-General in Council is therefore of opinion that the time has now arrived when further practical development may be afforded to the intentions of Lord Mayo's Government, and that the Provincial Governments should no longer exclude from all consideration the mass of taxation under Local and Municipal management together with the similar resources still retained in provincial control, and ignore the question of Local Self-Government. The Provincial Government, while being now largely endowed from Imperial sources, may well, in their turn, hand over to local self-government considerable revenues, at present kept in their own hands, but similar in kind to many which have long been locally managed with success by Committees, partly composed of non-official members and subject only to a general remedial control reserved to the State by the Legislature. At the same time, such items should be generally made local as the people are most likely to be able to understand the use of and to administer well. His Excellency would therefore invite the Local Governments to undertake a careful scrutiny of Provincial, Local and Municipal accounts, with the view of ascertaining (1) what items of receipt and charge can be transferred from 'Provincial' to 'Local' heads, for administration by Committees comprising non-official and, wherever possible elected members, and what items already 'Local', but not so administered, might suitably be so; (2) what re-distribution of items is desirable, in order to lay on Local and Municipal bodies those which are best understood and appreciated by the people; (3) what measures, legislative or otherwise, are necessary to ensure more Local Self-Government. Incidentally to the scrutiny they will probably notice, and might carefully consider (4) ways of equalising Local and Municipal taxation throughout the Empire, checking severe or unsuitable imposts, and favouring forms most in accordance with popular opinion or sentiment. The Government of India have already made some preliminary enquiries in the same direction, the results of which will shortly be communicated to the several Local Governments for consideration in conjunction with their own."

2. Accordingly on the 10th October 1881 letters were addressed to the various Local Governments indicating those branches of expenditure which appeared to the Government of India most suited for local control, and inviting each Government to examine any other heads of accounts which might seem to cover items capable of transfer to such control. It was pointed out that it was not the intention of the Government of India that the proposed transfer of the control of expenditure of a specially local character to local bodies should involve any addition to existing local burdens; and it was, therefore, shown to be necessary to arrange for the simultaneous transfer of receipts sufficient to meet any net balance of additional expenditure which in any instances might arise. The receipts to be thus transferred should, it was suggested, be such as to afford a prospect that, by careful administration, with all the advantages due to local sympathy, experience and watchfulness, they would be susceptible of reasonable increase. In cases where larger assignments of funds were required, the receipts from pounds, or a share of the assessed taxes collected within the jurisdction of local body, were indicated as suitable sources of revenue to be made over. But on this, as on other points a wide discretion was left to the Local Governments.

3. As regards the character of the local bodies to whom those powers of control and administration were to be entrusted, it was remarked that already in most parts of British India there were in existence Municipal Committees whose powers might in many cases be advantageously extended, and District Committees for various purposes,

which might very well be consolidated into single homogeneous working bodies, with ancillary subordinate committees for each tahsil or sub-division of the district. It was suggested that the Magistrate and Collector should be President of the District Committee, and the Assistant or Deputy Magistrate in charge of the sub-division, President of the subordinate committees but in each case the local bodies should, it was said, comprise persons not in the service of Government, and elected or nominated, as might seem best, in a proportion of not less than from one-half to two-thirds of the whole numbers. For the satisfactory development of this plan, it was admitted that legislation would probably be necessary in most provinces, and the Local Government were invited in their replies to explain the general outlines which such legislation should follow. In regard to this it was said—

"Special attention will be required in settling the relations between the various local bodies and the officers of the general administration, and in providing for a certain measure of control and inspection on the part of Government. It would be hopeless to expect any real development of self-Government, if the local bodies were subject to check and interference in matters of detail; and the respective powers of Government and of the various local bodies should be clearly and distinctly defined by statute so that there may be as little risk of friction and misunderstanding as possible. Within the limits to be laid down in each case, however, the Governor-General in Council is anxious that the fullest, possible liberty of action should be given to local bodies."

4. The policy thus enunciated by the Government of India has on the whole, been loyally, and in some cases warmly accepted by the Local Governments, several of which have already drawn up schemes for giving effect to it, and have submitted these for the Government of India. The Governor-General in Council desires to acknowledge the care and thought with which some of these schemes have been worked out. Upon each the Government of India will communicate hereafter its views in detail to the local Government concerned. Meantime, however, it will be convenient that the Governor-General in Council should explain somewhat more fully than he has hitherto done, the general mode in which he would wish to see effect given to the principle of Local self-Government throughout British India outside the Presidency Towns. This is the more necessary, as further considerations of the subject and examination of the schemes prepared for the different provinces have suggested the propriety of certain modifications of the plan sketched out in the Circular letters of the 10th October last.

5. At the outset, the Governor-General in Council must explain, that in advocating the extension of local self-Government, and the adoption of

this principle in the management of many branches of local affairs, he does not suppose that the work will be in the first instance better done than if it remained in the sole hands of the Government District officers. It is not, primarily, with a view to improvement in administration that this measure is put forward and supported. It is chiefly desirable as an instrument of political and popular education. His Excellency in Council has himself no doubt that in course of time, as local knowledge and local interest are brought to bear more freely upon local administration, improved efficiency will in fact follow. But at starting, there will doubtless be many failures, calculated to discourage exaggerated hopes, and even in some cases to cast apparent discredit upon the practice of self-Government itself. If, however the officers of Government only set themselves, as the Governor-General in Council believes they will, to foster sedulously the small beginnings of independent political life; if they accept loyally and as their own the policy of the Government, and if they come to realise that the system really opens to them a fairer field for the exercise of administrative tact and directive energy than the more autocratic system which it supersedes, then it may be hoped that the period of failures will be short, and that real and substantial progress will very soon become manifest.

6. It is not uncommonly asserted that the people of this country are themselves entirely indifferent to the principle of self-Government; that they take but little interest in public matters; and that they prefer to have such affairs managed for them by Government officers. The Governor-General in Council does not attach much value to this theory. It represents no doubt the point of view which commends itself to many active and well-intentioned District officers; and the people of India are, there can be equally no doubt, remarkably tolerant of existing fact. But as education advances, there is rapidly growing up all over the country an intelligent class of public-spirited men whom it is not only bad policy, but sheer waste of power, to fail to utilise. The task of administration is yearly becoming more onerous as the country progresses in civilisation and material prosperity. The annual reports of every Government tell of an ever-increasing burden laid upon the shoulders of the local officers. The cry is everywhere for increased establishments. The universal complaint in all departments is that of over-work. Under these circumstances it becomes imperatively necessary to look around for some means of relief; and the Governor-General in Council has no hesitation in stating his conviction that the only reasonable plan open to the Government is to induce the people themselves to undertake, as far as may be, the management of their own affairs; and to develop,

or create if need be, a capacity for self-help in respect of all matters that have not, for imperial reasons, to be retained in the hands of the representatives of Government.

7. If it be said that the experiments hitherto made in this direction have not been encouraging, the Governor-General in Council must avow his belief that the principle has not as yet been, in any general or satisfactory fashion, fully and fairly tried. There is reason to fear that previous attempts at Local self-Government have been too often overridden and practicaly crushed by direct, though well-meant, official interference. In the few cases where real responsibility has been thrown upon local bodies and real power entrusted to them, the results have been very gratifying. There is even now a vast amount of assistance rendered to the administration by Honorary Magistrates, Members of Municipal Corporations and other Committees; and there is no antecedent improbability in the theory that if non-official auxiliary agency were more thoroughly organised and more fully trusted, there would be a speedy and marked improvement, not only in its amount, but in its efficency.

8. Holding therefore, that it is the duty and interest of the ruling power to take care that the further advance which it is now proposed to make in the direction of Local self-Government shall be, though cautious, yet at the same time real and substantial, the Governor-General in Council will proceed to indicate, for the guidance of the Provincial Administration, the general principles upon which, in the judgment of the Government of India, these measures should be shaped. The subject may, for the purposes of this Resolution, be divided into two parts—the first, relating to the mode in which Local Boards, whether Municipal or District, should generally be constituted; and the second, to the degree of control which the Government should retain over such bodies, and the manner in which that control should be exercised.

9. In regard to the first of these points, the Governor-General in Council would observe that he is quite aware of the absurdity of attempting to lay down any hard and fast rules which shall be of universal application in a country so vast, and in its local circumstances so varied, as British India. It would be unreasonable to expect that any uniform system of Local Government could be applied with equal success in Provinces differing as the Punjab, for instance, from Madras, or Bengal from Burmah. A large latitude of application must, therefore, in every case be left to the local authorities. Indeed, we are really as yet so much in the infancy of self-Government, and have, perhaps so little knowledge of the directions in which it would naturally develop itself among the people, that there is a distinct advantage in having different

schemes tried in different places, in order to test, by practical experience, what arrangements are best suited to the ways of thinking, habits, and other idiosyncrasies of the heterogeneous populations of the Empire. But there are, nevertheless, fundamental principles which, after every allowance has been made for local peculiarities, must be universally followed and frankly adopted, if the system is to have anywhere a fair trial.

10. The Government of India desires, then, that while maintaining and extending, as far as practicable, the plan of municipal Government in the cities and towns of each Province, the Local Governments will also maintain and extend throughout the country, in every district where intelligent non-official agency can be found, a net work of Local Boards, to be charged with definite duties and entrusted with definite funds. The Governor-General in Council considers it very important that the area of jurisdiction allotted to each Board should in no case be too large. If the plan is to succeed at all, it will be necessary to secure among the members both local interest and local knowledge. Experience proves that District Committees are, as a rule, very badly attended by members not actually residing in the vicinity of the headquarters' station. Those who do attend have frequently no intimate acquaintance with the wants of outlying parts of the district. The consequence is, either that undue attention is given to the requirements of the immediate neighbourhood of the central station, or that the business falls entirely into the hands of the District officer, the Committee contenting itself formally endorsing his proposals. Modifying, therefore, to some extent the suggestions made in paragraph 8 of the Circular letters of the 10th October last, the Governor-General in Council desires that the smallest administrative unit—the sub-division, the taluka or the tahsil—shall ordinarily form the maximum area to be placed under a Local Board. He would not indeed object to even smaller jurisdiction were these deemed suitable. In some Provinces it may be found possible to leave this sub-divisional Boards to their own independent working, arranging for a periodical District Council, to which delegates from each Local Board might be sent, to settle such common matters as the rate of land-cess to be levied during the year, allotment to be made of district funds, and other questions of general interest. In other Provinces, again, it may be thought best to have a District Board with controlling power over the smaller Local Boards. But whatever system is followed, the cardinal principle, which is essential to the success of self-Government in any shape, is this, that the jurisdiction of the primary Boards must be so limited in area as to ensure both local knowledge and local interest on the Part of each of the members.

11. The Municipal Committees will, of course, remain the Local Boards for areas included within town limits. The relations between such Municipal Boards and the Sub-divisional or District Boards within whose jurisdiction the towns lie, must be carefully settled in each case. In some instances the Town Boards will be left entirely independent and apart. In others it may be found desirable to give the Rural Boards a certain share in the settlement of questions of common interest. In others, again, the Town Boards would be required to send delegates to the District Board or Council.

12. The Local Boards, both urban and rural, must everywhere have a large preponderance of non-official members. In no case ought the official members to be more than one-third of the whole, unless in places in which the elective system is followed, when there would be no ground for objecting to an elected member merely on the ground that he was in the service of Government. The Governor-General in Council is disposed to think that the non-official members of the Boards should hold office for at least two years after election or appointment; but probably the best plan to follow would be that of the compulsory retirement by rotation of a fixed proportion of members, those retiring being eligible to sit again. A detail of this description may, however, fitly be left to the Local Government.

13. Members of the Boards should be chosen by election wherever it may, in the opinion of the Local Governments, be practicable to adopt that system of choice The Governor-General in Council does not require the adoption of the system of election in all cases, though that is the system which he hopes will ultimately prevail throughout the country, and which he wishes to establish now as widely as local circumstances will permit. Election in some form or other should be generally introduced in towns of any considerable size, but may be extended more cautiously and gradually to the smaller Municipalities and to backward rural tracts. Even as regards these last, however, the Governor-General in Council is disposed to think that if the Government officers cordially accept the principle, and set themselves to make it successful, a great advance might be made with comparatively little difficulty. Thus when the Local Governments had determined the nature of the qualifications suited to such a district (and these might ordinarily at first be fairly high); each Sub-Divisional Officer might be instructed to prepare a list or register of candidates qualified to sit upon the Local Board and might invite all those residing in any particular area, such as a Police (thana) jurisdiction, to meet him on a day fixed at some convenient spot near their homes. He might then explain to them the objects of Government, and the nature of the duties they were invited to undertake, and call

upon them to elect then or on a future day the number of representatives that had been fixed for the area in question. In the course of a few years, when the members of the Board find that they have real powers and responsibilities entrusted to them, any Government interference will become unnecessary. The electors may safely then be left to conduct their own elections under such rules as may be from time to time laid down.

14. As to the system of election to be followed, the Governor-General in Council would here also leave a large discretion to the Local Governments. Experience is wanting to determine the most suitable general system for each province ; and it is desirable that a variety of plans should be tried in order to a future comparison of results. The simple vote, the cumulative vote, election by wards, election by the whole town or tract, suffrage of more or less extended qualification, election by castes or occupation—these and other methods might all be tried. New methods unthought of in Europe, may be found suitable to India ; and after a time it will probably be able to say what forms suit best the local peculiarities and idiosyncrasies of the different populations. The Provincial Governments should, through their District officers, consult the leading Natives of each locality, not only as to the possibilities of introducing the elective system, but as to the arrangements most likely to meet their local circumstances, and should use every effort to make the schemes adopted as consonant as possible to the feelings and habits of the people.

15. Doubtless the first consequence of this mode of proceeding will be that the electoral system, viewed as a whole, will present for a time a very diversified appearance, and in some places arrangements made will turn out badly and call for change ; but the Governor-General in Council is not disposed to attach undue importance to this. The problem before the Government is one of no slight difficulty; being that of discovering in what manner the people of the town and district of British India can be best trained to manage their own local affairs intelligently and successfully. The attempts hitherto made with this object have met with but little success. The best men in many cases do not present themselves as candidates for Municipal Office. The number of voters is generally insignificant compared with the number on the registers. And yet there can be no doubt that among the more intelligent classes of the community there is a real and growing interest being taken in administrative matters. It may be suspected, therefore, that the cause of comparative failure in the efforts hitherto made is to be found rather in the character of those efforts than in the nature of the object pursued. They have been, it seems to the Governor-General in Council, wanting to a great degree in earnestness and in real endeavours to adopt

the system adopted to the feelings of the people by whom it has to be worked. If this is so, the remedy must lie in ascertaining by patient and practical experiment how best to call forth and render effective desire and capacity for self-government which all intelligent and fairly educated men may safely be assumed to possess.

16. With a view to stimulating the candidature of men of respectable standing in Native society, and to mark the importance of the functions of these Local Boards in the eyes of Government, the Governor-General in Council is pleased to direct that the courtesy titles of "Rai (or Rao) Bahadur or Khan Bahadur" shall in all official correspondence be applicable to Native members of all Local Boards during their term of office.

17. Turning now to the second division of the subject—the degree of control to be retained by the Government over the Local Boards, and the manner in which that control should be exercised—the Governor-General in Council observes that the true principle to be followed in this matter is that the control should be exercised from without rather than from within. The Government should revise and check the acts of the local bodies but not dictate them. The executive authorities should have two powers of control. In the first place their function should be required in order to give validity to certain acts, such as the raising of loans, the imposition of taxes in other than duly authorised forms, the alienation of Municipal property, interference with any matters involving religious questions or affecting the public peace, and the like. (The cases in which such sanction should be insisted upon would have to be carefully considered by each Government, and they would at the outset be probably somewhat numerous, but, as the Boards gained in experience, might be reduced in number.) In the second place, the Local Government should have power to interfere either to set aside altogether the proceedings of the Board in particular cases, or, in the event of gross and continued neglect of any important duty, to suspend the Board temporarily, by the appointment of persons to execute the office of the Board until the neglected duty had been satisfactorily performed. That being done the regular system would be re-established, a fresh Board being elected or appointed. This power of absolute supersession would require in every case the consent of the Supreme Government. A similar power is reserved to the Executive Government under several English statutes; and if required in England, where Local self-Government is long established and effective, it is not probable that it could be altogether dispensed with in India. It should be the general function of the executive officers of Government to watch, especially at the outset, the proceedings of the Local Boards, to point out to them matters calling for their consideration,

to draw their attention to any neglect of duty on their part, and to check by official remonstrance any attempt to exceed their proper functions or to act illegally or in an arbitrary or unreasonable manner.

18. It does not appear necessary, for the exercise of these powers, that the chief executive officers of towns, sub-divisions or districts should be Chairmen or even members of the Local Boards. There is, indeed, much reason to believe that it would be more convenient that they should supervise and control the acts of those bodies, without taking actual part in their proceedings. The Governor-General in Council is aware that many high authorities hold that the District officer should always be *ex-officio* Chairman of all the Local Boards within the district, and should directly guide and regulate their proceedings. This was indeed the view taken by the Government of India itself in the Circular letters of the 10th October last, so far as the constitution of district Boards was concerned. But even then the Governor-General in Council did not see his way to accepting the principle in the case of Muncipal Boards; and further consideration has led him to the belief, that on the whole, it is better to lay down no such general rule in the case of any class of Local Boards. There appears to him to be great force in the argument that so long as the chief executive officers are, as a matter of course, Chairmen of the Municipal and District Committees, there is little chance of these Committees affording any effective training to their members in the management of local affairs, or of the non-official members taking any real interest in local business. The non-official members must be led to feel that real power is placed in their hands, and that they have, real responsibilities to discharge. It is doubtful whether they have under present arrangements any sufficient inducement to give up their time and attention to the transaction of public business. There is this further objection to the District officer acting as Chairman, that if the non-official members are independent and energetic, risk may arise of unseemly collision between the Chairman and the Board. The former would be in a far more dignified and influential position if he supervised and controlled the proceedings of the Board from outside, acting as arbiter between all parties, and not as leader of any.

19. The Governor-General in Council, therefore, would wish to see non-official persons acting wherever practicable, as chairmen of the Local Boards. There may, however, be places where it would be impossible to get any suitable non-official Chairman, and there may be districts where the chief executive officer must for the present retain these duties in his own hands. But His Excellency in Council trusts that the Local Governments will have recourse sparingly to the appointment of executive officers as chairmen of Local Boards; and he is of opinion that

it should be a general rule that when such an officer is Chairman of any Local Board, he shall not in that capacity have a vote in its proceedings. This arrangement will, to some extent, tend to strengthen the independence of the non-official members, and keep the official Chairman, where there must be such, apart from the possible contentions of opposing parties.

The appointment of Chairman should always be subject to the approval of the Local Government, but need not be always made by it. The Governor-General in Council would be glad to see the Boards allowed, in as many cases as possible, to elect each its own Chairman. But this matter is one which must be left to the discretion of Local Governments.

20. These, then, are the principles upon which the Governor-General in Council desires to see the experiment of Local self-Government introduced throughout the several provinces of India ; and he would ask the Local Governments to revise their several schemes and shape any proposed legislation in general accordance with these principles. On such of the local schemes as have already come before the Government of India separate orders will, as already intimated, be passed in accordance with the foregoing exposition of policy. There are, however, one or two points to which attention has been drawn by a perusal of the orders of the Local Governments, which, though matters of detail, are still of sufficient importance to warrant their being noticed in this Resolution.

21. In the orders of the 10th October last the Government of India laid special stress on the importance of entrusting to the Local Boards, not merely the expenditure of fixed allotments of funds, but the management of certain local sources of revenue. Sufficient regard does not as yet appear to have been paid to this part of the scheme. Not only should every Local Board have the entire control over the proceeds of all local rates and cesses levied within its jurisdiction for its own special purposes, but along with the charge of any expenditure that is at present Provincial should be transferred where possible, the management of equivalent revenue. The License Tax assessments and collections for example, might very well be made over to the Local Boards, municipal and rural, in many parts of the country, subject to the control provided by the existing law. Pounds and ferry receipts have been already indicated as suited for transfer. The allotment of lump grants from Provincial revenues should be reserved as much as possible to balance receipts and expenditure of the Local Boards. The Governor-General in Council hopes that this part of the scheme will receive very careful consideration from all Local Governments, with a view to giving full effect to the policy which the Government of India has laid down on this point.

22. Another point deserving of notice is the control that should be exercised over the execution of local works. It will not always be possible for a Local Board to entertain a competent engineer of its own: and in any case when Government buildings and important works of other kinds are made over, for maintenance, there must be some effective guarantee for thoroughness of execution. It will probably be most convenient that, while all subordinate establishments are entirely under the control of the Boards, Government should supply the District Engineer, and furnish professional supervision, the Boards defraying in such manner as may be determined by the Local Governments with reference to the amount of work done for each Board, the payments to be made to Government on this account. Care must, however, be taken that the Boards are left unfettered in the initiation and direction of operations and that the Engineer is placed in the position of their servant and not of their master. The power of check vested in the District officer will suffice to remedy any carelessness or improper working on the part of the Boards. If this arrangement be carried out, it will probably be found possible to make over to the charge of the Boards most of the public buildings in the districts, and other works of various kinds which would otherwise have to be kept in the hands of the Government officers. Double establishments will thus be avoided, and public money saved.

B—THE INDIAN LEGISLATURES

I

GENERAL

The Indian Legislative Councils consist at present of the Imperial Legislative Council, legislating generally for the whole of British India and the Provincial Legislative Councils of Madras, Bombay, Bengal, Bihar, the United Provinces, the Punjab, Burma and Assam. They are formed in the case of the Imperial and in Presidency Governments by the addition of members, nominated and elected in accordance with the Regulations under the Indian Councils Act, 1909, " for the better exercise of the power of making laws and regulations vested in the Governor-General in Council" or Governor-in-Council as the case may be, under sections 10 and 29 of the Indian Councils Act 1861; and in the case of the other Provincial Governments and Administrations, they are constituted under sections 44 and 46 of the said Act, the proclamations under which specify the number of Councillors whom the Lieutenant-Governor (or Chief Commissioner under the Government of India Act 1912) " may nominate for his assistance in making laws and regulations."

All the present Legislative Councils have been called into existence by the Governor-General in Council under section 8, clause (2) of that Act, on the dates which were appointed by the Governor-General for the coming into operation of this Act as respects these Legislative Councils as previously constituted ; all the nominated members thereof went out of office, and by the Regulations which the Governor-General in Council was empowered to make new Councils were constituted in accordance with their provisions. The Legislative Councils in conformity therewith consist of the ordinary and extraordinary members of Council where they exist, and of the additional members, official and non-official, elected or nominated, as the case may be according to the strength thereof prescribed by the Regulations, but subject to the maxima prescribed in the schedule to the Act of 1909.

The additional members of these Legislative Councils are thus called together to the Council by notifications issued under sec. 8 (2) of the Indian Councils Act, 1909 and Regulation XVIII of the Regulations made by the Governor-General in Council for the nomination and election of additional members, while the Governor-General in the case of the Legislative Council of the Governor-General and the Governor or Lieutenant-Governor, or Chief Commissioner in the case of Provincial Councils, together with the ordinary members of Council, are thus ex-officio Members of the Council assembled for making laws and regulations. The Governor or Lieutenant-Governor of the Province in which a meeting of the Imperial Legislative Council is held is also ex-officio an extraordinary member of the Council. The following table gives the necessary particulars regarding the constitution of the Indian Councils :—

Number.	Province.	Maximum number of Additional Members prescribed by the Act of 1909.	Maximum of Additional Members allowed by the Regulations: Cols. 6 & 11.	Strength of the Councils under the Regulations.							Total Strength: Cols. 5, 6 and 11.
				Ex-officio.	Elected.	Nominated.					
						Officials.		Non-officials.	Experts.	Total.	
						Law Officers.	Others.*				
1	2	3	4	5	6	7	8	9	10	11	12
1	India ...	60	60	8	27	...	28	5	...	33	68
2	Madras...	50	45	4	21	1	16	5	2	24	49
3	Bombay	50	45	4	21	1	14	7	2	24	49
4	Bengal...	50	50	4	28	...	16	4	2	22	54
5	Bihar ...	50	41	4	21	...	15	4	1	20	45
6	U. P. ...	50	49	1	21	...	20	6	2	28	50
7	Punjab...	30	26	1	8	...	10	6	2	18	27
8	Burma...	30	17	1	1	...	6	8	2	16	18
9	Assam ...	30	25	1	11	...	9	4	1	14	25

* The numbers in this column represent the maximum of Official Members permitted under the Regulations.

II

THE CONSTITUTION OF THE COUNCILS

(i) THE REGULATIONS

The General charactor of the composition and features of the Indian Legislative Councils and the general conditions governing the same will be gathered from the following text of the Regulations for the nomination and election of additional members of the Legislative Council of the Governor-General which is published *verbatim.* The Provincial Regulations are *mutatis mutandis*, similar :—

Number of Members

I. The Additional Members of the Legislative Council of the Governor-General shall ordinarily be sixty in number, and shall consist of—

A.—Members elected by the classes specified in Regulation II, who shall ordinarily be twenty-seven in number ; and

B.—Members nominated by the Governor-General, who shall not exceed thirty-three in number, and of whom—.

(*a*) not more than twenty-eight may be officials, and

(*b*) three shall be non-official persons to be selected—

(i) one from the Indian commercial community,

(ii) one from the Muhammadan community in the Punjab and

(iii) one from the landholders in the Punjab :

Provided that it shall not be lawful for the Governor-General to nominate so many non-official persons under these Regulations that the majority of all the Members of the Council shall be non-officials.

Elected Members

II. The twenty-seven elected Members specified in Regulation I shall be elected as follows, namely :—

(i) By the non-official Additional Members of the Council of the Governor of Fort St. George ... ... 2 Members.

(ii) By the non-official Additional Members of the Council of the Governor of Bombay ... ... 2 Members.

(iii) By the non-official Additional Members of the Council of the Governor of Fort William in Bengal ... 2 Members.

(iv) By the non-official Members of the Council of the Lieutenant-Governor of the United Provinces of Agra and Oudh ... ... 2 Members.

(v) By the non-official Members of the Council of the Lieutenant-Governor of the Punjab ... ... 1 Member.

(vi) By the non-official Members of the Council of the Lieutenant-Governor of Burma ... ... 1 Member.

(vii) By non-official Additional Members of the Council of the Lieutenant-Governor of Bihar and Orissa ... 1 Member.

(viii) By the non-official Members of the Council of the Chief Commissioner of Assam ... ... 1 Member.

(ix) By the District Councils and Municipal Committees in the Central Provinces ... ... 1 Member.

(x) By Landholders in the Presidency of Fort St. George. 1 Member.

(xi) By Landholders in the Presidency of Bombay ... 1 Member.

(xii) By Landholders in the Presidency of Bengal ... 1 Member.

(xiii) By Landholders in the United Provinces of Agra and Oudh ... ... 1 Member.

(xiv) By Landholders in Bihar and Orissa ... ... 1 Member.

(xv) By Landholders in the Central Provinces ... ... 1 Member.

(xvi) By the Muhammadan community in the Presidency of Fort St. George ... ... 1 Member.

(xvii) By the Muhammadan community in the Presidency of Bombay ... ... 1 Member.

(xviii) By the Muhammadan community in the Presidency of Bengal ... ... 1 Member.

(xix) By the Muhammadan community in the United Provinces of Agra and Oudh ... ... 1 Member.

(xx) By the Muhammadan community in Bihar and Orissa. 1 Member.

(xxi) By the Bengal Chamber of Commerce ... ... 1 Member.

(xxii) By the Bombay Chamber of Commerce ... ... 1 Member.

In addition to the Members specified in the foregoing part of this Regulation, a second Member shall be elected at the first, third and succeeding alternate elections by the Muhammadan members of the class specified in sub-head (xiii), and at the second, fourth and succeeding alternate elections, by the class specified in sub-head (xviii).

Explanation.—The expression "alternate election" shall not be deemed to include elections to fill casual vacancies.

Electorates and electoral procedures

III. The election of the Members specified in Regulation II shall be effected by the electorates, and in accordance with the procedures respectively prescribed in the Schedules to these Regulations.

Ineligible candidates.

IV. No person shall be eligible for election as a Member of the Council if such person—

(*a*) is not a British subject, or

(*b*) is an official, or

(*c*) is a female, or

(*d*) has been adjudged by a competent Court to be of unsound mind, or

(*e*) is under twenty-five years of age, or

(*f*) is an uncertificated bankrupt or an undischarged insolvent, or

(*g*) has been dismissed from the Government service, or

(*h*) has been sentenced by a Criminal Court to imprisonment for an offence punishable with imprisonment for a term exceeding six months, or to transportation, or has been ordered to find security for good behaviour under the Code of Criminal Procedure, such sentence or order not having subsequently been reversed or remitted, or the offender pardoned, or

(*i*) has been debarred from practising as a legal practitioner by order of any competent authority, or

(*k*) has been declared by the Governor-General in Council to be of such reputation and antecedents that his election would, in the opinion of the Governor-General in Council, be contrary to the public interest :

Provided that, in cases (*g*), (*h*), (*i*) and (*k*), the disqualification may be removed by an order of the Governor-General in Council in this behalf.

Qualification of candidates

V. No person shall be eligible for election under any sub-head of Regulation II unless he possesses the qualifications prescribed for candidates in the Schedule regulating elections under that sub-head.

Disqualifications of voters

VI. No person shall be qualified to vote at any election held under these Regulations if such person—

(*a*) is a female, or

(*b*) is a minor, or

(*c*) has been adjudged by a competent Court to be of unsound mind.

Oath of office

VII. Every person, who is elected or nominated under these Regulations to be a Member of Council, shall before taking his seat make, at a meeting of the Council, an oath or affirmation of his allegiance to the Crown, in the following form, namely :—

I, A. B., having been $\frac{\text{elected}}{\text{nominated}}$ an Additional Member of the Legislative Council of the Governor-General, do solemnly swear (*or* affirm) that I will be faithful and bear true allegiance to His Majesty the King, Emperor of India, His heirs and successors, and that I will faithfully discharge the duty of the office upon which I am about to enter.

Power to declare seats vacant

VIII. (1) If any person,—

(*a*) not being eligible for election, is elected under these Regulations, or

(*b*) having been elected or nominated, subsequently becomes subject to any of the disabilities stated in clause (*d*), (*f*), (*g*), (*h*) or (*i*) of Regulation IV, or fails to make the oath or affirmation prescribed by Regulation VII within such time as the Governor-General in Council considers reasonable,

the Governor-General shall, by notification in the *Gazette of India*, declare his election or nomination to be void or his seat to be vacant.

(2) When any such declaration is made, the Governor-General shall, by notification as aforesaid, call upon the electorate concerned to elect another person within such time as may be prescribed by such notification, or shall nominate another person, as the case may be.

(3) If any person elected at such fresh election is not eligible for election, the Governor-General may nominate any person who is eligible for election by the electorate concerned.

Candidates elected by several electorates

IX. (1) If any person is elected by more than one electorate, he shall, by notice in writing signed by him and delivered to the Secretary to the Government of India in the Legislative Department, within seven days from the date of the publication of the result of such elections in the *Gazette of India*, choose, or in his default the Governor-General shall declare, for which of these electorates he shall serve, and the choice or declaration shall be conclusive.

(2) When any such choice or declaration has been made, the votes recorded for such person in any electorate for which he is not to serve shall be deemed not to have been given, and the candidate, if any, who, except for the said votes would have been declared elected for such electorate, shall be deemed to have been duly elected for the same.

Term of office

X. (1) Save as otherwise provided in these Regulations, the term of office of an Additional Member shall be three years, commencing from—

(*a*) in the case of a nominated Member, the date of the publication in the *Gazette of India* of the notification by which he is nominated,

(*b*) in the case of an elected Member, the date of the publication in the *Gazette of India* of the result of the election, or, where the result of such election has been so published before the vacancy has occurred, from the date on which such vacancy occurs :

Provided that official Members and Members nominated as being persons who have expert knowledge of subjects connected with proposed or pending legislation shall hold office for three years, or such shorter period as the Governor-General may at the time of nomination determine:

Provided further that in the event of a Legislative Council being constituted for the Central Provinces, the term of office of the Member elected by the class specified in sub-head (ix) of Regulation II shall expire on such date as the Governor-General in Council may, by notification in the *Gazette of India*, direct.

(2) A Member elected or nominated to fill a casual vacancy occurring by reason of absence from India, inability to attend to duty, death, acceptance of office or resignation duly accepted, or otherwise, or a Member nominated on failure of an electorate to elect an eligible person, shall hold office so long as the Member whose place he fills would have been entitled to hold office if the vacancy had not occurred.

Vacancies

XI. (1) When a vacancy occurs in the case of a Member who represents any interest specified in Regulation II, or at any time within three months of the date when such a vacancy will occur in the ordinary course of events, the Governor-General shall, by notification as aforesaid, call upon the electorate concerned to elect a person for the purpose of filling the vacancy within such time as may be prescribed by such notification.

(2) When a vacancy occurs in the case of a nominated Member, the Governor-General may nominate any person to the vacancy :

Provided that when a casual vacancy occurs—

(*a*) in the case of an elected Member, the election shall always be made by the same electorate as that which elected the Member whose place is to be filled, and shall be subject to the same conditions in respect of eligibility of candidates for nomination as those which governed the election of such Member, and

(*b*) in the case of a Member nominated as representing any class specified in Regulation I, sub-head B, clause (*b*), the person nominated shall be selected from the same class.

Failure to elect

XII. If within the time prescribed by a notification issued under Regulation VIII, clause (2), or Regulation XI, clause (1), the electorate concerned fails to elect, the Governor-General may nominate at his discretion any person who is eligible for election by such electorate.

Quorum

XIII. The power of making laws and regulations, and of transacting other business vested in the Legislative Council of the Governor-General shall be exercised only when fifteen or more Additional Members of the Council are present.

Corrupt practices

XIV. (1) No election shall be valid if any corrupt practice is committed in connection therewith by the candidate elected.

(2) A person shall be deemed to commit a corrupt practice within the meaning of these Regulations—

(i) who, with a view to inducing any voter to give or to refrain from giving a vote in favour of any candidate, offers or gives any money or valuable consideration, or holds out any promise of individual profit, or holds out any threat of injury, to any person, or,

(ii) who gives, procures or abets the giving of a vote in the name of a voter who is not the person giving such vote.

And a corrupt practice shall be deemed to be committed by a candidate if it is committed with his knowledge and consent, or by a person who is acting under the general or special authority of such candidate with reference to the election.

Explanation.—A "promise of individual profit" includes a promise for the benefit of the person himself, or of any one in whom he is interested.

Non-compliance with rules

XV. No election shall be invalid by reason of a non-compliance with the rules contained in the Schedules to these Regulations or any mistake in the use of Forms annexed thereto, if it appears that the election was conducted in accordance with the principles laid down in such rules, and that such non-compliance or mistake did not affect the result of the election.

Disputes as to validity of elections

XVI. (1) If the validity of any election is brought in question by any person qualified either to be elected or to vote at such election on the ground of the improper rejection or reception of a nomination or of a vote, or of any corrupt practice in connection with such election, or for any other cause, such person may, at any time within fifteen days from the date of the publication of the result of such election in the *Gazette of India*, apply to the Governor-General in Council to set aside such election.

(2) The Governor-General in Council shall, after such inquiry (if any) as he may consider necessary, declare, by notification as aforesaid,

whether the candidate whose election is questioned or any or what other person was duly elected, or whether the election was void.

(3) If the election is declared void, the Governor-General shall. by notification as aforesaid, call upon the electorate concerned to elect another person within such time as may be prescribed by such notification.

(4) If within the time so prescribed the electorate fails to elect, the Governor-General may nominate any person who is eligible for election by such electorate.

Finality of decisions

XVII. The decision of the Governor-General in Council on any question that may arise as to the intention, construction or application of these Regulations shall be final.

First elections

XVIII. (1) As soon as conveniently may be after these Regulations come into force, a Council shall be constituted in accordance with their provisions.

(2) For this purpose the Governor-General shall, by notification as aforesaid, call upon the electorates referred to in Regulation III to proceed to elect Members in accordance with these Regulations within such time as may be prescribed by such notification.

(3) If within the time so prescribed any such class fails to elect, the Governor-General may nominate at his discretion for a period not exceeding six months any person who is eligible for election by such class.

[The Regulations framed by the Governor-General in Council for the nomination and election of Additional Members for the Provincial Legislatures are similar. Regulations I and II, prescribe the strength of the Councils and the proportion of elected to nominated Members. The proviso to Regulation I does not provide for an official majority in the Councils as in the case of the Imperial Legislature, but for a non-official majority in the following terms: "Provided that it shall not be lawful for the Governor or Lieutenant-Governor, as the case may be, to nominate so many officials under these regulations that the majority of all the Members of the Council shall be officials." As in the case of the Imperial Legislative Council, it is provided by Regulations II and III in each of the Provincial Regulations that the elected Members specified in Regulation I shall be elected by the electorates in accordance with the procedures respectively prescribed in the schedules to the Regulations. The schedules and the electorates for the election of Members to all the Councils, Imperial and Provincial, are summarised in full in the next section. The rest of the Regulations IV—XII, XIV—XVIII are identical in terms with those made for the Imperial Legislature, reproduced above, with the substitution of the words, 'Governor' or 'Lieutenant-Governor', for the words 'Governor-General' and of 'Governor-in-Council' for 'Governor-General in Council' as the case may be.

In the case of nominations to the Provincial Legislatures, it is provided in the Regulations that Members to the Provincial Legislative Councils of the United Provinces of Agra and Oudh, Behar, and Assam and Burma should be nominated by the respective Lieutenant-Governors with the sanction of the Governor-General. No sanction is required in the case of nominations made to their Legislative Councils by the Governors of Madras, Bombay and Bengal.

In the Regulation corresponding to Regulation XIII of those relating to the Imperial Council fixing the quorum for Legislative Meetings, in the Regulations of each Province, the quorum has been fixed as follows:—

Excluding the President, 10 or more Members in the Legislative Councils of Madras, Bombay, Bengal, United Provinces of Agra and Oudh and Behar and 8 or more Members in that of the Punjab and Assam and 6 in that of Burma].

(ii) THE CLASSIFICATION OF MEMBERS

EX-OFFICIO MEMBERS

By virtue of the Indian Councils Act of 1861, the ordinary members of the Council of the Governor-General, Governor or Lieutenant-Governor as the case may be, or as they may be called for purposes of convenience, members of the Executive Councils of the various administrations, are ex-officio members of the several Legislative Councils.

NOMINATED MEMBERS—OFFICIALS

There are no special qualifications prescribed in the case of officials nominated to the Indian Councils. There is absolutely no restriction in choice ; as a general rule, Secretaries to Government in the various departments and heads of administrative departments are nominated to the Council. There have been instances when, in order to make up the number of officials, or for other reasons, Principal of a Government Arts College, or a mofussil Government pleader, has been so appointed.

NOMINATED MEMBERS—NON-OFFICIALS

As in the case of officials who are nominated to the Councils, there are no qualifications prescribed in the case of non-officials who may be appointed to the Councils under the Regulations. The Regulations of most of the Councils require that, in exercising the power of nomination care should be taken that certain special interests are represented in the Councils. The object of allotting a certain number of seats in the Councils to be filled in by nomination of non-officials is to enable such special interests as have not organised themselves sufficiently well to be conferred the privilege of election, to be represented in the Councils. The heads of administrations, in whom is vested the power of nominations, could also nominate to the Councils persons who, in their opinion, possess exceptional merit and ability and who could not get into the Councils by the door of election.

The Regulations have laid down that non-officials should be selected from the classes mentioned against each Council :—

1. The Imperial Legislative Council :—
   (a) One Member from the Indian Commercial Community.
   (b) One Member from the Muhammadan Community in the Punjab and
   (c) One Member from the land holders in the Punjab.
2. The Madras Legislative Council :—
   One Member from the Indian Commercial Community.
3. The Bengal Legislative Council :—
   (a) One Member from the Indian Commercial Community and
   (b) One Member from the European Commercial Community carrying on business outside Calcutta and the Municipality of Chittagong and not connected with tea-planting.
4. The United Provinces Legislative Council :—
   One Member from the Indian Commercial Community.
5. The Burma Legislative Council :—
   (a) Four Members from the Burmese population.
   (b) One Member from the Indian Commercial Community.
   (c) One Member from the Chinese Community.
   (d) Two Members to represent other interests.

EXPERTS

Experts who may be nominated to the Councils may be either officials or non-officials and are intended to be appointed in connection with proposed or pending legislation in regard to which they have special knowledge.

ELECTED MEMBERS

In the composition of every representative body, the question as to who are the voters, is always treated as distinct from the question into what groups shall they be combined. In constitutions which proceeded in early days on a full faith in democratic principles, the latter question was treated as of no importance or as of but secondary importance, for it was assumed that the interests of the masses of the people were fundamentally identical and the main question is only that of enlarging the basis of representation. This fundamental indentity is now seen to be subject to the conflict of human interests and in the formation of constituencies and groups of voters are sought results and remedies in the direction of equal or effective representation. The relative advantages of the *scrutin de liste* and *scrutiu'd arroundissementare* still unsettled in France, where this problem of single electoral districts or large areas choosing a number of representatives apiece is complicated by that of proportional representation. The arrangement of the constituencies on the basis of wealth as in the three-class system of Prussia in preference to the grouping of voters on the basis of their natural economic relations into urban and rural constituencies as in England, has given rise to suggestions of possible groupings on the basis of occupations and on the basis of opinions by some form of proportional representation ; the electoral system in India does not, however, proceed on any such defined principles but in addition to partaking of principles of minority and class representation adds those of communal representation.

(iii) THE ELECTORATES AND ELECTORAL AREAS

The distribution of elective seats in India in respect of the various Legislative Councils is based, only to a limited extent, on the principle of territorial division followed in countries where representative institutions have advanced very much. The granting of the privilege of election to certain classes and special interests has made the application of this principle impossible in India. In the United Kingdom, for instance, the country is divided into separate electoral divisions each with its own distinctive name, returning one member each to the Parliament. twenty-three boroughs, the City of London and the Universities of Oxford, Cambridge and Dublin making the twenty-seven cases of constituencies returning two members each. There is not in England, as there is in India, any representation of communities or organised bodies of men marked off from each other either by religious differences or the existence of special or peculiar interests, a number of men being grouped together only for the purpose of election. The only case in India in which an approach is made to the priniciple of territorial representation is the division of each province for which a Legislative Council is constituted, into groups consisting of one or more administrative units—districts—the local bodies in each of which are together entitled to return a member to the Legislative Council. The electorates of the various Legislative Councils in India may be considered under the heads of (i) general electorates, (ii) class electorates comprising (*a*) Landed Interests and (*b*) Muhamadans and (iii) special electorates comprising (*a*) the Presidency Corporations, (*b*) the Universities, (*c*) Commerce, (*d*) Trade, (*e*) Planting and (*f*) Port Trusts and other Interests.

(i) GENERAL ELECTORATES

(*a*) The Imperial Legislative Council (13) :—

In Madras, Bombay, Bengal and the United Provinces of Agra and Oudh, the non-official Members of the Provincial Legislative Councils elect two Members each for the Viceroy's Council and have cumulative vote, so as to afford an opportunity to a strong minority to secure one of the seats.

In the Punjab, Behar, Assam and Burma, the non-official Members of the Provincial Legislative Councils elect one Member each to the Viceroy's Council.

In the Central Provinces the votes of twenty-two delegates from the District Councils and twenty-eight delegates from Municipal committees elect one Member.

(*b*) The Madras Legislative Council :—

Nine members are elected by Municipalities and District and Taluk Boards and certain other electors and, it is provided in Schedule III of the Madras Regulations that one shall be elected for each of the following groups of districts :

(1) Ganjam and Vizagapatam ;

(2) Godaveri, Kistna and Guntur ;

(3) Nellore, Cuddapah and Chittore ;

(4) Kurnool, Bellary and Anantapur ;

(5) Nellore, Chingleput and South Arcot ;

(6) Salem, Coimbatore and the Nilgiris ;

(7) South Canara and Malabar (including Anjengo and Tangasseri) ;

(8) Tanjore and Trichinopoly ;

(9) Madura, Ramnad and Tinnevelly.

(*c*) The Bombay Legislative Council :—

Eight Members are elected by the Municipalities and by District Local Boards as follows :—

The Municipalities of the Southern, Northern, Central and Sind Divisions, each one 4

The District Local Boards of the Southern, Northern, Central and Sind Divisions, each one 4

(*d*) The Bengal Legislative Council :—

Eleven or ten members are elected by the Municipalities and District Local Boards as follows :—

by Municipal Commissioners : 1 Member from the Presidency, Burdwan, Dacca and Rajshahi Divisions at every election ; 1 from the Chittagong Division at every alternate election and in addition 1 Member to be returned by the Municipalities of the Presidency and Burdwan Divisions alternately :— 6 or 5 Members ;

by District and Local Boards (1 for each Division) 5 Members.

(*e*) The United Provinces Legislative Council :—

Thirteen Members are elected by Municipalities and District Boards as follows :—

Four Members are elected by the large Municipalities alternately by the four Municipal Boards forming each of the following groups :—

Group (1)—the Municipal Boards of Meerut, Agra, Allahabad and Lucknow ; and

Group (2)—the Municipal Boards of Bareilly, Cawnpore, Benares and Fyzabad.

Of the nine Members to be elected by the District Boards and smaller Municipalities, one Member is elected for each of the Meerut, Agra, Rohilkhand, Jhansi, Allahabad, Benares, Gorakhpur, Lucknow and Fyzabad Divisions.

(*f*) The Behar Legislative Council:—

Ten Members are elected by Municipalities and District Boards as follows:—

Municipal Commissioners (one from each Division) 5

District Boards (one from each Division) 5

(*g*) The Punjab Legislative Council:—

Six Members are elected by Municipal and Cantonment Committees and District Boards as follows :—

Municipal and Cantonment Committees 3

District Boards 3

(*h*) The Assam Legislative Council :—

Four members are elected by Municipalities and Local Boards as follows :—

Municipal Commissioners (one for each Division) 2

Local Boards (one for each Division) 2

(ii) CLASS ELECTORATES

(a) LANDED INTERESTS :—

1. The Imperial Legislative Council :—

Landholders, of certain specified qualifications which will be referred to in detail presently, return one member each from Madras, Bombay, Bengal, the United Provinces, Behar, and the Central Provinces.

2. The Madras Legislative Council (5):—

Two Members are elected by Zamindars, of whom one is elected for each of the following groups of districts :—

Group (1)—Ganjam, Vizagapatam, Godaveri, Kistna, Guntur, Nellore, North Arcot, Chittore, Cuddapah, Kurnool, Bellary and Anantapur.

Group (2)—Madras, Chingleput, Salem, Coimbatore, South Canara, Malabar (including Anjengo and Tangasseri), the Nilgiris, South Arcot, Tanjore, Trichinopoly, Madura, Ramnad, and Tinnevelly.

Three members are elected by landholders other than Zamindars in each of the following groups of districts :—

Group (i)—Ganjam, Vizagapatam, Godaveri, Kistna, Guntur, Nellore, North Arcot, Chittoor, Cuddapah, Kurnool, Bellary and Anantapur.

Group (ii)—Madras, Chingleput, Salem, Coimbatore, the Nilgiris, South Arcot, Tanjore, Trichinopoly, Madura. Ramnad and Tinnevelly.

Group (iii)—Malabar (including Anjengo and Tangasseri) and South Canara.

3. The Bombay Legislative Council (3):—

The Sardars of the Deccan, the Sardars of Gujarat and the Jagirdars and Zamindars of Sind elect one member each.

4. The Bengal Legislative Council (4 or 5) :—

The landholders of the Presidency, Burdwan, Rajashahi and Dacca Divisions return one Member each and those in the Chittagong Division return one member at each alternate election.

5. The United Provinces Legislative Council (2) :—

Two members are elected. one each by the landholders of Agra and of Oudh.

6. The Behar Legislative Council (5) :—

The Landholders of each of the five Divisions return one member.

7. The Assam Legislative Council (2) :—

The Landholders of each of the two Divisions return one Member.

(b) THE MUHAMMADAN COMMUNITY :—

1. The Imperial Legislative Council (5) :—

The Muhammadan Community in each of the Provinces of Madras, Bombay, Bengal, Behar and the United Provinces elect one member.

2. The Madras Legislative Council (2) :—

Two members are elected by the Muhammadan Community, one by each of the following groups of districts :—

Group (1)—Ganjam, Vizagapatam, Godavari, Kistna, Guntur, Nellore, Madura, Chingleput, North Arcot, Chittoor, Cuddapah, Kurnool, Bellary and Anantapur.

Group (2)—Salem, Coimbatore, South Canara, Malabar (including Anjengo and Tengasseri), the Nilgiris, South Arcot, Tanjore, Trichinopoly, Madura, Ramnad and Tinnevelly.

3. The Bombay Legislative Council (4) :—

Four members are elected by the Muhammadan Community, one for each of the Southern, Northern, Central Divisions and the city of Bombay.

4. The Bengal Legislative Council (5) :—

The Muhammadan Community of each of the five Divisions elect a Member.

5. The United Provinces Legislative Council (4) :—

Four Members are elected by the Muhammadan Community, one each for the following four groups :—

The Meerut and Agra divisions ;

The Rohilkhand and Kumaun divisions ;

The Lucknow and Fyzabad divisions ;

The Allahabad, Jhansi, Benares and Gorakhpur divisions.

6. The Behar Legislative Council (4) :—

Four Members are elected by the Muhammadan Community as follows :—

Patna, Tirhut and Bhagalpur divisions 1 each 3

Orissa and Chota Nagpur divisions voting jointly 1

7. The Assam Legislative Council (2) :—

Two Members are elected by the Muhammadan Community, one by each division.

(iii) SPECIAL ELECTORATES

(*a*) THE CITY CORPORATIONS :—

The following City Corporations send one Member each to the Legislative Councils mentioned against them :—

(1) Madras—The Corporation of Madras ;

(2) Bombay—The Corporation of Bombay ;

(3) Bengal—The Corporation of Calcutta.

(*b*) THE UNIVERSITIES :—

The following Universities send one Member each to the Legislative Councils mentioned against them :—

(1) Madras—The University of Madras ;

(2) Bombay—The University of Bombay ;

(3) Bengal—The University of Calcutta ;

(4) The United Provinces—The University of Allahabad.

(*c*) COMMERCIAL INTERESTS :—

The following Chambers of Commerce send one Member each to the Legislative Councils mentioned against them :—

(1) India—The Chamber of Commerce, Calcutta and Bombay.

(2) Madras— " Madras.

(3) Bombay— " in Bombay and Karachi and the Indian Commercial Community.

(4) Bengal—The Chamber of Commerce (2 Members)......Calcutta.

(5) The United Provinces—The Upper India Chamber of Commerce.

(6) Punjab—The Punjab Chamber of Commerce.

(7) Burma—The Burma Chamber of Commerce.

(*d*) THE TRADES :—

The following trading interests return one Member each to the Legislative Councils mentioned against them:—

(1) Madras—The Madras Trades Association.

(2) Bengal—The Calcutta Trades Association.

(*e*) PLANTING INTERESTS :—

The following planting interests return one Member each to the Legislative Councils mentioned against them:—

(1) Madras—The Planting Community.

(2) Bengal—The Tea Planting Community.

(3) Behar—The Planting Community.

(4) Assam—The Tea Planting Community.

(*f*) PORT TRUSTS AND OTHER INTERESTS :—

The following bodies representing special interests return one Member each to the Legislative Councils as under :—

(1) Bombay—The Millowner's Association of Bombay and the Millowner's Association of Ahmedabad respectively.

(2) Bengal—The Port Commissioner of Chittagong.

The Municipal Commissioners of the Calcutta Coporation exclusive of Government nominees.

(3) Behar—The Mining Community.

(iv) THE ELECTORAL FRANCHISE

In conferring on the persons or classes of persons the right to vote for a representative to the legislatures, the Regulations have not proceeded on any uniform principle of property or residential qualification, but have varied them according to the circumstances and conditions of the several groups of constituencies in the several Provinces. The object sought to be attained appears to have been more to obtain a workable electorate from the classes out of which it is formed, which could be expected to elect a candidate representative of that group, than to confer upon the citizens in that group a right to vote and a voice in the selection of representatives to the legislature. Generally speaking, apart from the disqualifications to vote applying to voters in all the constituencies as provided for by Regulation, such as those arising from conviction for offences, insolvency, insanity, corrupt practices etc., a right to vote in India depends on a property qualification as evidenced by the payment of taxes, rents or land-revenue, though in the case of Muhammadan electorates, the standard of this qualification is generally lower than in the case of others. This property qualification is ascertained either directly as in the case of the landed classes electorates or indirectly in the territorial electorate, through membership in local bodies, which always implies property qualifications. In addition to this, the receipt of government pensions, civil and military as well as the holding of titles hereditary as well as conferred by government, gives the franchise to their recipients in the different electorates and in different degrees. Nor, except to a limited extent, have the principles of " one man, one vote, " " one vote, one value, " been followed in the bestowal of the franchise.

The following is an analysis and summary of the rules as to the franchise under the several schedules to the Regulations :—

(i) GENERAL ELECTORATES

So far as the Imperial Legislative Council is concerned, the franchise in regard to the general electorates is exercised, as already stated, by non-official members of the Local Legislative Councils, except in the Central Provinces, where it is conferred on 50 delegates, 22 of whom are selected by District Councils and 28 by Municipal Committees, from among members thereof other than officials appointed by name or *ex-officio*.

In the case of other Local Legislative Councils, the franchise is territorial in character and is generally exercised by non-official members of local bodies.

(1) MADRAS

The election is made by the non-official members of Municipal Councils and District and Local Boards and certain other electors. The electors are those who

(*a*) on the 30th June preceding the publication of the roll, were non-official members of a Municipal Council or a District or Taluk Board within the electoral area concerned, or

(*b*) have been non-official members of a Municipal Council or a District or Taluk Board within the electoral area concerned for an aggregate period of not less than three years during the decade expiring on the said date, or

(*c*) are not qualified to vote at an election held under any other Schedule annexed to these Regulations and are holders of any title conferred or recognised by the Government (higher in rank than the title of Rao Sahib) or are Members of the Order of the Star of India or of the Order of the Indian Empire, or are holders of the Kaiser-i-Hind medal.

(2) BOMBAY

The Member to be elected by each of the groups of Municipalities or District Local Boards is elected by the votes of delegates to be selected from among themselves in the manner described below, by the non-official Members of all the Municipalities or District Local Boards of the group :—

Municipalities

	Number of delegates
Where the population of the Municipality—	
exceeds 5,000, but does not exceed 10,000	1
Do. 10,000 do 20,000	2
and for every 10,000 or part thereof in excess of 20,000...	1

District and Local Boards

	Number of delegates
Where the population of the district—	
does not exceed 1,00,000	1
where it exceeds 1,00,000 but does not exceed 2,00,000.	2
and for every 1,00,000 or part thereof in excess of 2,00,000	1

The population of each Municipality or district is deemed to be that stated in the returns of the most recent official census.

(3) Bengal

The following procedure is adopted:—

Municipalities

The number of votes assigned to each Municipality is determined in accordance with the following scale, namely:—

		Rs.		Rs.
Municipalities with a local income of...		5,000 &	less than	10,000—1 vote.
Do	do	10,000	do	20,000—2 votes.
Do	do	20,000	do	50,000—3 ,,
Do	do	50,000	do	80,000—4 ,,

and for every additional Rs. 30,000 or part thereof in excess of Rs. 80,000 —1 vote.

The number of votes to which each Municipality is entitled on the said scale is notified from time to time by the Local Government in the Local Official Gazette.

To determine the candidate to whom, or, where two Members are to be elected for the Division concerned, the two candidates to each of whom the votes assigned to each Municipality in accordance with the above rule are to be given, an election is held, by the Commissioners qualified to vote, other than officials appointed by name or *ex-officio*, of each of the notified Municipalities in each of the said Divisions.

No such Commissioner has in any one Division more votes than the number of Members to be elected for the Division.

The candidate or each of the two candidates, according as one or two Members are to be elected for the Division, to whom the largest number of votes is given by the Commissioners at any such election, is deemed to have obtained the number of votes so assigned to the Municipality in which such election has been held.

District and Local Boards

The number of votes assigned jointly to the District Board and the Local Boards in each district is determined in accordance with the following scale:—

		Rs.	
District Boards with an annual income (exclusive of opening balances and receipts from loans)	not exceeding	75,000	... 1 vote.
Do	exceeding 75,000 but less than	1,25,000	... 2 votes.
and for every additional Rs. 50,000 or part thereof in excess of		1,25,000	... 1 vote.

The number of votes to which the District Board and the Local Boards in each district are jointly entitled on the said scale is notified from time to time by the Local Government in the Local Official Gazette.

To determine the candidate to whom the votes jointly assigned to the District Board and Local Boards in each district in accordance with rule 3 is given, an election is held, in the manner hereinafter prescribed, by the persons (hereinafter referred to as electors) who are members, other than officials appointed by name or *ex-officio*, of the District Board and Local Boards of each district of the said Divisions and are qualified to vote.

No elector has more than one vote in any one Division.

The candidate to whom the largest number of votes is given by the electors at any such election is deemed to have obtained the number of votes so assigned jointly to the District Board and Local Boards holding such election.

(4) THE UNITED PROVINCES.

In the United Provinces the following plan is adopted :—

The Large Municipalties

The four Members are elected alternately by the four Municipal Boards forming each of the said groups (See page cxxix), the Municipal Boards in group (1) having the first right of election.

The members, other than (*a*) the Chairman, if an official, and (*b*) the members appointed ex-officio, of each of the four Municipal Boards forming a group, elect one member.

The Smaller Municipalities and District Boards

The Members are elected by the votes of delegates, to be selected by the Members other than the Chairman, if an official, and the Members appointed ex-officio, of all District Boards and such Municipal Boards within the said Divisions as are established for towns forming district head-quarters or containing more than twenty thousand inhabitants according to the returns of the most recent official census, or are named in the notification of the Lieutenant-Governor of the United Provinces of Agra and Oudh No. 44-C III-807-A, dated the 19th day of July, 1899.

Provided that nothing in this rule is deemed to apply to any Municipal Board which,—

(*a*) at the time of holding an election under this Schedule to fill a casual vacancy, is already represented by a Member elected for the larger Municipalities, or

(b) at the time of holding an election to fill a vacancy other than casual is entitled to elect a Member for the larger Municipalities.

The number of delegates which such District and Municipal Boards are entitled respectively to select is in accordance with the following scale :—

For districts with a population		Delegates.
	of under... 500,000 ...	... 2
Do.	from 500,000 to 750,000	... 3
Do.	„ 750,000 to 1,000,000	... 4
Do.	„ 1,000,000 to 1,250,000	... 5
Do.	„ 1,250,000 to 1,500,000	... 6
Do.	over 1,500,000 ...	... 7

For towns containing		Delegates.
	not more than 20,000 inhabitants	... 1
Do.	between 20,000 and 50,000 inhabitants	... 2
Do.	„ 50,000 and 100,000 do ...	... 3
Do.	over 100,000 do ...	... 4

(5) BIHAR AND ORISSA

The following plan is adopted :—

Municipalities

The number of votes assigned to each Municipality is determined in accordance with the following scale, namely :—

		Rs.		Rs.
Municipalities with a local income of		5,000 &	less than	10,000—1 vote.
Do	do	10,000	do	20,000—2 votes.
Do	do	20,000	do	50,000—3 „
Do	do	50,000	do	80,000—4 „

and for every additional Rs. 30,000 or part thereof in excess of Rs. 80,000—1 vote.

The number of votes to which each Municipality is entitled on the said scale is notified from time to time by the Local Government in the Local Official Gazette.

To determine the candidate to whom the votes assigned to each Municipality in accordance with the above rule is given, an election is held, by the Commissioners qualified to vote, other than officials appointed by name or *ex-officio*, of each of the notified Municipalities in each of the said Divisions.

No such Commissioner has more than one vote in any one Division.

The candidate to whom the largest number of votes is given by the Commissioners at any such election is deemed to have obtained the number of votes so assigned to the Municipality in which such election has been held.

District Boards

The number of votes assigned to each District Board is determined in accordance with the following scale :—

		Rs.		
District Boards with an annual income (exclusive of opening balances and receipts from loans)	not exceeding	75,000	...	1 vote.
do	exceeding 75,000 but less than	1,25,000	...	2 votes.
and for every additional Rs. 50,000 or part thereof in excess of		1,25,000	...	1 vote.

The number of votes to which each District Board is entitled on the said scale is notified from time to time by the Local Government in the Local Official Gazette.

To determine the candidate to whom the votes assigned to each District Board in accordance with the above rule is given an election is held, by the persons who are members, other than officials appointed by name or *ex-officio*, of each District Board of each of the said Divisions and are qualified to vote.

No elector has more than one vote in any one Division.

The candidate to whom the largest number of votes is given by electors at any such election is deemed to have obtained the number of votes so assigned to the District Board holding such election.

(6) THE PUNJAB

The three members for municipal and Cantonment Committees and three members for District Boards are elected by members of these bodies, classified into three groups (the Cis-Sutlej Central and Western groups) other than those appointed *ex-officio*.

(7) ASSAM

Municipalities

The number of votes which the Commissioners of each Municipality are entitled to give is regulated by the local income possessed by it according to the following scale :—

Municipalities with an annual local income of less than			
		Rs. 10,000 ...	1 Vote.
Do.	do.	Rs. 10,000 and less than Rs. 20,000 ...	2 Votes.
Do.	do.	Rs. 20,000 and less than Rs. 50,000 ...	3 "
Do.	do.	Rs. 50,000 and less than Rs. 80,000 ...	4 "
and for every additional Rs. 30,000 or part thereof in excess of Rs. 80,000 ...			1 Vote.

By " local income " is meant the total income of the Municipality excluding the opening balance of the municipal fund, grants and contributions, and receipts under the account heads " Extraordinary " and " Debt."

The number of votes to which each Municipality is entitled on the said scale is notified from time to time by the Local Government in the Local Official Gazette.

Local Boards

The election is made by the votes of the members of the Local Boards in the Division other than (*a*) the Chairman, if an official, and (*b*) officials appointed by name or *ex-officio* to be such members.

The number of votes which the members of each Local Board is entitled to give is regulated by the ordinary income possessed by it as follows, namely :—

One vote if the ordinary income of the Board does not exceed Rs. 1,00,000, and one additional vote for every additional Rs. 1,00,000 or portion thereof.

By " ordinary income" is meant the total income of the Board, excluding the opening balance, and entries under the account head " Debt."

The number of votes to which the Members of each Local Board are entitled is notified from time to time by the Local Government in the Local Official Gazette.

(ii) THE CLASS ELECTORATES.

(*a*) LANDED INTEREST

(1) The Imperial Legislative Council

Taking next the class electorates for the election of the members of the Imperial Legislative Council, it is found that the franchise is conferred on all landholders in each of the Provinces of Madras, Bombay, Bengal, United Provinces of Agra and Oudh, Bihar and Orissa and the Central Provinces.

(i) The landholders who elect an Additional Member from Madras must

(*a*) possess an annual income, calculated according to certain rules, of not less than fifteen thousand rupees from land situated within the Presidency; or

(*b*) receive from Government a *malikhana* allowance the annual amount of which is not less than fifteen thousand rupees.

(ii) The landholders who elect a Member from Bombay must be

(*a*) Jagirdhars and Zemindars of Sind,

(*b*) Sardars of Gujerat and

(*c*) Sardars of the Deccan.

The Jagirdars and Zemindars of Sind elect one Member in the first year, the third year and so on.

(iii) The landholders who vote in Bengal must be those who

(*a*) pay land-revenue or road and public works cesses as follows:—

(1) In the case of the Presidency, and Burdwan forming one group-land-revenue amounting to not less than ten thousand rupees, or road and public works cesses amounting to not less than two thousand five hundred rupees per annum, and

(2) In the case of the Rajshahi, Dacca and Chittagong Divisions forming another group-land revenue amounting to not less than five thousand rupees or road and public works cesses amounting to not less than one thousand two hundred and fifty rupees per annum, or

(*b*) hold titles conferred or recognised by the Government not lower in rank than that of a Raja or Nawab.

(iv) From the United Provinces for the election of a Member by landholders of Agra and Oudh the election is made

(*a*) by the British Indian Association of Oudh at an extraordinary general meeting,

(*b*) by members qualified to vote in the Agra Province who must.

(1) own in that province land in respect of which land revenue amounting to not less than ten thousand rupees per annum is payable; or

(2) own in that province land free of land revenue, if the land revenue nominally assessed on such land in order to determine the amount of rates payable in respect of the same, either taken by itself or in addition to land revenue payable in respect of other land by such owners amounts to not less than ten thousand rupees per annum; or

(3) hold the title of Maharaja, Rajah or Nawab conferred or recognised by the Government ;

(4) hold the title of Rajwar, Rai Bahadur, Rao Bahadur, Rai, Mirza, Khan Bahadur Chaudhri or Diwan, if hereditary and recognised by the Government.

(v) The landholders who elect a member from Bihar and Orissa must

(*a*) pay land-revenue amounting to not less than ten thousand rupees, or road and public works cesses amounting to not less than two thousand five hundred rupees per annum ; or

(*b*) before the date of the Notification hold titles conferred or recognised by the Government not lower in rank than that of Raja or Nawab.

(vi) In the Central Provinces, the landholders who elect a Member must be persons

(*a*) whose land is assessed to land-revenue at not less than five thousand rupees per annum ; or

(*b*) whose names are entered in the Durbar list prepared under the authority of the Local Government ; or

(*c*) who hold the office of Honorary Magistrate.

(2) The Madras Legislative Council

Zemindars.

The election of two Members, one for each group, is made by all zamindars qualified to vote and having a place of residence within the electoral area concerned, who—

(*a*) possess an annual income, calculated as provided in rules 4, 5 and 6, of not less than three thousand rupees derived from an estate situated within the Presidency of Fort St. George, or

(*b*) receive from Government a malikana allowance the annual amount of which is not less than three thousand rupees.

The annual income of a zamindar from his estate is taken to be the annual rental upon which he pays land-cess under the Madras Local Boards Act, 1884, excluding the peshkish or similar charge payable by him to Government.

If in any case it is not possible to calculate income from land, the Collector is to determine such income for the purposes of these rules upon the best information available.

In all cases, the income is calculated on the figures of the latest fasli year for which figures are available or, in cases where figures for the fasli year are not available, then, proportionately, on the figures of the latest period for which figures are available.

In calculating the annual income of zamindars.—

(*a*) income derived from an estate shall not be reckoned along with income derived from any land other than an estate, but it may be reckoned along with a malikana allowance ; and

(*b*) in no case shall income derived from a portion of an estate which is not separately registered in the office of a Collector be taken into account.

Landholders (other than zamindars)

The election is made by all landholders other than zamindars qualified to vote and having a place of residence within the electoral area concerned who possess an annual income, calculated as provided in rules 4 and 5, of not less than one thousand rupees derived from land situated within the Presidency of Fort St. George and not forming an estate.

For this purpose the annual income of landholders other than zamindars is calculated as follows :—

(*a*) the income of ryotwari holders cultivating their own lands is taken to be equal to twice the assessment fixed on the land so cultivated ;

(*b*) the income of ryotwari holders who have leased their lands to tenants is taken to be equal to the assessment fixed on the land so leased ;

(*c*) the income of holders of *inams* is taken to be equal to the rental value on which the land-cess is calculated under section 64 of the Madras Local Boards Act, 1884, excluding the *peshkish. jodi*, quit-rent or similar charge payable to Government ;

(*d*) the income of tenants of *zamindars* and *inamdars* is taken to be equal to two-thirds of the annual rent value of the lands held by such tenants as determined under section 64 of the Madras Local Boards Act, 1884 :

Provided that to the income of tenants holding land free of rent or at a favourable rent calculated as provided in clause (*d*) there is added the difference between the rent if any actually charged and the rent ordinarily payable for land of similar description and with similar advantages in the village or in neighbouring villages ;

(*e*) in the case of sub-tenants, the income is taken to be equal to half the income as determined for the superior tenant.

If, in any case, a separate water-rate or second-crop charge is payable to Government or to a superior holder in respect of any land, such water-rate and charge is regarded as forming part of the assessment or rental value, as the case may be, in calculating income under this rule :

Provided that a landholder who collects water-rate or second-crop charge from another person on behalf of Government is not entitled to have anything so collected taken into account when his income is fixed under this rule.

If, in any case, it is not possible to calculate income from land in accordance with sub-rule (1) of this rule, the Collector is to determine such income for the purposes of these rules upon the best information available.

In all cases the income is calculated on the figures of the latest fasli year of which figures are available or, in cases where figures for the fasli year are not available, then, proportionately, on the figures of the latest period for which figures are available.

In calculating the annual income of landholders for the purposes of ruls 3—

(*a*) income derived from an estate is not to be reckoned along with income derived from any land other than an estate;

(*b*) subject to the provisions of clause (*a*), incomes derived from more than one parcel of land, however held, may be reckoned together provided that, in the case of joint holders of land or joint family under the Marumakkatayam or Aliyasantanam law the income derived therefrom is not added to any income derived from other land unless the holder of the latter has been nominated, or is entitled, under those rules to represent the joint holders or family in respect of the former land.

(3) The Bombay Legislative Council

Sardars of the Deccan

The election of one Member by this body is made by all persons who are qualified to vote and whose names appear in the list for the time being in force under the Resolution of the Government of Bombay in the Political Department No. 2363, dated 23rd day of July 1867.

Sardars of Gujerat

The election by this body is made by all persons who are qualified to vote and whose names appear in the list for the time being in force under the Resolution of the Government of Bombay in the Political Department No. 6265, dated the 21st day of September 1909.

Jagirdars and Zamindars of Sind.

The election of the Member is made by all persons qualified to vote who are—(*a*) Jagirdars of the first or second class, or (*b*) Zamindars who for the three years preceding the preparation of the electoral roll have paid not less than one thousand rupees per annum as ordinary land revenue: Provided that no elector is to have more than one vote though he may possess more than one of the qualifications above described.

(4) The Bengal Legislative Council

The election is made by landholders qualified to vote and having a place of residence within the Division concerned who—

(*a*) in the case of the Presidency and Burdwan Divisions, hold in their own right, as proprietors, one or more estates or shares of estates and pay in respect thereof land-revenue amounting to not less than six thousand rupees or road and public works cesses amounting to not less than one thousand five hundred rupees per annum; or

(*b*) in the case of the Rajshahi, Dacca or Chittagong Division, hold in their own right one or more estates or shares of estates as proprietors, or one or more permanent tenures or shares of such tenures held direct from such proprietors and pay in respect thereof land-revenue amounting to not less than three thousand rupees or road and public works cesses amounting to not less than seven hundred and fifty rupees per annum; or

(*c*) before the date of the Notification held titles conferred or recognised by the Government not lower in rank than that of Raja or Nawab:

Provided that no landholder is to have more than one vote in any one Division though he may possess more than one of the qualifications above described.

(5) The United Provinces Legislative Council

Landholders of Agra

The election is made in the Province of Agra by all persons qualified to vote and having a place of residence in the Province who—

(*a*) in that Province own land in respect of which land-revenue amounting to not less than five thousand rupees per annum is payable, or

(*b*) in that Province, own land free of land revenue if the land-revenue nominally assessed on such land in order to determine the amount of rates payable in respect of the same, either alone or together with any land-revenue payable in respect of other land by such owners, amount to not less than five thousand rupees per annum, or

(*c*) hold the title of Maharaja, Raja or Nawab if conferred or recognised by the Government, or

(*d*) hold the title of Rajwar, Rao Bahadur, Rai Bahadur, Mirza, Khan Bahadur, Choudhri, or Dewan, if hereditary and recognised by the Government:

Provided that no elector shall have more than one vote though he may possess more than one of the qualifications described above.

Landholders of Oudh

The election of a member is made by the British Indian Association of Oudh at an extraordinary general meeting in the manner laid down for the time being in the bye-laws of the said Association for carrying resolution or recording decision upon questions of business brought before that body ;

Provided that, where an equality of votes is found to exist between any candidates and the addition of a vote will entitle any of the candidates to be declared elected, the determination of the person to whom such one additional vote is deemed to have been given is made by lot to be drawn at such meeting and in such manner as the Chairman thereof may determine.

(6) The Bihar Legislative Council

The election is made by landholders qualified to vote and having a place of residence within the division concerned, who—

(*a*) pay either land-revenue or road and public works cesses as follows, namely —

(i) in the case of the Patna, Tirhut and Bhagalpur Divisions, pay land-revenue amounting to not less than four thousand rupees or road and public works cesses amounting to not less than one thousand rupees per annum ; and

(ii) in the case of the Orissa and Chota Nagpur Divisions, pay land-revenue amounting to not less than six thousand rupees or road and public works cesses amounting to not less than five hundred rupees per annum ; or

(*b*) before the date of the Notification held titles conferred or recognised by the Government not lower in rank than that of Rajah or Nawab :

Provided that no landholder is to have more than one vote in any one Division though he may possess more than one of the qualifications above described.

(7) The Assam Legislative Council

The election is made by landholders qualified to vote and having a place of residence within the Division concerned, who—

(*a*) hold in their own right as proprietors within the Division one or more estates or shares of estates, and pay in respect thereof land-revenue amounting to not less than five hundered rupees or local rates amounting to not less than one hundred and twenty-five rupees per annum ; or (*b*) hold titles conferred or recognised by the Government not lower in rank than that of Rajah or Nawab :

Provided that no elector is to have more than one vote in any one Division though he may possess more than one of the qualifications above described.

Explanation.—For the purposes of this rule—

(1) a manager or a trustee or the holder of a religious endowment, such as a *mahant* or a *gosain* or the *mutawali* or manager of a Muhammadan *wakf*, is not as such to be deemed to be a person who holds estates in his own right within the meaning of this rule ;

(2) where an estate or a share of an estate is held by two or more persons jointly, it is to be assumed, until the contrary is shown, that they hold equal shares ;

(3) the term "local rates" refers to the rates levied by Government under the Assam Local Rates Regulation, 1879 ;

(4) the term "proprietor" includes "landholders" as defined in the Assam Land and Revenue Rugulation, 1886.

(*b*) THE MUHAMMADAN COMMUNITY

(1) The Imperial Legislative Council

(i) The Muhammadans in Madras who vote for an additional Member must be those who—

(*a*) are landholders possessing an annual income from land situated within the Presidency of Fort St. George of not less than three thousand rupees ; or

(*b*) pay on their own account income-tax on an income of not less than six thousand rupees ; or

(*c*) are members of the Legislative Council of the Governor of Fort St. George; or

(*d*) are Ordinary or Honorary Fellows of the University of Madras; or

(*e*) are holders of any title conferred or recognised by the Government, or are members of the order of the Star of India or the Indian Empire or holders of the Kaisar-i-Hind Medal ; or

(*f*) are in receipt of pensions of Rupees fifteen per mensem and upwards for service as Gazetted or Commissioned Officers of Government.

(ii) The Member to be elected in Bombay for Muhammadan Community is elected by the Muhammadan non-official Additional Members on the Provincial Council.

(iii) The Muhammadans who vote for a Member in Bengal must be those who—

(*a*) are members of the Legislative Council of the Lieutenant-Governor of Bengal; or

(*b*) are holders of any title conferred or recognised by the Government, or are members of the Order of the Star of India or of the Order of the Indian Empire or holders of the Kaiser-i-Hind Medal; or

(*c*) are Ordinary or Honorary Fellows of the University of Calcutta; or

(*d*) own in their own right, and not in a fiduciary capacity, land or a share in land in respect of which land or share road and public works cesses amounting to not less than one hundred and eighty-seven rupees, eight annas are payable per annum to Government, either directly or through a superior landlord; or

(*e*) held in their own right, and not in a fiduciary capacity, as permanent tenure holders, one or more tenures held direct from the Zemindar, or shares of such tenures, in respect of which tenures or shares road and public works cesses amounting to not less than one hundred and eighty-seven rupees, eight annas are payable per annum; or

(*f*) have during the financial year immediately preceding that in which the election is held paid on their own account income-tax on an income of not less than six thousand rupees per annum; or

(*g*) are in receipt of pensions for service as gazetted or commissioned officers of the Government:

Provided that no elector shall have more than one vote though he may possess more than one of the qualifications above described.

(iv) The Muhammadans who vote for a Member in the United Provinces must be those who—

(*a*) own land in respect of which land-revenue amounting to not less than ten thousand rupees is payable per annum; or

(*b*) own land free of land-revenue if the land-revenue nominally assessed on such land in order to determine the amount of rates payable in respect of the same, either taken by itself or in addition to land-revenue payable in respect of other land by such owners, amounts to not less than ten thousand rupees per annum; or

(*c*) have during the financial year immediately preceding that in which the election is held paid on their own account income-tax on an income of not less than ten thousand rupees per annum; or

(*d*) are Members of the Legislative Council of the Lieutenant-Governor of the United Provinces of Agra and Oudh; or

(*e*) are Ordinary or Honorary Fellows of the University of Allahabad; or

(*f*) are Trustees of the Muhammadan Anglo-Oriental College, Aligarh; or (*g*) are holders of any title conferred or recognised by the Government, or are members of the Order of the Star of India or the Order of the Indian Empire or holders of the Kaisar-i-Hind Medal ; or

(*h*) are in receipt of pensions for service as gazetted or commissioned officers of the Government ; or

(*i*) are Honorary Assistant Collectors, Honorary Magistrates or Honorary Munsifs :

Provided that no elector shall have more than one vote though he may possess more than one of the qualifications above described.

(v). The Muhammadans who elect a Member for Bihar and Orissa should be those who—

(*a*) are members of the Legislative Council of the Lieutenant-Governor of Bihar and Orissa ; or

(*b*) are holders of any title conferred or recognised by the Government, or are members of the Order of the Star of India or of the Order of the Indian Empire, or holders of the Kaisar-i-Hind Medal ; or

(*c*) are Ordinary or Honorary Fellows of the University of Calcutta ; or

(*d*) own in their own right, and not in a fiduciary capacity, land or a share in land in respect of which land or share land-revenue amounting to not less than seven hundred and fifty rupees is payable per annum ; or

(*e*) own in their own right, and not in a fiduciary capacity, land or a share in land in respect of which land or share road and public works cesses amounting to not less than one hundred and eighty-seven rupees eight annas are payable per annum to Government, either directly or through a superior landlord ; or

(*f*) have during the financial year immediately preceding that in which the election is held paid on their own account income tax on an income of not less than six thousand rupees per annum ; or

(*g*) are in receipt of pensions for service as gazetted or commissioned officers of the Government :

Provided that no elector is to have more than one vote though he may possess more than one of the qualifications above described.

(2) The Madras Legislative Council

The election is made by all Muhammadans qualified to vote and having a place of residence within the electoral area concerned, who—

(1) are landholders possessing an annual income from land situated within the Presidency of Fort St. George of not less than five hundred rupees ; or

(2) have during the financial year immediately preceding that in which the election is held paid on their own account income-tax on an income of not less than two thousand rupees ; or

(3) are ordinary or honorary Fellows or registered graduates of the University of Madras ; or

(4) are holders of any title conferred or recognized by the Government or members of the Order of the Star of India or the Order of the Indian Empire or holders of the Kaiser-i-Hind Medal ; or

(5) are in receipt of pensions of rupees fifteen *per mensem* and upwards, for service as gazetted or commissioned officers of Government.

(3) The Bombay Legislative Council

The election is made by all Muhammadans qualified to vote and having a place of residence in the Division for which the election is being held who—

(*a*) hold alienated or unalienated land assessed at or of the assessable value of not less than one hundred rupees or in the City of Bombay of a rateable value of not less than two thousand and five hundred rupees as determined in accordance with the provisions of Chapter VIII of the City of Bombay Municipal Act, 1888, for the purposes of that Act; or

(*b*) being sharers in joint estates are entitled to a share which would as separate holding qualify them to vote under sub-clause (*a*); or

(*c*) have during the financial year immediately preceding that in which the election is held paid on their own account income-tax on an income of not less than one thousand rupees per annum, or in the City of Bombay two thousand rupees per annum; or

(*d*) are practising Advocates or Attorneys or ;

(*e*) are holders of any title conferred or recognised by the Government or are Members of the Order of the Star of India or of the Order of Indian Empire. or holders of the Kaiser-i-Hind Medal or;

(*f*) hold diplomas in medicine or engineering granted at least five years previously by any Institution in the British Empire recognised by the Local Government for this purpose ; or

(*g*) are conciliators under the Deccan Agriculturists' Relief Act, 1879 ; or

(*h*) are Justices of the Peace or Honorary Magistrates; or

(*i*) are graduates of five years' standing of any University in the British Empire :

Provided that no elector is to have more than one vote though he may possess more than one of the qualifications above described.

(4) The Bengal Legislative Council

The election is made by the votes of Muhammadans qualified to vote and having a place of residence in the electoral area concerned, who—

(*a*) hold a title recognised or conferred by the Government or are members of the Order of the Star or India or the Order of the Indian Empire, or hold a Kaisar-i-Hind Medal; or

(*b*) are Ordinary or Honorary Fellows of the University of Calcutta; or

(*c*) are Honorary Magistrates; or

(*d*) are in the service of Government on a salary of rupees two thousand or more per annum; or

(*e*) are Barristers-at-law, Attorneys-at-law, Vakils, or Pleaders; or

(*f*) are graduates of any University or Institution recognised by the Government in the United Kingdom or British India; or

(*g*) are licentiates or diploma holders in Surgery or Medicine of any University or Institution, recognised by the Government in the United Kingdom or British India; or

(*h*) (i) are lincentiates in engineering of any University recognised by the Government in the United Kingdom or British India; or

(ii) have passed the examination appointed by the Council of the Institute of Civil Engineers, London, for candidates for Associate Membership of that Institute, or any examination recognised by the said Council as exempting such candidates from the examination first mentioned; or

(1) in the case of the Presidency and Burdwan Divisions, are teachers in any institution maintained or aided by the Government or affiliated to or recognised by the University of Calcutta or recognised by the Director of Public Instruction:

Provided that such teachers are not less than thirty years of age and receive a monthly salary of not less than fifty rupees in Calcutta, or not less than twenty-five rupees in any place other than Calcutta;

(2) in the case of the Rajshahi, Dacca and Chittagong Divisions, are teachers in any high school recognised by the University of Calcutta, or by any college affiliated thereto or by any Madrassa recognised by the Government, and hold certificates of having passed the final examination of a recognised Madrassa; or

(*j*) are Registrars authorised to act under the Bengal Muhammadan Marriages and Divorces Registration Act, 1876; or

(*k*) are holders in their own right, as proprietors or permanent tenure holders, of one or more estates or shares of estates or of one or more permanent tenures held direct from such proprietors, or of shares of such tenures, and pay in respect thereof—

(i) in the Presidency or Burdwan Division, land-revenue amounting to not less than one hundred and twenty-five rupees per annum or road and public works cesses amounting to not less than thirty-one rupees four annas, per annum ; or

(ii) in the Rajshahi, Dacca or Chittagong Division, land-revenue amounting to not less than one hundred rupees per annum or road and public works cesses amounting to not less than fifty rupees per annum ; or

(*l*) have during the financial year immediately preceding that in which the election is held paid on their own account income-tax on an income of not less than three thousand rupees in Calcutta, two thousand rupees in other parts of the Presidency Division, or in the Burdwan Division, or one thousand rupees in the Rajshahi, Dacca or Chittagong Division ; or

(*m*) are in receipt of pensions from the Government as gazetted or commissioned officers of Government or of not less than fifty rupees per mensem :

Provided that no elector is to have more than one vote though he may possess more than one of the qualifications above described ; and if an elector is entitled to vote in any one of two or more Divisions, he may, by intimation in writing given to the Returning Officer not later than such date as the Local Government may prescribe, choose, or in his default, if intimation of such default is given to the Returning Officer or to the Local Government by any other elector within sufficient time to admit of orders being passed, the Local Government shall fix the Division in which he is to vote, and his name will be entered in the electoral roll for that Division only.

Explanation.—For the purposes of this rule—

(1) in determining the eligibility of a landholder as an elector, only land-revenue or road and public works cesses payable in respect of his own personal share shall be taken into account, and

(2) "holder in his own right" include *mutawalli* or manager of a wakf estate, but shall not include a trustee or manager of an estate other than a wakf estate.

(5) The United Provinces Legislative Council

The election is made by all Muhammadans qualified to vote and having a place of residence in the United Provinces of Agra and Oudh who—

(a) own land in respect of which land-revenue amounting to not less than three thousand rupees per annum is payable ; or

(b) own land free of land-revenue if the land-revenue nominally assessed on such land in order to determine the amount of rates payable in respect of the same either alone or together with any land-revenue payable in respect of other land by such owners, amounts to not less than three thousand rupees per annum ; or

(c) have during the financial year immediately preceding that in which the election is held paid on their own account income tax on an income of not less than three thousand rupees per annum ; or

(d) are Members of the Legislative Council of the Lieutenant-Governor of the United Provinces of Agra and Oudh ; or

(e) are Ordinary or Honorary Fellows of the University of Allahabad ; or

(f) are Trustees of the Muhammadan Anglo-Oriental College, Aligarh ; or

(g) are holders of any title conferred or recognised by the Government, or are members of the order of the Star of India or the Order of the Indian Empire or holders of the Kaisar-i-Hind Medal ; or

(h) are in receipt of pensions for service as gazetted or commissioned officers of the Government ; or

(i) are Honorary Assistant Collectors, Honorary Magistrates or Honorary Munsifs ; or

(j) are graduates of five years' standing of any University in the British Empire :

Provided that no elector shall have more than one vote though he may possess more than one of the qualifications above described.

(6) The Bihar Legislative Council

The election is made by the votes of all Muhammadans qualified to vote and having a place of residence in the electoral area concerned, who—

(a) hold a title recognized or conferred by the Government or are members of the Order of the Star of India or the Order of the Indian Empire, or hold a Kaisar-i-Hind Medal ; or

(b) are Ordinary or Honorary Fellows of the University of Calcutta ; or

(c) are Honorary Magistrates ; or

(d) are in the service of Government on a salary of Rs. 2,000 or more per annum ; or

(e) are graduates of ten years' standing of any University in the United Kingdom or British India ; or (*f*) are teachers in any institution maintained or aided by the Government or affiliated to, or recognized by, the University of Calcutta, or recognized by the Directer of Public Instruction :

Provided that such teachers are not less than thirty years of age, and receive a monthly salary of not less than twenty-five rupees ; or

(*g*) are Registrars, authorised to act under the Bengal Muhammadan Marriages and Divorces Registration Act, 1876 ; or

(*h*) own land in respect of which land-revenue amounting to not less than one hundred and twenty-five rupees in the Orissa and Chota Nagpur Divisions, and two hundred and fifty rupees in the Patna, Tirhut and Bhagalpur Divisions, is payable per annum ; or

(*i*) own land in respect of which road and public works cesses amounting to not less than thirty-one rupees and four annas in the Orrisa and Chota Nagpur Divisions, and sixty-two rupees and eight annas in the Patna, Tirhut and Bhagalpur Divisions are payable per annum to Government either directly or through a superior landlord ; or

(*j*) have during the financial year immediately preceding that in which the election is held, paid on their own account income-tax on an income of not less than two thousand rupees in the Orissa and Chota Nagpur Divisions, and four thousand rupees in the Patna, Tirhut and Bhagalpur Divisions ; or

(*k*) are in receipt of a pension from the Government of not less than fifty rupees per mensem or as gazetted or commissioned officers of the Government :

Provided that no elector shall have more than one vote though he may possess more than one of the qualifications above described, and if an elector is entitled to vote in any one of two or more Divisions, he may, by intimation in writing given to the Returning Officer not later than such date, as the Local Government may prescribe, choose or in his default, if intimation of such default is given to the Returning Officer or to the Local Government by any other elector within sufficient time to admit of orders being passed, the Local Government shall fix the Division in which he shall vote, and his name shall be entered in the electoral roll for that Division only.

(7) The Assam Legislative Council

The election made by the votes of Muhammadans qualified to vote and having a place of residence in the Division concerned, who—

(*a*) hold titles conferred or recognised by the Government ; or

(*b*) hold the Kaisar-i-Hind Medal ; or

(*c*) are members of the Order of the Star of India or the Order of the Indian Empire ; or (*d*) are Ordinary or Honorary Fellows of the University of Calcutta ; or

(*e*) are graduates of any University in the United Kingdom or British India ; or

(*f*) are Honorary Magistrates ; or

(*g*) hold certificates that they have passed the final examination of a recognised Madrassa, and are teachers in any High School recognised by the Calcutta University, or any College affiliated thereto, or any Madrassa recognised by the Government ; or

(*h*) are Registrars authorised to act under the Bengal Muhammadan Marriages and Divorces Registration Act, 1876 ; or

(*i*) are holders in their own right as proprietors within the Division of one or more estates or shares of estates and pay in respect thereof land-revenue or local rates amounting to not less than fifty rupees per annum ; or

(*j*) are *jotedars* in the district of Goalpara paying rent amounting to not less than two hundred and fifty rupees per annum ; or

(*k*) have during the financial year immediately preceding that in which the election is held, paid on their own account income-tax on an income of not less than one thousand rupees per annum ; or

(*l*) are in receipt of pensions from the Government of not less than fifty rupees per mensem :

Provided that no elector is to have more than one vote though he may possess more than one of the qualifications above described, and if an elector is entitled to vote in either of the Divisions, he may, by intimation in writing given to the Returning Officer not later than such date as the Local Government may prescribe, choose, or in his default, if intimation of such default is given to the Returning Officer or to the Local Government by any other election within sufficient time to admit of orders being passed, the Local Government shall fix the Division in which he shall vote, and his name shall be entered in the electoral roll for that Division only.

(iii) THE SPECIAL ELECTORATES

(*1*) *The Universities*

The Franchise in the University electorates of all the provinces is bestowed on all the ordinary, honorary and extra-ordinary Fellows of the several Universities concerned viz., Madras, Bombay, Calcutta, Allahabad, and the Punjab Universities.

(2) *Trade and Commerce*

In the constituencies created for the representation of Trade and Commerce, European and Indian, for the Imperial Legislative Council, viz., the Chambers of Commerce of Bengal, and Bombay, the franchise is to be exercised by their members in the same manner as is adopted by them for the election by them of Port Trustees *i.e.* the Commissioners for the Ports of Bombay, and Calcutta respectively.

[Indian trade and commercial interests, it will be recollected, are provided for by the nomination to the Imperial Council of one additional Member.]

In the constituencies for the representation and commerce, European and Indian, in the Provincial Legislative Councils, viz., in the Chambers of Commerce of Madras, Bombay, Bengal, Karachi, Upper India, Punjab, Burma, and in the Trades Associations of Madras and Calcutta, the Mill-owner's Associations of Bombay and Ahmedabad (electing alternately), the franchise of their members is to be exercised in the same manner as that which they adopt at special meetings held for the election of their own office-bearers. In the Indian Merchant's Chamber and the Native Piece-goods Association which together elect a member to represent Indian Commerce in the Bombay Legislative Council they exercise their franchise at business meetings of their bodies by electing ten delegates each.

(iv) OTHER SPECIAL INTERESTS

(a) *Calcutta City*

In the special additional electorate created in Bengal for the representation of Calcutta City, the franchise is conferred on those who are Commissioners of the Calcutta Corporation, other than those appointed by the Local Government, and is to be exercised at special meetings convened of the said electors.

(b) *Planters*

1. In the electorate representing the planting interests in Madras, the franchise is conferred on each Planters' Association affiliated to the United Planter's Association of Southern India, who are to exercise it by ascertaining the candidate selected at meetings held for the purpose and the result ascertained according to the value given to their votes in the same way as at general meetings of the United Planters' Association.

2. In Bengal, in the constituency for representing the Tea Planting Community, the franchise is conferred on all managers of tea gardens whose area is not less than 100 acres and is situated within the Province.

3. In Bihar, the franchise in the Planters' electorate is conferred on the Members of the Bihar Planters' Association.

4. In Assam, the franchise of the Planting Community Electorates is conferred on the Members of the Assam Valley Branch of the Indian Tea Association, the Surma Valley Branch thereof, to elect one each in every election and to elect one additional Member alternately in the same way as at business meetings of the Branches.

(c) *Mining*

In the electorate for the mining interests represented in the Bihar Council, the franchise is conferred on the Members of the Indian Mining Association, to be exercised at a special general meeting of the Association.

(v) ELECTORAL PROCEDURE

All the elections to the various Legislative Councils, Provincial and Imperial, have to begin and to take place in pursuance of notifications which must be issued by the Governor-General or the Governor as the case may be, calling upon the electorates mentioned, prior to the expiry of the term of office of the several members thereof or on the occurrence of any vacancies in consequence of death, resignation, or otherwise, calling upon the electorates concerned to elect in accordance with the Regulations the Member or Members assigned to them by a certain date to be fixed by the Notification. As the terms of office of Members of the Legislative Councils have generally been now adjusted so as to expire at or about the same time, the Notifications issued in this country in respect of elections, to that extent, are calculated to bring about a kind of general elections to the councils. They may therefore, be said to roughly correspond to the writs issued under the great seal in England from the Crown Office and directed to the returning officers of each of the constituencies.

There is, however, a preliminary work to be attended to each year with reference to the constituencies concerned, as in England, which is the revision of the several electoral rolls wherever such electoral rolls have to be maintained for the purposes of election.

This work has to be done annually and is begun by the publication of draft electoral rolls in the month of July, on which objections are heard and decided by the Collector of each district every year, so as to admit of the final electoral roll being published by the 1st of October. This work corresponds, no doubt, to that which is performed by the revising Barristers in England, but the procedure is much more summary and involves far less elaborate procedure or proceedings than those which usually take place in England under the control of party organizations and otherwise.

The electoral rolls then constitute at the time of every election conclusive evidence of the right to vote of those claiming to vote and the elections therefore are conducted in accordance therewith. In the case of elections where no electoral roll is necessary it is connected in accordance with the special procedure prescribed in each case and referred to above.

The actual election proceedings every three years thus begin, with the nomination of candidates made in writing by at least two voters in due form. If only one person is nominated for a seat, or only two where there are two seats, the candidates are forthwith declared elected; but if more candidates are nominated, the voters have then to proceed to an election on the dates fixed for the recording of their votes.

The method of voting in India is of three kinds according to the nature of the constituency. In all cases, votes are allowed to be recorded before the Returning Officer and in some cases it is obligatory. In other cases, votes are recorded before Attesting Officers who have to attest the votes recorded and transmit the same to the Returning Officers. In the remaining cases, votes may also be recorded and sent to the returning officer by registered post. The method of voting is, as in England, by ballot, though the safeguards for securing secrecy cannot be said to be as complete in India as in England. In the bulk of the Electorates, the returning and the attesting Officers are the district and divisional executive officers in the several districts. In others, it is the chief ministerial or the executive officer of the constituency concerned or where this is unsuitable, it is the Secretary to the Government in the Legislative Department himself.

On the declaration of the results on the date fixed by the returning officers concerned the validity of elections can be contested as in England either on the ground of the improper rejection, or reception of a nomination or of a vote or on the ground of any corrupt practices committed in connection with such election or for any other sufficient cause as provided in the Regulations. No cases have arisen in India so far as to any corrupt practices employed in the elections so far held, but even in cases where the elections have been contested on other grounds the fact that the decision of the matter has lain under the Regulations with the chief executive authority of the Province, and not with the Courts, has not tended to make the procedure on scrutiny and objection, as judicial as it has come to be in England.

The definition of corrupt practices in the Regulations is taken from the Bombay District Municipalities Act; but though it covers false personation on the part of a voter and the use of threats of injury as well as the actual purchase of votes by the candidate or his agent, yet the refinements and developments to which the law as to corrupt practices in elections has attained in England, are yet unknown in the elections to the legislatures in India. In England, corrupt practices usually come under the heads of bribery, undue influence, personation, and treating. The first three are covered by the definition of corrupt practices contained in the Indian Councils Regulations, but treating, as such, is not specifically mentioned therein, though it is apprehended it would come under the head of offering any promise of individual profit or any valuable consideration. Bribery, of course, is well understood and in England the offence is defined in great detail for, as Professor Lawrence Lowell put it as there are seven recognised kinds of his lines so the English statutes describe seven distinct methods of bribery. Treating, however, does not imply a specific contract to vote for a specific return, but relies for its effect upon the sense of good honour and gratitude which it puts the voters in. In England, besides corrupt practices which on account of the specific proofs required are not easily brought home to candidates or their agents, there are other processes by which general attempts to demoralize the constituencies by lavish expenditure of money to individuals or classes therein are prohibited as an illegal practices—such as gifts to individual voters ; where there is no immediate contract, stringent provisions are also made making it obligatory on members to make returns of their election expenditure, and provisions are also made defining what are authorised expenses at elections.

The very attempt at such elaborate definitions has only increased corresponding attempts at clever evasions, and it cannot be said that.

though electoral morality has very much improved since the degenerate days of Old Sarum, the present law as such has not ensured the purity of elections. Such practices as nursing constituencies and such difficulties, trouble and expense as are involved in election-petitions with the uncertainty of results attaining thereof have to a large extent, stood in the way of a more rigorous enforcement of election morality on the part of the Courts than would otherwise have been the case. The whole subject of corrupt practices and the election morals is however, one which is yet to arise in any tangible shape in the Legislative Council elections in India.

III

PRACTICE AND PROCEDURE OF THE LEGISLATURES

(i) RULES OF LEGISLATIVE BUSINESS IN THE IMPERIAL COUNCIL

In exercise of the power conferred by the Indian Councils Act, 1861, section eighteen, the following rules have been made by the Council of the Governor-General assembled for the purpose of making laws and regulations at the meetings held on the eleventh day of February 1873 and sixteenth day of February 1883 and have received the assent of the Governor-General.

I. Preliminary

1. These rules supersede the rules for the conduct of business at the meetings of the Council as amended on the 17th day of December 1862, and the 28th day of February 1868.

2. In these rules—

"Council" means the Council of the Governor-General of India for the purpose of making laws and regulations: "President" means the Governor-General or (during the time of his visit to any part of India unaccompanied by his Council) the President nominated by the Governor-General in Council, under the Indian Councils Act, 1861, section six; or, in the absence of both the Governor-General and the President so nominated, the Senior Ordinary Member of the Council present and presiding :

"Member" means a Member of the Council, whether ordinary, extraordinary, or additional :

"Secretary" means the Secretary to the Government of India in the Legislative Department, and includes every person for the time being exercising the functions of his office : and "Local Governments" include a Chief Commissioner.

II. Meetings of the Council

3. The Council shall ordinarily meet at 11 A. M., and shall not prolong its sitting after 4 P. M., unless the President otherwise direct.

4. The quorum shall be seven, including the President.

5. The Commander-in-chief shall sit on the right of the President, the Governor or Lieutenant-Governor shall sit opposite the President : the Law Member shall sit wherever it may be convenient; and, subject to these provisions the Members shall sit according to seniority, the Junior Member being on the left of the President.

6. The President may adjourn, without any discussion or vote, any meeting or business, whether there be a quorum present or not, to any future day or to any part of the same day.

7. The President shall preserve order, and all points of order shall be decided by him, no discussion thereupon being allowed.

8. A Member desiring to make any observations on any subject before the Council shall address the President without rising from his chair.

9. On all matters brought before the Council, after the Member who makes a motion has spoken, each Member consecutively, beginning with the Member on the left of the President, may make such observations as he thinks proper.

After all the Members in turn have had an opportunity of speaking, the Mover may speak once by way of reply, and any other Member may, with the permission of the President, speak once by way of explanation.

Provided that, if the matter be an amendment of a bill, the Member in charge of the bill shall be entitled to speak next after the Mover of the amendment.

10. When, for the purpose of explanation during discussion, or for and other sufficient reason, any Member has occasion to ask a question of another member on any measure then under the consideration of the Council, he shall ask the question through the President.

11. Any member may speak at the request and on behalf of another Member who is unable to express himself in English.

12. On every motion before the council, the question shall be put by the President, and shall be decided by a majority of votes.

In case of a division, the votes shall be taken by the Secretary in consecutive order, beginning with the Member on the left of the President.

After the question is put no further discussion upon it shall be allowed.

13. Any member may ask for any papers or returns connected with any bill before the Council. The President shall determine, either at the time or at the meeting of the Council next following, whether the papers or returns asked for can be given.

14. Communications on matters connected with any bill before the Council may be addressed, either in the form of a petition to the Governor-General in Council, or in a letter to the Secretary, and must in either case be sent to the Secretary. Ordinarily such communications will not be answered.

Except in the case of the High Court at Fort William, such communications from courts, officials, or public bodies shall ordinary be sent through the Local Government.

15. The Secretary shall either cause such communications to be printed and send a copy to each Member, or circulate them for the perusal of each Member.

III. Introduction and Publication of Bills

16. Any member desiring to move for leave to introduce a bill in accordance with the provisions of section 19 of the Indian Councils Act shall give the Secretary at least three days' previous notice of the title and object of the bill.

If such motion be carried, the bill with a full statement of objects and reasons shall, if not already prepared, be prepared by the Member or (if he so desire) by the Secretary in consultation with the Member.

17. The Secretary shall then cause the bill, together with the statement of objects and reasons, to be printed, and shall send a copy to each Member.

If any of the members are unacquainted with English, he shall also cause the bill and the statement of objects and reasons to be translated into Hindustani for their use.

17A. The Council may, at any time after leave to introduce a bill has been granted, direct that the bill be published in such manner as the Council thinks fit.

18. When a bill is introduced, or on some subsequent occasion, the Member in charge of it shall make one or more of the following motion :—

(a) that it be referred to a Select Committee, or

(b) that it be taken into consideration by the Council either at once, or at some future day to be then mentioned, or

(c) that it be circulated for the purpose of eliciting opinion thereon.

19. No such motion shall be made until after a copy of the bill and a copy of the statement of objects and reasons have been furnished to each Member. Any Member may object to the motion unless such copies have been furnished to him at least seven days previously ; and such objections shall prevail unless the President, in exercise of his power to suspend any of these rules, allows the motion to be made.

20. On the day on which such motion is made or on any subsequent day to which the discussion is postponed, the principle of the Bill and its general provisions may be discussed.

21. When any motion mentioned in Rule 8 is carried, the bill shall, together with a statement of its objects and reasons, be published in English in the *Gazette of India.*

The bill and statement shall also be published in such official gazettes and in such vernacular languages (if any) as the Council in each case decides to be necessary for the purpose of giving notice to the communities affected by the bill.

For this purpose the Council shall make an order at the meeting at which motion is carried, and may, from time to time, on the motion of any Member, vary or cancel such order.

22. The Governor-General, if he see fit, may order the publication of a bill, together with the statement of objects and reasons which accompanies it, in such Gazettes and languages as he thinks necessary, although no motion has been made for leave to introduce the bill.

In that case it shall not be necessary to move for leave to introduce the Bill ; and if the bill be afterwards introduced, it shall not be necessary to publish it again.

IV. Select Committees

23. The Law Member shall be a Member of every Select Committee.

The other Members of every committee shall be named by the Council when the bill is referred, or at any subsequent meeting.

The Law Member, and in his absence the Member in charge of the bill, shall be chairman of the Committee, and, in the case of an equality of votes, the chairman shall have a second or casting vote.

24. After publication of a bill in *Gazette of India* the Select Committee to which the bill may have been referred shall make a report

Such report shall be made not sooner than three months from the date of the first publication in the *Gazette of India*, unless the Council orders the report to be made sooner.

Reports may be either preliminary or final.

The Select Committee shall in their report state whether or not, in their judgment, the bill has been so altered as to require re-publication, whether the publication ordered by these rules or by the Council has taken place and the date on which the publication has taken place, or where publication in more than one Gazette or in more than one language is ordered, the date on which the publication in each such Gazette and each such language has taken place.

If, in the judgment of the Committee, the bill has been so altered as to require re-publication, the Secretary shall send a copy of the altered bill to the Secretary of the Department to which it pertains.

When the Committee recommend the re-publication of a bill which was originally ordered by these rules or by the Council to be published in more than one Gazette or in more than one language, they shall, in the absence of anything to the contrary in their report, be taken to recommend that the bill be re-published in every such Gazette and every such language.

If the Committee are of opinion that it is unnecessary to re-publish the bill in any such Gazette or in any such language, they shall, in their report, state the grounds of the opinion.

25. The Secretary shall cause every report of a Select Committee to be printed, and shall send a copy of such report to each member, and, if the Committee or the President so direct, the Secretary shall cause the report, with the amended bill, to be published in the *Gazette of India*.

If any of the members present are unacquainted with English he shall also cause the report to be translated into Hindustani for their use.

26. The report of the Select Committee on a Bill shall be presented to the Council by the Member in charge of the bill, and shall be taken into consideration by the Council as soon as conveniently may be ; but any Member may object to its being so taken into consideration when he has not been furnished for a week with a copy of the report ; and such objection shall prevail, unless the President, in exercise of his power to suspend any of these Rules, allows the report to be taken into consideration.

V. Consideration and Amendments of bills

27. When a bill is taken into consideration by the Council, any Member may propose an amendment of such bill.

28. If notice of such amendment has not been sent to the Secretary at least three days before the meeting of the Council at which the bill is to be considered, any Member may object to the moving of the amendment, and such objection shall prevail, unless the President, in exercise of his power to suspend any of these rules, allows the amendment to be moved.

The Secretary shall cause every such notice to be printed, and shall send a copy for the information of each Member.

If any of the Members present are unacquainted with English, he shall also cause every such notice to be translated into Hindustani for their use.

29. Amendments shall ordinarily be considered in the order of the clauses to which they respectively relate.

29A. Notwithstanding anything in the foregoing rules, it shall be in the discretion of the President, when a motion that a bill be taken into consideration has been carried, to submit the bill, or any part of the bill, to the Council section by section ; when this procedure is adopted the President shall call each section separately, and, when the amendments relating to it have been dealt with, shall put the question that this section or (as the case may be, this section as amended) shall stand part of the Bill.

30. Any Member may move that a bill which has been amended by the Council or by a Select Committee be re-published or re-commit-

ted, and, if the Council so decide, the President may order the bill to be re-published or re-committed, as the case may be.

31. If no amendments be made, when a bill is taken into consideration by the Council, the bill may at once be passed.

If any amendment be made, any Member may object to the passing of the bill at the same meeting; and such objection shall prevail, unless the President, in exercise of his power to suspend any of these rules, allows the bill to pass.

Where the objection prevails, the bill shall be brought forward again at a future meeting, and may then be passed with or without further amendment.

VI. Passing of bills and publication of Acts

32. When a bill is passed by the Council, a copy thereof shall be signed by the President, and, when the Governor-General has declared his assent thereto, such copy shall be signed by the Governor-General and the bill shall be published as soon as possible in the official Gazettes under the signature of the Secretary, as an Act of the Governor-General in Council.

Such publication shall be made in the *Gazette of India* in English and in the official Gazettes of the Local Governments in English and in the principal Vernacular languages spoken in the territories subject to such Governments respectively :

Provided that, when the Act does not apply to the whole of British India, it shall be published only in the *Gazette of India* and in the Gazettes of the Local Governments to whose territories it applies.

VII. Duties of Secretary

33. At least two days before each meeting of Council, the Secretary shall send to each Member a list of the business to be brought forward at such meeting.

34. The Secretary shall keep a journal, in which all the proceedings of the Council shall be fairly entered.

The journal shall be submitted after each meeting to the President for his confirmation and signature, and, when so signed, shall be the record of the proceedings of the Council.

35. The Secretary shall also prepare a report of the proceedings of the Council at each of its meetings, including an abstract of the observations of the Members, and publish in the *Gazette of India* as soon as possible after the meeting. He shall send a copy of such report to each member and also to the Permanent Under-Secretary of State for India.

36. In addition to the other duties specially required by these rules, it shall be the duty of the Secretary—

1st, to draft all bills originated by the Government of India, the statements of their objects and reasons, and the reports of the Select Committee to which such bills are referred ;

2nd, to take charge of the copies of the bills signed by the Governor-General and of all the other records of the Council ;

3rd, to keep the books of the Council ;

4th, to keep a list of the business for the time being before the Council ;

5th, to superintend the printing of all papers printed in pursuance of these rules ;

6th, to assist the Council and all Committees in such manner as they may direct ;

7th, to send to the Secretary of the Department to which the bill pertains, any bill which an additional Member has obtained leave to introduce under Rule 16 ;

8th, to examine all bills deposited by Additional Members, and report to the President on those which contain clauses touching on subjects coming within section 19 or section 22 of the Indian Councils Act, 1861 ;

9th, to write all letters which the Council, or the President, or any Select Committee, or the Law Member, directs to be written.

37. It shall be the special duty of the Assistant Secretary in the Legislative Department to translate into Hindustani, Bills, Statements of Objects and Reasons, Reports of Select Committees and Amendments of Bills, to explain papers to the Members unacquainted with English, and otherwise to assist them in such manner as they may require.

VIII. Miscellaneous

38. Strangers may be admitted into the Council Chamber during the sittings of the Council on the order of the President.

Application for orders of admission is to be made to the Secretary.

39. The President on the motion of any Member, may direct, at any time during a sitting of the Council, that strangers withdraw.

40. Any paper relating to any measure before the Council may be published by order of the President. Copies of papers so published shall be sold at such rates as may be fixed by the Secretary.

41. Any bill respecting which no motion has been made in the Council for two years may, by order of the President, be removed from the list of business.

42. The President, for sufficient reason, may suspend any of the foregoing rules.

(ii) INSTRUCTIONS TO LOCAL GOVERNMENTS

Legislative Department of Government of India to be addressed

1. (1) Every communication made by a Local Government to the Government of India asking for leave to introduce a bill, or regarding a bill which has been introduced, in the Local Council, or submitting a law for the assent of the Governor-General under section 40 of the Indian Councils Act, 1861, shall be addressed to the Secretary to the Government of India in the Legislative Department.

(2) Nothing in this rule shall be construed to apply to any correspondence or communication regarding a proposal for legislation in a Local Council, unless and until the stage is reached at which leave to introduce a bill is asked for. All correspondence before that stage shall be conducted with the executive department of the Government of India to which the subject belongs.

Draft bills to be ordinarily reported to Secretary of State and Government of India before introduction

2. (1) Save as otherwise provided in these rules, every draft bill, with all necessary papers connected therewith, shall, before introduction, be transmitted with a despatch to the Secretary of State.

(2) In the case of a Madras or Bombay draft bill, the despatch shall be addressed by the Local Government to the Secretary of State direct, a copy thereof and of its enclosures being forwarded for information with a covering letter to the Legislative department of the Government of India.

(3) In the case of a draft bill other than a Madras or Bombay draft, the Local Government shall forward the draft, with all necessary papers connected therewith, to the Legislative department of the

Government of India, and the requisite despatch shall forthwith be addressed by the Government of India to the Secretary of State, a copy thereof being forwarded for information to the Local Government.

[1. Copies of all papers including previous correspondence should be forwarded to the Government of India when reference is made to it under this rule.

2. Where the legislation proposed involves substantial question of principle, leave to introduce a bill should not be asked for under this rule until such questions have been settled in communication with the executive department of the Government of India to which the subject belongs.

3. The usual number of spare copies of the draft bill and the connected papers should accompany the despatch to the Secretary of State and forty spare copies should accompany the letter to the Legislative department of the Government of India.]

Previous sanction when to be applied for in certain cases

3. (1) Where a draft bill contains penal clauses, the previous sanction of the Government of India thereto shall be expressly applied for when the draft is reported to the Legislative department of the Government of India under sub-section (2) or sub-section (3) of rule 2, as the case may be .

(2) Where a draft bill contains provisions which, under section 43 of the Indian Councils Act, 1861, or section 51 of the Indian Councils Act, 1892, require the previous sanction of the Governor-General, such previous sanction shall likewise be expressly applied for when the draft is forwarded to the Legislative department of the Government of India as aforesaid.

Procedure after report of draft bill to Secretary of State and Government of India

4. When a draft bill has been reported to the Secretary of State and the Government of India under rule 2, it shall not be introduced in the Local Council until the receipt of a communication from the Legislative department of the Government of India intimating that the penal or other clauses (if any) requiring previous sanction are sanctioned and that the Secretary of State and the Government of India have no present intention of interfering with the measure :

Provided that, if no such communication and no orders to the contrary are received within two months from the date of the despatch transmitting the draft bill to the Secretary of State and, if such previous sanction (if any) as is referred to in rule 3, sub-section (2), has been obtained, the bill may be introduced and proceeded with on the assumption that the penal clauses (if any) are approved and that there is no present intention, on the part of either the Secretary of State or the Government of India, of objecting to the measure :

Provided, also, that the omission of either the Secretary of State or the Government of India to communicate any remarks regarding a measure dealt with under this and the foregoing rules shall not be taken to imply final approval of the measure, and shall not be regarded as in any way affecting the right of the Governor-General to withhold his assent therefrom under section 40, or that of Her Majesty to signify the disallowance thereof under section 41, of the Indian Councils Act, 1861.

[1. In submitting bills to the Government of India, their attention should be drawn to all clauses which appear to require sanction under this section.

2. Although the Governments of Madras and Bombay address the Secretary of State direct, the replies of the Secretary of State are, "to obviate all chance of concurrent or conflicting action" by arrangement addressed to the Government of India for communication to the Local Government concerned.

3. The previous sanction here referred to is required by Act of Parliament and cannot, therefore, be dispensed with].

5. (1) The following shall be excepted from the operation of rules 2, 3 and 4, namely :—

Exceptions from foregoing rules

(*a*) draft consolidation bills, pure and simple, consolidating acts of the local council concerned ;

(*b*) cases in which the approval of the Secretary of State and the Government of India to the principle of the legislation proposed has already been obtained and a further reference is, in the opinion of the Local Government, unnecessary ;

(*c*) cases in which the legislation proposed is, in the opinion of the Local Government, of a purely formal or unimportant character; and

(*d*) cases in which the legislation proposed cannot, in the opinion of the Local Government, be, without serious evil, delayed in order to admit of a prior report to the Secretary of State and the Government of India.

(2) In every such case as aforesaid, the draft bill may be introduced forthwith :

Provided that, where such a draft bill contains penal clauses, the

Legislative department of the Government of India shall be applied to for sanction thereto, and the bill shall not be introduced until the receipt of such sanction or the expiration of one month from the date of the application therefor without the receipt of any reply from the Legislative department of the Government of India :

Provided, also, that, where such a draft bill contains provisions which, under section 43 of the Indian Councils Act, 1861, or section 5 of the Indian Councils Act, 1892, require the previous sanction of the Governor-General, such previous sanction shall be applied for and obtained from, the Legislative department of the Government of India before the introduction of the bill.

Procedure in exceptional cases

6. (1) Where a draft bill is dealt with under rule 5 and introduced without a prior report to the Secretary of State and the Government of India, a copy of it and of all necessary papers connected therewith shall forthwith be transmitted to the Secretary of State with a full explanatory despatch.

1. The examination, by the Legislative department of the Government of India, of the bills of a Local Council does not ordinarily extend to matters of form and details of drafting. For these the Local Government concerned is held responsible.

2. See second foot-note to rule 4, *ante*.

(2) The instructions contained in sub-sections (2) and (3) of rule 2 shall apply, *mutatis mutandis*, in the case of every despatch issued under sub-section (1) of this rule.

(3) Where a draft bill is dealt with under rule 5, no reply to the explanatory despatch referred to in sub-section (1) of this rule need be awaited before the bill is further proceeded with.

Amendments in Council

7. (1) Where, after a bill has been introduced in a Local Council whether as an exceptional measure dealt with under rule 5 or otherwise, an amendment is proposed in it which the Local Government is prepared to accept, but which, owing to its being outside the principle of the bill as introduced or for any other reason, it considers that it cannot accept without a reference to the Government of India, the requisite steps should be taken to delay the progress of the bill through Council pending the result of a reference to the Legislative department of the Government of India.

(2) Where a reference is made to the Legislative department of the Government of India under this rule, the amendment so referred

should not be accepted until the receipt of a favourable reply, or until the expiration of one month from the date of the reference without the receipt of any such reply.

(3) Where a reference is made under this rule, and the Government of India consider that the amendment so referred is one which ought not to be accepted without a further reference to the Secretary of State an intimation to that effect will be sent to the Local Government by the Legislative department of the Government of India. The Secretary of State shall then be addressed by the Government of India, and the amendment shall not be accepted until intimation of the arrival of a favourable reply from the Secretary of State is received by the Local Government from the Legislative department of the Government of India, or until the expiration of two months from the date of the reference made by the Local Government without the receipt of any further communication on the subject from the Legislative department of the Government of India.

(4) Where in the course of a bill through Council an amendment is proposed which requires any such previous sanction as is referred to in rule 3, such previous sanction shall be applied for to, and obtained from, the Legislative department of the Government of India before the bill so amended is passed.

Marginal references to clauses

8. In every draft bill a reference shall be added on the margin of each clause to show whether it is based on any, and, if so, on what, provision of the existing law. Such marginal references may be retained during the progress of the bill through the local council, but shall be removed from the copy submitted, in the event of the passing of the measure, for the assent of the Governor or Lieutenant-Governor, as the case may be, and also from that submitted to the Legislative department of the Government of India for the assent of the Governor-General.

(iii) RULES OF LEGISLATIVE BUSINESS IN THE PROVINCIAL COUNCILS

The following are the rules for the conduct of Legislative business of the Madras Legislative Council :—

I. Definitions

1. In these rules—

"Council" means the Council of the Governor of Fort Saint George for the purpose of making laws and regulations.

" Meeting " means a meeting of the Council.

"President" means the Governor of Fort Saint George or, in his absence, the senior Civil Ordinary Member of Council present.

"Member" means an Ordinary or Additional Member of the Council.

"Secretary" means the Secretary or the Under or Assistant Secretary to the Government of Madras in the Legislative Department.

"Bill" means a proposed enactment in any stage before it has received the assent of the Governor.

In the computation of "clear days", Sundays and holidays are not excluded.

II. Summoning and adjournment of Council

2. The times and places of meetings shall be fixed by the Governor, and the Secretary shall notify the same in the *Fort Saint George Gazette* and to each Member by letter.

3. When the business before a meeting is concluded, the President shall declare the meeting dissolved. The President may adjourn without any discussion or vote, any meeting or business, to any future day or to any part of the same day. The Council also may, upon motion made and carried, adjourn any meeting or business.

4. A motion that any meeting or business be adjourned or that the Council pass to the business next in order in the statement of business, may be moved at any time and without previous notice as a distinct question, but not so as to interrupt a speech. If the motion is carried, the Council shall adjourn the meeting or business, or the further consideration of the business then under discussion shall be dropped, as the case may be.

5. A motion of the kind referred to in the last preceding rule shall take precedence of any other motion then before the Council and, if such motion is rejected, no similar motion shall be made until after the lapse of what the President shall deem to be a reasonable time nor by the Member by whom the previous motion was made.

6. If, at the time appointed for holding a meeting or adjourned meeting as aforesaid, or if at any time after the commencement of business at such meeting, the quorum required by section 48 of the Indian Councils Act, 1861 (that is to say, the Governor or some Ordinary Member of Council and four or more Members of Council), is not present, the Members present shall, without proceeding to business of any kind, adjourn until again summoned by the Governor, and the fact shall be noted by the Secretary in the Journal of the Council.

III. Course of Business

7. At least three clear days before the date fixed for a meeting the Secretary shall send to the Madras address of every Member a printed statement of the business to be transacted at such meeting.

8. No business which is not entered in the printed statement of business prepared under Rule 7, shall be transacted at any meeting unless the permission of the Governor has been obtained previously to the meeting.

9. The President shall have power to regulate the order in which business is transacted, but, ordinarily, the succession of business shall be as described in Rule 10.

10. After the President has taken the chair—

(1) the Secretary shall report the names of the Members (if any) who have taken their seats for the first time ;

(2) the discussion of the annual Financial Statement and the asking of questions under section 2 of the Indian Councils Act, 1892 shall then take place ;

(3) the President shall report to the Council the Acts which have received the assent of the Governor-General under section 40 of the Indian Councils Act, 1861, or which have been disallowed by the Governor-General or by Her Majesty, since the last meeting;

(4) the Secretary shall report to the Council the Acts which have received the assent of the Governor under section 39 of the Indian Councils Act, 1861, and the Bills which have been disallowed by the Governor since the last meeting ;

(5) the Secretary shall report to the Council the petitions and other communications relating to the business of the Council which have been received by him since the last meeting and shall, if necessary, read such petitions and communications to the Council ;

(6) members desirous of obtaining leave to introduce Bills shall move that such leave be granted ;

(7) the Council shall then proceed to dispose of the business left unfinished at the last meeting, if any ; and, this being done,

(8) the Council shall proceed to deal with the remaining business for the day.

IV. Regulation of Discussions

11. The President shall preserve order and shall decide all points of orders submitted for his decision by the Members and all questions

connected with the interpretation of these rules. There shall be no discussion on any point of order and the President's decision shall be final.

12. Any Member may draw the attention of the President to a violation of order and, while he is doing so, all other Members shall remain silent.

13. In discussing questions coming before the Council for consideration, a Member shall speak from his place, shall rise when he speaks, and address the President. The President also shall rise when he addresses the Council.

At any time, if the President rises, any Member speaking shall immediately resume his seat.

14. Members may read their speeches and may also read, as part thereof, passages from books or papers bearing upon the question under discussion.

15. No Member shall speak except upon business which is at the time regularly before the Council or, by special permission of the President, in explanation of what he said in a previous debate.

16. Except in discussing amendments, when the Council is settling the several clauses of a Bill, no Member other than the Mover shall speak more than once upon a question ; but the Mover shall, if he has spoken to the question when making his motion, be allowed a reply.

Provided that, if the matter before the Council be an amendment of a bill, the Member in charge of the bill shall be entitled to speak next after the Mover and Seconder of the amendment.

17. A Member who has spoken upon a motion may speak again upon any amendment of that motion. A Member may also speak again in order to explain what he has previously said, if it has been misunderstood.

18. When, for the purpose of explanation or for any other reason, a Member has occasion to ask of another Member a question relative to the business before the Council, he shall ask the question through the President.

19. Every matter which comes before the Council for decision shall be decided in accordance with the majority of votes after (1) motion has been made and seconded and (2) the question has been put by the President.

20. No discussion whatsoever shall take place after the question has been put by the President.

21. The votes of the Members may be taken by voices or by division or by name but they shall be taken by division or by name if Member so desires. The method of taking votes by division or by name shall be in accordance with the instructions of the President.

22. Any Member may ask for any papers, returns or information connected with the business before the Council and the President shall determine whether such papers, returns or information can be furnished.

V. *Motions generally*

23. Members who wish to make any motion at any meeting must give notice of their intention at the next preceding meeting or must send such notice in writing to the Secretary at least six clear days before the day fixed for the meeting at which they intend to make the motion : Provided that the President may, at his discretion, permit a motion to be made of which such notice has not been given.

24. All motions of which notice is given under the preceding rule shall be entered in the statement of business prepared by the Secretary under Rule 7.

25. No motion shall be taken into consideration by the Council unless it is seconded.

26. A motion of which due notice has been given may, in the absence and at the request of the Member by whom notice was given, be made by any other Member ; but if not so made, or if a Member announces his intention of withdrawing a motion standing in his name, the motion may be made by any other Member and, if not so made, shall not be put unless the Council otherwise orders.

27. If amendments of any motion are moved, the President, when taking the sense of the Council thereon, shall recite the terms of the original motion and of the amendments proposed and it shall be in his discretion to put first to the vote either the original motion or any of the proposed amendments thereon.

28. A purely verbal amendment of a motion may be moved at any time during the discussion upon the motion and without previous notice, but no amendment which is substantially the negative of a motion shall be taken into consideration by the Council.

29. A motion shall not be taken into consideration by the Council if it substantially raises a question already disposed of at the meeting or is inconsistent with any resolution already passed thereat.

30. If any motion, as made, involves several points, the

President may, at his discretion, divide it, so that each point may be determined separately.

VI. Introduction of Bills

31. Any Member may move at a meeting of the Council for leave to introduce a bill in accordance with section 38 of the Indian Councils Act, 1861 ; provided that at least six clear days' previous notice of the title and subject of the bill has been given to the Secretary.

32. If the motion for leave to introduce a bill be carried, the Mover shall send the Bill, together with a full statement of the objects of and reasons for the proposed measure and any connected papers, to the Secretary, who will forthwith cause the bill, the statement of objects and reasons and the connected papers to be printed and communicated to each of the Members, and will also cause the bill and the statement of objects and reasons to be published in the *Fort Saint George Gazette* in English and in such Vernacular languages as the Governor may direct.

33. The Governor may, at his discretion, direct the Secretary to publish any bill, together with a statement of the objects of and reasons for it, in the *Fort Saint George Gazette* in English and in such Vernacular languages as he thinks necessary, although leave to introduce the Bill has not been applied for under Rule 31 ; and the Secretary shall publish it accordingly and shall send a copy of the bill and of the statement of objects and reasons to each of the Members. When a Bill has been published under this rule, it shall not be necessary to move under Rule 31 for leave to introduce it.

34. At any time after leave to introduce a Bill has been granted under Rule 32 or after publication has been ordered under Rule 33, the Member in charge of the Bill may introduce it after giving six clear days' notice to the Secretary ; provided that no Bill shall be introduced until fifteen clear days from the date of its publication under Rule 32 or Rule 33, as the case may be.

When introducing a Bill, the Member in charge of it shall move that the Bill be read in Council. The principle of the Bill and its general provisions may then be discussed, and, if the motion be carried, the Secretary shall read the title of the Bill. The Council shall then consider the question of referring the Bill to a Select Committee and, if the question be decided in the affirmative, the Council shall appoint the Committee and may further direct that its report shall be submitted within a specified period.

35. At any time during the progress of a Bill the Member in charge of it may move, for permission to withdraw it, and, if such permission is granted, the Bill shall be withdrawn accordingly. The Member in charge of a Bill which has been published under Rule 33, but which has not been introduced and read in Council, may withdraw the same without further formality than a mere announcement of the withdrawal to the Council.

VII. Select Committees

36. Select Committees may be appointed by the Council for any purpose connected with the business of the Council and may sit and submit their reports although the Council is adjourned.

37. When a Bill has been referred to a Select Committee for consideration, it shall be the duty of the Committee to discuss each clause of the Bill and to recommend to the Council such amendments as seem to it to be advisable.

38. If the Council has fixed a period within which the Select Committee shall submit its report upon a Bill and the Committee is unable for any reason to submit its report within that period, the Governor may from time to time extend the period on the application of the Member in charge of the Bill.

39. The report of the Select Committee shall be signed by all the Members of the Committee or by a majority of them; but any Member of a Select Committee may record his views in a separate minute.

40. The report of the Select Committee appointed to consider a Bill shall contain particulars of the principal amendments proposed and of the reasons for such amendments, or it may contain a recommendation that the Bill under consideration be abandoned.

41. The report of the Select Committee, any minutes that may have been recorded by individual Members of the Committee and (if the Bill has been amended) the Bill as amended by the Committee shall be printed and copies furnished to each Member of the Council. The report and minutes (if any) and (if the bill has been amended) such portion thereof as may have been amended, shall also, unless otherwise directed by the Select Committee, be published in the *Fort Saint George Gazette* in the languages in which the original Bill was published.

42. No business shall be transacted at any sitting of the Select Committee unless a majority of Members of the Committee is present.

43. The Member in charge of a Bill shall invariably be a Member and, also, the Chairman of the Select Committee appointed to consider that Bill and shall have power to report to the Governor the name of any Member of the Select Committee who neglects or is unable to attend its sittings and the Governor may thereupon appoint, out of the Members of the Council, an additional member to the Select Committee.

44. A Select Committee may, for the purpose of obtaining information, invite any person to be present at its sittings.

45. While a Select Committee is sitting to consider a Bill, all communications relating to Bills which are received by the Secretary shall be referred to it.

VIII. Passing of Bills

46. When a Bill has been introduced and read in Council under rule 34 and the Council has decided that it is not necessary to refer it for consideration to a Select Committee, the Council shall not proceed to take the Bill into consideration until the expiration of fifteen clear days from the date on which the Bill was read under rule 34.

In this case it shall not be necessary to make, on the day on which the Bill comes on for consideration, a formal motion that the Bill be taken into consideration.

47. When a Bill has been referred to a Select Committee under rule 34. it shall not be taken into consideration by the Council unless copies of the report of the Select Committee and (if the Bill has been amended) of the Bill as amended shall have been sent to the Madras address of each of the Members of the Council at least fifteen clear days beforehand and, in cases in which the Select Committee has not dispensed with the publication referred to in rule 41, until the expiration of twenty-one clear days from the date of such publication. Subject to these conditions, the Member in charge of a Bill, when presenting the report of the Select Committee to the Council, may move either that the Bill and report be taken into consideration at once or that the consideration of them be postponed to a subsequent meeting.

The discussion upon a motion under this rule that a Bill be taken into consideration shall not extend to the principle of the Bill.

48. Any Member wishing to propose an amendment affecting the

substance of a Bill shall send a copy of the proposed amendment to the Secretary in accordance with Rule 28 and the Secretary shall enter the same in the printed Statement of Business preparep under Rule 7; but it shall not be necessary to give previous notice of amendments of a purely verbal character or of amendments consequential upon, or moved in respect of, amendments which have been carried.

49. Proposed amendments of Bills shall not be moved until the Bill is actually taken into consideration and, when moved, they shall be considered in the order of the sections to which they relate.

Proposed amendments of Bills shall be governed by Rules 25, 26, 27, 29 and 30 relating to motions.

50. The President may declare that a proposed amendment of a Bill shall be discussed or put to the vote on the ground that it is irrelevant or incomplete or that an amendment identical in substance with it has been previously disposed of by the Council in considering the same Bill.

51. If no amendments, other than purely verbal amendments and (if the Bill has been referred to a Select Committee) the amendments proposed by the Select Committee, be made in a Bill by the Council on the day upon which it is taken into consideration, the Bill may, upon motion made, be passed at once. If, however, amendments other than purely verbal amendments or, amendments proposed by the Select Committee are made, any Member may object to the passing of the Bill at the same meeting ; and such objection shall prevail unless the Council, upon motion made, otherwise orders.

52. If the objection referred to in the last preceding rule prevails, the motion that the Bill be passed shall be taken into consideration again at a subsequent meeting and the Bill may then be passed either with or without further amendment; provided that, at this stage, no amendment may be moved without the permission of the President.

IX. Final Stages of Bills

53. When a Bill has been passed by the Council, the Secretary shall revise and complete the marginal abstracts and the numbering of the sections thereof and shall submit it immediately to the Governor for a declaration under section 39 of the Indian Councils Act, 1861, that he assents to, or withholds his assent from, the same.

54. The assent or dissent of the Governor shall be enfaced upon

the bill and the fact communicated to the Council at its next meeting by the Secretary.

55. When an Act has received the assent of the Governor-General under section 40 of the Indian Councils Act, 1861, it shall be published in the *Fort Saint George Gazette*, in English and the Vernacular languages of the parts of the Presidency affected by its provisions, as an Act of the Governor in Council assented to by the Governor-General and having the force of law. Such publication shall be deemed to be the publication referred to in section 40 of the Indian Councils Act, 1861.

56. The assent or dissent of the Governor-General or the dissent of Her Majesty to an Act shall be announced by the Governor to the Council as soon as conveniently may be and such assent or dissent shall be recorded in the journal of the Council.

57. No Member shall make any motion upon, or otherwise bring under the consideration of the Council, the exercise by Her Majesty, the Governor-General or the Governor of the prerogative of withholding assent to an Act or Bill.

X. *Rules relating to Petitions*

58. Petitions to the Council must—

(1) relate to some matter actually under the consideration of the Council ;

(2) be addressed to the "Governor, in Council";

(3) be dated and signed by the petitioner or petitioners ;

(4) be in respectful and temperate language; and

(5) conclude with a distinct prayer.

59. If a petition is not in conformity with the preceding rule, or if the Secretary sees reason to doubt the authenticity of any signature appended thereto, he shall certify the same on the back of the petition and report the fact to the Council. The Council may, thereupon reject the petition, which shall then be returned to the petitioner or petitioners with a statement of the reason for such rejection.

60. If the petition is in conformity with Rule 58, the Secretary shall, if necessary, make an abstract of it and bring the petition under consideration by reading it, or the abstract, before the Council, which shall deal with the petition in such manner as it may deem proper.

XI. Admittance of Strangers

61. Persons desirous of admission into the Council Chamber during the sittings of Council shall make application to the Secretary who will take the orders of the President thereon.

62. The President may at any time during a sitting of the Council direct that all strangers withdraw.

63. If a Bill which peculiarly affects private interests be under the consideration of the Council or of a Select Committee thereof and if any person whose interests are so affected apply to the Council or Select Committee for permission to be heard, either personally or by Counsel, on the subject of the Bill, the Council of Select Committee may, upon the motion of any Member direct that the petitioner or his Counsel be heard at the meeting at which the motion is made or at and on some future specified time and day; and if the petitioner or his Counsel is not present at the said meeting or does not appear at and on the said time and day, as the case may be, the permission granted by the Council or Select Committee shall be held to have lapsed.

64. Except as provided in Rules 44 and 63, no stranger shall be permitted to address the Council or any Select Committee.

65. Any Member may move that the hearing of any person who has been permitted under Rule 63 to address the Council or a Select Committee shall cease if such person is irrelevant or unduly prolix, or for any other sufficient reason.

XII. Duties of the Secretary

66. The Secretary shall be bound to perform the following duties in addition to those specified in the preceding rules:—

(1) to take charge of the records of the Council;

(2) to keep the prescribed books;

(3) to attend all meetings and to take minutes of the proceedings;

(4) to superintend the printing of all papers ordered to be printed;

(5) to note in bills the amendments ordered by the Council and to scrutinize all Bills and Acts in view to preventing typographical errors;

(6) to prepare and revise the marginal abstract of Bills and Acts and the headings and arrangement of the chapters and the numbering of the sections thereof;

(7) to attend the sitting of Select Committees and to draw up the reports of Select Committees when required so to do;

(8) to carry on correspondence under the orders of the Council ;

(9) to help, when required to do so, in the framing of Bills;

(10) to generally assist the Council.

XIII. Books and Records

67. A journal shall be kept containing a brief abstract of the proceedings of the Council. This journal shall be submitted as soon as possible after each meeting to the President for his confirmation and signature.

68. Besides preparing the above journal the Secretary shall publish in the *Fort Saint George Gazette* in English, as soon as may be after the conclusion of each meeting, an account, which should be as full as possible, of the proceedings of the Council.

69. A register and index of letters and petitions addressed to, or despatched under orders of, the Council shall be maintained.

XIV. General

70. The Council may, on a motion and at any time, suspend the operation of any of the foregoing rules.

71. Any Bill respecting which no motion has been made in the Council for the space of two years may, by order of the President, be removed from the list of business and the fact of such removal shall be announced by the President to the Council.

72. A Member in charge of a Bill may entrust it to any other Member and the Member to whom it is so entrusted shall be the Member in charge of the Bill for the purposes of these rules.

73. Any Member may apply to the Secretary for any papers, returns of information connected with the business before the Council and the Governor shall determine whether such papers, return or information can be furnished.

[Similar rules have been framed for the other Provincial Legislative Councils, and they follow the main lines which have been laid down for the Imperial Legislative Council, subject to the statutory limitations imposed by the Indian Councils Acts. The stages in the process of Law-making and the methods of enactment in the Indian Councils are not exactly the same as that which obtains in the British Parliament, but the principles are the same. An interesting comparison was made between the two in this respect in a speech delivered by Sir John Muir-Mackenzie in

June 1910 on a motion for the revision of the Rules of Business of the Bombay Legislative Council on the expansion of that Council under the Indian Councils Act, 1909 :—

"The existing rules for the conduct of the business of this Council were last amended in 1896. The passing of the Indian Councils Act 1909, has necessitated some minor alterations in the rules, and Government think that this opportunity should be taken also to remedy certain defects which have been found to exist in those of the rules, which refer to the conduct of legislation. The present rules on this subject are obscure and unsatisfactory in many ways, especially in respect of the character of amendments and the stages at which they may be moved. This uncertainty is a constant source of trouble and the rules ought to be completely recast. The following is a succinct account of the procedure in respect of Bills in the House of Commons :—

1 Leave to intoduce :—Now obsolete, save in the case of important Government measures. 2 First reading:—Now mere matter of form—No amendment or debate. 3 Second Reading:—Debate on principles of Bill—Discussion of details and amendments of clauses not allowed—The passing of a second reading settles the principles of a Bill. 4 Reference to Committee of the whole (House) or one of the recently created Standing Committees, which is a substitute for the Committee of the whole. At this stage the Bill is considered in detail, clause by clause, amendments of clause are made, and new clause may be added. 5 Report stage :—Bills reported from the Committee of the whole with amendments, or from a Standing Committee with or without amendment, come before the House for review of the work done in Committee—A Bill is not considered clause by clause, but amendments may be made and clauses added. 6 Third Reading :—Verbal amendments only permitted—It will be apparent that our procedure is very different from that of the House of Commons. Against six or possibly seven stages, we have five :— (1) Introduction.— In most cases effected by publication. (2) First Reading.—Not a formality as in the House of Commons. (3) Reference to Select Committee. (4) Second Reading. (5) Third Reading—Our rules seem to have been framed on the supposition that our stages correspond to those in the House of Commons of the same value. Thus our Second Reading settles the principles of a Bill, because that is done by a Second Reading in the House of Commons. This is of course a complete mistake. Our First Reading corresponds with the Second Reading of the House of Commons, our Second Reading with the Report stage and the Third Readings alone are the same. Hence the First Reading should decide the principles of the Bill, upon which no debate should afterwards be permitted. At the Second Reading amendments

must be limited to alterations of clauses which do not affect the principles of a Bill; and at the Third Reading verbal amendments only should be allowed as at present. We propose then that the existing rules dealing with legislation should be revised on these lines ".]

(iv) EXTRACTS FROM LEGISLATIVE STANDING ORDERS

A.—PROCEDURE WITH REGARD TO BILLS BEFORE THEIR INTRODUCTION INTO THE VICEROY'S COUNCIL

I.—No. 9, Dated, India Office, London, the 31st March 1874.

From—Her Majesty's Secretary of State for India.

To—His Excellency the Right Honorable the Viceroy and Governor-General of India in Council.

My attention has been drawn to the great number and importance of the measures recently passed by the Council of the Governor-General for making Laws and Regulations, which have been brought for the first time to the official knowledge of the Secretary of State for India through enactments sent hither for Her Majesty's approval or disallowance, under section 21 of the Indian Councils Act. The Government of India appears to have taken upon itself the entire responsibility for nearly the whole of these measures throughout their course. The policy embodied in them was no doubt maturely considered in the first instance by the Governor-General in his executive capacity and in Executive Council when this policy was determined upon. Bills to give effect to it were drafted in your Legislative Department, and were subsequently introduced into the Legislative Council by the Law Member or by some other Member of Council, or by some gentleman who acted as the organ of the Government. In their passage through the legislature they appear to have remained in charge of some representative of the Governor-General in Council up to the time of their final enactment. There is no question that, if measures of equally great moment to the fortunes and interests of the Indian Empire had been adopted by the Governor-General, not in the Council for making Laws and Regulations, but in Executive Council, they would have been reported to me in full detail at a much earlier stage and I see no sufficient reason why the circumstance, often quite accidental, that Your Excellency's orders take a legislative form should deprive me of all official information concerning them until a period at which it becomes peculiarly difficult to deal with them. Among many inconveniences which attend the present course of proceeding, it may be pointed out that, if the Secretary of State advises Her Majesty to disallow an enactment under section 21 of the Indian Councils Act, he may be annulling, on the score of a single objectionable provision, the results of much conscientious labour on the part of the Legislature, and of much technical skill bestowed by the Legislative Department; and, further, that unless a measure is reserved under section 20 of the above Act for Her Majesty's pleasure (a course which appears to be very rarely followed) its disallowance may cause great difficulty and confusion by rendering useless course of administrative actions which have been entered upon on the footing of the law. It adds to the force of these observations that of late there has been a considerable increase in the number of petitions and representations addressed to the Secretary of State by natives of India and others on the subject of intended legislative measures, concerning which his information is at least imperfect.

2. The present practice appears to be a departure from older precedents. I observe that as recently as 1868, despatches were addressed by the then Government of India to Sir Stafford Northcote (Home Department, Legislative, 30th June 1868; Home Department, Public, 6th November 1868, in which full information was given to him respecting important legislation which was at that time contemplated, and in which his opinion on its policy was invited. I consider that a return to this method of proceeding would be attended with advantage, and I request therefore that Your Excellency in Council will observe in future the following rules with reference to all intended legislative measures which are at the same time of importance and are not urgent.

3. Whenever the Governor-General in (Executive) Council has affirmed the policy and expediency of a particular measure, and has decided on submitting it to the Council for making Laws and Regulations, I desire that a despatch may be addressed to me stating at length the reasons which are thought to justify the step intended to be taken, and the mode in which the intention is to be carried out. This despatch must be accompanied by a copy of the Bill drafted in your Legislative Department, or should be followed by such copy with as brief delay as possible. I do not propose to reply at once in all cases to this communication, but I request that Your Excellency will mention in it the date at which it is intended that the Bill referred to shall be submitted to the Legislative Council, and that this date may be so fixed as to afford me sufficient time to address to you on the contemplated measure such observations as I may deem proper, if I should desire to observe upon it.

4. I have excepted from the above directions measures of slight importance (of which I am aware that a considerable number pass the Legislative Council annually), and measures urgently requiring speedy

enactment. I leave Your Excellency to judge of the degree of importance which will bring a given case within the rule I have laid down, and of the degree of urgency which will withdraw another case from it. In the event, however, of your omitting to give me previous information of an intended enactment on the ground that it is urgently required, I request you to communicate to me subsequently the grounds of the opinion on which you have acted.

5. It is, of course, conceivable that a Bill of which I have approved, or which has been modified in conformity with my desire, may be materially changed during its passage through the Legislative Council. It appears to me that, as a fact, that body early alters Government measures on points of principle ; but if the case to which I am referring should happen, I do not apprehend that your Excellency would have any practical difficulty in delaying the progress of the bill until I have a fresh opportunity of expressing my opinion.

6. In making these observations I have not failed to bear in mind the correspondence which took place in 1870 between my predecessor and the Government of Lord Mayo respecting the powers of the Council for making laws and regulations, but it does not appear to one that the questions discussed in that correspondence are raised by the rules which I have requested your Excellency to observe.

7. It is my intention to send a copy of this despatch (omitting the last two paragraphs) to the Governors in Council of Madras and Bombay for their guidance in matters of legislation, and I request you to transmit a copy (with the like omission) to the Lieutenant Governor of Bengal, to whose legislative measures I wish my directions *mutatis mutandis*, to apply.

II.—No. 45, Dated Fort William, the 28th July 1874.

From—The Government of India in the Home Department.

To—Her Majesty's Secretary of State for India.

We have the honour to acknowledge the receipt of your Lordship's despatch Legislative) No. 9 of the 31st March 1874.

2. In that despatch the following rules are prescribed for the guidance of the Government of India, the Governments of Madras and Bombay, and the Lieutenant-Governor of Bengal in matters of legislation :—

(1) Whenever the Government, in its executive capacity, has decided to submit a measure of importance, which is not urgent, to the Council for making laws and regulations, a despatch is to be addressed to the Secretary of State, stating at length the reasons for the measure and the manner in which its objects are to be carried out. The despatch

is to be accompanied, or followed soon after, by a draft of the bill proposed to be introduced.

(2) When this course is not followed, because a measure of importance is urgently required, the grounds of the opinion on which the Government has acted are to be subsequently communicated.

3. In communicating the motive for these rules and instruction, the despatch alludes to the great number and importance of the measures recently passed by the Council of the Governor-General for making laws and regulations which have been brought for the first time to the official knowledge of the Secretary of State through enactments sent home under section 21 of the Indian Councils Act. And your Lordship observes that our present practice in regard to communications with the Secretary of State upon important legislative measures appears to have departed from older precedents. It is added that there has been a considerable increase in the number of petitions and representations addressed to the Secretary of State by Natives of India and others on the subject of intended legislative measure, concerning which his information was at best imperfect.

4. We have no record of the petitions and representations on the subject of intended legislative measures to which your Lordship refers, and we know only one instance of a representation recently made to your Lordship regarding measures under our consideration. In fact, during the last two years, few measures of importance have been introduced into the Legislative Council of the Governor-General ; and official consultations have passed between the Secretary of State and the Government of India in respect to several measures, either introduced or under consideration, during that period. We are not aware that there has been any deviation from former practice in this respect, and we can certainly affirm that none has been intended.

5. Your Lordship's despatch explains that the degree of importance which will necessitate reference of a measure to the Secretary of State before its introduction to one Legislative Council is left to be determined by our judgment. We see no difficulty in giving effect to your Lordship's wishes as thus understood. We assume that they do not contemplate the examination and criticism of the drafts of bills on points of form or detail, and that only their general object and scope would form the subject of correspondence. We believe that we could place before your Lordship sufficient reasons to show that any further discussion of bills previous to their introduction would be likely to cause serious inconvenience. But from the tenor of your Lordship's despatch we do not infer that any argument upon this point is required from us.

6. We observe, however, that your Lordship sees no sufficient reason why the circumstance that our orders take a legislative form should deprive the Secretary of State of all official information concerning them, until a period at which it becomes peculiarly difficult to deal with them. There is, of course, a distinction which has been observed from the earliest constitution of our Indian Governments, between measures that are put in force by the executive and those that are committed to legislation. It may be true that this distinction makes no difference in the expediency of taking the opinion of the Secretary of State in Council upon any important legislative measure before its policy has been affirmed by the Executive Government. On the other hand when that policy has been settled and announced, and when the measure founded upon it is under consideration by the Council of the Governor-General, which, when assembled for the purpose of making laws, includes additional members, and deliberates in public, we apprehend that the question of subsequent reference to the Secretary of State then takes a different aspect.

7. If any important alteration on a point of principle in a bill of which the Secretary of State has approved, or which has been modified in conformity with his desire, should be made during its passage through the Legislative Council your Lordship apprehends that there will be no practical difficulty in delaying the progress of the bill until the Secretary of State has had a sufficient opportunity of expressing a further opinion.

8. Alterations of great importance, proposed or made during the passage of a bill through the Legislative Council, would be considered by the Government in its executive capacity. Such alterations may be equivalent to measures which, if they had been affirmed before the introduction of a bill, it would have been proper in our judgment to communicate to the Secretary of State. In that case and in the absence of any practical difficulty as to delaying the progress of the bill, we should refer these alterations to the Secretary of State, we do not gather that your Lordship requests us to frame any rule for the purpose of regulating the manner in which rare cases of this kind should be dealt with in the Legislative Council. In order, however, to guard against risk of misapprehension upon a matter which might materially affect the position of the Legislative Council, we desire to add the expression of our opinion that such a rule would be open to objections which we have not considered necessary on the present occasion to discuss ; while the application of your Lordship's directions to any wider class of cases than that to which we have alluded would be likely to give rise to difficulties. We shall be prepared to state our reasons at length if your Lordship should entertain any doubt upon this part of the subject.

9. We foresee considerable impediments to the application of the rules prescribed by your Lordship's despatch to the legislative business of the presidencies of Madras and Bombay and of the Lieutenant-Governorship of Bengal.

10. By the Indian Councils Act, 1861, the Governor-General has certain defined powers with regard to the legislation of the two presidencies and the Lieutenant-Governorship. Under the 43rd section, no bill which affects certain subjects specified in the section (in fact, no bill of real importance) can be taken into consideration except with the Governor-General's previous sanction; and under the 40th section, Acts when passed are to be transmitted to him, and upon his assent they become valid, subject to subsequent disallowance by the Crown.

11. While the law remains as it is, we cannot avoid the conclusion that these rules will invest the Home Government and the Government of India with a concurrent authority that might be exercised simultaneously in different directions upon these matters. The Governor-General will not be relieved from the responsibility which devolves upon him by law of giving or withholding his sanction to the introduction of certain classes of bills, or from giving or withholding his assent to all Acts. On the other hand, the rules now under discussion have been framed with the object of enabling the Secretary of State to express an opinion upon the propriety of introducing certain bills into the Local Councils and upon important alterations made during their progress. It is obvious that, if the opinion expressed by the Secretary of State to the Local Government should in any case differ from that of the Governor-General, the position of the Governor-General would be embarrassing. We consider that such concurrent, and possibly conflicting, action might complicate proceedings, and that the application of the rules to the business of the Local Councils would eventually be found to require an alteration to be made in the law.

12. We have also to observe that, by the Legislative Despatch No. 35 of December 1st, 1862 all bills which contain penal clauses are ordered to be submitted for the previous sanction of the Government of India to those clauses before being introduced into the local legislatures. For reasons similar to those which have been given above in respect to the Governor-General's previous sanction required by statute, we should exercise the executive power henceforward with much hesitation if the Local Governments were simultaneously consulting the Secretary of State, upon the Bill containing the penal clauses. But we think that the free exercise of this power is very useful in controlling the unnecessary multiplication of petty penal enactments and in preserving a general equality of punishments prescribed in different

provinces for similar classes of offences. It has been often used with advantage, and we recommend that it be continued in our hands.

13. Moreover, it is in our judgment inexpedient, upon general grounds, to place restrictions upon the direct power to control and guide the proceedings of the local Legislatures, which the present law and practice entrust to the Governor-General, or to the Government of India. We are opposed for many reasons to anything which would bring about such a change. Bills introduced into and Acts passed by, the local legislatures require careful consideration as to their bearing towards the laws that have been passed by the Legislative Council of India ; they often impose Local and Municipal taxes which are intimately connected with imperial taxation and imperial finance, for which we are primarily responsible ; and they frequently deal with matters of considerable importance to the supreme Executive Government. For these considerations it appears to us that the Governor-General and the Government of India should be left to discharge the duties which have been imposed upon them by the Indian Councils Act and by existing administrative regulations. And we therefore trust that your Lordship will agree with us that the rules respecting the communication of bills to the Secretary of State cannot be applied without embarrassment to the legislative measures of the Local Governments.

14. In conclusion, we enclose a list of the business now before the council of the Governor-General for the purpose of making laws and regulations, together with a minute written by the Hon'ble Mr. Hobhouse, which will afford a full explanation of the several measures included in the list.

III.—No. 33 (Legislative), Dated India Office, London, the 15th October 1874.

From—Her Majesty's Secretary of State for India.

To—The Government of India.

I have received and considered in Council Your Excellency's despatch Home Department, Public, of July 28th, No. 45 of 1874.

2. In my despatch of 31st March 1874, to which you reply, I requested Your Execllency to furnish me (save in cases of urgency) with full and timely information concerning the policy of all important measures which, it was your intention to submit to your council for making laws and regulations. Your Excellency now intimates that you see no difficulty in complying with this request, and you further state that, where alterations of great importance have been made in a bill during its passage through the Legislative Council, you will, in the absence of any practical difficulty as to delaying the progress of the

measure, communicate such alterations to the Secretary of State. But in regard to this last point you do not think it expedient that there should be any fixed rule for the purpose of regulating the manner in which cases of the kind should be dealt with in the Legislative Council. You have rightly gathered from my language that I do not consider such a rule necessary or desirable.

3. Your Excellency, however, foresees considerable impediments to the application of the rules prescribed in my despatch to the legislative business of the presidencies of Madras and Bombay, and of the Lieutenant-Governorship of Bengal. You observe that, by the 43rd section of the Indian Councils Act, 1861 no bill which affects certain subjects specified in the section can be taken into consideration without the previous sanction of the Governor-General, whose assent to an enactment of a Local legislature is also rendered necessary by the 40th section of the same statute. You apprehend that the control over local legislation thus reserved by law to the Governor-General may be interfered with or weakened if the Local Governments are instructed to supply the Secretary of State with the same information respecting their bills which I have requested you to furnish concerning legislative measures which Your Excellency's Government may have in contemplation. I am unable to perceive that any evil can arise from my being kept informed respecting all intended Indian Legislation. My possession of that information will not diminish the power now vested in Your Excellency by law of rejecting, either before or after its enactment, any legislative proposal of the Subordinate Governments. The circumstance that in any given case a discretion has been given to the Governor-General by statute will at all times have due weight attached to it by the Secretary of State when the question of commenting on a particular measure is under consideration. At the same time, to obviate all chance of concurrent or conflicting action, I will always state to Your Excellency's Government, and not to that of Madras or Bombay, any objections I may think it right to make to their legislative proposals.

4. The object of the instructions which I have given to Your Excellency on this subject is not to fetter the discretion which the law has vested in the various legislative authorities of India, nor in any case to renounce, on behalf of the crown, the power of disallowance which belongs to it. I therefore think it desirable to add that the mere fact of my not having replied to a despatch explaining to me the policy of any intended legislation is not to be regarded as necessarily implying on the part of Her Majesty a final approval of such legislation. Considerations may arise in particular cases which may make it expedient

to defer the expression of my opinion until the period at which the measure is sent to England for the assent or disallowance of the Crown.

IV.—No. 72, Dated Fort William, the 24th December 1874.

From—The Government of India in the Home Department.

To—Her Majesty's Secretary of State for India.

We have the honour to acknowledge Your Lordship's despatch (Legislative), No. 33, dated 15th October last.

2. With respect to communication with the Secretary of State in Council after a measure has once been publicly launched, and while it is in the hands of the Legislative Council, we understand Your Lordship to make full allowance for the practical difficulties which we pointed out in our despatch of the 28th July. Subject to such difficulties, we shall bear carefully in mind Your Lordship's wish to receive intelligence of any alterations of great importance that may be made in a bill in such time as will enable the Secretary of State in Council to express an opinion before the measure has passed into law.

3. With regard to the receipt of answers to the communications which will be made to Your Lordship upon proposed legislation, we still feel some difficulty. We do not mean to suggest that the Secretary of State should, by the expression of his opinion upon any measure before its introduction, forestall or prejudice the exercise of his important function of advising the Crown when the measure has reached its maturity; but the object of the instructions now under consideration is to afford time for intervention in case the Secretary of State in Council thinks fit to intervene, and that time must vary according to the pressure of business in the India Office, and according to the difficulty presented by the measures themselves. We should be rather at loss to judge of the time required for the contemplated purpose in each particular case; and we need hardly say that when a measure is once determined on, and a bill drawn to carry it into effect, it is desirable to proceed with it so as to give room for the smallest amount of inconvenience resulting from the frequent changes in Indian official life. We would suggest to Your Lordship that the difficulty we are now speaking of would be reduced to a minimum if, instead of a date being fixed by us with respect to each measure, it were understood that whenever no reply is received to a communication within two months after it has been despatched, or whenever the reply is a simple acknowledgment of receipt, we shall take it as an intimation that the Secretary of State in Council wishes to reserve the expression of his opinion until the measure comes up in a natural state for the pleasure of the Crown. We say only two months, because if more time should be required for consideration, we could be

so informed either by a despatch or by telegraph, and we should hold our hands accordingly. Such an understanding would be in accordance with the principles expressed in Sir C. Wood's despatch No. 58, dated 31st December 1863.

4. Your Lordship has assured us generally that the instructions which have been given with regard to legislation are not intended to fetter the discretion which the law has vested in the various legislative authorities of India, and in particular that their application to legislation in the local Legislative Councils "will not diminish the power now vested in the Governor-General by law of rejecting, either before or after its enactment, any legislative proposal of the subordinate Governments."

These observations, coupled with the arrangement mentioned at the end of the 3rd paragraph of the despatch under reply, appear to us to obviate the difficulties which we apprehended from the application of the distinctions to the legislative business of the Local Governments.

We presume that Your Lordship intends that, not only any objections which may be made by the Secretary of State in Council to measures proposed, but, also any concurrence which may be expressed to their introduction, will be stated through this Government and not to the Local Governments directly.

B.—PROCEDURE WITH REGARD TO BILLS BEFORE THEIR INTRODUCTION INTO THE MADRAS PROVINCIAL LEGISLATIVE COUNCIL

1. All bills relating to the matters specified in section 43 of the Indian Councils Act, 1861, should be submitted for the sanction of the Governor-General before they are taken into consideration in the Legislative Council or forwarded for report to the Secretary of State.

[Government of India, Home, dated 7th July 1875, No. 1130, recorded in G. O., dated 15th September 1875, No. 48, Legislative, and despatch from Secretary of State to Government of India, No. 50, dated 7th October 1875, in G. O., dated 11th January 1876, No. 4, Legislative].

2. The same rule applies under the instructions of the Secretary of State of the 1st December 1862 to all bills containing penal clauses.

Extracts from Secretary of State's despatch to the Government of India, No. 35, dated 1st December 1862, recorded in G. O., dated 22nd January 1863, No. 92, Judicial.

"2. Cases no doubt will occasionally occur where special legislation by the Local Governments for offences not included in the Penal Code will be required. In these cases the general rule should be to place such cases under penalties already assigned in the code to acts of a similar character. This mode of legislation, though an addition to, cannot be deemed an alteration of, the Penal Code. But if any deviation is considered necessary, then the law requires that your previous sanction should be obtained.

"3. It was the intention of Her Majesty's Government that, except in local and peculiar circumstances, the code should contain the whole body of penal legislation, and that all additions or modifications suggested by experience should, from time to time, be incorporated in it. And the duty of maintaining this uniformity, of course, devolves upon Your Excellency in Council.

"4. As a general rule for the guidance of the local Councils it would probably be expedient, and this appears also to be your own view, that all bills containing penal clauses should be submitted for your previous sanction."

(See also Government of India, Home, dated 7th July 1875, No. 1130, in G. O., dated 15th September 1875, No. 48, Legislative, and Despatch from Secretary of State to Government of India, No. 50, dated 7th October 1875, in G. O., No. 4, dated 11th January 1876, Legislative).

3. Funds have been created by various laws and orders, the appropriation of which is restricted to defined purposes. It is often found inconvenient that the action and discretion of the executive authority should be thus hampered and confined : moreover, such funds are apt to be forgotten and sometimes misused. The Governor-General in Council has, therefore, been pleased to decide that in future no provision should be made in any bill to be introduced into any Legislative Council in India for the creation of such a fund until the expediency of the measure has been specially considered in the Financial Department of the Government of India. As a rule, objections are felt to the creation of such funds, and especially to their creation by an act of the legislature unless in any case, as in that of the University Fee Fund, the assets and liabilities are altogether separate and distinct from the general assets and liabilities of the State.

(Government of India, Financial Resolution, dated 19th June 1877, No. 1275 in G. O., Financial, dated 5th July 1877, No. 1843).

4. Section 67 of the Indian Penal Code as amended by Act VIII of 1882, provides that if an offence is punishable with fine only, the imprisonment which the Court imposes in default of payment of the fine shall be simple. The word "offence" in that section has by section 21 of Act X of 1886 been so defined as to denote a thing punishable under a local or special law as well as under the code; and an enactment of the local legislature prescribing rigorous imprisonment, or imprisonment,

rigorous or simple, at the discretion of the Magistrate in default of payment of fine, where the offence is punishable with fine only, would now be open to objection under section 42 of 24 and 25 Vict., Cap. 67, as being in conflict with a law passed by the Governor-General in Council after the passing of that statute.

(Government of India, Legislative, dated 31st May 1886, No. 1076, in G. O., Legislative, dated 17th June 1886, No. 120.)

5. The legislative Department is not in respect of Government measures an originating or initiating department, and its proper function in respect of such measures is to clothe with a technical shape projects of law of which the policy has been affirmed elsewhere. Accordingly all legislative proposals emanating from Local Governments and Administrations should be addressed, not to the Legislative Department, but to the proper Executive Department of the Government of India. When once a measure has been referred to the Legislative Department that department corresponds directly with the Local Governments and Administrations, and all correspondence with Her Majesty's Government relating to bills and Acts of the Imperial and Local Councils is conducted in the Legislative Department.

(Government of India, Home, dated 12th July 1874, No. 2301, in G. O., Judicial, dated 24th July 1873, No. 1162).

6. Bills brought before the Legislative Council will be translated into the vernaculars and circulated with the District as well as the Fort St. George Gazettes.

(G. O., dated 16th February 1883, No. 39, Legislative).

7. Bills emanating from non-official members of the Council should after introduction be dealt with in the same way as measures brought forward by Government.

(Government of India, Legislative, No. 1430, dated 14th August 1888, in G. O., dated 4th September 1888, No. 70, Legislative.)

8. Whenever the Government in its executive capacity has decided to submit a measure of importance, which is not urgent, to the Council for making laws and regulations, a despatch is to be addressed to the Secretary of State, stating at length the reasons for the measure and the manner in which its objects are to be carried out. The despatch is to be accompanied or followed soon after by a draft of the bill proposed to be introduced.

When this course is not followed, because a measure of importance s urgently required, the grounds of the opinion on which the Government has acted are to be subsequently communicated.

(Secretary of State's Despatch, No. 9, dated 31st March 1874, in

G. O., dated 22nd July 1874, No. 28, Legislative and G. O., dated 16th January 1875, No. 3, Legislative.)

9. The bill should not be proceeded with in the Legislative Council until a communication has been received from the Government of India in the Legislative Department to the effect either that the Secretary of State has no objection to the proposed bill, or that no reply has been received from the Secretary of State within two months from the date of the report.

(Government of India, Home, No. 1130, dated 7th July 1875, in G. O., dated 15th September 1875, No. 48, Legislative.)

10. Any objections which may be made by the Secretary of State in Council to legislative measures proposed by Local Governments, as well as any concurrence which may be expressed therewith, are, as a rule, conveyed through the Government of India.

(Government of India Despatch to Secretary of State, dated 24th December 1874, No. 72, in Legislative G. O., dated 16th January 1875, No. 3, Secretary of State's Despatch to Government of India, dated 11th February 1875, No. 8, in Legislative G. O., dated 1st May 1875, No. 29.)

11. The report of a bill or amendment to the Secretary of State and the receipt of no opinion adverse to it from him is not to be considered as necessarily implying on the part of Her Majesty a final approval of such legislation; considerations may arise in particular cases which may make it expedient to defer the expression of the Secretary of State's opinion until the period at which the measure is sent to England for the assent or disallowance of the Crown.

(Government of India, Home, dated 7th July 1875, No. 1130, in G. O., dated 15th September 1875, No. 48, Legislative.)

12. Copies of bills pending before the Legislative Council should be transmitted to the Secretary of State, in all their stages, with connected papers.

(Secretary of State's Despatch, No. O, dated 11th May 1882, in G. O., dated 22nd June 1882, No. 39, Legislative.)

13. When a bill which has been approved by the Secretary of State is materially changed during its passage through the Legislative Council, the progress of the bill should be delayed as provided in para. 5 of the despatch from the Secretary of State dated 31st March 1874, No. 9, in G. O., dated 12th July 1874. No. 28, until the Secretary of State has a fresh opportunity of expressing his opinion.

14. The decision as to whether any measure has or has not undergone such material change during its passage through the Council as to bring it within the preceding rule, rests with the Local Government and in the despatch forwarding an amended bill to the Secretary of State

in accordance with para. 2 of the Government of India Despatch to the Secretary of State dated 24th December 1874, No. 72, in G. O., dated 16th January 1875, No. 3, it should mention what the decision is, and whether it is intended to proceed with the bill at once or to delay the progress of the measure until the receipt of a communication from the Secretary of State or the Government of India as the case may be.

(Government of India, Legislative, dated 14th August 1888, No. 1430, in G. O., dated 4th September 1888, No. 70, Legislative.)

15. When a letter is despatched to the Secretary of State relating either to a bill or an amendment, copies of the letter, with enclosures, should be sent to the Government of India in the Legislative Department for information.

(Government of India, Home, dated 7th July 1875, No. 1130, in G. O., dated 15th September 1875, No. 48, Legislative.)

16. The Government of India in the Legislative Department is to be supplied with 27 copies

(1) of every bill and accompaniments referred to in the foregoing paragraph including the covering letter ;

(2) of every bill, with annexure, which is despatched to the proper Executive Department of the Government of India for the previous sanction of the Governor-General under section 43 of the Indian Councils Act, or of the Government of India under the instructions of the Secretary of State of the 1st December 1862 ;

(3) of every bill submitted for the assent of the Governor-General under section 40 of the Indian Councils Act, together with the papers specified in the margin.

	No. of Copies.
Bill as introduced	27
Annexure	27
Reports of Select Committees	27
Amended bills	27
Paper (printed) relating to Bills	27 each
Bill as passed	27
Abstract of proceedings of Legislative Council connected with each stage of the measures ...	each 27

(Government of India, Legislative, dated 14th July 1879, No. 751, in G.O., dated 1st August 1879, No. 97, Legislative, as modified by Government of India, Legislative, dated 14th May 1889, No. 1020, G.O., dated 27th May 1889, No. 14, Legislative.)

17. If in any case Abstract Proceedings of the Legislative Council are forwarded with a bill under the foregoing rule, such extracts only of the proceedings as refer to the bill should accompany it and not the entire proceedings of the day.

(Government of India, Legislative endorsement, dated 23rd December 1886, No. 2524, in G.O., dated 10th January 1887, No. I. R., Legislative Government of India, Legislative, dated 25th April 1888, No. 727, in G.O., dated 17th May 1888, No. 47, Legislative. Government of India, Legislative, dated 30th June 1888, No. 1118, in G-O., dated 14th July 1888, No. 57, Legislative.)

18. When any bill either pending before, or about to be introduced into the Legislative Council, is submitted for the consideration of the Government of India or for previous sanction, or when any bill is passed and is submitted for the assent of His Excellency the Governor-General, any existing law on which any of the sections are based should be noted in the margins of those sections.

(Government of India, Legislative, dated 19th December 1878, No. 1584, in G. O., dated 26th December 1878, No. 185).

19. Two or more bills forwarded for His Excellency the Governor-General's assent should not be sent under one covering letter, but each bill is to be forwarded separately, so that it may be dealt with in the department to which it appertains, and the disposal of one bill may not be delayed for the consideration of another.

(Government of India, Home Department, Official Memorandum, Nos. 738-39, dated 6th February 1869, in G. O., dated 18th February 1869, No. 68, Legislative.)

20. It may happen that the Governor-General may find it inexpedient to sanction an Act having retrospective effect, and may consequently have to refuse his assent, therefore Acts should be so framed as to enable the assent of His Excellency the Governor-General to be procured before the date fixed for their coming into force.

(Government of India, Legislative, dated 15th January 1883, No. 113, in G. O., dated 30th January 1883, No. 23, Legislative.)

21. The Governor-General having once formally disallowed a bill, it is impossible for him to revoke that disallowance. The bill has ceased to have any validity and cannot be revived except by re-introduction as a new bill into the local Legislative Council.

(Government of India, Home, dated 22nd January 1883, No. 508, in G. O., dated 4th February 1883, No. 173, Judicial.)

22. When Local Governments have occasion to introduce bills which may possibly conflict with some Statute or Act of the Governor-General in Council which the Local Legislature is precluded from affecting or restrict the jurisdiction of the High Court, it is recommended that copies of the bills be first submitted to His Excellency the Governor-General in Council for examination through the Legislative

Department. It is not the desire of the Government of India to press this suggestion on Local Governments ; but if any Local Government thinks fit to act on it in any case, it will arrange for the examination of the draft submitted and for communicating at an early date the result of its examination.

(Government of India, Legislative, dated 23rd May 1879, No. 570, in G. O., dated 9th June 1879, No. 73, Legislative.)

[Similar Standing orders have been framed from time to time in regard to the Legislative business in the other Provincial Legislative Councils.]

(v) RULES FOR THE DISCUSSION OF THE BUDGET

(a) IN THE IMPERIAL LEGISLATIVE COUNCIL

In exercise of the powers conferred by section 5 of the Indian Councils Act, 1909, the Governor-General in Council has, with the sanction of the Secretary of State for India in Council, made the following rules authorising, at any meeting of the Legislative Council of the Governor-General, the discussion of the annual financial statement of the Governor-General in Council.

DEFINITIONS

1. In these rules—

(1) "President" means—

(a) the Governor-General, or

(b) the President nominated by the Governor-General in Council under section 6 of the Indian Councils Act, 1861, or

(c) the Vice-President appointed by the Governor-General under section 4 of the Indian Councils Act, 1909, or

(d) the Member appointed to preside under rule 27 ;

(2) "Member in charge" means the Member of the Council of the Governor-General to whom is allotted the business of the Department of the Government of India to which the subject under discussion belongs, and includes any Member to whom such Member in charge may delegate any function assigned to him under these rules ;

(3) "Finance Member" means the Member in Charge of the Finance Department of the Government of India ;

(4) "Secretary" means the Secretary to the Government of India in the Legislative Department, and includes the Deputy Secretary and every person for the time being exercising the functions of the Secretary ;

(5) "Financial Statement" means the preliminary financial estimates of the Governor-General in Council for the financial year next following ; and

(6) "Budget" means the Financial Statement as finally settled by the Governor-General in Council.

A.—THE FINANCIAL STATEMENT

General order of discussion

2. (1) On such day as may be appointed in this behalf by the Governor-General, the Financial Statement with an explanatory memorandum shall be presented to the Council every year by the Finance Member, and a printed copy shall be given to every member.

(2) No discussion of the Financial Statement shall be permitted on such day.

3. (1) On such later day as may be appointed in this behalf by the Governor-General, the first stage of the discussion of the Financial Statement in Council shall commence.

(2) On this day, after the Finance Member has stated any changes in the figures of the Financial Statement which circumstances may since have rendered necessary and has made any explanations of that Statement which he may think fit, any Member shall be at liberty to move any resolution entered in his name in the list of business relating to any alteration in taxation, any new loan or any additional grant to Local Governments proposed or mentioned in such statement or explanatory memorandum, and the Council shall thereupon proceed to discuss each such resolution in the manner hereinafter prescribed.

4. (1) The second stage of the discussion of the Financial Statement shall commence as soon as may be after all the resolutions which may be moved as aforesaid have been disposed of.

(2) In this stage each head or group of heads specified in the statement contained in the Schedule appended to these rules as being open to discussion, shall be considered separately according to such grouping as the member in charge may determine.

(3) The consideration of a particular head or group of heads shall be introduced by the member in charge with such explanations, supplementing the information contained in the Financial Statement, as may appear to him to be necessary.

(4) Any Member shall then be at liberty to move any resolution relating to any question covered by any such head or group of heads

which may be entered in his name in the list of business, and the Council shall thereupon proceed to discuss every such resolution in the manner hereinafter prescribed.

Subjects excluded from discussion

5. No discussion shall be permitted in regard to any of the following subjects, namely :—

(*a*) any subject removed from the cognizance of the Legislative Council of the Governor-General by section 22 of the Indian Councils Act, 1861 ; or

(*b*) any matter affecting the relations of His Majesty's Government or of the Governor-General in Council with any Foreign State or any Native State in India ; or

(*c*) any matter under adjudication by a Court of Law having jurisdiction in any part of His Majesty's Dominions.

Resolutions

6. No resolution shall be moved which does not comply with the following conditions, namely :

(*a*) it shall be in the form of a specific recommendation addressed to the Governor-General in Council :

(*b*) it shall be clearly and precisely expressed and shall raise a definite issue :

(*c*) it shall not contain arguments, inferences, ironical expressions or defamatory statements, nor shall it refer to the conduct or character of persons except in their official or public capacity ;

(*d*) it shall not challenge the accuracy of the figures of the Financial Statement ; and

(*e*) it shall be directly relevant to some entry in the Financial Statement.

7. A Member, who wishes to move a resolution, shall give notice in writing to the Secretary at least two clear days before the commencement of the stage of the discussion to which the resolution relates, and shall together with the notice submit a copy of the resolution which he wishes to move.

8. The President may disallow any resolution or part of a resolution without giving any reason therefor other than that in his opinion it cannot be moved consistently with the public interests or that it should be moved in the Legislative Council of a Local Government.

9. (1) No discussion in Council shall be permitted in respect of any order of the President under rule 8.

(2) A resolution that has been disallowed shall not be entered in the proceedings of the Council.

10. Resolutions admitted by the President shall be entered in the list of business in such order as he may direct.

Discussion of Resolutions

11. (1) After the mover of a resolution has spoken, other Members may speak to the motion in such order as the President may direct and thereafter the mover may speak once by way of reply.

(2) No Member other than the mover and the Member in charge shall speak more than once to any motion except with the permission of the President for the purpose of making an explanation.

12. No speech, except with the permission of the President, shall exceed fifteen minutes in duration.

Provided that the mover of a resolution, when moving the same, and the Member in charge may speak for thirty minutes.

13. The discussion of a resolution shall be limited to the subject of the resolution, and shall not extend to any matter as to which a resolution may not be moved.

14. A Member who has moved a resolution may withdraw the same unless some Member desires that it be put to the vote.

15. When, in the opinion of the President, a resolution has been sufficiently discussed, he may close the discussion by calling upon the Mover to reply and the Member in charge to submit any final observations which he may wish to make:

Provided that the President may in all cases address the Council before putting the question to the vote.

16. If any resolution involves many points, the President at his discretion may divide it, so that each point may be determined separately.

17. (1) Every question shall be resolved in the affirmative or in the negative according to the majority of votes.

(2) Votes may be taken by voices or by division and shall be taken by division if any member so desires.

(3) The President shall determine the method of taking votes by division.

18. (1) The President may assign such time as with due regard to

the public interests he may consider reasonable for the discussion of resolutions or of any particular resolution.

(2) Every resolution which shall not have been put to the vote within the time so assigned shall be considered to have been withdrawn.

19. Every resolution, if carried, shall have effect only as a recommendation to the Governor-General in Council.

20. When a question has been discussed at a meeting of the Council, or when a resolution has been disallowed under rule 8 or withdrawn under rule 14, no resolution raising substantially the question shall be moved within one year.

B.—THE BUDGET

21. (1) On or before the 24th day of March in every year the Budget shall be presented to the Council by the Finance Member, who shall describe the changes that have been made in the figures of the Financial Statement, and shall explain why any resolutions passed in Council have not been accepted.

(2) A printed copy of the Budget shall be given to each member.

22. (1) The general discussion of the Budget in Council shall take place on such latter day as may be appointed by the President for this purpose.

(2) At such discussion, any member shall be at liberty to offer any observations he may wish to make on the budget, but no member shall be permitted to move any resolution in regard thereto, nor shall the budget be submitted to the vote of the Council.

(3) It shall be open to the President, if he thinks fit, to prescribe a time limit for speeches.

23. The Finance Member shall have the right of reply, and the discussion shall be closed by the President making such observations as he may consider necessary.

C.—GENERAL

24. (1) Every Member shall speak from his place, shall rise when he speaks and shall address the chair.

(2) At any time, if the President rises, any Member speaking shall immediately resume his seat.

25. (1) Any Member may send his speech in print to the secretary not less than two clear days before the day fixed for the discussion of a resolution, with as many copies as there are members and the Secretary shall cause one of such copies to be supplied to every Member.

(2) Any such speech may at the discretion of the President be taken as read.

26. (1) The President shall preserve order, and all points of order, shall be decided by him.

(2) No discussion on any point of order shall be allowed unless the President thinks fit to take the opinion of the Council thereon.

(3) Any Member may at any time submit a point of order to the decision of the President.

(4) The President shall have all powers necessary for the purpose of enforcing his decisions.

27. The Governor-General may appoint a member of the Council to preside in his place, or in that of the Vice-President, on any occasion on which the Financial Statement or the Budget or any portion thereof is discussed in the Council.

28. The President, for sufficient reason, may suspend any of the foregoing rules.

THE SCHEDULE

Heads open to or excluded from discussion under Rule 4

A. REVENUE		B. EXPENDITURE	
Heads open to discussion	*Heads not open to discussion*	Heads open to discussion	*Heads not open to discussion*
I.—Land Revenue	*IV.—Stamps*	1.—Refunds and Drawbacks	*2.—Assignments and Compensations*
II.—Opium	*VII.—Customs*	3.—Land Revenue	*13.—Interest on debt*
III.—Salt	*VIII.—Assessed Taxes*	4.—Opium	*23.—Ecclesiastical*
V.—Excise	*XI.—Tributes from Native States*	5.—Salt	*25.—Political*
VI.—Provincial Rates	*XVI-A.—Courts**	6.—Stamps	*27.—Territorial and Political Pensions*
IX.—Forest	*XXXII.—Army*	7.—Excise	*38.—State Railways.‡*
X.—Registration	*XXXIII.—Marine*	8.—Provincial Rates	*42.—Major Works: Interest on Debt*
XII.—Interest	*XXXIV.—Military Works*	9.—Customs	*46.—Army*
XIII.—Post Office	*All purely Provincial revenue and revenue accruing from divided heads in Provinces possessing Legislative Councils*	10.—Assessed Taxes	*46A.—Marine*
XIV.—Telegraph		11.—Forests	*47.—Military Works*
XV.—Mint		12.—Registration	*47A.—Special Defences*
XVI-B.—Jails		14.—Interest on other obligations	*All statutory charges*
XVII.—Police		15.—Post Office	*All Purely Provincial expenditure and expenditure accruing under divided heads in Provinces possessing Legislative Councils*
XIX.—Education		16.—Telegraphs	
XX.—Medical		17.—Mint	
XXI.—Scientific and other Minor Departments		18.—General Administration †	
XXII.—Receipts in aid of Superannuation, etc.		19 A.—Courts of Law †	
XXIII.—Stationery and Printing		19 B.—Jails	
XXIV.—Exchange		20.—Police	
XXV.—Miscellaneous		22.—Education	
XXVI.—State Railways		24.—Medical	
XXVIII.—Subsidised Companies		26.—Scientific and other Minor Departments	
		28.—Civil Furlough and Absentee Allowances	

A. REVENUE		B. EXPENDITURE	
Heads open to discussion	*Heads not open to discussion*	Heads open to discussion	*Heads not open to discussion*
XXIX.—Irrigation, Major Works XXX.—Minor Works and Navigation XXXI.—Civil Works		29.—Superannuation Allowances and Pensions 30.—Stationery and Printing 31.—Exchange 32.—Miscellaneous 33.—Famine Relief 34.—Construction of Protective Railways 35.—Construction of Protective Irrigation Works 36.—Reduction or avoidance of Dept. 40.—Subsidised Companies; Land, etc. 41.—Miscellaneous Railway Expenditure 42.—Irrigation: Major Works—Working expenses 43.—Minor Works and Navigations 45.—Civil Works 48.—State Railways; Capital Expenditure not charged to Revenue. 49.—Irrigation Works; Capital Expenditure not charged to Revenue	

* Mainly Court-fees and fines.

† These heads include certain statutory charges, which will be excluded from debate.

‡ This head deals purely with interest, sinking funds and annuities.

(b) IN THE PROVINCIAL COUNCILS

Rules for the Discussion of the Annual Financial Statement in the Legislative Council of the Governor of Fort Saint George :—

Definitions

1. In these rules—

(1) " Finance Committee" means the Committee of the Council appointed under Rules 2 and 3 to consider and revise the Draft Financial Statement ;

(2) "President" means—

(a) the Governor, or

(b) the Vice-President appointed by the Governor under section 4 of the Indian Councils Act, 1909, or

(c) the Member appointed to preside under Rule 36 ;

(3) " Finance Member" means the Member of the Governor's Council to whom the business of the Financial Department is allotted ;

(4) " Member in charge" means the Member of the Governor's Council to whom is allotted the business of the Department of the Local Government to which the subject under discussion belongs, and includes any Member to whom such Member in charge may delegate any function assigned to him under these rules ;

(5) " Draft Financial Statement" means the preliminary financial proposals of the Governor in Council for the financial year next following ;

(6) " Revised Financial Statement" means the Draft Financial Statement as revised by the Local Government with the approval of the Government of India after considering the proposals of the Finance Committee ;

(7) " Budget" means the Financial Statement as finally sanctioned by the Government of India, after amendment with reference to resolutions passed in Council and accepted by the Local Government or to any special circumstances not previously foreseen ; and

(8) " Secretary " means the Secretary to the Madras Legislative Council, and includes every person for the time being exercising the functions of the Secretary.

The draft financial statement

2. On a day not later than the 5th day of January in every year, the Governor shall appoint a Finance Committee for the purpose of

discussing the Draft Financial Statement and making proposals with reference thereto for the consideration of the Local Government.

3. (1) The Finance Committee shall consist of not more than twelve members of whom not more than half shall be nominated by the Governor.

(2) The remaining members of the Committee shall be elected by the non-official members of Council by votes given under such procedure as the Governor in Council may from time to time prescribe by notification 1 in the *Fort St. George Gazette*.

4. The Finance Member shall be the Chairman of the Committee, and in the case of an equality of votes on any matter shall have a second or casting vote.

5. (1) On a day not later than the 18th day of January in every year, the Local Government shall refer to the Finance Committee the Draft Financial Statement.

(2) The draft shall comprise tabular statements showing—

(*a*) the opening balance of the Provincial account,

(*b*) the estimated Provincial revenue under the various major heads of account,

(*c*) the estimated Provincial expenditure, under specific major heads, on existing establishments and schemes and on new schemes the cost of which is not considerable or which the Local Government considers to be of an absolutely obligatory character,

(*d*) the amounts available for maximum recurring expenditure and for total expenditure upon other new schemes, the latter being provisionally included under a head 'Unallotted Expenditure', and

(*e*) the estimated closing balance.

(3) There shall be appended to the Draft Financial Statement a memorandum indicating as fully as possible the manner in which the Local Government provisionally proposes to allot the sum available for total expenditure on new schemes referred to in clause (*d*) of sub-rule (2), and also indicating, if thought desirable, alternative methods of distributing this expenditure. In respect of each suggestion thus made, the maximum recurring expenditure, and the total expenditure, (*a*) recurring and (*b*) non-recurring, which it is proposed to incur in the next financial year, should be separately stated.

6. (1) The Finance Committee shall consider how the proviso (*d*) made under the head 'Unallotted Expenditure' referred to in clause one of sub-rule (2) of Rule 5 shall be distributed among the specific major heads and to what purposes the sums thus allotted should be applied:

Provided that—

(i) the total provision for recurring and non-recurring expenditure on new schemes shall not exceed the amount entered in the Draft Financial Statement as available for these purposes; and

(ii) the limit of recurring expenditure shall be determined with reference to the maximum amount which a scheme will eventually involve, any difference between this figure and the recurring expenditure required to be provided in the Draft Financial Statement under discussion being made up by addition to non-recurring expenditure.

(2) It shall also consider the estimates of revenue and expenditure referred to in clauses (*b*) and (*c*) of sub-rule (2) of Rule 5 and recommend such amendments in them as seem to it to be advisable, so long as these do not materially affect heads of revenue and expenditure which the Local Government shares with the Government of India:

Provided that any recommendation likely to reduce the estimated closing balance referred to in Rule 5 (2) (*e*) shall be accompanied by proposals for a counterbalancing increase in revenue or reduction in expenditure referred to in clause (*c*) or (*d*) of sub-rule (2) of Rule 5.

7. (1) The proceedings of the Committee shall be private and informal.

(2) They shall begin not later than the 20th day of January and be completed not later than the 27th day of the same month.

(3) Free discussion shall be allowed, but the Chairman may disallow discussion upon any particular item when he thinks that it cannot be continued with advantage.

(4) Where the question of making any particular provision in the estimates coming within the scope of the Committee's functions is in dispute, the Member in charge shall be heard in its support, and the Committee shall then proceed to vote, the decision being by majority of votes.

8. The Finance Committee shall submit to the Local Government, not later than the 28th day of January, a report indicating the changes which it recommends in the Draft Financial Statement.

9 After considering the proposals of the Committee, the Local Government shall embody its own conclusions in the Draft Financial

Statement, and shall refer the statement thus amended to the Government of India.

The revised financial statement

10. (1) The Revised Financial Statement shall be presented to the Council on a day not later than the 13th day of March.

(2) It shall comprise a memorandum by the Finance Member explaining the general financial situation of the province in the current and ensuing years, together with memoranda explaining the estimates of revenue and expenditure under the various major heads, or groups of major heads.

(3) A week before the Revised Financial Statement is presented to the Council, copies of the amended Draft Financial Statement, as provisionally approved by the Government of India at the time, shall be supplied to the Members with a note that the figures and remarks contained in it are liable to alteration.

(4) Copies of the Revised Financial Statement, together with copies of a memorandum detailing the alterations made in the Statement of which copies have been previously supplied under sub-rule (3), shall be supplied to the Members not later than the day preceding that on which the Statement is presented to the Council.

11. (1) On the day when the Revised Financial Statement is presented to the Council, each head or group of heads in the Statement, which is specified in the schedule appended, to these rules as being open to discussion, shall be considered separately according to such grouping as the Member in charge may determine.

(2) The consideration of each such head or group of heads shall be introduced by the Member in charge with such explanations supplementing the information contained in the Revised Financial Statement, as may appear to him to be necessary.

(3) Any Member shall then be at liberty to move any resolution relating to any question covered by any such head or group of heads which may be entered in his name in the List of Business and the Council shall thereupon proceed to discuss every such resolution in the manner hereinafter prescribed.

12. No discussion shall be permitted in regard to any of the following subjects, namely :—

(*a*) any subject removed from the cognizance of the Legislative Council of the Governor by section 43 of the Indian Councils Act, 1861; or (*b*) any matter affecting the relations of His Majesty's Government, or of the Governor-General in Council, or of the Governor in Council with any Foreign State or any Native State in India, or relating to the internal affairs of any such Native State ; or

(*c*) except with the sanction of the Governor, any matter which is the subject of discussion between the Governor-General in Council or the Secretary of State and the Local Government ; or

(*d*) any matter under adjudication by a Court of Law having jurisdiction in any part of His Majesty's dominions.

13. No resolution shall be moved which does not comply with the following conditions, namely:—

(*a*) it shall be in the form of a specific recommendation addressed to the Governor in Council ;

(*b*) it shall be clearly and precisely expressed and shall raise a definite issue ;

(*c*) it shall not contain arguments, inferences, ironical expressions or defamatory statements, nor shall it refer to the conduct or character of any person except in his official or public capacity ;

(*d*) it shall not challenge the accuracy of the figures of the Revised Financial Statement ;

(*e*) it shall be directly relevant to some entry in the Revised Financial Statement ;

(*f*) it shall not criticise any decision of the Government of India in respect of Provincial finance ; and

(*g*) if it would in itself have the effect of causing the total expenditure of the Presidency to exceed the amount sanctioned by the Government of India, it must propose some counterbalancing reduction in the estimate so as to avoid such excess.

14. A Member, who wishes to move a resolution, shall give notice in writing to the Secretary, prior to the date on which the Revised Financial Statement is presented to the Council, and he shall at the same time submit a copy of the resolution which he wishes to move :

Provided that the President may fix a date after which no such notice of resolution may be received.

15. The President may disallow any resolution or part of a resolution without giving any reason therefor other than that in his opinion it cannot be moved consistently with the public interests or that it should be moved in the Legislative Council of the Governor-General.

16. (1) No discussion in Council shall be permitted in respect of any order of the President under Rule 15.

(2) A resolution that has been disallowed shall not be entered in the proceedings of the Council.

17. Resolutions admitted by the President shall be entered in the List of Business in such order as he may direct.

Discussion of resolutions

18. (1) After the mover of a resolution has spoken, other Members may speak to the motion in such order as the President may direct, and thereafter the mover may speak once by way of reply.

(2) No Member other than the mover and the Member in charge shall speak more than once to any motion except, with the permission of the President, for the purpose of making an explanation.

19. No speech, except with the permission of the President, shall exceed fifteen minutes in duration :

Provided that the mover of a resolution, when moving the same, and the Member in charge may speak for thirty minutes.

20. The discussion of a resolution shall be limited to the subject of the resolution, and shall not extend to any matter as to which a resolution may not be moved.

21. A Member who has moved a resolution may withdraw the same unless some Member desires that it be put to the vote.

22. When, in the opinion of the President, a resolution has been sufficiently discussed, he may close the discussion by calling upon the mover to reply and the Member in charge to submit any final observations which he may wish to make :

Provided that the President may in all cases address the Council before putting the question to the vote.

23. If any resolution involves many points, the President at his discretion may divide it, so that each point may be determined separately.

24. (1) Every question shall be resolved in the affirmative or in the negative according to the majority of votes.

(2) Votes may be taken by voices or by division and shall be taken by division if any Member so desires.

(3) The President shall determine the method of taking votes by division.

25. (1) The President may assign such time as with due regard to the public interests he may consider reasonable for the discussion of resolutions or of any particular resolution.

(2) Every resolution which has not been put to the vote within the time so assigned shall be deemed to have been withdrawn.

26. Every resolution, if carried, shall have effect only as a recommendation to the Governor in Council.

27. When a question has been discussed at a meeting of the Council or when a resolution has been disallowed under Rule 15 or withdrawn under Rule 21, no resolution raising substantially the same question shall be moved within one year.

28. The discussion of the Revised Financial Statement shall be closed not later than the 16th day of March or if the discussion commences before the 13th day of March, then on the third day of the discussion.

The Budget

29. (1) On such day as may be appointed in this behalf by the Governor, the Budget shall be presented to the Council by the Finance Member who shall describe the changes that have been made in the figures of the Revised Financial Statement, and shall explain why any resolutions passed in Council have not been accepted.

(2) A printed copy of the Budget shall be given to each Member.

30. (1) The general discussion of the Budget in Council shall take place on such later day as may be appointed by the President for this purpose.

(2) At such discussion, any Member shall be at liberty to offer any observations he may wish to make on the Budget, but no Member shall be permitted to move any resolution in regard thereto, nor shall the Budget be submitted to the vote of the Council.

(3) It shall be open to the President, if he thinks fit, to prescribe a time-limit for speeches.

31. The discussion shall be limited to those branches of revenue and expenditure which are under the financial control of the Local Government, and it will not be permissible to enter upon criticisms of Imperial Finance.

32. The Finance Member shall have the right of reply, and the discussion shall be closed by the President making such observations as he may consider necessary.

General

33. (1) Every Member shall speak from his place, shall rise when he speaks and shall address the chair.

(2) At any time, if the President rises, any Member speaking shall immediately resume his seat.

34. (1) Any Member may send his speech in print to the Secretary not less than two clear days before the day fixed for the discussion of a resolution, with as many copies as there are Members, and the Secretary shall cause one of such copies to be supplied to every Member.

(2) Any such speech may, at discretion of the President, be taken as read.

35. (1) The President shall preserve order and all points of order shall be decided by him.

(2) No discussion on any point of order shall be allowed unless the President thinks fit to take the opinion of the Council thereon.

(3) Any Member may at any time submit a point of order to the decision of the President.

(4) The President shall have all powers necessary for the purpose of enforcing his decisions.

36. The Governor may appoint a Member of the Council to preside in his place, or in that of the Vice-President, on any occasion on which the Revised Financial Statement or the Budget or any portion thereof is discussed in the Council.

37. The President for sufficient reason may suspend any of the foregoing rules.

SCHEDULE

Heads open to or excluded from discussion under rule 11

Revenue

Heads open to discussion.

- I.—Land Revenue.
- V.—Excise.
- IX.—Forest.
- X.—Registration.
- XII.—Interest.
- XVI-B.—Jails.
- XVII.—Police.
- XVIII.—Ports and Pilotage.
- XIX.—Education.
- XX.—Medical.
- XXI.—Scientific and other Minor Departments.
- XXII.—Receipts in aid of Superannuation, etc.
- XXIII.—Stationery and Printing.
- XXV.—Miscellaneous.
- XXIX.—Irrigation, Major Works.
- XXX.—Minor Works and Navigation.
- XXXI.—Civil Works.

Heads not open to discussion.

- *IV.—Stamps.*
- *VI.—Provincial Rates*
- *VIII.—Assessed Taxes.*
- *XVI.A.—Courts.*[1]
- *XXVI.—State Railways.*
- *All purely Imperial revenue*

Expenditure

Heads open to discussion.

- 1.—Refunds and Drawbacks.
- 3.—Land Revenue
- 6.—Stamps.
- 7.—Excise.
- 8.—Provincial Rates.
- 10.—Assessed Taxes.
- 11.—Forest.
- 12.—Registration.
- 18.—General Administration.[3]
- 19-A.—Courts of Law.[3]
- 19-B.—Jails.
- 20.—Police.
- 21.—Ports and Pilotage.
- 22.—Education.
- 24.—Medical.
- 26.—Scientific and other Minor Departments.
- 29.—Superannuation-allowances and Pensions.
- 30.—Stationery and Printing.
- 32.—Miscellaneous.
- 33.—Famine Relief.
- 36.—Reduction or Avoidance of Debt.
- 40.—Subsidized Companies : Land, etc.
- 41.—Miscellaneous Railway Expenditure,
- 42.—Irrigation : Major Works—Working Expenses.
- 43.—Minor Works and Navigation.
- 44.—Construction of Railways charged to Provincial revenues.
- 45.—Civil Works.

Heads not open to discussion.

- *2.—Assignments and Compensations.*
- *13.—Interest on debt.*
- *25.—Political.*
- *42.—Major Works; Interest on debt.*
- *All statutory charges.*
- *All purely imperial expenditure.*[4]

---

1. Mainly Court-fees and fines.
2. Purely Imperial heads of account are omitted from this list, *e.g.*, II, III, XI, XIII, XIV, etc.
3. These heads include certain statutory changes, which will be excluded from debate.
4. Purely Imperial heads of account are omitted from this list, *e.g.*, 4, 5, 9, 15, etc.

Notification No. 37, dated 31st December 1909

With reference to Rule 3 of the above rules, His Excellency the Governor in Council, is pleased to fix the strength of the Finance Committee *ex-officio* and to prescribe the following rules of procedure for the election of the six non-official Members of the Committee :—

Rules of Procedure for the Election of six non-official Members of the Finance Committee.

1. The election of Non-Official Members of the Finance Committee shall be made at a meeting of the non-official Additional Members of the Legislative Council, at which the Finance Member shall preside.

2. The Members shall, one by one, proceed to the Secretary to the Legislative Council, who shall be seated in a place screened from observation and receive from him printed list of the non-official Additional Members eligible for election.

3. Each Member has six votes. He shall vote by placing the mark opposite the names of six of the members whose candidature he supports and shall then hand the list back to the Secretary.

4. When all the members present have recorded their votes, the Secretary shall report the fact to the President who will then proceed to the voting table and, with the Secretary count the votes and announce the result.

5. In the event of there being a number of votes so that the inclusion of all of them would bring the total to more than six, the President shall, by lot, select from them such a number as will bring the total to six only. [The Rules for the discussion of the Budget in the Provincial Councils are *mutatis mutandis* the same].

(vi) RULES FOR THE DISCUSSION OF MATTERS OF GENERAL PUBLIC INTEREST

IN THE IMPERIAL LEGISLATIVE COUNCIL

No. 24.—In exercise of the powers conferred by section 5 of the Indian Councils Act, 1909, the Governor-General in Council has, with the sanction of the Secretary of State for India in Council, made the following rules authorising at any meeting of the Legislative Council of the Governor-General the discussion of any matter of general public interest :—

DEFINITIONS

1. "In these rules—

(1) "President" means—

(*a*) the Governor-General, or

(*b*) the President nominated by the Governor-General in Council under section (a) of the Indian Councils Act, 1861, or

(*c*) the Vice-President appointed by the Governor-General under section 4 of the Indian Councils Act, 1909, or

(*d*) the Member appointed to preside under rule 27 ;

(2) "Member in charge" means the Member of the Council of the Governor-General to whom is allotted the business of the Department of India to which the subject under discussion belongs, and includes any member to whom such member in charge may delegate any function assigned to him under these rules ; and the Secretary.

(3) "Secretary" means Secretary to the Government of India in the Legislative Department, and includes the Deputy Secretary and every person for the time being exercising the functions of the Secretary.

MATTERS OPEN TO DISCUSSION

2. Any matter of general public interest may be discussed in the Council subject to the following conditions and restrictions:—

3. No such discussion shall be permitted in regard to any of the following subjects, namely :—

(*a*) any subject removed from the cognizance of the Legislative Council of the Governor-General by section 22 of the Indian Council Act, 1861 ; or

(*b*) any matter affecting the relations of His Majesty's Government or of the Governor-General in Council with any Foreign State or in any Native State or in any Native State in India ; or

(*c*) any matter under adjudication by a Court of Law having jurisdiction in any part of His Majesty's Dominions.

RESOLUTIONS

4. Subject to the restrictions contained in rule 8, any Member may move a resolution relating to a matter of general public interest:—

Provided that no resolution shall be moved which does not comply with the following conditions, namely :

(*a*) it shall be in the form of a specific recommendation addressed to the Governor-General in Council;

(*b*) it shall be clearly and precisely expressed and shall raise a definite issue ; and

(*c*) it shall not contain arguments, inferences, ironical expressions or defamatory statements, nor shall it refer to the conduct or character of persons except in their official or public capacity.

5. A Member, who wishes to move a resolution, shall give notice in writing to the Secretary, at least fifteen clear days before the meeting of the Council at which he desires to move the same, and shall together with the notice submit a copy of the resolution which he wishes to move :

Provided that the President may allow a resolution to be moved with shorter notice than fifteen days, and may, in any case, require longer notice or may extend the time for moving the resolution.

6. (1) The Secretary shall submit every resolution of which notice has been given to him in accordance with rule 5 to the President, who may either admit it or, when any resolution is not framed in accordance with rule 4, cause it to be returned to the Member concerned for the purpose of amendment.

(2) If the Member does not, within such time as the President may fix in this behalf, re-submit the resolution duly amended, the resolution shall be deemed to have been withdrawn.

7. The President may disallow any resolution or part of a resolution without giving any reason therefor other than that in his opinion it cannot be moved consistently with the public interest or that it should be moved in the Legislative Council of a Local Government.

8. (1) No discussion in Council shall be permitted in respect of any order of the President under rule 6 or rule 7.

(2) A resolution which has been disallowed shall not be entered in the proceedings of the Council.

9. Resolutions admitted by the President shall be entered in the list of business for the day in the order in which they are received by the Secretary :

Provided that the President may give priority to any resolution which he may consider to be of urgent public interest, or postpone the moving of any resolution.

DISCUSSION OF RESOLUTIONS

10. The discussion of resolutions shall take place after all the other business of the day has been concluded.

11. (1) After the mover of a resolution has spoken, other Members may speak to the motion in such order as the President may direct, and thereafter the mover may speak once by way of reply.

(2) No Member other than the mover and the Member in charge shall speak more than once to any motion, except, with the permission of the President, for the purpose of making an explanation.

12. No speech, except with the permission of the President, shall exceed fifteen minutes in duration :

Provided that the Mover of a resolution, when moving the same, and the Member in charge may speak for thirty minutes.

13. (1) Every Member shall speak from his place, shall rise when he speaks and shall address the chair.

(2) At any time, if the President rises, any Member speaking shall immediately resume his seat.

14. (1) Any Member may send his speech in print to the Secretary not less than two clear days before the day fixed for the discussion of a resolution, with as many copies as there are members and the Secretary shall cause one of such copies to be supplied to each Member.

(2) Any such speech may at the discretion of the President be taken as read.

15. The discussion of a resolution shall be limited to the subject of the resolution, and shall not extend to any matter as to which a resolution may not be moved.

16. When a resolution is under discussion any Member may, subject to all the restrictions and conditions relating to resolutions specified in rules 3 and 4, move an amendment to such resolution.

Provided that an amendment may not be moved which has merely the effect of a negative vote.

17. (1) If a copy of such amendment has not been sent to the Secretary at least three clear days before the day fixed for the discussion of the resolution, any Member may object to the moving of the amendment ; and such objection shall prevail unless the President in exercise of his power to suspend any of these rules allows the amendment to be moved.

(2) The Secretary shall, if time permits, cause every amendment to be printed and send a copy for the information of each Member.

18. A Member who has moved a resolution or an amendment of a resolution may withdraw the same unless some Member desires that it be put to the vote.

19. When, in the opinion of the President, a resolution and any amendment thereto have been sufficiently discussed, he may close the discussion by calling upon the Mover to reply and the Member in-charge to submit any final observations which he may wish to make :

Provided that the President may in all cases address the Council before putting the question to the vote.

20. (1) When an amendment to any resolution is moved, or when two or more such amendments are moved, the President shall, before taking the sense of the Council thereon, state or read to the Council the terms of the original motion and of the amendment or amendments proposed.

(2) It shall be in the discretion of the President to put first to the vote either the original motion or any of the amendments which may have been brought forward.

21. If any resolution involves many points, the President at his discretion may divide it, so that each point may be determined separately.

22. (1) Every question shall be resolved in the affirmative or in the negative according to the majority of votes.

(2) Votes may be taken by voices or by division and shall be taken by division if any Member so desires.

(3) The President shall determine the method of taking votes by division.

GENERAL

23. (1) The President may assign such time as with due regard to the public interests he may consider reasonable for the discussion of resolutions of any particular resolution.

(2) Every resolution which shall not have been put to the vote within the time so assigned shall be considered to have been withdrawn.

24. Every resolution, if carried, shall have effect only as a recommendation to the Governor-General in Council.

25. When a question has been discussed at a meeting of the Council, or when a resolution has been disallowed under rule 7 or withdrawn under rule 18, no resolution or amendment raising substantially the same question shall be moved within one year.

26. (1) The President shall preserve order, and all points of order shall be decided by him.

(2) No discussion on any point of order shall be allowed unless the President thinks fit to take the opinion of the Council thereon.

(3) Any Member may at any time submit a point of order to the decision of the President.

(4) The President shall have all powers necessary for the purpose of enforcing his decisions.

27 The Governor-General may appoint a Member of the Council to preside in his place, or in that of the Vice-President, on any occasion on which a matter of General public interest is discussed in the Council.

28. The President, for sufficient reason, may suspend any of the foregoing rules.

[The Rules for the discussion of matters of general public interest in the Provincial Legislative Councils are, *mutatis mutandis*, the same as those for the Imperial Council with the proviso that no resolutions will be permitted relating to subjects removed from the cognizance of the Provincial Legislative Councils under section 43 of the Indian Councils Act 1861, in addition to those mentioned in Rule 3 above].

(vii) RULES FOR THE ASKING OF QUESTIONS

IN THE IMPERIAL LEGISLATIVE COUNCIL

In exercise of the power conferred by section 5 of the Indian Councils Act 1909, the Governor-General in Council has, with the sanction of the Secretary of State for India in Council, made the following rules authorising the asking of questions at any meeting of the Legislative Council of the Governor-General :—

1. In these rules—

(1) "President" means—

(*a*) the Governor-General, or

(*b*) the President appointed under section 6 of the Indian Councils Act, 1861, or

(*c*) the Vice-President appointed by the Governor-General under section 4 of the Indian Councils Act, 1909.

(2) "Member in charge" means the Member of the Council of the Governor-General to whom is allotted the business of the Department

of the Government of India to which the subject of the question belongs, and includes any Member to whom such Member in charge may delegate any function assigned to him under these rules ; and

(3) "Secretary" means the Secretary to the Government of India in the Legislative Department, and includes the Deputy Secretary and every person for the time being exercising the functions of the Secretary.

2. Any question may be asked by any Member subject to the following conditions and restrictions :—

3. No question shall be permitted in regard to any of the following subjects, namely :—

(*a*) any matter affecting the relations of His Majesty's Government or of the Governor-General in Council with any Foreign State or with any Native State in India, or

(*b*) any matter under adjudication by a Court of law having jurisdiction in any part of his Majesty's Dominions.

4. No question shall be asked unless it complies with the following conditions, namely :—

(*a*) it shall be so framed as to be merely a request for information,

(*b*) it shall not be of excessive length.

(*c*) it shall not contain arguments, inferences, ironical expressions or defamatory statements, nor shall it refer to the conduct or character of persons except in their official or public capacity, and

(*d*) It shall not ask for an expression of an opinion or the solution of a hypothetical proposition.

5. In matters which are or have been the subject of controversy between the Governor-General in Council and the Secretary of State or a Local Government no question shall be asked except as to matters of fact, and the answer shall be confined to a statement of facts.

6. A member who wishes to ask a question shall give notice in writing to the Secretary at least ten clear days before the meeting of the Council at which he desires to put the question and shall, together with the notice, submit a copy of the question which he wishes to ask.

Provided that the President may allow a question to be put with shorter notice than ten days and may in any case require longer notice or may extend the time for answering a question

7. (1) The Secretary shall submit every question of which notice has been given to him in accordance with rule 6 to the President, who may either allow it or, when any question is not framed in accordance with rules 4 and 5, cause it to be returned to the Member concerned for the purpose of amendment.

(2) If the Member does not, within such time as the President may fix in this behalf, resubmit the question duly amended the question shall be deemed to have been withdrawn.

8. The President may disallow any question, or any part of a question, without giving any reason therefor other than that in his opinion it cannot be answered consistently with the public interest or that it should be put in the Legislative Council of a Local Government.

9. No discussion in Council shall be permitted in respect of any order of the President under rule 7 or rule 8.

10. Questions which have been allowed shall be entered in the list of business for the day and shall be put in the order in which they stand in the list before any other business is entered upon at the meeting.

11. Questions shall be put and answers given in such manner as the President may in his discretion determine.

12. Any Member who has asked a question may put a supplementary question for the purpose of further elucidating any matter of fact regarding which a request for information has been made in his original question.

13. The Member in charge may decline to answer a supplementary question without notice, in which case the supplementary question may be put in the form of a fresh question at a subsequent meeting of the Council.

14. These rules, except rules 6 and 7, apply also to the supplementary questions:

Provided that the President may disallow any supplementary question without giving any reason therefor.

15. The President may rule that an answer to a question in the list of business for the day shall be given on the ground of public interest even though the question may have been withdrawn.

16. No discussion shall be permitted in respect of any question or of any answer given to a question.

17. All questions asked and the answers given shall be entered in the proceedings of the Council:

Provided that no question which has been disallowed by the President shall be so entered.

18. The President may assign such time as with due regard to the public interests, he may consider reasonable for the putting and answering of questions.

[The Rules for the asking of questions in the Provincial Legislative Councils are, *mutatis mutandis*, the same as those for the Imperial Council.]

INDEX

A

B

C

D

E

F

G

H

I

MADRAS : THE GUARDIAN PRESS, MOUNT ROAD